LETTERS OF LOVE AND DUTY:
THE CORRESPONDENCE OF
SUSANNA AND JOHN MOODIE

Susanna and John Moodie, two of their sons,
and an unidentified child, c.1860

Letters of Love and Duty

The Correspondence of Susanna and John Moodie

EDITED BY
CARL BALLSTADT,
ELIZABETH HOPKINS,
AND MICHAEL PETERMAN

UNIVERSITY OF TORONTO PRESS
Toronto Buffalo London

ISBN 0-8020-5708-X

∞

Printed on acid-free paper

Canadian Cataloguing in Publication Data

Moodie, Susanna, 1803–1885
Letters of love and duty : the correspondence of
Susanna and John Moodie

Includes index.
ISBN 0-8020-5708-X

1. Moodie, Susanna, 1803–1885 – Correspondence.
2. Moodie, J.W. Dunbar (John Wedderburn Dunbar),
1797–1869 – Correspondence.
3. Authors, Canadian – 19th century – Correspondence.
4. Ontario – Social life and customs.
I. Moodie, J.W. Dunbar (John Wedderburn Dunbar), 1797–1869.
II. Ballstadt, Carl, 1931–   . III. Hopkins, Elizabeth.
IV. Peterman, Michael A., 1942–   . V. Title.

PS8426.063Z54 1993   C813'.3   C92-095697-1
PR9199.2.M66Z48 1993

This book has been published with the help of
a grant from the Canadian Federation for the Humanities,
using funds provided by the Social Sciences and
Humanities Research Council of Canada.

Contents

Illustrations

Acknowledgments

D URING THE FIVE YEARS it has taken to prepare this volume, we have come to know and appreciate the work and assistance of many colleagues, archivists, librarians, and researchers. In particular we thank Gary Boire, Betsy Boyce, Gerry Boyce, Ruth Bradley-St Cyr, Jean Cole, Gordon Dibb, Martin Dowding, Lois Foster, Carole Gerson, Anne Goddard, Linda Hoad, Claude Le Moine, Charles Longley, Lorna Knight, Mary Lu MacDonald, John Martyn, Doug McCalla, Jean Rainwater, Colin Read, Peter Rochon, Charles G. Roland, Paul Romney, Gordon Roper, Ron Stagg, Lianna Van der Bellen, Barbara Wilson, the staffs of the Metropolitan Toronto Reference Library's Baldwin Room, the Archives of Ontario, and the Archives of the American Antiquarian Society of Worcester, Massachusetts. We are also very grateful for the patient technical support of Pat Cheuk, John Dawson, Shirley Hill, Jim Savary, and George Seravalle.

Without a grant from the Social Sciences and Humanities Research Council and the time and facilities provided by our three universities, McMaster, Trent, and York, this work could not have been completed. We wish to thank these institutions and the public which funds them for assisting us so generously.

We appreciate the patience and helpful advice of Ken Lewis and of Gerry Hallowell of University of Toronto Press. And for sharing the domestic load so that we could pursue the project, not to mention for their interest and encouragement, we express our gratitude and love to Cara, Dorothy, and Tony.

Toronto
December 1992

Editorial Preface

I N THE SUMMER OF 1987, about eighteen months after the publication of *Susanna Moodie: Letters of a Lifetime*, we learned that
the National Library of Canada had just acquired a hitherto
unknown collection of Moodie papers from the estate of Patrick
Hamilton Ewing, who had died at his home in Upper Red Hook, New
York, in March 1986. Mr Ewing was a great-great-grandson of John and
Susanna Moodie. A descendant of their eldest daughter, Katie Vickers,
he had somehow escaped our net when we were canvassing Moodie
descendants for letters during the preparation of *Susanna Moodie:
Letters of a Lifetime* (1985). A quick visit to Ottawa that summer
revealed the new collection contained letters, manuscripts, and other
documents that once belonged to the Moodies, including seventeen
'new' letters written by Susanna.

What to do? We were in the midst of editing the large correspondence of Susanna's sister, Catharine Parr Traill, but the new letters,
with their important revelations concerning the Moodies' life in the
bush, the basis of *Roughing It in the Bush*, were tantalizing. The
relationship between Susanna and her husband, which had been so
shadowy in her famous book and even in the letters we had earlier
collected, was brought to life in the new discovery and had to be
shared. In 1987 the 150th anniversary of the Mackenzie rebellion was
upon us, and John Moodie's militia activities during and after the
rebellion were finally apparent in his letters home to Susanna. Other
facets of their lives, such as those revealed by John Moodie's correspondence with Robert Baldwin about life as a public servant in
Belleville or by the Moodies' writings on spiritualist activities, also
warranted attention. The fuller story begged to be told, and so this
second volume of Moodie letters came to be.

Unlike *Letters of a Lifetime* this new volume tells the Moodies'
story more in John's than in Susanna's words. The nature of the companionship they shared was inextricably related to his roles as a soldier, settler, public servant, and writer. John Moodie's correspondence
offers a unique and immediate view of nineteenth-century social and
political concerns and events in Canada and abroad. Whether he is
propounding his views on the settlement and development of the
young colony, describing the machinations of small-town political life,
or delving into the mysteries of spiritualism, his letters are a valuable
addition to the record of the interests and opinions of those early
British emigrants whose efforts helped to lay the foundations of the
emerging nation.

The sections in this volume delineate the changing phases and
interests of the Moodies' lives: the days of their courtship and emigration; the periods apart from each other during and after the Rebellion
of 1837; life in Belleville as public figures in their respective ways;
their involvement with spiritualism; their retirement and eventual
separation by death. The essays and notes which accompany each
division are intended to provide information useful for understanding
the letters themselves. As a general rule we have tried to find some
identification for every name which appears in the letters, though we
have not always been successful. Rather than announce throughout the
text where information was not found, we ask the reader to assume
this when we offer no footnote or comment in the essays. We trust the
index will assist in bringing together what we have been able to learn
about names and places mentioned in the letters. Much more might
be written about the Moodies and the people they mention, but we
have tried, in the interests of length and space, to restrain the urge to
overshadow the correspondence with biography.

Throughout the volume we have generally referred to the Moodies
as 'John' and 'Susanna' in order to distinguish them from each other,
but when no confusion was possible we have used the surname alone.
There has been a convention of referring to Susanna Moodie as Mrs
Moodie because she frequently referred to herself that way and because
that form of address seemed to capture something of her personal and
temporal milieu. It is inappropriate and unnecessary to maintain this
convention in current scholarship.

Deciding how to refer to John Wedderburn Dunbar Moodie has been
an interesting problem. Susanna and others like Thomas Traill and
Agnes Strickland often referred to him simply as 'Moodie,' but this
creates obvious problems. In our first volume we took our cue from

Susanna's early references to him as 'Dunbar' in letters written during the courtship. But she referred to him either as 'Moodie' or 'John' in letters written after their marriage. Family pride, or perhaps the importance of stressing J.W.D. Moodie's connections with the titled Dunbar family of Scotland at times when their fortunes might be influenced by it, conditioned their use of 'Dunbar.' For example, he usually expanded his simple signature of 'J.W.D. Moodie' to 'J.W. Dunbar Moodie' when petitioning government or men of influence, or when seeking to legitimize a relationship with public figures like Robert Baldwin. Or perhaps the Moodies themselves simply learned to avoid confusion in the personal realm after the birth of their eldest son, whom they called 'Dunbar.' In any event, our choice of 'John' is supported by Donald Moodie's letters to his brother as well as the majority of Susanna's personal references to her husband.

As in the first collection, we have undertaken to transcribe the manuscript material as closely as print will permit, without editorial correction or change. Two categories of accidentals have been regularized in accordance with the 'house' style of University of Toronto Press: single quotation marks have been used throughout, with double quotation marks for interior quotes; and commas and periods have been placed inside closing quotation marks throughout. As well, to avoid needless confusion for the reader, we have silently added opening or closing quotation marks and parentheses when they were missing in the original. Otherwise, where we have made intrusions, these are indicated by square brackets. Empty square brackets indicate an illegible word or a gap in the manuscript.

Both Moodies were generally consistent and correct in grammar, spelling, and punctuation, and their handwriting remained fairly legible until old age. What idiosyncrasies they do exhibit (John often reversed *ei*, and Susanna's commas and periods can easily be confused with dashes) simply add to the impression of the letters' immediacy and the couple's frankness, affection, and humour. Susanna often underlined phrases to reveal their irony, and John was fond of puns, making observation of his spelling a particular delight.

The letter headings, which are irregular in both completeness and position (sometimes appearing at the end rather than the beginning of a letter), have been regularized for ease of reference. We have used square brackets to indicate dates and places missing in the manuscripts and footnoted the evidence for such interpretations. A few of the letters exist only as fragments, and this is indicated by the presence of ellipses at the beginning or end of the fragment.

The transcription of letters from manuscript and newspaper sources is sometimes delicate work, and, while we have tried to ensure accuracy at each stage of reproduction, errors may have crept in, for which we accept responsibility.

Much still remains to be discovered and told of the Moodies' lives – the appearance of new Moodie material after the publication of our first volume has taught us to be cautious – but we trust the letters of this volume will add substantively to their story and to the reader's picture of a significant period in Canadian history.

Abbreviations

AO	Archives of Ontario
DCB	*Dictionary of Canadian Biography*
DNB	*Dictionary of National Biography*
DSAB	*Dictionary of South African Biography*
LC	Susanna Moodie. *Life in the Clearings.* Ed. Robert L. McDougall. Toronto 1959
LOL	*Susanna Moodie: Letters of a Lifetime.* Ed. Carl Ballstadt, Elizabeth Hopkins, and Michael Peterman. Toronto 1985
MR	National Archives, Militia Records, RG 9
NA	National Archives, Ottawa
PHEC	National Library, Patrick Hamilton Ewing Collection
RIB	Susanna Moodie. *Roughing It in the Bush.* Ed. Carl Ballstadt. Ottawa 1988
TFC	National Archives, Traill Family Collection, MG 29, D 100

1830–1837

'I care for no luxuries, dearest'

JOHN WEDDERBURN DUNBAR MOODIE met Susanna Strickland in the early summer of 1830. He was a thirty-six-year-old retired lieutenant of the 21st Royal North British Regiment of Fusiliers and friend of Thomas Pringle (1789–1834), whom he had met in South Africa and with whom he shared an interest in the anti-slavery movement. She was a twenty-six-year-old aspiring writer, visiting London in search of literary opportunities. Pringle, a Scot residing in Hampstead on the outskirts of London after his return from South Africa, had been elected secretary of the Anti-Slavery League in 1827 and eked out a living as a writer and an editor of journals and annuals such as the *Athenaeum* and *Friendship's Offering*. Susanna became acquainted with him when she submitted poems for his consideration.[1] Pringle took a paternal interest in her, and she occasionally stayed with the Pringles at their Hampstead home in 1830 and 1831. Under their influence she, too, became involved in the anti-slavery movement, anonymously transcribing the stories of two black slaves, Ashton Warner and Mary Prince (who was a servant in the Pringle household), for publication by the League.[2]

Both Susanna and John had experienced youthful attractions to others. Susanna had an unhappy attachment to a man named Asker during 1828 (*LOL*, 25–6), and John in his 'Narrative of the Campaign in Holland'[3] refers to a brief infatuation with 'A.R.' shortly after his enlistment in the 21st Regiment at Fort George on the Moray Firth in Scotland. But in the summer of 1830, during long rambles on Hampstead Heath,[4] the two shared their interests in writing and the anti-slavery movement with the kindly encouragement of their mutual friends the Pringles, and fell in love.

Moodie belonged to an impoverished but ancient family of Scottish gentry whose home seat, Melsetter, was located at Long Hope on the Orkney island of Hoy. As described in a mid-century gazetteer, 'from the house of Melsetter to the romantic fishing-hamlet of Rackwick, is an uninterrupted series of stupendous rock-scenery, occasionally exceeding 500 feet in the height, – sometimes perpendicular and smooth, – in other places rent, shivered, and broken down in huge fragments, – occasionally overhanging the deep, and frowning on the stormy surges of the Pentland Firth.'[5] As Moodie told Richard Bentley in a long autobiographical letter (Letter 70), he was born 7 October 1797, the youngest of the five sons of Major James Moodie of Melsetter. Two brothers, Thomas and James, died in military service in India. Benjamin, the eldest, sold Melsetter and emigrated to South Africa, where he undertook to bring the first relatively large group of

Melsetter House, Hoy, Orkney Islands

evicted Scottish tenants to settle at the Cape in 1817. A successful settler himself, he was joined by his two younger brothers, John and Donald, in 1819 and 1820 respectively. In later years Benjamin became an active supporter of the British philanthropic organization, the Children's Friend Society, himself bringing twenty-one children to the Cape and raising them until they were old enough to be employed.[6] Donald Moodie became a public figure in South Africa, holding several government positions, including that of colonial secretary (1846–51), and translating 'a monumental source-book' of early Dutch records dealing with relations between the colonists and the aboriginal tribes.[7] John Moodie's adventures would take him further afield.

Raised and educated as a gentleman, John at age sixteen entered the army, in which service he received a severe wound in the left wrist while trying to take the Waterpoort Gate at the British attack on Bergen op Zoom in Holland on 8 March 1814. Retired on half pay after the Napoleonic Wars and unlikely to inherit whatever remained of the family estate from his uncle, Sir Alexander Dunbar, the twenty-five-year-old John emigrated to South Africa, where he eventually joined his older brother Donald in farming a grant of two lots in Groote Valley.[8] While in South Africa he became acquainted with Thomas Pringle, at the time a Capetown editor. But Pringle's frustrations with the tightly controlled publishing scene in South Africa led to his return to London in 1826. Four years later Moodie also returned to England to publish a book about his South African adventures and to seek a wife:

This was my case in South Africa. I had plenty of land, and of all the common necessaries of life; but I lived for years without companionship, for my nearest English neighbour was twenty-five miles off. I hunted the wild animals of the country, and had plenty of books to read; but, from talking broken Dutch for months together, I almost forgot how to speak my own language correctly. My very ideas (for I had not entirely lost the reflecting faculty), became confused and limited, for want of intellectual companions to strike out new lights, and form new combinations in the regions of thought; clearly showing that man was not intended to live alone. Getting, at length, tired of this solitary and unproductive life, I started for England, with the resolution of placing my domestic matters on a more comfortable footing. (RIB, 232–3)

Susanna was raised and educated in an atmosphere of middle-class respectability and gentility made possible by her father's success in business. His premature death in 1818, however, considerably reduced the large family's circumstances, leaving them with the manor and farm of Reydon Hall in Suffolk but very little money. Susanna's two younger brothers set out to make their own fortunes. Tom Strickland became an officer in the Merchant Navy, sailing for the East India Company; and Samuel Strickland emigrated in 1825 to Upper Canada, where he initially settled with friends, Colonel James Black and his family, in Darlington Township in the Newcastle District. Soon after his arrival Samuel married Emma Black, one of James's daughters, and on his own began clearing a lot in Otonabee Township near Peterborough. Emma died in childbirth in 1826, and Samuel remarried in 1828 to Mary Reid, the daughter of Robert Reid, a prominent settler in Douro Township. In 1829 he joined the Canada Company, for which he worked in Guelph and Goderich, and then returned in 1831 to clear a new farm on the banks of the Otonabee River in Douro, near present-day Lakefield.[9]

Of the six Strickland sisters, all but Sarah (nicknamed 'Thay') embarked on careers as writers and editors in the busy world of

Susanna Strickland, c.1828

London magazines and giftbooks. The two oldest sisters, Eliza and Agnes, soon established themselves in London and would eventually become well known for their biographies of British royalty. Jane Margaret pursued her own literary career from Reydon, where she remained with their mother. Sarah married Robert Childs, one of the Bungay family of Nonconformist publishers. He died in 1839, and she married the Anglican Canon Richard Gwillym of the parish of Ulverston five years later. Catharine and Susanna, the youngest sisters, remained primarily at Reydon Hall until their marriages, writing books for children, contributing to annuals and magazines, and, in the case of Susanna, gradually developing as a poet and story writer.[10]

Just prior to her visit to the Pringles in May 1830, Susanna had converted from the Church of England to the Congregational denomination under the guidance of Pastor Andrew Ritchie of Wrentham, a village near Reydon. As her courtship with John Moodie progressed, Pastor Ritchie's apparent disapproval disturbed Susanna (Letter 3) and brought forth her fiancé's 'disgust and indignation.' However, as her sister Catharine reported on 16 July 1830, 'in spite of the warning of her good padre and her Southwold friends to love none but a good man of their church poor Susie has become a convert to Lieut. Dunbar Moodie.'[11] On 2 July 1830, notwithstanding their poor financial situation, John asked for her hand in marriage. In her reply Susanna's mother, Elizabeth Strickland, noting John's social position with approval, assessed the couple's economic prospects:

My daughter's happiness is too dear to me to admit of any opposition to her inclination in a union with a gentleman of family and high moral character. In a prudential point of view your income is at present too confined to support a wife, and I am sorry it is not in my power to augment it. My daughter upon the demise of two aged relatives is entitled to the eighth part of six thousand pounds funded property. Under her late father's will (upon my decease) she claims a child's share in the estate on which I reside with the prospect of further contingencies. (PHEC, no. 135)

By the end of July, John had determined to visit his uncle in Caithness to discuss family finances and to try to collect his share of a debt owed by a Mr Threpland. Letters 2 and 3 give a glimpse of some of his adventures as well as of the couple's plans and feelings during this separation, which Susanna expected to last until the spring of 1831 (LOL, 52). She suggests they look after an elderly aunt in order to acquire a home; he favours renting a small house in the Orkneys until their fortunes improve. In January 1831, however, Susanna reported to her friends, poet James Bird and his wife, Emma, of nearby Yoxford, that their marriage plans were broken: '... our engagement was too hasty. I have changed my mind. You may call me a jilt a flirt or what you please, I care not. I will neither marry a soldier nor leave my country for ever and feel happy that I am once more my own mistress' (*LOL*, 55). The reason for this break was that John had raised the prospect of emigration to South Africa:

... when I left South Africa it was with the intention of returning to that colony, where I had a fine property, to which I was attached in no ordinary degree, on account of the beauty of the scenery and delightful climate. However, Mrs. Moodie, somehow or other, had imbibed an invincible dislike to that colony, for some of the very reasons that I liked it myself. The wild animals were her terror, and she fancied that every wood and thicket was peopled with elephants, lions, and tigers, and that it would be utterly impossible to take a walk without treading on dangerous snakes in the grass. (*RIB*, 233)

Apparently a compromise was reached, however, and in the early spring Susanna described their marriage to James Bird:

Tell dearest Emma, a piece of now old news, that I was on the 4th instant at St. Pancras Church made the happiest girl on earth, in being united to the beloved being in whom I had long centred all my affections. Mr. Pringle 'gave me' away, and Black Mary, who had treated herself with a complete new suit upon the occasion, went on the coach box, to see her dear Missie and Biographer wed. I assure you, that instead of feeling the least regret at the step I was taking, if a tear trembled in my eyes, it was one of joy, and I pronounced the fatal obey, with a firm determination to keep it. My blue stockings, since I became a wife, have turned so pale that I think they will soon be quite white, or at least only tinged with a hue of London smoke. (*LOL*, 60–1)

After a brief residence at Middleton Villa in London the newly-weds moved to a cottage in Southwold to await the birth of their first child, Catherine Mary Josephine, who would be born on 14 February 1832. Possibly as a result of their compromise John pursued various strategies that would allow them to remain in Britain. He made several trips to London to meet his uncle, Sir Alexander Dunbar, and to explore opportunities for employment in Britain, either as soldier, police magistrate, or literary man, as well as to arrange publication of

his *Ten Years in South Africa.*[12] Disappointed in such prospects, he
began to reconsider the alternative of emigration. Attracted in various
ways by the opportunities available in Upper Canada, where Susanna's
brother was already living and where, as a retired officer, he was
entitled to a government grant of four hundred acres of land, he
abandoned his plans to return to South Africa: 'At last, between my
wife's fear of the wild animals of Africa, and a certain love of novelty,
which formed a part of my own character, I made up my mind, as they
write on stray letters in the post-office, to "try Canada"' (*RIB*, 234).

Having resolved upon emigration as a means 'to procure a sufficient
subsistence by farming' (Letter 7) and thus a secure future, John began
to make arrangements with characteristic enthusiasm. Although the
surviving letters written during the pre-embarkation period do little
more than hint at the extent of those preparations, Susanna's novel
Flora Lyndsay (1854) makes clear that his planning was extensive. In
addition to making the necessary trips to London to arrange for passage,
he laid the foundation for a proper reception in his new role as settler
by soliciting a letter of introduction from Lord Lynedoch to Sir John
Colborne, lieutenant-governor of Upper Canada from 1828 to 1836.

He sought to inform himself about the colony of Upper Canada as
well. Some sense of that endeavour is conveyed in the first chapter of
Flora Lyndsay, which includes a debate between wife and husband on
the subject of emigration, showing the reluctance of the one and the
determination of the other. The chapter ends with the husband's
departure to talk with a man from Canada who is visiting in Britain
while Flora silently admits 'the logic of her husband's argument.' The
man consulted was Robert Reid, Samuel Strickland's father-in-law and
'a successful settler in Upper Canada for twelve years,' from whom the
Moodies received information in August 1831 and again in March 1832
on 'the advantages of Emigration' (*LOL*, 63, 67). Discussions with Reid
would have augmented details that John had obtained through letters
received from Susanna's brother and the James Black family (*LOL*, 42).
But these were not the only experienced emigrants on whose advice
John relied. As Susanna notes in her sketch of Tom Wilson in
Roughing It in the Bush, John went to Yoxford to hear a lecture by
William Cattermole and probably to buy his book, *Emigration: The
Advantages of Emigration to Canada*. It is based on two lectures
delivered in May of that year in Colchester and Ipswich, but he was
promoting it and its subject in Suffolk villages like Yoxford in the
spring of 1832 (see *RIB*, 55, 62).

While the book and, doubtless, the lectures provided Moodie with encouraging particulars and statistical information on the procedures for emigration and settlement, in his enthusiasm he overlooked the fact that Cattermole addressed himself specifically 'to the agricultural population, because it is them I most wish to see emigrate.' He emphasized the necessity of 'habits of industry' and, in his conclusion, advised 'no Englishman or European whatever to go into the bush, it is quite unnecessary now, when towns are springing up in all directions.' Setting sail from Leith, Scotland, on 1 July 1832 and arriving in Cobourg, Upper Canada, on 9 September, Moodie initially followed Cattermole's advice. Since settlement 'on a small improved farm' could be done at fairly low cost, John lost no time in establishing the family on a cleared farm in Hamilton Township (see *RIB*, 68, 82, and *LOL*, 71). However, the Moodies were eventually to neglect Cattermole's advice and leave the environs of Cobourg, which Cattermole had described as 'a very fine and flourishing village, in which many half-pay officers of his Majesty's Army and Navy are comfortably settled,'[13] to move to the backwoods, in which an early optimism about their situation and prospects would give way to a considerable disenchantment with the opportunities offered the settler in Upper Canada.

Sometime during the previous year Susanna's sister Catharine had met Thomas Traill, a widowed Orkneyman and fellow officer of John Moodie, at the Pringles' in London. She had spent the spring of 1831 in the city with her aunt, Rebecca Leverton, in Bedford Square and later in the year travelled in England with her. Her brief courtship with Traill resumed early in 1832 and culminated in their marriage in St Margaret's Church at Reydon on 13 May 1832. They too determined to emigrate to Canada, and, after a farewell visit to Traill's family and his two sons, who were to remain in Scotland, they set sail from Greenock in mid-July, landing at Montreal in mid-August (see *LOL*, 70).

At the end of 1833, about the time the Moodies were preparing to move to the backwoods, John was still buoyant about his prospects in Upper Canada. In Letter 10 to James Traill (1794–1873), a London police magistrate for whom he is proposing to purchase land,[14] he reports his own recent acquisition of two hundred acres in Douro Township and outlines his plans to become a land agent or speculator in partnership with his brother-in-law, Samuel Strickland. The proposal is both ironic and novel. The irony is that Moodie is arranging his own removal to the backwoods at the very time when he seems to recognize the greater appeal and value of cleared lands to prospective

British capitalists. The novelity lies in his endeavour, not to lure monied emigrants, but to attract British capital for the purchase and subsequent rental of land, charging 3 per cent plus travelling expenses for his own services as agent. While James Traill could not afford to become a speculator, Moodie clearly hoped that he himself would have success in such enterprise.

Although the land agency scheme apparently did not mature, John did invest money in the hope of good return. His chapter 'The Land-Jobber' in *Roughing It in the Bush* recounts how he entrusted the sale of his army commission early in 1834 to the speculator Mr Q——, storekeeper Charles Clark of Cobourg, in exchange for twenty-five shares valued at £25 each in the company that was building the steamship *Cobourg*. It turned out to be a much lamented investment and, as John notes, resulted only in loss. It did not, however, entirely dampen his search for an appropriate venture.

Letter 11 reveals that his correspondence with James Traill entailed a proposal to write a book on emigration and settlement in Upper Canada as a kind of sequel to the manuscript on the Cape colony that Richard Bentley would publish as *Ten Years in South Africa* (1835). It was the resurrection of an idea that he had tried first with Smith and Elder in London in the midst of his arrangements for emigration. Clearly, he hoped that a literary career could be nurtured even in the midst of the trials of a settler.

Beginning on 25 October 1834 the New York *Albion*, a newspaper on which the Moodies relied for much of their news both of Britain and the New World, began carrying advertisements for the Colony of the Rio Grande and the Texas Land Company. The advertisements provided the details of emigration plans and costs, together with information about the 'Empressario Dr. Beales.' Interested parties were advised to write to the secretary and counsel, Charles Edwards, in New York for 'maps of the Colony, together with a printed description of the climate, resources, and general face of the country, made by persons who have visited the lands.'

In spite of Moodie's assertion to Richard Bentley (Letter 11) that he was enjoying success in his backwoods settlement, actual conditions were already leading him, and others like him, to become increasingly sceptical about prospects in Douro and conditions in Upper Canada. John responded to the Texas Land Company advertisements in the *Albion* with some alacrity. A letter from Charles Edwards dated 15 January 1835 includes an apology for the delay in his reply because John's letter 'has been in the hands of one & the pocket of another'

The Moodies' Douro property, showing their dug well
in the foreground

before coming to the secretary (PHEC, no. 11). The letter indicates that Moodie, in replying to the advertisement, sought to extricate himself from his deteriorating circumstances by exploiting his capabilities and reputation as a writer and at the same time acquiring new land, perhaps, in greener pastures. Apparently Moodie offered to write a book for the Texas Land Company in exchange for passage to the colony and lands on which to settle. Edwards's reply was encouraging:

We have a knowledge of you as a literary man; & your lady is spoken highly of, by Dr. Bartlett of the Albion – who is one of our directors.

I am inclined to believe our Board would cheerfully find you a passage from this Port to Texas; and guarantee to take a liberal number of Copies of any work you might write upon the Country. – A Country, by the bye (& do not lose sight of the hint!) which no scientific man has written about: – perhaps, the only spot in the world upon which a book has not been perpetrated.

We have honorable men connected with our Company; and I can assure you the society of such a man as Dr. Beales is to be coveted.

His outlay is great. If it were not so, we should offer terms which, I am satisfied, you would instantly Embrace. Even as it is, we should be pleased to hear from you more definitely; and I will promise to be as frank in my answer. (PHEC, no. 11)

Optimistically construing Edwards's letter as a near definite offer, Moodie pressed for particulars. He was disillusioned of his expectations by the secretary's reply of 3 March: 'I fear, dear Sir the terms of my first letter may have been too strong – or, you have given me too sanguine an answer. I should not be authorized in offering you any *salary* situation. The inducements of the Company would be these: a free passage – subscription for a large number of Copies of any work you might publish – & a gift of land when you were about to settle' (PHEC, no. 12). He added that the company was pleased with the prospects of having a man such as Moodie join the enterprise, but he reiterated that it was beyond the company's means to 'go into expenses.'

The lack of a salary may have dampened Moodie's enthusiasm for the time being, but late in the year or early in 1836 he received a letter from Dr Beales himself inquiring whether he thought it worth his while to come to Upper Canada to promote his venture and to sell 'script' and shares (PHEC, no. 3). He informed Moodie that he sought men 'of capital and influence' who might buy shares, valued at £300 each and including full title to six hundred acres, and hence acquire an interest in 'pushing on Emigrants' to the Texas grants. In order to solicit his interest further, Beales offered 10 per cent of all sales that Moodie might make. By 1836, however, Moodie could no longer seize this opportunity to become a 'land-speculator,' were he still so inclined, in view of his increasingly precarious financial circumstances. For the Moodies the Texas scheme seems to have ended there.[15]

Susanna's Letter 33 makes it clear that for others the Texas prospect was still alive; it was entertained by Thomas Traill and the Crawfords (Letters 33 and 35), amongst others in the Peterborough area. Nor was it simply personal failure in Upper Canada that made the Texas emigration scheme tempting to such people. Inhabitants of the district had been optimistic that the passion for canal building in the Great Lakes region would extend to the Trent-Otonabee river system. Between 1833 and 1835 N.H. Baird's survey of the rivers was under way, and residents of the townships along the proposed navigation route attended an information meeting in Peterborough on 30 October 1835.[16] Unfortunately the economy of Upper Canada, sparked by the tide of emigration early in the decade, faltered in the wake of the economic downturn or 'panic' of late 1836 and 1837 in both Britain and America. For people of the Newcastle District one of the effects of that economic crisis and the political unrest that led to rebellion in the Canadas late in 1837 was the deflation of ambitious hopes to build a navigational system from the mouth of the Trent River through the inland lakes and rivers north and west to Georgian Bay. People like the Moodies and Traills, well situated as they were on the Otonabee River, were optimistic that such a system, opening up trade to the back country and the west, would be their economic salvation, as, indeed, it might have been. With the failure of that prospect they were compelled to seek other options.

Though Moodie's flirtation with Texas resettlement soon came to an end, he continued to attend to Upper Canadian realities, including such matters as the need for internal improvements to stimulate the economy. He had pursued his early ambition of adding his own statement to the literature of emigration to the Canadas by writing to Richard Bentley (Letter 11), but Bentley replied in April 1835 'that so much has lately been written on that country, as to make it doubtful how far such a book would succeed here.' He did add, however, that he would be happy to see such a manuscript should John carry out his plan.[17] Moodie's long letter to James Traill, dated 8 March 1836 (Letter 14), appears to be the draft of that plan and a continuation of the kind of reportage he provided in earlier letters to the London police magistrate. It has a rambling and impulsive quality that suggests that he was adopting the epistolary form, as others had done, to reflect his own experience and to provide a treatise on the economics of emigration in relationship to the present state of Upper Canada. Whether or not it was ever sent to James Traill, the letter is a significant document conveying an intelligent assessment of Moodie's time and place; moreover, it is a valuable piece for a number of specific reasons.

Foremost amongst these is the relationship of the letter to three of the chapters that John Moodie contributed to *Roughing It in the Bush*: 'The Village Hotel,' 'The Land-Jobber,' and 'Canadian Sketches.' Like the chapters the letter offers extensive commentary on such topics as land speculators, mostly with respect to their negative effect, government land policy, the cost of settled and wild lands, the type of emigrant best suited to Upper Canada, and the economic prospects of the colony in view of population, trade, and internal improvements. In addition the treatise offers themes that pervade the whole book. These include the too 'sanguine anticipation' of the Moodies about Upper Canada, duped as they were by the exaggerated accounts of the colony; an emphasis on the folly of the gentleman of modest means who settles in the backwoods, such location being suitable only for the labourer; and the disappointment and misery experienced by refined persons who choose remote and romantic situations.

While the letter shows how rapidly the Moodies' hopes for prosperity and happiness dissipated in the backwoods, it also reveals that they kept abreast of current affairs. Not only does the letter contain specific knowledge of conditions in Upper Canada, but it reveals considerable awareness of comparative circumstances in the United States, doubtless another indication that the *Albion* was close at hand. The political disturbances in Upper and Lower Canada that Moodie refers to in his letter were faithfully reported in that paper. Those events were also to bring about the next dramatic change in the circumstances of John and Susanna Moodie.

1 For example, the *Athenaeum* (3 April 1830) carried an advertisement for Susanna's *Enthusiasm, and Other Poems* (London 1830).
2 *The History of Mary Prince, a West Indian Slave* (London 1831) and *Negro Slavery Described by a Negro: Being the Narrative of Ashton Warner, a Native of St. Vincent's* (London 1831)
3 'Narrative of the Campaign in Holland in 1814' was published in the *United Service Journal* (1830), 385–404, and in John Henry Cooke, ed., *Memoirs of the Late War* (London 1831).
4 In *North American Quarterly Magazine* 6 (July 1835) the following poem appears: 'Lines: On a bunch of withered flowers, gathered on Hampstead Heath, and presented to the Author, by J.W.M. in the spring of 1830.'

5 *The Topographical, Statistical, and Historical Gazeteer of Scotland*, 2 vols (Edinburgh 1848), 1: 809

6 In Letter 14 John Moodie suggests a similar arrangement with the Children's Friend Society for Canada.

7 *DSAB*, 2: 487–91

8 *Ibid.*, 3: 626. In 1828 John purchased Donald's farm.

9 See Samuel Strickland, *Twenty-Seven Years in Canada West* (London 1853).

10 See *LOL*, 2–17; and Carl Ballstadt's dissertation, 'The Literary History of the Strickland Family' (University of London, 1965).

11 Ipswich Public Record Office, Suffolk, Glyde Collection; see also NA, Susanna Moodie Collection, reel A–1182.

12 Richard Bentley finally published John's *Ten Years in South Africa, Including a Particular Description of the Wild Sports* in 1835.

13 William Cattermole, *Emigration: The Advantages of Emigration to Canada* (London 1831), 26

14 James Traill of the Hobbister branch of the Traills was a distant relative of Thomas Traill of Westove, Catharine's husband. See William Traill, *A Genealogical Account of the Traills of Orkney* (Kirkwall 1883).

15 Dr John Charles Beales's land was located south of the grant of Stephen F. Austin and south of the Rio Colorado. On 30 March 1835 Austin wrote to another of his colleagues in that part of Mexico: 'I am very happy to hear that Doctor Beales is going on prosperously with the settlement of the families he contracted with the State Government, and that he expects them out from Ireland and Germany in a short time. I wish him every success in his enterprise, for it is an arduous one ...' Beales's colony was not, however, successful. It failed in the period of economic stagnation that followed the 'panic of 1837.' Ironically, it was the same prolonged economic depression that was prompting Upper Canadian settlers to look for alternative locations. See *The Papers of the Texas Revolution, 1835–1836*, ed. John H. Jenkins (Austin 1973), 1:49; Bobby D. Weaver, *Castro's Colony: Empresario Development in Texas, 1842–1865* (Texas 1985), 15; and J.S. Bartlett's letters to the Moodies in PHEC.

16 Cobourg *Star*, 30 Oct. 1835

17 British Library, Richard Bentley Archives, Add. MS 46, 640, f. 134 (microfilm L81, 135)

---

1 John Moodie to Susanna Strickland

92 Upper Seymour Street
Euston Square
My Dear Friend,   [summer 1830][1]

Will you allow me to see you alone? If you are engaged now, let me know when – I cannot meet you in presence of a third person

y^{rs} afft^y
J.W.D.M.

1 This note was probably written early in the summer of 1830 not long after John and Susanna had met.

2 John Moodie to Susanna Strickland

Scrabster[1]

My Dearest Susanna   19th August 1830

I had expected to hear from you soon after my arrival here, and therefore delayed writing for a few days, but I know my Susie will be anxious to have some account of my voyage which was happily terminated on last Saturday being two weeks from the day we sailed from Gravesend. It would not make a bad article to send to some of the periodicals were I capable of doing justice to all the little incidents in the course of it. A fishing smack is I believe the most uncomfortable conveyance in existence and tho' I am by no means particular as to my comforts and knew them of old yet I confess I felt my landing like a release from the pains of Purgatory. But I am so fond of adventures that I was by no means without my enjoyments, particularly in observing the manners and habits of my *messmates* for *all hands* met together at meals. We had a fair wind as far as the Firth of Forth which we reached after two days sail, and enjoyed a fine view of the coast most of the way with many a town and fine old castle. But I could hardly distinguish the coast of Suffolk from the distance, and a haze which veiled from my anxious view the spot which is dearest to my heart – perhaps my dear girl was walking on the beach – that vile mist! – I felt as if my heart could have leaped ashore and taken up its abode with yours for ever – Ah! would to God this wretched corporeal frame which occasions me so much suffering were as free and insubstantial as my Spirit: – how delighted and swiftly would it fly to the arms of my beloved Susie – to bask in her sunny smiles what countless kisses would I imprint on her dear lips – kind heaven which has often preserved me from danger and misery give me only her I love; I ask no more for this world to make me happy! Believe me you are indeed with me when I lie down and when I rise my thoughts are still with you – you still are present in my dreams with your smiles and the looks you wore when first I loved you and your eyes still rest on me with that expression which spoke to my heart that you loved again. Alas

my dearest, how long shall my arms on awaking from some sweet
dream of you return empty to my breast. My kind uncle remains as
he ever did to take an affectionate interest in all my concerns and
approves of my choice and would I am persuaded assist us if he
could, but he is not a man to talk of what he would do. I have seen
but few of my old friends or connections as yet. My kind friend
Lord Caithness[2] is expected north soon; when he arrives I shall see
him and if he can be of any service to me I know he will spare no
trouble to forward my views – he is a particular friend of the kings
and will it is thought be one of the Sixteen Scotch Peers. The
climate here is by no means agreeable and the season particularly
cold. I can hardly write, my fingers are half frozen as you will
perceive by this miserable scrawl which you must decipher as you
best can. In going north we were detained for more than a week at
Fort George[3] in the Murray Firth where I had first joined the 21st
reg[t]. We anchored between the walls and the beautiful village of
Rosemartney. I can hardly describe my feelings in thus unexpectedly
revisiting the scene of the happiest part of my life – the country was
much improved green fields where formerly were extensive mosses
– so painful were my sensations that I could not for two days
summon resolution to land. I thought on my poor comrades then
bouyant with youth and spirits nine-tenths of whom are now under
the sod. I cried like a child when I saw the furze and tufts of Scotch
fir where I had sported with my companions. I saw the well known
cottage where she dwelt who to my boyish ideas was all perfection,
who first taught me to sigh. What a melancholy history is that of [a]
Seventeen year [old] soldier. A.R.[4] I have alluded to in my account
[of the camp]ai[g]n in Holland – her parents compelled her to marry
when scarce Sixteen to a veteran officer of fifty who was [and] he is
now Fort Major of Fort George – shortly after the marriage her
father who had gone to dine with a friend in the Fort was found
dead not a hundred yards from his own cottage which death
prevented him from reaching. I went to see Mrs. R. who is a
melancholy widow of sixty, and next called to surprise A.R. what a
change – scarcely thirty years of age, from a lovely girl she has
become a tall spare figure. I gathered her history by half sentences
from her sister who walked over with me – she has lost her health
and has four children – sorrow was painted in her face – my heart
bled for her – she saw it, and I saw the tear rise in her eye but she
checked the feeling and attempted to look cheerful but it would not
do – I soon took my leave of her – thank God I did [not] see her

husband as I could hardly have been civil to a man who cou[ld ta]ke
a woman's hand [on] the terms he recieved A's. Now my dearest
[Susie] you will say 'what is all this to me entertaining me with his
first love' but I never told that love even to her who was the object
of my first tears – & I know you will forgive my feeling keenly for
an unhappy girl who deserved a better fate, and you know that I can
feel as warmly towards yourself as I ever did to another. You see
my dearest girl that I can have no concealment with you. I am
impatient to hear from you, and do pour out your heart as freely as I
do mine to you let us drink from the same cup – we have both
tasted unhappiness and now let our spirits be mingled for we must
endeavour to make up for what we have already suffered by the
happiness we expect to enjoy in each others arms. And now farewell
my beloved Susie. May God bless you with health and comfort you
in this vale of tears – continue to love me as I believe you do at
present and let us trust in God to make us both happy in this world
if it is his will – & I remain, My Dearest Susanna

> yours ever Affectionately
> *J.W. Dunbar Moodie*

PS Mrs. Pringle desires me to tell you that they could not manage to
write you before leaving London being so much occupied with
preparations for their departure. They were to [leave the] day after I
left London

> J.W.D.M.

I believe you already have my direction. If not, direct to J.W.
Dunbar Moodie Esqr Scrabster, Thurso Caithness, W.B.

I have begun to write an account of my voyage which if I can make
it readable I shall send to some friend in London to get something
for it if possible – my dear Susie you must do me a little favor, if
you are in the humour of painting[5] will you send me one of your
pretty little birds done in your best stile, for the Chief of the
Dunbar's my dear Uncle, which will gratify him exceedingly. You
can paint it perhaps on a part of your letter so that it may be cut
out. I have been reading a history of the Dunbars which is full of
romance and instances of heroism particularly of the celebrated

defence of the castle of Dunbar by *Black Agnes*[6] the Countess of Dunbar against the English army – it is a fine subject for a tale. I am going to make extracts from a box full of charters and old letters as old some of them as the 14th century. What a treat to an antiquarian! Farewell my Susie

J.W.D.M

1 The site of an anchorage under high cliffs on the western part of the interior of Thurso Bay on the north coast of Caithnesshire.

2 John Anstruther, on the deaths of his mother, Grizzel-Maria Thomson, daughter of Henry St Clair, and his grand uncle, Colonel James Paterson St Clair, became heir-general of the Earls of Orkney and Lords Sinclair. Sinclair was the name of the Caithness lords. It was presumably expected that he would become one of the sixteen Scottish peers in the British House of Lords, the representation set by the Act of Union in 1707. The sixteen peers were chosen by the other lords in open election. See Sir Bernard Burke, *A Genealogical History of the Dormant, Abenant, Forfieted and Extinct Peerages of the British Empire* (Baltimore 1987).

3 On the Moray Firth in County Nairn, Parish of Ardersier. Its building commenced in 1748 on a site at which 'the ramparts' on three sides 'rise almost out of the sea.' The fort was capable of housing three thousand men, and it included 'elegant accommodation for the Governor and other officers.' See *A Survey of the Province of Moray, Historical, Geographical and Political* (Aberdeen 1798); and *The Topographical, Statistical, and Historical Gazeteer of Scotland*, 2 vols (Edinburgh 1848), 1:614.

4 In 1814 John's regiment had been stationed at Fort George and embarked from it to begin 'foreign service' in Holland. John writes of that embarkation and of the girl he left behind at the beginning of his 'Narrative of the Campaign in Holland in 1814, with Details of the Attack on Bergen-Op-Zoom': 'As for the officers, most of us being young fellows, and single, we had little to damp our joy at going on foreign service. For my own part, I confess I felt some tender regrets in parting with a fair damsel in the neighbourhood, with whom I was not a little smitten, but I was not of an age to take these matters long to heart, being scarcely sixteen at the time. Poor A—— R—— has since been consigned, by a calculating mother, to an old officer, who had nearly lost his sight, but accumulated a few thousand pounds in the West Indies' (*United Service Journal and Naval and Military Magazine* [1830], Part 2, 385).

5 See *LOL*, 16, 198–9.

6 Actually the Countess of March, who, in the absence of her husband, led the defence of Dunbar Castle against the English army during a siege of nineteen weeks, from late 1337 through the early part of 1338. According to one verse account of the defence, the castle was seated on a promontory projecting into the sea and connected to the mainland by a bridge of rock. See *Black Agnes; or, The Defence of Dunbar* (London 1804).

3 John Moodie to Susanna Strickland

My Dearest Susie:

Scrabster
7th September *1830*

On recieving your former letter I sat down to endeavour to cheer your heart after the sufferings you had experienced but alas! my love, I had nothing to communicate regarding my prospects of a more encouraging nature than what you already knew, & on second thoughts I determined to delay writing for a few days until I could get an answer to a proposal I had made to Mr. Heddle,[1] my brother in law, who is now in Orkney.

Ah! my dearest girl how I grieved to hear of your illness. What would I have given to have been with you, to have supported your aching head in my arms. Every day of absence, every line I read of your dear letters augments my love and esteem for you and when I think that much of your sufferings have been occasioned by your affection for me, my heart would indeed be cold if I did not love you more than ever. I now indeed feel that life has no enjoyments for me while absent from you. What toils could I not endure what sacrifices could I not make to clasp my Susie once more to my heart, to press those dear lips to mine. My whole soul is absorbed in one sweet dream of you – you must and shall be mine. I cannot describe the anxiety I feel on your account – For God's sake my dearest, endeavour to calm your mind and despise the opinions of those who would reduce your best and most exalted feelings to their own standards. The most dangerous of all decievers are those who first decieve themselves. I believe Mr. R[2] to be in many respects a good and an honest man, but you must excuse me dear Susan when I say that I consider him as a man whose mind is perverted by fanaticism. This is really the most charitable construction that I can put on his conduct. The passage you quoted from his letter when I first read it excited the most unqualified disgust and indignation, and I am most glad that you resented it as you did. You owed it to your own insulted dignity and wounded feelings and I trust you will not again be troubled with his interference. Do not mistake me dearest, I feel but for your own happiness in the matter. As for myself individually tho' in [his] persecuting you I indeed feel wounded in the tenderest part – every other feeling for such people

is absorbed in contempt. I believed that my Susie knows me too
well to think that I would wish her to marry me if she thought she
was violating her principles in doing so. Indeed much as I love you I
could not urge it on such terms. I shall never quarrel with my own
darling's enthusiasm but at the same time remember that in this
world where the feeling mind has so much to suffer, a little
indifference is also a most useful quality to enable us to pass thro'
it in tranquility and make us independent of others who would
poison our enjoyments every moment of our lives. But I am
encroaching on Mr R's privilege of preaching – would to God that I
could act up to my own doctrines. It would have saved me many a
bitter pang. It is now time that I should tell you what I have been
doing and mean to do. I have been trying to raise the wind which is
no easy matter for a poor man. I am in want of a lever and a
fulcrum, so that if old Archimedes was alive I doubt whether he
would find it much easier to assist me in this respect, than to
succeed in his own plan of raising the world. I have been
recommended to endeavour to enter into a compromise with Mr.
Threpland,[3] a gentleman who is indebted to our family in the sum
of £3000, to avoid the expense and delay of a law suit should he
contest the claim. I have in consequence requested my friend Mr.
George Traill[4] (who has just been elected M.P. for Orkney) to write
to Mr. Threpland on the subject as the mutual friend of both parties
to endeavour to get the business settled by compromise. I have also
written to Mr Heddle to get him to join me in the application to
Mr. Threpland, as he is interested in the matter thro' his wife. If he
will do this it will be a *matter* of great importance to me as he is
rich and can pursue his claim legally should Mr. Threpland refuse
payment. I have not yet recieved an answer from Mr. Heddle but I
shall see Traill before I close my letter and shall tell you what he
says. At all events should Heddle not be inclined to assist me in
this respect I shall try *to see* what I can do without him, and I feel
that the happiness of both of us is so much involved in our speedy
union that I am prepared to make any sacrifice if it can be brought
about by this means. Should this means fail, my friend James Traill
in London (brother of the M.P.) offered to assist me in getting a loan
of £100 but I would rather avoid contracting any debts if I can help
it. Should your Aunt relish the plan you mentioned in your last
letter I have little doubt that we could manage to live as comfortably as either of us care about, provided we can get a cheap
house, and I think we could contrive to make her more comfortable

than she would be with strangers. I am fond of old people
particularly when they are intelligent and I really hope she would
consent to your proposal. Our chief expense would then be the
furniture we might require. I care for no luxuries, dearest, let me
but press you to my heart and I will live upon those dear lips, and
these worldly cares would be forgotten. My uncle is very much
pleased with your letter and desires to be most kindly remembered
to you. How shall I thank you my sweet Susie for your verses on
such an unworthy subject. The last is beautiful in particular. Would
to God that the hand which wrote them was now within mine, how
would I resist writing in such sweet numbers what I so truly feel
and would write had I language to express how I love you. You say
Susie that you are working a watch guard for me of silk – could you
not make me a hair one? You know from whose head it must be cut
– But do not spoil your sweet locks for it. The story about the Duke
of Clarence and my uncle is quoted correct and shows with many
other early anecdotes of him that he is an excellent hearted man for
all that has been said against him. You are too romantic, dear. I
must tell you once for all my love, that I will not father any of your
bairns unless I write at least one half of them and stand by while
you write the other half. I am glad you have begun your larger work
as it will amuse your mind. Only keep the characters true to nature
and themselves and give them sufficient individuality and I am sure
you will succeed. As it is a romance some allowance must be made
for improbability of incidents, but you must look to the characters
principally for shewing your skill and talents. If they must be high
coloured let them be a[t] least naturally sensational. I feel so lost
and out of my element when away from you, love that were I
capable of writing anything tollerable, I could not do it now. I have
long been intending to write a personal narrative of my residence
and adventures at the Cape but I know not when I shall be able to
settle myself to the task. I can do nothing in that way unless I am
perfectly easy in my mind at the time. Your last letter dated 21st
Augst, recieved yesterday – by the bye, dearest in both your last
letters you wrote a good deal which might be read without opening
the seal by simply squeezing the sides. There are many prying
people here as well as at other places. And from the appearance of
the letters I rather suspect someone had been looking into them.
You must not write a word, dear, in your next on that part that can
be seen from without. Remember me most kindly to your mother

and your sisters and believe me ever My Dearest Susanna, Your faithful and affectionate

J.W. Dunbar Moodie

I have just learned that Lord Caithness is not to be one of the sixteen Peers and I think there is no chance of his being in Caithness soon. However it is not improbable that I shall be obliged to go to Edinburgh to look after the money I mentioned, when I shall most likely see him. My uncle Dunbar[5] has every chance of succeeding to a property of £3000 a year if he follows up the matter. There is no doubt that he is the next heir of entail, and so well aware is the present possessor of the weakness of his title to the estate that he is selling every movable he can but he will have to refund. My uncle has also become entitled to take up *two Baronetcies* by the failure of heirs male. I think I told you that he is now the head of the family, so that much property may yet revert to his family on the failure of heirs. He is proceeding very quietly in getting his claims established, never mentioning the subject to any one. I have hardly seen any of my friends here yet but I intend to see my Grand Uncle Lord Duffus[6] as soon as I can. Perhaps he may be able to be of use to me.

1st Oct.
My own ... My beloved Susie, I have just returned from Orkney and found my dearest's letter. Its contents did not at all surprise me. Ah! My dear, how anxious I feel regarding your health. I am most unhappy in being the cause (tho' innocent one) of suffering to one whom I so dearly love, but I thank God you did not know the cause of my silence. The truth is I have been given up for lost by my friends in Caithness for the last three weeks. My old craze for boat sailing siezed me one day and I went with a young man who had bought a small vessel from a cousin of mine to take a sail along the Caithness side of the Pentland Firth intending to be back in a few hours. The weather was delightful and the rocks of my native isle looked so grand and beautiful that I could not resist the temptation to pay them a visit and see my excellent friend the clergyman of Hoy. Many a time, Susie, I wished you had been with us to enjoy the stupendous views we had of the western rocks towering up to the height of a thousand feet from the ocean. It would have

transported your mind beyond itself. I felt proud of having been
nursed amid scenes exceeding in grandeur the wild imagination of
the poet. Our vessel was about 24 feet in length and was only half
decked, and our crew consisted of my companion, a young man of
very little experience in boating and of none of the Pentland Firth,
and a little boy not worth his salt for all the work he could do.
I of course played the part of steersman and pilot as being best
acquainted with the coast and my companion managed the sails. We
had just rounded the promontory of Rora-head when the wind began
to blow with great violence with heavy squalls from the mountains.
We took in our gaff-topsail which we had hitherto carried and
proceed[ed] along the rocks towards Hoy mouth. Once or twice
we were nearly laid on one broadside with the gusts from the
mountains but we were obliged to carry sail to stem the tide and get
in before dark. Unfortunately I had been misinformed regarding the
time of low water. I had depended on having the flood tide to carry
us in at Hoy mouth before dark. We were consequently not able to
beat up against the ebb tide which was running out like a river
between the islands (you are perhaps aware that the tides here run
at the rate of from 3 to 9 miles an hour at this place). After being off
and on for some time until the ebb tide was exhausted we were
beating up between the islands of Hoy and Gremsay, the channel
between which is very narrow from the outlying rocks on the Hoy
side, when my companion took it into his head to knock up and
contrary to my remonstrances took in the fore sail without which
(being sloop rigged) she would not come about, in consequence of
which proceeding she twice missed stays and went ashore on the
very worst part of the island of Gremsay. Fortunately there was not
any sea from its being low water or we must inevitably have been
provided for. My companion dropped the anchor, which was the last
instance of presence of mind he showed on the occasion. While we
were lying thumping on the rocks in this manner, I percieved a boat
pulling up along the rocks towards us but from the darkness of the
night they did not percieve us at first. On hailing them they came
towards us when I recognized the voice of my friend the clergyman
of Hoy, who happened to be returning from Stromness and was
about to stand over to Hoy before they heard us call to them. The
worthy minister was quite astonished at being saluted by name as
he did not know my voice and did not know that I was in the
country. The old man was rejoiced to see me and to have it in his
power to assist us. His boat was crowded with men and women

who all knew me. It would have done your heart good to see us shaking hands and to hear the heart felt welcomes I recieved from our poor islanders – kind hearted souls they completely reconciled me to my country which only a sudden but irresistible impu[l]se tempted me to revisit.

We stowed the women into our little vessel to be out of the way while the boat proceeded to carry out a spare anchor which we fortunately had to endeavour to haul out the vessel from the rocks – in the meantime the kind clergyman went ashore to get more assistance. My companion remained quiet from being quite un-prepared for difficulties which I was glad of as I could now do as I liked and was most anxious to get him out of the scrape his obstinacy and inexperience had got him into. I made the boat take up the anchor which was first dropped and carry it out to the whole length of the cable and before the other boat had come to our assistance I had the vessel hauled out quite clear of the rocks, and with the assistance of the head sails we got into Stromness. It blew at this time a perfect hurricane so that my friend the clergyman was obliged to remain all night in the island of Gremsay which is not a mile from his own house in Hoy. Next day we crossed over to Hoy where we have been detained for the last three weeks from a continuance of bad weather which prevents the post from leaving Orkney. It would have been of no use writing from there as we intended returning to Caithness as soon as it was possible to cross the Pentland Firth which you know is a very dangerous place in bad weather. As soon as we could we proceeded to Long-hope which was part of my father's property, where we were again detained for some days by bad winds. I cannot describe the kindness of the poor people. Some of them shed tears when they saw me, saying that 'they never expected to see one of our family again.' I could not pass a cottage without shaking hands with my old acquaintances. A poor old woman near a hundred years of age, who had been a servant of my grand fathers, sent her grand daughter to me with a pair of *worsted stockings* in a present. She was not able to come herself. I could not wound her feelings by offering her a return for this genuine instance of kindness, but went to see the poor woman and recieved her blessing. Ah! my Susie had you been with me this would indeed have been one of the happiest moments of my life. I left Orkney under painful circumstances and certainly did not expect to find such attachment remaining towards my family and myself. If my dear Susie lived here she would be adored by the poor people. I have been thinking if we could manage to live here for some time we might buy a little place which might be improved in value. The clergyman acting here is a man after my own heart and is beloved by the people. He visits them all in health and in sickness. Having studied medicine he prescribes and gives them medicine gratis. You may therefore easily concieve his moral influence with his extensive flock. He is a son of the clergyman of Hoy. Hamilton is his name.[7] I have not yet seen Mr. Heddle, but I am going today to see Mr. Traill when I expect to hear what he intends doing. If not I shall go to Orkney again in a few days. I have written this long story about my adventure in Orkney to amuse you and exculpate myself from the charge of neglect. My dearest do not conjure up imaginary ills to distress your mind. Do not fancy that I can love you less because you love me more. My happiness is yours and all I desire is to be in any situation that will make you happy. Write me what your aunt says to your proposal. I shall be glad to come into any arrangement you may make for I feel we cannot live but in each other arms. That cough you complain of allarms me – for heavens sake my dearest girl take care of yourself and avoid catching cold. Before concluding my letter I shall have seen Traill who has been every day in Thurso inquiring about me since I left Caithness.

Castle-Hill 2nd October 1830 –
My dearest I am now with my friend Traill who will frank my letter for me. Heddle has recieved my letter but has not thought proper to answer it. I fear from what he tells me that there is but little chance of getting the money due to our family as the *Bond* is *amissing* and payment will doubtless be refused until it is produced. I intend going over to Orkney in a few days – Unless your aunt will agree to your proposal I fear we must wait for better times. However, my love I shall strain every nerve to find means of being united forever to my beloved Susie. It is not impossible that I may be able to get a house cheap in Orkney in the mean time, and living is not dear in this country. Farewell dearest love and believe me ever your sincere and affectionate,

J.W. Dunbar Moodie

1 Robert Heddle of Melsetter was married to Henrietta Moodie, John's sister.
2 John is referring to Pastor Andrew Ritchie.

3 In PHEC, no. 98, John Phin, an Edinburgh lawyer who corresponded on matters related to Melsetter, mentions a Sir Patrick Murray Threpland Rudge, the proprietor of Toftingall. Apparently the Moodie family had some claim against him, but it is not clear that this is the same Mr Threpland mentioned by John.

4 George Traill (1787–1871) was a member of the Ratter and Hobbister branch of the Traill family.

5 *A Dunbar Pedigree*, prepared by William Jaggard, does not list an Alexander Dunbar having entitlement to any traditional Dunbar properties; for example, Grangehill or Earnehill or Durn. Although Grangehill, the area from which John Moodie's mother came, had been acquired by Mark Dunbar, Baronet of Durris and Grangehill, in 1592, by the early eighteenth century it is not cited in connection with the main Dunbar inheritance. Presumably some Dunbars still lived in the area and claimed association with the main line. See *A Dunbar Pedigree: A Biographical Chart Tracing the Descent of the Dunbar Family, through Fourteen Successive Centuries, form the early English and Scottish Kings*, prepared by William Jaggard, author of 'Shakespearean Bibliography' (n.p., n.d.).

6 Benjamin Dunbar, Lord Duffus, of Hempriggs Castle (1761–1843). See *Complete Peerage*, 4:498.

7 *The Edinburgh Almanack, or Universal Scots Register for 1828* (Oliver and Boyd, 1827), 397, lists G. Hamilton as the incumbent for Graemsay in Cairston Presbytery, Synod of Orkney.

---

4 John Moodie to Susanna Moodie

My Dearest Susie,   [Spring, 1831][1]

I have just called on Cap‍ᵗ. Pigot[2] at his lodgings but the curmudgeon had not the decency to ask me to dine with him.

Major Dundas[3] is in London with Mrs. D. but will be back at 1/2 5. I have determined to wait for him. If he cannot offer me a bed I shall be back tonight but you must not be anxious if I should not come as I shall not refuse a bed if he offers it.

> I remain Dearest Susy
> Yours Affectionately
> *J.W.D. Moodie*

Don't sit up for me after 11

1 The letter suggests that Susanna and John are married and living in their first home, Middleton Villa in Pentonville.

2 Captain Hugh Pigot, brother of Major General Richard Pigot and Major George Pigot, both prominent Cape settlers during John's residence in South Africa. See

postscript to Letter 7; and *The Journals of Sophia Pigot*, ed. Margaret Ranier (Capetown 1973.)

3 Major William Bolden Dundas (1785–1858) was another Scot who had spent some time at the Cape of Good Hope, arriving in 1822 and serving as both a soldier and administrator. From 1828 to 1830, when he returned to England, he was military secretary to the governor of South Africa. During 1839–52 he would serve as inspector of artillery in Britain. See *DSAB*, 3:247.

5 John Moodie to Susanna Moodie

110 Seymour Street
Euston Square
My Dearest Suky,   [early March 1832][1]

I arrived safe here yesterday morning unburked[2] and uncholera'd what a fortunate fellow I am. I did not get a wink of sleep on the coach and I dressed myself and breakfasted immediately and proceeded in search of Nunky and found him at the Craven Hotel.[3] By way of refreshing myself after my want to rest I sat up drinking sundry liquors with the old gentleman till one this morning when I went to bed and slept sound till 6. I am just going to call on Katy and shall finish my dispatch there if I am allowed. I have not seen Traill yet but shall today if possible. My Grand Uncle Lord Duffus is in town. I shall go and see him when I have time. The folks here do not seem to care much about the cholera. You must not be anxious about me as I shall carefully avoid any suspicious places. I shall try and get a frank from G. Traill to whom you may direct your letters (George Traill, Esq. M.P. 2 Cleveland Court – S^t. Jame's). I have just seen Katy – she returns with me to Reydon. Now my dear Suky I have nothing further to tell you so God bless you

Yours affectionately
J.W. Dunbar Moodie

Write me in a day or two and tell me how you are getting on – love to 'Thay' etc. etc.

1 This letter prompts Susanna to comment to Emma Bird: 'Moodie is in London, he was forced to leave me ten days after my confinement to meet his uncle,

Mr. Dunbar, who after coming upwards of six hundred miles on his journey to see us, fell ill in Town ...' (*LOL*, 66).

2 A reference to Burke and Hare, notorious Scottish murderers who attacked travellers to obtain bodies for anatomical study.

3 During the nineteenth century there was, and there remains today, a Craven Hotel at 38 Craven Street, London WC2.

---

6 John Moodie to Susanna Moodie

110 Seymour Street
Euston Square

My Dearest Hunchy   Friday M^g 1832

Don't expect a long letter for I am pressed for time. I was delighted to hear that you and little Dab-chick are getting on so swimmingly. You must not mind the squalls of your little kitten for it is the way with our family to make a noise when they do not get their own way – even after they grow up. We shall probably have some worse squalls in crossing the Atlantic which are much more dangerous than these domestic ones – for tho' baby may be often subject to these little storms of passion – and be moreover *somewhat* leaky as nurse must know – they only afford her an opportunity to shew the strength of her little timbers. I have my M.S. to Elder to examine. Colburn[1] from press of business could not attend to it. James Traill says that it is a *very* creditable performance this is a good deal from him. My friend *Gemman* Traill[2] is afraid to come to London for fear of his boys getting Cholera. I have written to tell him how groundless his fears are, and to urge him to come to Southwold and talk the matter over with me etc. etc. etc. etc. Miss Talbent is getting on with Mrs. Stones business[3] and I hope we shall get it settled very soon. Katy and I shall if possible start from here on Monday but do not be fancying that we are *burked* if we do not make our appearance on Tuesday. I delivered dear Goodings[4] letter. I do not know what I should buy for her worthy her acceptance but she must take the will to please for the deed if I do not find something pretty. I wish to God you were here to choose yourself for a more stupid and worse person to attend to these matters you could not have found than myself. I shall try and find something for Thay. I am thinking of buying one of these shawl gown pieces for her which would make rather a show in Southwold – it will not cost

above 30/ I am quite puzzled what to buy for little Dab-chick's
Godmother Mary. Her hand you know is rather large and I might be
liable to give offence by seeming to know it. Burn this letter without letting any body read it and I shall do my best. God bless you
and Dab-chick Love to dear Thay – to dear Goody etc.

Yours affectionately
J.W. Dunbar Moodie

I have seen Joe Linder[5] he is pretty well now. I shall see him again
to day. I left a note for Marshall[6] but have not heard from him yet. I
have but small hopes of making him bleed.

1 John would have approached Henry Colburn because he was the publisher of the
  United Service Journal, in which John's 'Narrative of the Campaign in Holland ...'
  had appeared in 1830.
2 The *Oxford English Dictionary* lists 'gemman' as a slang form of 'gentleman.'
3 In a letter of 1 June 1833 (PHEC, no. 112) Agnes Strickland refers to an Ethelinde
  Talbent as the residual legatee in a family will. It is unknown, though, exactly
  what 'Mrs. Stone's business' referred to here was.
4 Susanna had asked her close friend Mary Gooding to be baby Catherine's
  godmother. *Flora Lyndsay* is dedicated to Mary Gooding.
5 Joe Linder later became head of the firm of Linder and Kingsley in Brooklyn, New
  York, where Moodie sought him out in 1856. See *LOL*, 167; and Agnes's letters
  (nos. 112, 116, 129) in PHEC.
6 W. Marshall, the publisher of the *Gem*, which included Susanna's 'The
  Disappointed Politician' in 1832. See *LOL*, 59.

---

7 John Moodie to Lord Lynedoch

Southwold – Suffolk
24th March 1832

My Lord,[1]

I feel that an apology is due for the liberty I have taken in venturing
to address your Lord[p] without having the honor of a personal introduction. But having had the honor of serving under your command
in the unfortunate attack on Bergen op Zoom in 1814 where I had
the satisfaction of opening the Waterpoort Gate and drawbridge
which was the only communication effected with the interior of
that place, as detailed in a Narrative of that attack lately published
with The Earl of Munsters account of the campaign in Portugal[2] – I

venture to hope that your Lord^P will feel inclined to favor my views in a matter totally unconnected with the Service, and where some acknowledgement of your Lordship's approbation of my conduct might prove useful in furthering my interest – or at all events would be highly gratifying to my feelings as a soldier who whenever opportunities have offered, has been zealous in the discharge of his duty.

Having vainly endeavoured to procure advancements in my profession, I am at length compelled to remove with my family to Upper Canada where I hope to procure a sufficient subsistance by farming – but having no friend who is able to furnish me with letters to Sir John Colburne the Governor of the Province, which is considered necessary to the respectability of a settler; I am encouraged by Your Lordship's character to solicit your kind assistance in this matter. Should your Lord^P deem it necessary I can produce strong testimonials as to character and intelligence from persons who have held important situations at the Cape of Good Hope where I have resided for many years – among these I may name Major Dundas of the Royal Artillery now at Woolwich and Mr. Justice Menzies,³ now Chief Justice of that colony. Testimonials in my favor from both these gentlemen have been lodged in the hands of the Commissioners of Police (Major Rowan and Mr Mayne) to whom I had formerly applied for employment in that establishment. It may be further necessary to state that I was severely wounded in the left wrist in the attack alluded to, in consequence of which I have been in a great measure deprived of the use of my arm – and for which I recieved a temporary pension which was discontinued after two years. With great respect

> I remain
> My Lord
> Your Lordships Most Ob^t Hum^bl Servt
> *J.W. Dunbar Moodie*
> Lieut. H.P. 21st Fusiliers

P.S. I may further refer Your Lord^P to Major General Richard Pigot to whom I am well known

J.W.D.M.

1 Cross-written over the top left corner of the first sheet is a note by Lord Lynedoch:

'Rec[d] 26th March – Ans[d] Do.Do. Wrote Sir John Colborne about him on 19th May – .' Although born a commoner, Thomas Graham, Baron Lynedoch (1748–1843), married a daughter of the Earl of Caithness and became commander of John's Scottish regiment. He was knighted after the Battle of Barraosa and elevated to the peerage.

2 Moodie's account had been republished in John Henry Cooke, ed., *Memoirs of the Late War* (London 1831), along with two other pieces.

3 Mr Justice William Menzies (1795–1850) was born in Edinburgh and graduated from the University of Edinburgh. He emigrated to South Africa in 1827 and became the senior puisne judge at the Cape. He laid the foundations of the legal system in South Africa. See *DSAB*, 3:601–2.

8 John Moodie to Susanna Moodie

Thursday May 24th 1832
25 Thavie's Inn[1]
Holborn Hill

My Dearest Susie,

I was delighted to hear from you and our dear little toddle. What a parcel of silly gawks you all were to go out in the boat without any occasion – you in particular. But never mind for that – it is the nature of you female creatures to do these extravagant things. I have had no rest for the soles of my feet since I came here, but I have got through a deal of work. I have paid Elder, Hodson, cum multis aliis. Your M.S.S. is in Elder's hands – mine in Colburn's *again*. Major Clerke[2] of the U.S. Journal has been my friend and spoke to the *great man* for me, and promises to aid me in every manner in his power. I look upon it as the next thing to being sold. I find that in spite of my shyness people are favorably impressed by my conversation, and seem to expect something from me. Elder is still much inclined to have the kind of work I mentioned on Canada. He has kindly advertised your poems in his list of books and still hopes to sell them. I therefore thought it best to have them in his hands. I have got a letter for Sir J. Colbourn from Lord Lynedoch which I have no doubt will be of service to us. I should have left London to night, but cannot till I see Lawrie[3] which will be tomorrow, so that I hope to start by the mail tomorrow night if possible.

I have sold out the £379 stock at 93 1/8 per cent, and paid £300 to a house here who have given me a letter of credit in Montreal for the am[t]. I have been infinitely bothered and worried. Yesterday I had to go with J. Linder to get a copy of our marriage register at St.

Pancras and had to petition the Governor of the Bank to allow me to sell out without getting a Power of Attorney from you which they wanted. I saw Mrs Leverton today for the first time, she is in high spirits and good humour and says that I have stolen a march on her with regard to Katy but she is well pleased on the whole with the match. I am glad Tom Traill is off. James Traill says he will raise the price of beef in Canada. Don't worry yourself with meeting me at Bird's, for I still hope to start from Southwold on Sunday. Bird talks of accompanying us to Edin^R. I breakfasted with Mr. Hodson this morning, he was very kind, and tho' he did not say much I could easily see that his opinion of Mr. Ritchie is much altered and by no means favorable to that sneaking *Gemman*. I have laid out a good deal of money but I don't think that I have taken many needless articles. I have nothing further to say but that I long to be again in the arms of my dearest Susie and to kiss my little toddle. God bless you dearest and believe me

Yours Affectionately
J.W. Dunbar Moodie

1 The oldest of the Inns of Chancery, located just south of Holborn Circus, this property became a public inn in the late eighteenth century. In Dickens's *Bleak House* Mr and Mrs Jellyby live at Thavie's Inn before finding permanent lodgings. The site was completely destroyed by bombing in 1940.
2 Sir Thomas Henry Shadwell Clerke (1792–1849). After losing his right leg during his army career, he became the first editor of Colburn's *United Service Magazine* in January 1829 and continued in that position until 1842.
3 Patrick Lawrie (1785–1869) was a Scot who would himself emigrate to the Cobourg area in 1835. He apparently had some South African connections for he was the agent by whom Moodie eventually received payment for his Groote Valley farm.

9 John Moodie to Sir John Colborne

York U.C.
15th October 1832[1]

To His Excellency Sir John Colborne K.C.B.[2] Lieutenant Governor of Upper Canada and Major General Commanding His Majesty's Forces therein.
– In Council

The Petition of John Wedderburn Dunbar Moodie of the 21st Regiment of Foot.[3]

Humbly Sheweth

That your Petitioner is a Native of Scotland. That he served seven years in His Majesty's Army, and that, he has not received any Lands or orders for Lands from the Crown.

Your Petitioner therefore humbly prays that Your Excellency will be pleased to grant him such allowance as is usually made to officers of his rank and Service.[4]

And Your Petitioner as in duty bound will every pray:

> J.W. Dunbar Moodie
> Lieut: Half Pay 21st Foot

1 NA, Upper Canada Land Petitions, 'M' bundle 17, RG 1, L 3, vol. 355a, 318
2 Knight Commander of Bath
3 Accompanying the petition is a letter from an officer of the Horse Guard, dated 26 May 1832. It testifies to the legitimacy of John's statement of service and reports 'favorably of his conduct.' He was appointed 2d lieutenant on 24 July 1813 and lieutenant on 5 May 1814; he was put on half pay on 25 March 1816.
4 A note on the document says, 'recommended in Council 27th Oct. 1832.'

---

10 [John Moodie to a friend in London][1]

> Newcastle District
> Upper Canada,
> 24th November 1833

... If you could make a trip out here next summer, *via New York by all means*, you would learn more of the actual state of this part of the colony in a few weeks' time than from all the books that have been written about it for the last ten years, and, I may add, from any one who has resided in it. Formerly, *your informant's* statements, however true they may have been, to a certain extent, several years ago, are now totally inapplicable to *Upper Canada*, or at least to this part of it, at the present day. I have had much conversation regarding the former state of the colony with the older settlers, and they all agree in stating that, until within the last four or five years, they were obliged to take goods in exchange for their wheat, etc., from the merchant; now, however, the case is totally altered, and MONEY can be readily obtained for most articles of *farm produce*. When the farmer happens to be in their debt, however, as *at home*, they frequently compel him to take goods in part payment, and allow a smaller price for their grain. Even making allowance for the difference of times, *your informant's* statement that not even value *in any shape* could be obtained for produce, I cannot help regarding as a great exaggeration. If this was the case, I would ask him how the inhabitants of the colony managed to *clothe them-selves*. As to *your informant's* other opinions, which only show his ignorance, I shall merely answer them by facts, which I engage myself to establish by the soundest of all proofs, viz. L.S.D. Your own doubts, I own, are only natural, but, from the arrangements I have made in your favour, you will not have ME to blame if you do not discard them. There is one thing I should state, which I believe I formerly mentioned, viz. that, notwithstanding the rapidly increasing value of land in most parts of the province, it will never do to force *a sudden sale*, as in such cases property is often sold at 1s.3d. below its market-price. Yesterday I completed a purchase for you of 227 acres of land, viz. 127 acres in Hamilton, about four miles to the eastward of Cobourg, and a 100 acres in Haldimand, about nine miles east from Cobourg and two miles and a half from the village of Grafton, near the shore of the Lake. The first mentioned place is to cost £600 currency, and the last mentioned £300, in all £900 currency, or, at the present rate of exchange, about £760 sterling. Each of these places contains about 70 acres of cleared land, free from stumps, and has small orchards of apple-trees, log-houses, barns, etc. My bargain with Mr. C., the seller, is that, if you are not pleased with your purchase, he will take back the land, and will return the price in two years, with 10 per cent. per annum for the use of the money. I have also had a lease drawn, subject to your approval, which will not be binding till the 1st of April next, in favour of Mr. ——, an experienced and substantial English farmer, who will take all the land for seven, fourteen, or twenty-one years, for the yearly rent of £80 currency, or nearly 9 per cent on the purchase-money. Mr. —— will at any time give up the lease on being paid at a fair valuation for his improvements. If you do not wish to take possession of the property for some years, I would strongly recommend you to grant a lease for seven years at least, as you must be well aware that justice will never be done to the land on shorter leases; and, on his own account, the tenant, in this case, will find it his interest to make improvements, which will cost you nothing, and the land be, consequently, increased in value, independently of the progressive increase in value in the lands in this part of the province, which I have formerly stated at 25 per cent. per annum, and which I still think I have not overrated. The country around these estates is beautiful, well cleared and fully settled, and the soil is generally excellent, particularly for grain crops. There is little expense and no uncertainty in titles in Upper Canada, if properly attended to. In the Lower Province it is other-wise. I have had the transfer duly effected, and shall forward you the title-deeds, if you desire it; in the meantime I send you a certificate from the Register-Office at Cobourg, where the transfer is recorded, *which alone* assures your title. By paying 1s.6d. at this office any person can ascertain whether any mortgages affect any property within the district, and at this office all transactions regarding land must by law be duly registered. The whole expense of transfer and recording is only £1:5:0 and lease 10s. You will perceive that I am most anxious to give you every satisfaction and security in the purchase I have effected for you, and I regret much that I could not venture to make any further purchases, at a time when there is a little temporary embarrassment in business, from a foolish panic, arising from a report that the British Government had refused to confirm the charter of the York Bank. Both of the places command a view of the Lake, and the scenery around is very beautiful. Lake Ontario has every appearance of a great ocean, with the exception of being less troubled, and the scenery on the shores of a softer character. The country through which the water communication will pass, between Lake Huron and Kingston, is generally very fine, and the difference of climate between it and the neighbourhood of Cobourg is hardly perceptible.

I shall now give you some account of my own proceedings since I wrote last, and detail my *future prospects*, in which I feel assured you will lend me your assistance, which I am determined to merit by the manner in which I shall conduct any commissions I may receive. Some time ago, by the death of a relation, I came in for a legacy, which enabled me to make some most desirable purchases of land at a sale of Government lands; I bought 200 acres of wild land in Douro, adjoining part of my grant which I had taken up in that township. As none of the neighbours who knew the land would oppose me, I got it at 20s. per acre, and immediately after the sale I was offered £2 per acre by a land speculator. I have contracted for clearing twenty acres and building a log-house there, where I intend to fix my future residence. I have sold my farm here for £200 and

800 acres of wild land, which is worth at least £400 more, in all £600, being better than double what my farm here cost a year ago. You will, say *this is pretty well*; but I have been favoured by the circumstance alluded to. I now come to my future plans, in which I think you can materially assist me without incurring any kind of responsibility. I propose, in conjunction with my brother-in-law, to undertake an agency business for investing money in *improved* lands for capitalists in England who may honour us with commissions for that purpose. My plan is shortly as follows; to make no purchases *until a good tenant is found*, who will pay a rent of from 6 to 8 per cent. on the price of the land for any term of years not exceeding twenty-one years. The price of the lands would not be payable until the purchase was affected, and clear titles made out and duly registered. We propose charging three per cent. on all transactions, with travelling expenses, which last would not be great. It would obviously be our interest, and we should make a point of managing the business in the most economical manner for the parties employing us. My brother-in-law has been several years employed by the Canada Company in locating settlers, &c. &c. and from his experience as a farmer is well qualified to form a correct judgement of the soil and situation of the lands, etc. As I have formerly stated, *wild lands* rise much more rapidly in value than improved lands, when judiciously chosen; but their ultimate rise in value, though certain, proceeds at a different rate, according to circumstances in different situations. Of course if employed to make purchases of wild lands, which is not a part of our immediate plan, we would require to examine the lands particularly, which would be attended with considerable difficulty from want of roads, etc. and a greater expense than in the first case. I should feel particularly obliged by your mentioning our proposal to any of your friends who might wish to purchase land in Canada (that is to say, in the neighbouring districts as regards Cobourg). I should state that, in *the first instance*, I would undertake to invest £5000 in land paying from 6 to 8 per cent. in rent in the immediate neighbourhood of Cobourg, Port Hope, etc. etc.; our future proceedings must be determined by circumstances. The society in the neighbourhood of your farms is much better than where I am. By-the-bye I should mention that though one of the farms is called 127 acres in the deed, it is supposed actually to contain about 150 acres. I trust my arrangements will give you satisfaction, and

I am, etc. etc.,

N.B. During last winter one house in Cobourg paid £4000 in *cash* for the article of wheat alone.

1 This unsigned letter was published in *Letters and Extracts of Letters from Settlers in Upper Canada* (London 1834) as 'Extracts of a Letter from a Half-pay Officer Settled in the Newcastle District, Upper Canada.' A portion of it was included in *The Valley of the Trent*, ed. Edwin C. Guillet (Toronto 1957), 73–4. That the letter was written by John Moodie is supported by both internal and external evidence. As reported in *Roughing It in the Bush*, the Moodies had recently received a legacy of £700, and John had purchased lot 20, concession 6, from Ephraim Sanford. This lot was adjacent to part of his government grant, lot 21, concession 6, to which the Moodies moved in February 1834. Samuel Strickland, like the proposed partner in the land agency business mentioned in the letter, had been in the employ of the Canada Company before settling in Douro. External evidence suggests that James Traill, brother of Thomas Traill and a magistrate at London's Union Hall Police Court, was the recipient of this letter or one like it. The 8 March 1836 letter to Traill included in this collection (Letter 14) refers to earlier letters written to him. On 23 March 1834 Traill wrote to Elizabeth Strickland: 'About 4 weeks ago I had a very full letter from Moodie from which I am very happy to collect that he is doing as well as he expected & has not lost his favourable opinion of Canada; nor his relish for his new mode of life. He has it in contemplation to undertake the duty of an agent for the purchase of land in Canada and has suggested my looking out amongst my friends here who have money to invest. I know no person in whom I would more implicitly confide, and if I had money in hand I am satisfied this is about the best way of turning it to account in the present state of this country & of Canada. But unfortunately I am a long way off yet from being a Capitalist, and fear Canada will be thoroughly settled before I am in a condition even to pay for my passage out there' (PHEC, no. 153). Furthermore, on 16 July 1834 Agnes Strickland in writing to Susanna says, 'The Canada Company are much pleased with Moodie's letter which has been printed' (PHEC, no. 115).

---

11 John Moodie to Richard Bentley

Township of Douro
Newcastle District
Upper Canada
9th Nov^r *1834*

Sir,

Several months ago I learned from my friend Mr. James Traill (now one of the Police Magistrates of London) that you had made an offer to him of publishing at your own risk; a M.S. of mine containing an Account of an eleven year's residence as a Settler at the Cape of Good Hope – allowing me one half of the profits, should the work prove successful. I immediately wrote him to conclude a bargain with you on these terms if you should not feel inclined to *purchase the M.S.* altogether. By a subsequent letter from my friend which I received a few days ago I am sorry to find that he has not *yet* come to any agreement with you. I have therefore determined to communicate directly with you my self – and if you are still inclined to publish the work on these terms I shall feel perfectly satisfied. As to the *title* of the work I leave that to your better judgement; I had called it 'The Colonist,' but I am sensible that is too general.

I have now been settled with my family in Canada for more than two years and having had every opportunity of becoming acquainted with the mode of life and prospects of a settler in all its details *from actual experience*, I think myself qualified to give a fair and impartial account of the country. It unfortunately, generally happens that most of those writers who have given an account of Canada have either been mere *'birds of passage,'* or, influenced by interested motives.

If you are inclined to treat with me for a work on Upper Canada I shall be happy to undertake it, – but my *time* is so valuable here that I could not afford to sacrifice it without a fair prospect of an adequate remuneration. My plan should be to give a plain unaffected narrative of the progress and proceedings of a settler in this colony whether he settled in the cleared and improved parts of the country or went into the back woods. I have tried both these kinds of settlement myself – hitherto successfully – and can therefore form a tollerable estimate of their respective advantages and disadvantages. My personal narrative would of course occupy a considerable portion of the work, and would be the more popular as containing, not mere *opinions* but my actual experience in the country. Should you prefer purchasing my Cape M.S. I should leave the price entirely to your own liberality.

I remain
Sir
Your ob^t. Servt.
J.W. Dunbar Moodie

via New York   Richard Bentley
                                             8 New Burlington Street
                                             London[1]

---

1 Note on envelope reads: 'J.W. Dunbar Moodie's African Narrative 1/2 profits.'

12 John Moodie to Sir John Colborne

Toronto
6th March 1835

To His Excellency Sir John Colborne, K.C.B. L[t] Governor of the Province of Upper Canada, and Major General Commanding His Majesty's Forces therein etc. etc. etc.[1]
The Petition of John W. Dunbar Moodie, late Lieutenant of Half Pay 21st Regiment.
Humbly Sheweth:
That your Petitioner having purchased at Public Sale, under the General Order from the Horse Guards dated 1st Aug[t] 1831 *Lots Nos.* 17 in the 3rd Con: of Verulam, the East half of lot No. 19 in the 8th Con: of Fenelon, the West part of lot No. 21 in the 6th Con: of Douro and the south half of No. 19 in the 4th Con: of Douro *in the Township of   in the County of* Northumberland *in the* Newcastle *District, and having resided in the said Lands since* 1[s]t November 1833
and improved the same, as will appear by the Certificate of Sam[l] Strickland & another *hereto annexed, humbly prays your Excellency will be pleased to direct a Patent for the same issue. And as in duty bound, Your Petitioner will ever pray,*

J.W. Dunbar Moodie

1 The italicized portions of this letter are the text of a petition form (NA, Upper Canada Land Petitions, 'M' bundle 19, RG 1, L 3, vol. 360, 33). Moodie made at least one other transaction for land, in Burleigh Township (see Upper Canada Land Petitions, 'M' bundle 19, RG 1, L 3, vol. 148).

13 John Moodie to James Herriot

Douro
Newcastle District
Sir,[1]   18th Nov[r] 1835

In answer to your enquiries I have no hesitation in stating that the erection of your mills at Selby has tended materialy to enhance the value of all lands in their neighbourhood for several miles round them, particularly in the Townships of Douro and Smith, and the inhabitants of Douro have been most essentially benefited by the excellent bridge you have erected across the Otonabee. I beg further to state that the improvements already mentioned, as also the commencement of a village at Selby have at a moderate computation raised the value of the lands within the distance of three or four miles, at least ten shillings per acre, and have greatly facilitated the settlement of the country.

> I remain
> Sir
> Yours Very Truly
> J.W. Dunbar Moodie

1 James Herriot was the 'enterprising young Scotchman' whom Catharine Parr Traill in *The Backwoods of Canada* described as 'the founder of the village' of Lakefield (then Selby). He had settled in Douro in 1833, establishing a sawmill, gristmill, and store at the narrowing of Lake Katchewanook into the Otonabee. For all his enterprise, however, Herriot was plagued by problems. Not only was his 'fine timber bridge' swept away in 1834 and again in the spring of 1835 but he seems never to have obtained clear title to the land on which he built his mills. James Thomson, another Scot, had been granted title to the former Crown land and had considerable leverage over Herriot when he ran into serious financial problems. Moodie's letter is one of a number of testimonials Herriot sought to support his petition claiming title to the land (see NA, Upper Canada Land Petitions, 'H' bundle, RG 1, L 3, vol. 238). When the notice was called on 1 August 1835, Thomson was apparently in control of the mills and managing the property for his own benefit. In July 1834 James Herriot married Francis Louise Irvine, daughter of William Irvine, staff physician to the forces, then living in Peterborough. Catharine Parr Traill describes Louisa Herriot's courage in her sketch 'Female Trials in the Bush,' *Anglo-American Magazine* 2 (1853), 426–30.

---

14 John Moodie to James Traill

> Douro – Newcastle Dist[t].
> U. Canada
> 8th March 1836

In my first letters from this colony, you would percieve that I indulged in a strain of sanguine anticipation, respecting my own prospects, and those of the country. *Then*, indeed, I had every reason

to do so, and even now, notwithstanding many cruel disappointments as respects myself, and numberless *individuals* round me, I
cannot allow my personal feelings and privations, so far to bias my
judgement as to make me retract much of what I have already
stated as to the *future* prospects of society here, or of the individuals, *in general*, of which it is composed. What I have erred in, – is
in supposing, not that emigration was in its infancy: – but that it
would be steadily progressive. In this opinion I was not singular as
all the most shrewd and intelligent settlers here indulged the same
expectations; and are now suffering in proportion as they acted upon
them. Before proceeding to particulars, I will now state one *broad
fact*, that should be always borne in mind in treating of Canada: –
that its *present* prosperity and progress in improvement must
depend *chiefly* upon emigration and the expenditure of imported
capital. This at first sight, may appear a very trite observation, but
obvious as it is, due weight has never been given to the circumstance; and emigrants and travellers have generally allowed themselves to be decieved into too sanguine expectations of the country
in respect to the profits of farming. Calculations on paper of the
profits arising from the clearing of land and farming in this colony
are always erroneous: – generally as to *assumed* facts; – and, I may
say, always, they turn out to be so in practice. The truth is, that
labour is so dear, and must continue so, while unoccupied land
remains on the North American continent; – that the profits arising
from its employment are very small, and subject to many contingencies. In other words, labour is invariably high, (bearing no proportion to profits) while agricultural produce is uncertain as to
quantity, and still more so as to the price it may yield. Still, there is
no question that industrious farmers may, and do succeed in obtaining a tolerably comfortable subsistance for themselves, and a similar
provision for their families; but it seldom happens that they can
save any money from the proceeds of their farms, and only when
they have labouring families to save them the expense of hiring.
The only classes who can make fortunes here are Store-Keepers, –
Land speculators, – Millers, – and I may add *Lawyers*: (a bad feature,
by the bye, in the colony). I may state as a general fact, that farmers
only profit by the labour of their own families. Most of them, however, fall into the mistake of occupying and clearing more land than
they can cultivate to advantage; – by which they only sink money
which is never redeemed, and increase their toils and cares. It is a
common error most people fall into with respect to Canada, to sup-

pose that wild land can be improved and afterwards sold at a price proportionate to the extent of clearing and improvements. As far as *my* observation extends, I have remarked that although a certain degree of improvement, – say, the erection of a log hut and clearing 20 or 30 acres, will greatly increase the *saleable* value of a lot of land, anything beyond this is so much money thrown away. This is easily accounted for when we consider, that *capital* here bears but a very small proportion to the quantity of *land* in the market. In many parts of the United States the case is otherwise, for there capital or money is much more abundant in proportion to land in the *older settled States*: – and I have been assured by many respectable and intelligent Americans that land is easily sold there at prices equivalent to the improvements. It is quite common, I am told, in the State of New York, for industrious men to purchase wild lands, and make extensive clearings, build good houses etc. on them by their own labour aided by borrowed capital, and sell them again with a handsome profit. When things come to this state here, which they certainly will in a few years, the progress of improvement will be prodigiously accelerated. I shall now endeavour to give you some account of the present state of the colony, which is greatly changed within the last three years. When I arrived in the Colony in 1832 the emigration was very great; – money in consequence was plentiful, and lands were very saleable and rapidly rising in price. Of this emigration, the Newcastle District, with its healthy climate, and magnificent chain of inland lakes and rivers, which might easily be rendered navigable, attracted a large portion. Almost unlimited credit was given by the Store-Keepers to the settlers on the security of the rising value of their lands. At the same time all who could command the requisite capital, were eagerly investing their money in land speculations, in the *then* well founded expectation of soon realizing a handsome return for their outlay. Could this emigration have been supported, the progress of improvement would have been most rapid and certain. All classes would have benefited by it; – the Store-Keeper, and the land speculator *immediately*, and the farmer would have been enabled to obtain a remunerating price for his farm produce, *on the spot*, without incurring the expense of carrying it to market over bad roads. Everything *then* wore such an aspect of prosperity, that we should not wonder that most of the older settlers, as well as the newcomers, could not distinguish that portion of it which was *real and permanent*, from what was only temporary, liable to interruption, or entirely illusive. In this general *mania*, (as

it now appears) the capital which in other circumstances would
have been employed in internal improvements, which would have
been beneficial to the community, as well as to the individual, was
generally diverted to land speculations, which, if they do not *always*
retard the settlement and improvement of the country (as many
people think) certainly have not hitherto forwarded these objects. In
the years succeeding 1832 emigration to this country has greatly
declined, and while the local demand for produce has been much
reduced, the low price of wheat in the English market, from a succession of favorable seasons, has prevented our farmers from realizing a remunerating price here for our staple article of export. Wheat
which formerly sold for 5/ per bushel (colonial currency) has
declined to 4/ and 3/9. The merchants of Quebec and Montreal who
supply the Upper Canada Store-Keepers became alarmed, and the
latter were compelled to call in all their outstanding debts. The
Banks at the same time ceased to discount and a general stagnation
of business of every kind was the consequence, which greatly
increased the general distress. Great quantities of land were forced
into the market, and farming stock of every kind was sold by the
Sheriffs at less than half price. The pernicious effect of *long credits*,
arising from the avarice of the merchants and founded on the
insecure basis of emigration, now became sufficiently apparent. The
want of emigration was, of course, most severely felt by the back-
wood settlers, who were thus deprived of a home market for their
grain, which, in general, bears a much higher price in new settlements than in the older ones, where it is raised for exportation. It
may be worthwhile to enquire into the causes which have occasioned the recent diminution in the emigration from the British
Islands. *Some* of the causes are sufficiently evident, and of the
others we can here only form conjectures. The prevalence of *Cholera* which has now entirely disappeared, certainly operated power-
fully in the first instance, and *afterwards*, it is probable, the disturbances in Lower Canada and the party violence in the Upper Province, which little as we think of them here, were certainly calculated to excite alarm at a distance, may have had their influence on
the minds of the people at home. The low price of wheat in England, however much it affected the interests of farmers *already
settled* in this Colony, could have no immediate influence in check-
ing emigration, excepting in so far as the manufacturing class are
concerned. There may be several minor circumstances that have
operated unfavorably with respect to the colony, arising from the

natural re-action after the false, exaggerated and interested accounts that have been published of the country etc. etc. which I shall not further advert to in this place. I have always thought honesty the best policy, and the more experience I have had of the world, the more I am convinced of the truth of the maxim, even in an *interested* point of view. In my desire to lower the extravagant expectations of intending emigrants, many people here would tell me that I am injuring the colony, and myself as a landholder in it; – but on the contrary I am convinced that I am serving *both* effectually by so doing. What I wish to see is a steady influx of industrious and enterprizing settlers of those classes *only* who are likely to benefit themselves by coming here. I would lay it down as an axiom, that this colony can recieve no permanent advantage by the emigration of individuals who are incapable of hard labour, or who have not sufficient capital to benefit themselves by its application. You will percieve from what I have already stated that this colony, for the last two or three years, has been passing through a very severe ordeal, but from what I shall now state, you will see that it has been a most *salutary* one. From the great decline of emigration the capital that would have been entirely absorbed in land speculation, has been diverted into new and more useful channels: – and people now see that their own spare capital can only be beneficially employed, and the prosperity of the country promoted by effecting internal improvements to facilitate the settlement of the wild lands, and the transportation of our superabundant produce to the markets on the sea coast. The construction of several rail-roads by private companies will immediately be commenced. One, in particular, from the town of London in the London District to the head of Lake Ontario, it is expected, will be commenced next summer; – and another from Lake Huron to Lake Ontario is also in *contemplation*. A company has also been formed at Cobourg in the Newcastle District for the construction of a railroad from that town on the shore of Lake Ontario, to the Rice Lake. This work will be commenced as soon as the snow is off the ground.

The Legislature are now fully alive to the importance and even necessity of these improvements, and last Session a large sum of money was granted for the improvement of the navigation of the St Lawrence below Kingston, and the work is already far advanced. Unfortunately on the confines of the *Lower Province* we are thwarted by the narrow policy and hostile feelings of the French Canadian party, which is opposed to emigration and all improvements. The only way that the completion of the navigation of the St Lawrence can be insured, would appear to be, – by attaching Montreal to the Upper Province, which by giving us a sea port would make us independent of the Lower Province altogether. Still we have a route open by the Rideau Canal which is in full operation. This present Session £16,000 has been granted to commence the canal on the River Trent, which will be continued through the Rice Lake, the Otonabee River, and an extensive chain of navigable lakes in the Newcastle District on to Lake Simcoe, and from thence to Lake Huron. The whole route has been surveyed and (though the report of the Engineer has not yet been made public) it appears that the whole route may be completed for about £500,000, and little more than half of that sum will open the navigation to Peterborough. This last mentioned work will be of immense importance to the colony, first, by opening a very extensive tract of fertile lands, and affording a profitable market for our white and red pine timber, for which there is a great demand in the U. States, to say nothing of the *English* market which we may lose: – and also by opening the shortest and safest route to the Western States on the borders of Lakes Huron, Michigan etc. These extensive improvements will of course attract emigrants to the points where they are in progress, while they will ensure their prosperity afterwards. The great mistake committed by European settlers of the *higher classes*, or who do not possess sufficient labour in their own families, is locating themselves in the backwoods at a distance from markets, which they too often are tempted to do by the low price of lands in such situations. This has been a fruitful source of disappointment and misery. Handsome fortunes have been, and may be realized by men of large capital purchasing extensive tracts of wild land, and selling them again when they have raised their price by forming a small settlement as a nucleus for further improvements. But this seldom succeeds *on a small scale*, because the personal expenses of the projectors absorb the profits. In all cases it is a work of *time* attended with considerable privation and discouragement in the first instance. Persons of small capital, say with from £1000 to £3000 would *generally* best consult their interests by settling themselves on cleared farms in good situations, even though they should purchase them at the rate of £4 or £5 per acre; – instead of purchasing wild lands in *remote situations*, where they would only have to pay 10/ per acre – unless, as I said before, they should have working families. If they possess this latter advantage with a little spare capital to defray their first expenses, they should certainly take to the woods, – and with a certain prospect of immediate success and a handsome provision for their families ultimately. One deplorable consequence of the exaggerated accounts of Canada has been that numbers of sanguine young men, the sons of gentlemen, and who, from their previous habits, are either unwilling or unable to work, have been induced to bury themselves in the woods at a great distance from markets, and where the expenses of clearing land and living have been so great that they have expended their whole capital, and have been ruined before they could reap any advantage by reselling their lands, or even obtain a bare subsistence from them. The worst of the matter is, that generally, they are so disgusted with the roguery and self-interested representations of almost every one they meet here, that they are affraid to listen to honest advice, and in attempting to judge for themselves, they, in most cases fall into the pit they wish to avoid. The only class of people who profit by wild lands (who cannot clear them by the labour of their own families) are those who never improve them, but sell them when their value is enhanced by settlements in their neighbourhood. This brings me to the subject of land speculations; – and there can be no doubt that, *in most cases*, they have greatly retarded the settlement of the country: – though I by no means think, that they should *necessarily* do so. In judging of this matter a distinction should be made between *resident* land speculators, and *absentees*. The evils arising from extensive tracts of land being held *in an unimproved state* by absentee proprietors, have been severely felt in many parts of the Colony, and the Legislature has very properly imposed a tax upon such lands, to pay which, they are sold from time to time in portions by the Sherriffs. This is an evil of the first magnitude, and I only regret that a more speedy remedy could not be found.

A great number of these absentee proprietors are officers in our Service and others in England and in different parts of the world; – so that individuals who might feel inclined to purchase from them cannot possibly find them out, or even *ascertain their names*. The obstacles that such lands oppose to the improvement of the roads, and the concentration of the population are too obvious to require any comment. The other class of land speculators, with which this Province abounds, are such as possess numerous *detached* tracts of wild land, and although resident in the colony do nothing towards their improvement. Of this class I may simply observe, – that if they do no good, they do no harm to the country: – for, in most

cases, they are glad to sell their lands as cheap, if not *cheaper* than
Government does at present. Most of these speculators have
obtained their land by purchasing *Military* grants, and those made to
U.E. Loyalists and their children who came here from the United
States at the time of the American Revolution. Very few of these
rights to draw land having been acted on by the *original* holders,
they were obtained at very low rates; – often for less than 1/4th of
the lowest Government prices: – and of course the speculators could
afford to undersell the Govt with a handsome profit to themselves.
In consequence of the great emigration some years ago, these speculators also purchased largely at the Government sales. These speculations were *encouraged* by the easy terms of payment allowed by
Govt which only required one fourth of the price to be paid at the
time of sale, and the remainder in three annual instalments. The
Government justly considered this as an evil; but the way they took
to check it was sufficiently short-sighted. They raised the upset
price of wild lands in remote situations from 5/ to 10/ per acre as
the *minimum* price. The consequence of this was that the spirit of
speculation was rather *increased* than diminished, – while the
poorer settlers were at the same time driven out of the market. The
natural consequence has been that the emigration reduced as it is
from other causes, has been diverted in a great measure to the U.
States where lands are sold much cheaper than here. Now, if instead
of raising the price of wild land they had only followed the example
of the U. States in making *the whole price* to be paid at the time of
sale, their object would have been attained much more effectually
than by the plan adopted. The last description of land speculators
are such as purchase an extensive tract of land from Govt and being
possessed of adequate capital, establish themselves on the land, and
encourage others by their improvements, – by making roads, – erect-
ing Mills, etc. – to follow their example and buy lands from them.
This is frequently done in the U. States, but not often in Canada,
from want of sufficient capital. Two settlements of this kind have
been formed in the Newcastle District: – one by Messrs Jamieson &
Wallace (gentlemen of considerable capital) at Cameron's Falls:[1] –
and another very recently by Admiral Vansittart, brother of Lord
Bexley, on Balsam Lake:[2] – both on the line of the Trent Canal,
which when finished will amply remunerate them for their outlay
and exertions, by the number of settlers it will draw to their lands.
Such settlements as these are most beneficial to the country, and
deserve every encouragement from our Government. These gentle-

men are *personally* resident on their lands; and it is evident that the
more *individuals* are interested in such enterprises, the sooner will
the lands be settled. A great error, in my opinion, has been committed by our Colonial Gov^t, – in opening too many *new townships*
at once for settlement, particularly when they are too far from markets for the superabundant produce of the settlers. So long as a constant influx of settlers can be maintained, the *local* demand for agricultural produce will create a temporary prosperity, – but unless
improvements in the means of transport keep pace with – or rather
in some degree precede the wants of the settlers: – the *first check*
the emigration may recieve, will necessarily produce a dreadful reaction, attended with the most ruinous consequences to the inhabitants. From the peculiar situation and form of this colony, with a
long line of frontier, bounded by navigable rivers and lakes; the emigration is subjected to the most capricious changes in its direction.
Sometimes emigrants crowd to one point, sometimes to another, as
they may happen to be influenced by vague or interested reports: –
water conveyance being so cheap *for passengers* on the great lakes
that the difference of expense is considered of small moment.[3]

Having already casually noticed the description of emigrants who
are most likely to succeed here; – as the subject is one of great consequence, both to the Colony and to several classes in Britain, who
look to this country for a provision for their rising families, I think
my time will not be entirely thrown away in entering more fully
into particulars. Canada has often been called the country *for the
poor man*. If it had been called the country for the laborious and
industrious man; a more precise idea would have been conveyed: for
the *poor man* here without industry, or who from habit or weakness
is unable to endure hard labour is indeed in a deplorable condition,
– and meets with no compassion. We want labour *first* to clear
away the woods, – and capital afterwards to enable the settlers to
stock their farms, and to improve the roads and other means of conveyance for the productions of the country. For the intermediate
class, those who *cannot* or *will not* work, and who have but little
capital (unless they betake themselves to mercantile pursuits) this
country presents few advantages. This description of emigrants
would better consult their interest and comfort by going to the Cape
or some other *Pastoral* colony, provided they have sufficient capital
to establish themselves; – and I may observe, by the way, that the
same capital that would be expended in purchasing a cleared farm,
or in clearing wild land here, would establish them much more

comfortably at the Cape. If such people *will* come to Canada, as I
have hinted before, they should purchase cleared farms, and they
will be cheaper even at £5 per acre, than wild land, at the lowest
price, which is cleared entirely by hired labour. A single labourer
can do but little in the woods. He may, indeed, chop down trees,
but he requires *two* more labourers with a Yoke of oxen to pile the
logs and burn them. Still there are a great many young men of a
superior class to labourers who can find no provision in Europe, and
yet do not possess sufficient capital to establish themselves on a
cleared farm here, or in any more distant colony. The necessity of
acquiring laborious habits is obvious in this case; – and if two or
three young men in this situation, would unite their means and purchase a sufficient extent of wild land, – say 200 or 300 acres, and
clear and cultivate them at first by their united labour, I have no
doubt that with proper management and *strict economy*, they
will be successful. The younger they are when they begin their
operations, the more cheerfully will they submit to the temporary
privations and toil of the woods. Before they make any bargain for
land, or begin to clear land *on their own account*, it would be a
great advantage to them to make a temporary arrangement with
some established settler *of their own class*, by assisting whom for a
few months, they would have time to make a better choice of land,
and acquire some knowledge of the mode of clearing land etc. and at
the same time save themselves the expense of living at *inns*, where
much of their means as well as time would be unprofitably dissipated. Next to common labourers *working* farmers with grown up
sons will most improve their condition here, with reference to their
former situation in England. With regard to settlers of the working
class, or common labourers, – they will at once be able to procure
employment and high wages in all parts of Upper Canada, and they
would do well to content themselves with working for others for a
year or two, before they think of going on their own lands. In most
cases they show an extreme anxiety to get to work on their own
lands, but it rarely happens, that when they start on their own
account, they have sufficient means to purchase provisions to support their families, until they can raise their first crops. The consequence is, that they lose a great deal of time, and are subjected to
numerous unnecessary hardships in seeking *occasional* employment
in the older settlements: – whereas, if in the first instance, they
merely secured their lands, and employed themselves and families
in earning wages for some time, they would *then* be enabled to pro-

ceed uninterruptedly in the cultivation of their own farms. This is a
truth acknowledged by them all after they have had some experience of the country. If they were obliged to pay up the whole price
of their lands at the time of sale, the evil would in a great measure
be removed, and the improvement of the *older settlements*, as well
as of the country generally be greatly accelerated. I was much gratified to find that my suggestions with regard to apprenticing
children to the settlers in this country had been adopted by the
'Children's Friend Society,' and the complete success of the experiment, should, I think, lead to a great extension of the system, and
to the organization of similar societies throughout the country. One
thing, however, I should observe, that it appears to me that Ten
Dollars a year with clothing (which is here rather expensive) is too
much to require *for Girls*; – as, in this part of the colony girls of 14
years of age can be had for from 1 1/2 Dollars to 2 Dollars per
month *without clothing*. I have no hesitation in saying that the system *can hardly be extended too far*, provided that due attention is
paid to a proper distribution of the children over every part of the
Colony, according to the existing demand for them; – for, from the
nature of the country, the more labour may be furnished to us, – the
more will be required in an increasing ratio, until all our best lands
are fully settled. Before I conclude this subject I think it is right to
allude to a very common mistake: vis. – that young men of idle and
dissipated habits are likely to change their mode of life in Canada.
The fact is, that in no country I have ever seen does *drunkenness*
prevail to such a degree as here. 'Temperance Societies' may, *for a
time* do some good; – but in general the remedy is about as effectual
as amputation of the leg would be for a sore foot. This vice prevails
most *in new settlements*. As the country becomes improved, and
the inhabitants of all classes less intermixed the people settle down
into more regular habits. No class of settlers are less likely to succeed in this colony, than the sons of gentlemen of fortune in England, who are not educated with a view to some profession. But if it
is found necessary to send them to the colonies for a provision, it
would be wise to accustom them *previously*, while they are still
young, to habits of *personal* exertion. A moderate knowledge of
mercantile business would also be extremely desirable. Previously to
settling in Canada they should be placed for some time with a
farmer at home, where they should not only learn something of the
theory of agriculture, but also learn to use their *hands*; – for manual
labour is much more required here than *head work*. In case of their

failure as farmers, a knowledge of *Book-Keeping* and writing a good hand, will secure them a *living* as clerks to Merchants or Store-Keepers. As new settlements are formed, there is always an opening for the establishment of *Stores*, which afford employment to a great number of young men, who would not be likely, or have not sufficient means to succeed as farmers. The time is not far distant when these matters will be better understood in Europe, and when *manual labour* will be held in more respect than it is at present. I must say for Canada, that in no country in the world is honest industry held in higher estimation, – or does a more sound and healthy state of feeling exist in regard to these matters. It must be admitted, (and we need not wonder at it) that the democratic feeling is often carried too far; – that the man of education and talent is thought less of than the industrious labourer: – but it must be remembered that learning and talent are not *necessary* here, to chop down trees, and prepare the way for civilization and refinement. Still on the other hand, we are free from a hundred prejudices that are prevalent in more complicated states of society. All honest occupations are held in equal honour, and the rich man *dare* not treat the poor man with contempt. While Canada certainly deserves the praise I have bestowed on it, there is still much in it to disgust men possessed of honourable feelings and highmindedness. There exists *no high standard* for character. The great mass of the population of all classes are continually under the influence of the most odious selfishness. *Friends* and *relatives*, as well as strangers are unhesitatingly sacrificed to the local interests of the settlers, and hundreds are every year misled and decoyed into misery or ruin by their false and exaggerated accounts of the country. The great mistake with regard to this colony appears to be, that individual prosperity is supposed to *keep pace* with the prosperity and improvement of the country, *as a whole*. We may clear land and produce grain, – construct canals and rail-roads to an immense extent; – and yet individual *profits*, – though greatly increased, may still be small and uncertain. This is a country capable (from the abundance of fertile lands) of supporting an immense population, but from the high rate of wages (arising from the quantity of unoccupied lands, – and the high price of imported goods) and the low price of grain in our home and foreign markets, profits must be almost nominal, as far as agriculture is concerned. It is notorious that wheat at the *present* prices, hardly pays the expence of raising it. If added to this our timber trade be ruined by the reduction of the duties that have hitherto protected it, the emigration will be diverted to the States, and our condition will be wretched indeed. We shall then be obliged to clothe ourselves in the coarse manufactures of the colony, as we shall not be able to buy British manufactures; and our trade will be reduced to a system of internal barter. Should matters come to this state (which God forbid) England will cease to have any interest in retaining Canada, and our boasted loyalty will rapidly evaporate. This is certainly the dark side of the picture, but it is the side presented to us at the present moment. I cannot, however, persuade myself that the country will be allowed to retrograde, or that our fields cleared with such toil will be allowed by Providence to lie waste. Many things may occur to give a stimulus to our industry. *Wheat* will probably rise somewhat in price: – and if *Potash* continues to increase in value, *it will soon pay the expense of clearing our lands*, as it did formerly in many cases. *Tobacco* is already cultivated to some extent in the Western Districts of the Upper Province where the climate is favourable for its production. Our Legislature have applied for a further reduction in the duty on this article, to enable the Canadian growers to compete with those of the United States. Should any disturbance occur with Russia, it may become an important consideration whether Canada may not supply a large portion of the *flax* and *hemp* used in the British manufactures. We have already several *Iron works* (mines and foundries) established in the colony, and if *Copper mines* can be found sufficiently rich to be worked with profit; – of which there is a great probability, – as also *coal* to work them, – of which *there is every indication*, a valuable export would be established. In speaking of coal I may mention one fact of which you may not be aware; that *even in the midst of the forest*, wood, from the quantity required during a long and severe winter, is a most expensive kind of fuel. About *one acre* of timber *yearly* is often consumed in a house with only two or three fires, and when it is considered that nearly *one half* of every 100 acres should be left *uncleared* for supplying firewood, the introduction of coal, besides the saving in expense, will enable the lands to support *twice* the population they can do at present. Canada, from the nature of its present population, cannot be expected to make such rapid and steady progress in improvement as the U. States, – where a large proportion of the inhabitants are *born and bred* in the country. To people of the latter description, the process of clearing and cultivating new lands is better understood, and is not attended with the same degree of suffering and privation, as it is to Europeans. The

great mass of *our* population, on the contrary are not natives of the
colony; – for the *French* Canadians are unenterprising, and have no
inclination to act as pioneers of the forest. We require a division of
labour in this respect here, as much as it is required in other matters in older countries. In a few years, however, when the children
of the present inhabitants are grown up to manhood, the case will
be altered. Then the clearing of land *for sale* to European farmers
will become a separate occupation, – and when this shall be the
case, the progress of the colony will be greatly accelerated, and most
of the hardships and privations attendant on new settlements will
disappear. It is a circumstance worthy of observation that the *first
settlements* are but rarely permanent ones, – in so far as the individuals are concerned – who form them. This by no means arises from
love of change, or a passion for clearing land, as is generally supposed, – but either from interest or necessity. If a fair calculation were
to be made of the labour or money expended in *clearing* land, it
would be found, that in no case, (at least in Canada) does the price
obtained for improvements of this kind fully remunerate the original settlers for their outlay. But as the families of the settlers
increase, the necessity of obtaining a larger extent of land to provide
for them is apparent; – and therefore they are obliged to sell their
improved farms at the price *they may be able to get for them*, that
they may purchase a greater extent of wild land where their improvements are recommenced. *Still, there is an actual loss*: – but
this loss falls very unequally on different classes of settlers, – as
money or *labour* only is employed. The capitalist sinks *money*
which is never fully redeemed, and he is often – when his means are
limited – compelled to sell his improved land to pay the debts he
has incurred during the progress of his improvements. The *poor
man*, on the other hand, whose capital is his *labour*, sells his 'bet-
terments' (as the Yankees call them) for a price, which though a
good deal less than he might have earned by working for a master at
the common rate of wages, enables him to purchase a larger extent
of land for his family, and to have also some *money capital* to commence with: – while his capital *in labour* is not diminished, – and
in most cases increased. From this statement the following con-
clusions may be deduced: *first* that *labour* is [more] efficient than
capital for clearing land in Canada, – and therefore that the *poor
labourer* will be more successful *in the backwoods*, than the capitalist *without labour*. Secondly: – that the *capitalist* without labour
will best consult his interest by purchasing the poor man's improvements, which as I have already stated, are generally sold somewhat

– I might say greatly below their actual value. As I have stated that, in all cases, there is an actual loss; or in other words, that the labourer does not obtain the marketable value of his labour, in clearing land *for sale*, it may be necessary to explain more fully the cause of this loss, and why it is submitted to on the part of the labourer. In the first place, the poor man just escaped from his European thraldom is eager to become his own master; – and even supposing that, at first, he is aware of the hardships and privations he must encounter in the woods, he is too anxious to have land of his own to regard them. Afterwards, as his family increases, and he wishes to sell his improvements, *there is not sufficient capital* in the colony in proportion to the land in the market to enable him to obtain the real value of the labour expended on his farm. Now taking the wages of a good labourer in the more improved parts of the country at £30 per ann. with his board, and supposing he worked for ten years it would yield him £300. If instead of working for wages he should buy 100 acres of wild land, say at 10/ per acre = £50: – and should in ten years clear 50 acres at £3 per acre (the lowest rate) = £150: – then he might sell his land with the improvements for £200 but, in most cases, it would scarsely fetch this price as such wild lands as he can obtain for 10/ per acre would generally be in a *remote situation* with respect to markets or water communication. His expenses in the backwoods, in the latter case, in clothing etc. would be much greater both from the nature of his work, and his distance from markets. In situations where cleared farms now fetch £5 per acre the country has been settled for 20 or 30 years, and buildings have been erected which would cost some hundred pounds – and morever most of them have orchards which are worth at least £100. There are particular situations where wild lands sell much higher, as on the banks of lakes or rivers, which are navigable or will soon be rendered so, – or in the neighbourhood of old settlements; – but the same calculations apply to them also. I am assured that in the State of New York on the opposite side of Lake Ontario, improved farms are frequently sold at £10 per acre; – ten years being given to pay up the whole sum with interest by yearly instalments: – yet people without any capital but their labour purchase these farms and pay their instalments regularly. This fact shows how very far we are behind the U. States in improvement. Such are the effects of capital, canals, and rail-roads: – and I may add, an enterprising and industrious *native* population. This circumstance also shows how much it is our interest to cultivate an intimate *commercial* intercourse with our brethren on the other side of *the Lakes*, and I fear, unless we do so, the productive powers of Canada will not for many years be fully developed. I do not believe that the U. States *as a nation*, have the smallest desire to take possession of Canada, and the more they may profit by our trade, the less interest will they have in increasing their already too extensive territory, in *this* direction. From motives of personal interest their subjects are eager to take shares in our canals and rail-roads; – *and if we would allow them*, by means of their capital, they would improve our country in these respects more than we are able to do without their aid. As our internal communications are extended, and a good understanding is cultivated with them, their capital will flow into the country, raise the value of our lands and facilitate their improvement. Besides the great internal demand for *Wheat* which the people of the States possess in their manufacturing districts, – which, generally speaking, are not well adapted for the production of that article, – and in the Southern States, where it is *more profitable* to cultivate tobacco, rice, cotton and sugar etc. – they have a more ready access than the people of Canada to the West Indies, and the *grazing* countries of South America, and of course as producers of *wheat* they have a great advantage over *us*. Our wheat and flour when imported into the United States are subject to a heavy duty; – but of late they are anxious to have them admitted free of duty for re-exportation, for the sake of the profit they will derive from its passing through the Erie Canal to the Atlantic. The measure has (I believe) been proposed in Congress, and in Canada we are equally anxious to take advantage of their favorable disposition.

Taking all things into consideration, our *prospects* in Canada are more favourable than, judging from the *present* state of matters we might be led to think; – and if we should have a steady emigration for a few years, we may attain to as great a degree of prosperity as our republican neighbours.

1 On 8 October 1834 the Cobourg *Star* reported on a visit by Sir John Colborne, accompanied by Thomas Stewart, to the 'back lakes,' including Cameron's Falls, of the Trent River system: 'of the natural advantages of the situation its proprietors, Messrs. Jamieson and Wallace, are preparing fully to avail themselves, having now in rapid course of execution extensive mills, a large substantial Building for a Hotel, &c' (Guillet, ed., *The Valley of the Trent*, 192).

2 In the mid-1820s Admiral Henry VanSittart purchased three thousand acres of land on the north side of Balsam Lake, which he later named Bexley Township in honour of his brother. Like Jamieson and Wallace he intended to develop an active settlement as a result of the opening of the Trent River system to full navigation.

3 At this stage of the letter eighteen lines are crossed out.

15 John Moodie to Sir Francis Bond Head

Douro, Newcastle Dist[r]
1st Jan[y], 1837

To His Excellency
Sir Francis Bond Head K.C.H. etc. etc. etc.[1]

May it please Your Excellency,

I feel that some apology is necessary for presuming to address Your Excellency without observing the usual form. Situated as I am without local interest of any kind, and relying for the success of my application, entirely on the favorable consideration with which the facts I am about to state, may be recieved; I felt I could not do better than submit my case directly to Your Excellency's attention, in the humble confiden[ce] that, though my application may prove unsuccessful, my motives, in making it, will plead my excuse.

I emigrated to this Colony in 1832, and having a small sum of money besides my Half-Pay as a reduced Lieutenant of the 21st Fusiliers, I purchased an improved farm near Cobourg, on which I lived for some months, with every prospect of supporting my family in independence; but being informed that an actual residence was indispensable, in order to secure a title to the wild lands I had drawn for my grant, I was compelled to dispose of my cleared farm under unfavorable circumstances to enable me to settle on a portion of my grant situated in the Township of Douro in the Newcastle District. I was not, at that time, aware of the fact, that a military grant on these terms hardly possessed any value to an individual unaccustomed to hard labour, or who had no family capable of assistance to him. I should still notwithstanding this circumstances have been enabled by my own labour joined to my income, to realize an independant subsistence, but for a Circular from the War-Office, which appeared in several papers calling on Half-Pay Officers either to hold themselves in readiness to serve, or to sell their Commissions. In either of these cases, circumstanced as I was, absolute ruin seemed to threaten me, and in my natural anxiety to secure myself against the worst contingency, I was induced to accept an offer made me by a speculator in Cobourg of 25 shares in the 'Cobourg' Steam-boat, – value £625 Cur[cy], – for the sum I might receive for my Commission. The person with whom I made this unfortunate bargain, and from which I might have receded in time, had I not considered myself bound in honor to adhere to my verbal agreement, promised to repay me whatever sum exceeding £600 St⁸ I might possibly receive for my Commission: – which promise, on recieving the unexpected sum of £700 St⁸ he forgot. Advantageous as this bargain appeared at the time, in consequence of the decline in emigration, and various circumstances unnecessary to detail here, for three years I have recieved no income whatever from the Steam-boat, and have not as yet been enabled even to dispose of any of my shares to meet the great expenses attending a settlement in the back-woods. During this period I have struggled with embarassments and difficulties of no ordinary description, and relying on my personal labour I have been enabled to procure a bare subsistance for my family, consisting of my wife and four infant children. Could I indulge the hope of being enabled to support my family on my land, I should not have wished to relinquish my present situation, which however uncongenial to my tastes and feelings, in many respects, – might ultimately have proved beneficial to my children; – but disabled as I am from a wound I received in the Service, and otherwise from the state of my health, unequal to the labo[ur] to which I am necessarily subjected, I feel it to be my duty to endeavour to rescue my family from the distress or ruin to which even a temporary illness might subject them.

Under the circumstances I have ventured to address myself to Your Excellency to solicit your indulgent consideration of my case in the event of any situation becoming vacant, which Your Excellency might deem me capable of filling.

Unknown as I am to Your Excellency I take the liberty of enclosing a testimonial, which I happen to have by me, from a friend at the Cape of Good Hope where I was formerly settled for more than ten years, and where one of my brothers has for some years held the situation of Protector of Slaves for the Eastern Districts.[2]

I have the Honor to be
Your Excellency's Most Obᵗ
Humble Servᵗ
J.W. Dunbar Moodie

1 Sir Francis Bond Head, Knight Commander of Hanover (1793–1875), served as
  lieutenant-governor of Upper Canada from 1836 to 1838 (*DCB*, 10: 342–5).
2 Donald Moodie held this post in the early 1830s (*DSAB*, 2:489).

1838

'To meet the rebels and invaders'

W HEN YOUNG JAMES CADDY rushed to Sam Strickland's farm, bearing the governor's proclamation 'calling upon the Royal Militia of Upper Canada to assist him in putting down the rebellion,' he found Strickland still at his winter ploughing. It was 7 December, the day of the first snowfall of 1837. The backwoodsmen of Peterborough and Northumberland counties were, according to Strickland, 'completely taken by surprise.'[1] Loyalty was very strong and generally unquestioned among people of Strickland's class, especially at that distance from Toronto, and the prevailing conservative papers, particularly the Cobourg Star, regularly satirized and mocked William Lyon Mackenzie's pronouncements and fomenting. Indeed the Cobourg Star had reported favourably on a loyal meeting held at Peterborough in April 1836. But if Strickland was caught off guard, it was only by news of armed rebellion in Toronto. For their part, the Moodies were paying close attention to political tensions, particularly in Lower Canada. In fact, the first of Susanna's loyal poems to be published, 'Canadians Will You Join the Band' was completed in Douro on 20 November 1837.

News of the actual rebellion and Sir Francis Bond Head's call for volunteers (issued on 5 December) took two days to reach the north Douro area. Both Sam Strickland and Susanna Moodie, writing their memoirs many years later, wrongly recall receiving news of the trouble on 4 December, 'that great day of the outbreak' (RIB, 432). A contemporary and therefore more reliable record is Catharine Parr Traill's journal. Her account of the rebellion days, intended as part of a book-length sequel to The Backwoods of Canada, was drawn from her extensive notes and prepared as a manuscript in the late 1830s.[2] According to Traill, Sam Strickland set off that same night – Thursday, 7 December – for Peterborough. Her own husband, Thomas, left early Friday morning, and both men joined the Peterborough Volunteers, who marched to Port Hope under Captain James Gifford Cowell,[3] uniting there with the 2d Northumberland Regiment commanded by Colonel Alexander McDonnell[4] and the 4th Northumberland under Lieutenant Colonel Robert Brown. While awaiting steamboat transportation at Port Hope, the loyal volunteers were disappointed by the news that their services were not in fact required in Toronto.

John Moodie's involvement in the response to the rebellion was somewhat delayed. In late October 1837 he had broken a bone in his lower leg when hit by the recoil of a snagged plough. As there was no medical aid in the vicinity, he had devised a cast of his own and was carrying on as best he could when news of the outbreak reached him on 8 December via Catharine Parr Traill. Though he had sold his military commission a few years earlier and was not in good condition to travel, Moodie set out on foot the next day for Peterborough. Once there, rather than accept a position guarding Government House (as Catharine hoped he would do), he rode out on a borrowed horse for Port Hope at the head of two hundred Smithtown volunteers charged with conveying two prisoners to the front.[5] Militia records show that he was made a captain in the 2d Regiment of Northumberland Militia; his commission is backdated '6 December 1837' (MR, 1 B 5, 6).

What happened to Moodie immediately thereafter remains unclear. Sam Strickland recalled that 'on Mackenzie's occupation of Navy Island, every colonel of a Militia regiment was ordered to send up to head-quarters a draft of men, in order to form a number of incorporated battalions for active service. The men required were to be drafted by ballot, unless sufficient volunteers offered their services.'[6] After being turned back at Port Hope and frustrated by their subsequent search of nearby townships for rebels, the loyal backwoodsmen of Peterborough, Durham, Northumberland, and Prince Edward volunteered 'almost to a man,' marching to Toronto under Lieutenant Colonel Brown in late December. There many of them were quick to enlist in the Queen's Own, one of the new incorporated battalions commanded by Lieutenant Colonel William Kingsmill of Port Hope.

Catharine's journal reports that Moodie rode home the night of 14 December, bringing clearer news of events and word of Thomas Traill's sprained ankle, the result of a fall from his horse while mustering with the volunteer militia who had been directed to search certain nearby townships (Ops and Mariposa) for 'skulking radicals,' including Mackenzie himself.[7] Susanna herself confirms this in Roughing It in the Bush; however, the joy she took in her reunion with her husband was short-lived, for he remained at home only until January. 'Several regiments of militia were formed to defend the colony,' she writes, 'and to my husband was given the rank of captain in one of those then stationed in Toronto' (RIB, 439).

The process of creating these new regiments was begun with a general militia order issued by Adjutant-General Richard Bullock on 30 December 1837. It was not until early January, however, that the Queen's Own Regiment of Militia was raised. In response, on 20 January 1838, Moodie left home for a second time, having been appointed effective 15 January 1838. Outfitting himself on his way, he arrived in Toronto in late January to find his corps billeted at the New British Coffee House, a favourite meeting place of military men located at the

Colonel William Kingsmill

southeast corner of King and York streets. Still not formally integrated into the Toronto garrison, which consisted mainly of the Queen's Rangers under Samuel P. Jarvis,[8] the Queen's Own were being trained by the demanding and experienced Lieutenant Colonel William Kingsmill (1794–1876), the son of a major and himself a retired British captain who had served in the 66th Regiment during the Napoleonic Wars. He had been customs collector at Port Hope at the time of the outbreak and had led a march of the 1st Durham Militia and Port Hope Rifles, totalling more than fifteen hundred men, to Toronto, arriving on Monday 11 December. Once there, he was in a good position to make his case for an important leadership role in forthcoming military plans.

Appointed colonel, commanding the Queen's Own and head-quartered in Toronto, Kingsmill, a noted disciplinarian, had to select, train, and organize a regiment of ten companies and some five hundred men. That process was well under way when John Moodie arrived in

Toronto. Though it meant disjunctions, uncertainty, and danger, Moodie welcomed the renewed privilege of rank and the promise of guaranteed remuneration through 1 July 1838. Likely, too, his experience as an officer made him a valuable addition. At the same time he seems to have known Kingsmill personally, either from his days in Hamilton Township near Port Hope or in connection with Kingsmill's purchase of land on the Otonabee in 1835.[9]

But not all was duty and drilling for Moodie. His two Toronto letters suggest a network of acquaintances, many of whom he had first come to know through earlier contacts, among them John Strachan (1778–1867),[10] the influential archdeacon of Toronto. Another was John Kent (1807–88), an ordained minister and skilled cricket player, who had emigrated to York in 1833 to join the staff of Upper Canada College, founded by Sir John Colborne in 1830. Located on King Street, the school had received government funding and had set out ostensibly to establish a high standard for education in Upper Canada, based on the traditional English blend of classical studies and 'healthy and manly games.' Staffed by a 'cargo of masters' from Oxford and Cambridge and clearly designed for the sons of Toronto's (York's) elite, it was not long in becoming a special target for reformers. In William Lyon Mackenzie's words, it was 'never intended for the people.'[11] An amiable teacher who combined literary interests with athletic skills, Kent headed the UCC boarding-school in 1838 and was an active member of Toronto's St George's Society. Four years earlier he had tried his hand at editing a literary periodical, the *Canadian Literary Magazine*, to which Susanna Moodie contributed, but it lasted only a few issues.[12] Kent would later serve as secretary to Sir George Arthur and as editor of the Anglican newspaper the *Church* (1841–3), often writing under the pseudonym of Alan Fairchild.

It may well have been Kent who introduced Moodie to the Rev. George Maynard, a flamboyant master of classics, who had arrived from Cambridge in 1836. Described in contemporary accounts as a dramatic dresser, eccentric teacher, and 'a vivid character,' Maynard was also a skilled violinist who shared with Moodie a love of music, wit, and camaraderie. Maynard's later troubles at Upper Canada College are nowhere noted in the surviving Moodie correspondence.[13]

Other than John Kent the most important Toronto literary connection for Moodie was Charles Fothergill (1782–1840),[14] a Yorkshireman who had first settled near Rice Lake in 1817. A naturalist, artist, land developer, businessman, politician, printer, and journalist, Fothergill led so various and checkered a career in Upper Canada that his many contributions are perhaps too easily overlooked, despite the fact that he actively represented Durham in the Assembly from 1824 to 1830 and was King's Printer and editor of the *Upper Canada Gazette* (1822–6) until he was dismissed without notice from that position.

The importance of Fothergill with regard to the Moodies must be measured both in terms of publishing opportunity and political outlook. Though his life in Upper Canada was characterized by 'an unbroken sequence of failures that were largely of his own making,' Fothergill was a cultivated and talented gentleman, a 'savant with a sense of public duty,' who could readily account for his difficulties in terms of political favouritism and patronage. In the years 1824–30 he had been 'the foremost exponent of "conservative reform" views in the province, and his image of gentility and respectability was useful to the emergent reform movement at a time when many people still equated "party" activity with disloyalty.'[15] Having purchased two newspapers in 1837, he combined them as the *Palladium of British America and Upper Canada Mercantile Advertiser*, and he published his first issue two weeks after the outbreak of the rebellion. He insisted 'from the start that the chief cause of this calamity was the unconstitutional domination of the provincial government by the "family compact." '[16] The *Palladium* briefly became one of the most prominent newspapers in the province and a focus for outspoken opposition to Upper Canada's prevailing leadership. At the same time it provided an important venue for the writing of Susanna and John, who were both firm British loyalists and conservatives at the time.

Most of Susanna's intensely patriotic and anti-rebellion poems first appeared in the *Palladium*, though the broken run of surviving issues forces one to rely in part on the reprinting of *Palladium* poems in other newspapers to document her contribution. The first issue of the *Palladium* (20 December 1837) contained Susanna's 'Canadians, Will You Join the Band – a Loyal Song.'[17] So popular was it that it was quickly reprinted in at least eight newspapers in Upper and Lower Canada, including the widely circulated Montreal *Transcript* (28 December 1837). The following Susanna Moodie poems also appeared in the *Palladium* (those marked by asterisks are attributed to the *Palladium* in reprintings, particularly in the *Transcript*):

'On Reading the Proclamation Delivered by William Lyon Mackenzie, on Navy Island' (17 January 1838)
'The Banner of England' (24 January 1838)
'War' (21 February 1838)

'The Avenger of Blood' (11 April 1838)
*'The Wind That Sweeps Our Native Sea' (May 1838)
*'Song: The Trumpet Sounds' (May 1838)
*'The Burning of the Caroline' (October 1838)
*'The Waters' (August 1839)

It is clear from such a record, incomplete as it likely is, that Susanna Moodie was strongly aroused by the challenge to British institutions and the threat of rebellion. Though several of these poems were simply republished from her English collection, *Enthusiasm* (1831), the events of December 1837 and the fact of her husband's involvement re-energized her desire to write. Her reflex was patriotic, polemical, even bloody-minded. Initially at least, she gave little thought to the ground swell of substantial political and economic unrest at work in the Canadas (*RIB*, 436). As John's letter of 7 February 1838 indicates, Charles Fothergill also published two of his poems, 'The Bears of Canada' and 'O Let Me Sleep,' that very day. The 'flaming' and 'far too complimentary' introduction in the *Palladium* reads as follows:

It may not be generally known that the gallant husband of Mrs. Moodie, now so well known throughout Great Britain and upon the Continent, as a poetess of distinguished rank, Captain Moodie, is also a poet, possessed of talents of a superior character, as will be fully acknowledged, on a perusal of the following specimens which we have obtained permission to publish in this number, and which we have selected from amongst several others in order to shew the versatility of talent which distinguishes the writer, who is well known in England, as an author of that delightful work, a 'Ten Years Residence in South Africa.'[18]

A week later Fothergill published two other John Moodie poems, 'Song: To the Woods' and 'Song: Och! now I'm intirely continted.'

Moodie was not, however, long in Toronto. A little more than a month after formally joining the Queen's Own, his company was one of three designated to relieve troops on duty along the Niagara frontier. Major George Elliott, an Irishman (d. 1844), whose 2d Durham Militia had also been incorporated into the Queen's Own, was put in charge. A Monaghan Township resident who represented both the Newcastle District and Durham County on the Legislative Council, he led his men out of Toronto so quickly that John Moodie had no time to complete arrangements to raise a subscription for 'poor Mrs. Lloyd,' the abandoned widow (Ella N——) in Dummer Township whom Susanna and Emilia Shairp had recently visited and sought to help. The details presented in Letter 17 provide a factual basis for the action described in Susanna's chapter in *Roughing It in the Bush* 'The Walk to Dummer.'

The three letters written by John Moodie from the Niagara District provide glimpses not only of the life of a militia officer but also of the continuing state of unrest along the American border in the first six months of 1838. He arrived at Chippewa on 10 March after a nine-day trek, returning home in the first week of August (*RIB*, 448). As Susanna also points out, however, John's plan to seek leave (Letter 19) was approved, and for 'one short, happy week' in early June he was able to be in Douro with his family. The rest of his fortnight leave of absence was spent in travel (*RIB*, 447).

At Chippewa the three companies of the Queen's Own reported to Lieutenant Colonel Kenneth Cameron in answer to his urgent request for reinforcements (MR, 1B5, 23).[19] A Scottish half-pay officer formerly of the 79th British Regiment and an old acquaintance of Moodie's, Cameron had been appointed by Sir Francis Bond Head as assistant adjutant-general and commander of the militia serving the Niagara frontier. As such, he not only commanded the 1st Regiment, Lincoln's Incorporated Militia, renamed the 1st Frontier Infantry on 22 January 1838, but also oversaw the border defence during and after Mackenzie's stay on Navy Island. Cameron's regiment was based at the town of Niagara (Niagara-on-the-Lake). He held a higher ranking than James Kerby,[20] who commanded the parallel 2d Regiment, itself renamed the Queen's Niagara Fencibles on 22 January. Cameron's health was precarious, however, and, shortly after Moodie's arrival on the Niagara frontier, at his own request, he was replaced by Kerby. Cameron sent the three companies on to Colonel James Kerby (1785–1854) at Fort Erie, where Kerby commanded his Niagara Fencibles. On 5 March, in fact, having received Cameron's orders in advance, Kerby wrote back, clarifying his plans for the new men: 'I shall delay placing these three companies on outpost duty for a few days, as it is necessary further arrangements should be made for their more immediate comfort.'[21]

Kerby himself was a Canadian of distinguished military background. Born in Sandwich (Windsor), Upper Canada, he was a very active businessman and public figure in the Niagara area. During the War of 1812 he had been twice voted the sword of honour by the Legislative Assembly and in 1815 was given the rank of major. Cruikshank cites his quick and effective mobilization of a rag-tag militia in Niagara in

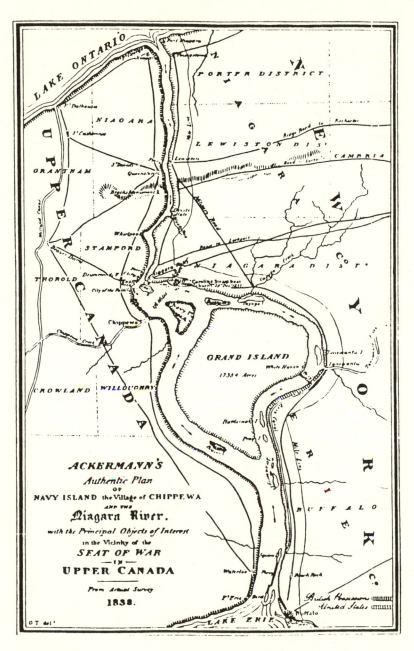

The Niagara frontier

early December 1837 as a crucial factor in discouraging invasion of the border areas by Mackenzie's American supporters. Like Cameron, Kerby was adamant that the Government provide additional troops to the area, given not only ample evidence of unrest among the Patriots and military mobilization in the United States but also the number of vulnerable locations for invasion along the border. Kerby had command of the three companies of the Queen's Own until the rest of the regiment under Kingsmill arrived in late May.

Under Kerby's direction the companies were dispersed along the border from Fort Erie to Point Abino. For several months John was billeted along with his lieutenant, Robert Hawthorn (d. 1839), formerly of the 27th Foot and the Cobourg Volunteers, at the homestead of Alexander, a Scottish settler, twelve miles west of Fort Erie and five miles east of Point Abino. Buffalo was visible across the lake at a distance of some eight miles. 'Alexander's Bay,' as he calls it, is not identifiable, however, as a post office or community.[22]

Beyond the daily patrols, militia duties on the Erie shore seem for Moodie to have been a frustratingly boring and enervating experience. Activities around Buffalo had to be closely monitored, for as Mary Beacock Fryer writes, 'Buffalo was fertile ground for the seeds of Mackenzie's propaganda. The city of 25,000 had many labourers, and sailors from the Erie Canal, who were unemployed during the winter months. Unemployment, especially among the young men, was unusually high owing to the economic recession of 1837.'[23] But while little of consequence was happening on the Canadian side, the militia commanders remained cautious. When it was argued in mid-March that the alarm was over and the Queen's Own companies could be relocated, Colonel Cameron replied on 19 March:

It is true the state of the ice does preclude the existence of any apprehension of an attack by means of a passage of it, but this frontier is not therefore less open to aggression; on the contrary the Americans possessing a decided superiority on Lake Erie and having Steam Boats and other Craft innumerable by which, when the Lake is navigable, a greater facility is afforded for transporting troops from a distance and striking a blow where we may least expect it. There is a district of Country in our rear which is considered generally disaffected, and I am consequently of opinion that the 3 Companies of the Queen's Own should *not* be withdrawn from this frontier.

It is also true that Sympathizing and Patriotism seem at present to be on the decline and going out of fashion on the opposite frontier, but how long will this state of things endure? So long as the American authorities can uphold the

Supremacy of the Laws; in other words as long as we are WELL ABLE to take care of ourselves and no longer![24]

When Sir George Arthur (1784–1854)[25] replaced Sir Francis Bond Head (23 March) as lieutenant-governor (1838–41), he too was optimistic that with the approach of spring he could significantly reduce the militia assigned to the Niagara district, thereby allowing farmers the opportunity to be home for the planting season. However, tensions and uncertainty in the area persisted; there were rumours of both small- and large-scale invasions by members of the Patriot movement south of the border,[26] fuelled in part by the publicity surrounding the impending executions in Toronto (12 April) of two of the leaders in the Mackenzie uprising, Samuel Lount[27] and Peter Matthews,[28] and the work of the Canadian Refugee Relief Association in the United States.

With pressures mounting Arthur countermanded his own orders to discharge most of the militia. While the 24th Company was returned to Toronto, the rest of the Queen's Own troops under Kingsmill were summoned to Niagara, in part because of Colonel Kerby's insistence on the need for garrisonlike reinforcements from Chippewa to Point Abino.[29] Returning from his fortnight's leave in Douro, John Moodie found himself reassigned to Drummondville (Niagara Falls), and suddenly involved in the immediate aftermath of what is now known as the Short Hills Raid, an attack on militia soldiers in the village of St John's in Pelham Township. On 20 June a group of Patriots led by James Morreau, Jacob Beamer, and Alexander McLeod came out of hiding in the Short Hills area of Pelham to surprise a small group of lancers at Osterhout's Tavern.[30] Moodie's letter provides not only his reconstruction of the attack and other related events but information garnered from interviews with captured Patriots, including the wounded Erastus Warner, a farmer from near Port Hope. Offering as well a feel for the mood of the moment – 'the papers talk of nothing but war war war' – he also includes a glimpse of the lack of discipline that seems to have characterized militia behaviour in both the lower and upper echelons and which was of considerable concern to Kerby as commander.

As dangerous as matters looked in late June, however, tensions in the Niagara area soon subsided. Sir George Arthur's prompt appearance in Pelham Township, the quick work of militia and reinforcements, and the promise to prosecute the Short Hills raiders significantly undermined the small base of support upon which the Patriots hoped to capitalize.

With the trials of the rebels, many of whom, as Colin Read has pointed out, were not Americans, but of British or Canadian birth, a kind of order was re-established and talk of invasion diminished (*RIB*, 448).[31] By early August Moodie was back in Douro, accompanied by *Roughing It in the Bush*'s J. E—— (the John Evans of Letter 20), whom Moodie had urged to join him at Niagara Falls. An Irishman who had come out to Canada to work under Sam Strickland before striking an amiable agreement to work Moodie's farm 'upon shares,' Evans – 'a gentleman in word, thought, and deed' – had brightened life for the Moodies (*RIB*, 418–19). He had left for Ireland in the early fall of 1837 to claim a legacy from his mother. In *Roughing It in the Bush* Susanna confuses his return to Douro in August 1838 in the company of John Moodie with his earlier return from Ireland (*RIB*, 448–9).

The autumn of 1838 was 'the happiest [harvest and season] we ever spent in the bush,' Susanna wrote retrospectively. With her husband home, with John Evans there to help, without servant problems, and with 'enough of the common necessaries of life,' the Moodies enjoyed a 'calm and healthful respose' (*RIB*, 449).

1 Samuel Strickland, *Twenty-Seven Years in Canada West* (London 1853), 2:259
2 TFC, vol. 3, 3413–14. This 'chapter' was added to the 1929 text of *The Backwoods of Canada* (Toronto 1929).
3 James Gifford Cowell (d. 1840), formerly a captain in the 1st Royal Regiment of Foot, became captain (subsequently lieutenant colonel) of the 2d Northumberland. He owned property in North Monaghan Township and had an interest in a brewery with James Duffie.
4 See *DCB*, 9:483.
5 *Backwoods of Canada*, 328
6 Strickland, *Twenty-Seven Years in Canada West*, 2:264
7 *Backwoods of Canada*, 332, 335
8 See *DCB*, 8:430–3.
9 In 1835 Kingsmill had purchased 350 acres from James Herriot on the Otonabee River at the site of present-day Lakefield (Land Registry Office, Peterborough, Ontario).
10 See *DCB*, 9:751–66.
11 Richard B. Howard, *Colborne's Legacy: Upper Canada College, 1829–1979* (Toronto 1979), 12
12 Poems by Susanna Moodie appeared in the issues of April and May 1833.
13 Howard, *Colborne's Legacy*, 49f. Maynard, who had a violent temper, strenuously objected to the appointment of Frederick Barron as headmaster in 1844. His 'persistent hostility' to Barron's leadership culminated in 1854 in Maynard's dismissal from the school.
14 See *DCB*, 7:317–21.
15 *Ibid.*, 319–20
16 *Ibid.*, 320
17 She dated the poem 20 November 1837. Fothergill was very complimentary about the 'beautiful and heart-stirring song' and about Moodie herself.

18 Some numbers of the *Palladium*, including those referred to here, are available in the Archives of Ontario.

19 E.A. Cruikshank, 'A Memoir of Colonel the Honorable James Kerby: His Life in Letters,' *Welland County Historical Society Papers and Records* 4 (1931), 160–4

20 See *DCB*, 8:465–7.

21 *Ibid.*

22 In a report of the 'state of Houses Public and Private, Point Abino,' Alexander's home is listed as accommodating sixteen soldiers, if necessary (MR, 1B1, 23).

23 Mary Beacock Fryer, *Volunteers and Redcoats, Rebels and Raiders: A Military History of the Rebellion in Upper Canada* (Toronto 1987), 55

24 Cruikshank, 'Memoir,' 165–6

25 See *DCB*, 7:26–31.

26 Calling themselves the 'Patriot Army of the Northwest,' the group aligned itself under the command of 'Major-General' Daniel McLeod in Lockport, New York. Through May and June in the wake of the executions of Matthews and Lount (12 April), the Patriots were very active in their fomenting and recruiting (Fryer, *Volunteers and Redcoats*, 87, 89).

27 See *DCB*, 7:518–19.

28 See *DCB*, 7:598–7.

29 Cruikshank, 'Memoir,' 198, 200

30 Colin Read, 'The Short Hills Raid of June, 1838, and Its Aftermath,' *Ontario History* 68, no. 3 (1976), 95. See also E.A. Cruikshank, 'A Twice-Told Tale,' *Ontario Historical Papers and Records* 23 (1926), 180–222; and Fryer, *Volunteers and Redcoats*, 86–92.

31 A general militia order issued by Sir John Colborne through Adjutant-General Richard Bullock on 22 June reduced the size of the incorporated regiments, effective 1 July. Directly contrary to Sir George Arthur's concern for increased forces in Niagara, the general order required each regiment to be reduced from ten to six companies, though 'the services of those who were discharged would be extended until 31 July' (Fryer, *Volunteers and Redcoats*, 89). Despite his confidence in being retained, Moodie was among those who were cut back.

---

16 John Moodie to Susanna Moodie

City of Toronto

My Dearest Susie,   7th Feb[y] 1838

I have been so bothered and hurried about with parades, drills, and other duties, which all fall upon my shoulders from the want of good subalterns and serjeants that I have not till this moment been able to settle myself sufficiently to write to you and our sweet babes. God bless you all. How I long to clasp you to my heart, my own good old wife, and to kiss my dear honest hearted Katie my light hearted Aggy, and sly Dunnie and my gentle generous Donald.[1] I have no occasion, considering the circumstances of the country to regret coming up here. Almost every one seems favorable to our corps being made permanent. Col. Kingsmill is well fitted for his situation and the progress of our officers and men in their drill is quite astonishing. In a few weeks our reg^t will be as effective as any reg^t of the line. We have to drill our companies separately twice a day and every night Col. Kingsmill drills the officers after dinner in a large room of the British Coffee house, where most of us are bil-letted. We pay 2/6 a piece with our rations to the landlord and are furnished with breakfast dinner lunch and tea in very respectable style, besides having our bedrooms and fire wood. In fact we have a regular Mess established drinking only two or three glasses of wine which will cost us about 6^d more, so that 3/- a day covers most of our expences. My pay is 13/4 a day. I have met with the greatest kindness from every one here. Our mess is close to the college and I have two or three friends there, who are always glad to see me whenever I can make it convenient to visit them in the evening. I have got acquainted with a man after my own heart in the Rev^d Mr Maynard one of the Masters of the College and a man totally without affectation or stiffness. Both he and his young wife are very musical and I take my flute in my pocket and go to enjoy their delightful society whenever I feel inclined. They are both extremely clever and lively. I saw our good little friend Kent yesterday and go to spend the evening with him tomorrow. I like my quarters so well that I shall be sorry to leave them. Perhaps you may have heard that a body of some 4000 or 5000 men are advancing to attack Montreal and it appears to me that a war with the States is almost inevitable. It is not unlikely that we may be marched to the lower Province before long, but the matter is quite uncertain. Col. Cowell is now here and returns to Peterboro the day after tomorrow. I shall endea-vour to send this by him. Every body here is delighted with your poetry. Fothergill seems most grateful for your assistance. In this days paper he inserts some of my verses 'The Bears of Can' & 'O let me sleep' with a flaming introduction. Far too complimentary for my tastes; but he means it kindly. If I knew that we should be per-manently fixed here, I should like to have you up with me, but at present it would be premature. My outfit at Cobourg cost me exact-ly £8 which I paid: I have also paid Conger & Gravely.[2] Dr Taylor[3] is attached to our Reg^t ('the Queen's Own') and squire Wood[4] is my Lieutenant. He is a forward impudent puppy and I have every now and then to give him a set down. On the whole tho' I have a great deal of trouble and responsibility I am very comfortable. If we should go into barracks and are likely to be kept up for any time I must endeavour to get you up here, – but we must have patience. I fear Traill would not much like our Colonel's discipline. He issues innumerable orders and interferes with every thing. In fact he is greatly disliked from his disagreeable temper. Still he is an excellent drill and is every way well calculated for breaking in our raw militia. I have not been able to settle myself to writing as yet, but I hope I soon shall. A young man who lives in this house accompanied an expedition to explore the course of the Ottawa and he has promised me a short paper on the subject. Crofton[5] offered me an acc^t of the present or (late) war, but I told him I should send it to the U.S. Journal who will pay him for it. I suppose you have got a boy to chop wood for you. I enclose you D^{rs}. 10 in this letter which Col. Cowell will give to Traill, or send by a safe hand. I shall send you more from time to time as you require it. Now my dear Susie do not stint yourself of comforts for I cannot bear to be pampered up while you are suffering any privation. I see no chance as yet of selling my Steam boat Stock. We must *wait* patiently on Providence. Now my dearest I must conclude my hurried letter to go to parade love to all friends and kiss my dear babes for me. Write me soon & Direct Capt Moodie. New British Coffee House Toronto.

> & I remain My Dearest Susie
> Yours Affe^{te} Husband
> *J.W. Dunbar Moodie*

P.S. 8th Feby. I have just heard that an express arrived last night continuing Sir F. Head as Governor till April when the Provinces will be united under *the* Governor Sir J. Colborne (it is believed). Sir J. Colborne is ordered to take *military possession* of the disputed territory. A war appears almost certain. I send this under a frank from my friend Gowan[6] who is just going to join his regiment at Brockville. Some people who came from Buffalo last night say that recruiting is proceeding actively there and that about 2000 had been enrolled. It is reported also that about 4000 Yankees with some deserters of the 32nd Reg^t as Colonels & Majors on their march to attack Montreal. Gowan tells me he had the report from a Serg^t of the 32nd *who saw them on the march*, and on whose veracity he can place entire reliance.

> *J.W.D.M.*

1 In February 1838 the Moodie children were Catherine (b. 1832), Agnes (b. 1833),

Dunbar (b. 1834), and Donald (b. 1836). Susanna was in her first month of pregnancy with John (b. 16 October 1838).

2 William Seymour Conger (1804–64) served as a captain in the Cobourg Rifles during the rebellion period and later held a variety of public positions in Cobourg and Peterborough. At the time of this letter advertisements in the Cobourg *Star* indicate that he operated a general store and the Albion Hotel (formerly the Steam Boat Hotel of *Roughing It in the Bush*) in Cobourg (see *DCB*, 9:149). William Gravely began as a private in the Cobourg militia and by the end of the rebellion had become a major, by which title he was known thereafter in his role as a prominent Cobourg citizen. An advertisement in the Cobourg *Star* of 24 May 1837 indicates that he was a partner in the Cobourg Medical Dispensary with a person named Jackson.

3 Dr William Henry Taylor of Peterborough (d. 1846) was appointed 'Asst Surgeon' of the Queen's Own by order of Richard Bullock, 23 February 1838 (MR, 1B1, 23).

4 Young William Wood, a near neighbour of the Moodies in the Douro backwoods, was appointed a lieutenant in the 2d Northumberland Militia (19 January 1838). He began service as an ensign in the Queen's Own and was promoted to lieutenant 1 February 1838. He seems to have left the province after the latter service (MR, 1B1, 29).

5 Described in the Cobourg *Star* (4 June 1845) as a former teacher and late editor of this paper, W.G. Crofton (1806?–70) was the first school superintendent of Cobourg, appointed from 1842 to 1845 by the Board of Police (David Calhan, 'Postponed Progress: Common Cobourg Schools, 1850–1871,' in *Victorian Cobourg: A Nineteenth Century Profile* [Cobourg 1976], 199). An Englishman with a military background, Crofton had been quartermaster with the Royal Cobourg Rifles but was injured in Toronto in 1840 (MR, 1B1, 41). He was also an author, occasionally using the pseudonym 'Uncle Ben.'

6 Ogle R. Gowan (1803–76) was an Irish journalist who emigrated to Upper Canada in 1829. Settling in the Brockville area, he continued in the newspaper business as an editor and proprietor and became a member of the Assembly for Leeds when the rebellion broke out. He was also a lieutenant colonel in the militia, raising a regiment in November 1838 in Brockville to counter the Patriots. Gowan is perhaps best known as the founder of the Orange Association in British North America (1830), of which he served as grand master until 1853. See *DCB*, 9:309–14; and Don Akenson, *The Orangeman: The Life and Times of Ogle Gowan* (Toronto 1986).

---

17 John Moodie to Susanna Moodie

City of Toronto
My Dearest Susie, 1ˢᵗ March *1838*

I have just time to write you a few lines before going to bed. Early tomorrow morning I start for the Niagara frontier – either to Chippewa, opposite Navy Island or to any other point where we may be most required. Three Companies of the 'Queen's Own' (as we are now called) recieved orders this morning to march under the command of Major Elliot and my comp^y is one of those selected for this service. I known my dearest Susie that you will be anxious, and it is useless to tell you not to be so. There are various reports of an intended attack from the other side, but none of them can be relied on. A war seems now inevitable sooner or later. I have no doubt that the result will be favorable – the rest is in the hands of Providence where we must leave it, in the firm belief that all will be ordered for the best, and will end *in good*. Though harassed with duties of various kinds I have not neglected to do all in my power for poor Mrs. Lloyd. I called on Dr Strachan and he recieved me most kindly, and entered warmly into our views. I thought it best to get him to interest himself in the business from the great influence he possesses rather than leave the matter to the uncertain effect of a newspaper advertisement. He begged to get the case written out and given to him today as he was anxious to procure subscriptions before the Parliament was dissolved. I was so busy today that I could not get the paper written out in time to send it to him, but I have left it with my kind friend Mr Maynard of the College who will send it to Dr. Strachan and has promised to do all in his power to forward the subscription. I wrote a few lines of my own as an introduction or heading and quoted a considerable portion of your communication, which I was obliged to curtail a little. It is rather unfortunate that I could not attend to it myself but I still think that a considerable sum will be procured, both through Dr Strachan and Maynard, and also from the Officers of our own Regiment. Write me soon my dearest, and tell me all about my sweet babes. How I long to see you all again. I feel like a guilty one when I think of your poor fare while I am living in comparative luxury. I trust my dear children are attending to their books & I expect to find a great improvement when I return to you again. Remember me most affectionately to Traill and Katie. I would have written to Traill but really I am not able to manage it just now. McDonnel told me, he had heard from him the other day. Remember me to good Jenny[1] and tell her not to spoil the little lamb Donald, my own sweet boy. God bless you all and keep you from all evils. And now good night my dear Susie and believe me

Ever Your Affectionate Husband
J.W. Dunbar Moodie

1 Jenny Buchanan, the Moodies' servant, was also a Dummer resident of Irish birth. She was 'a striking instance of the worth, noble self-denial, and devotion which are often met with – and, alas! but too often disregarded – in the poor and ignorant natives of that deeply-injured and much-abused land' (*RIB*, 500). Jenny first worked for Captain Lloyd, serving his turbulent household for five years before joining the Moodies in the summer of 1837.

18 John Moodie to Susanna Moodie

My Dearest Susie,

12 miles above Fort Erie
Niagara District
13th March *1838*

I wrote you a few lines from Toronto before starting for this place. We left Toronto on the 2nd Inst and arrived here on the 10th. We were transported in Sleighs to Chippewa opposite the Falls of Niagara. I had just time to get a glimpse of the Falls from above before the evening closed, so that I cannot attempt to give you any description of them. We were hurried off next morning to Fort Erie 17 miles which distance we had to *march* thro' the most detestable roads of slushy snow and greasy clay and were tollerably soaked with soft snow & rain on the way. The Commander of the Forces Col. Cameron was an old acquaintance of mine formerly a Capt in the 79th Regt at Edinb where our Regiments lay together. As soon as he heard my name, he put me in mind of our former acquaintance, but 22 years had completely obliterated all recollection of his features tho' I had a perfect recollection of him otherwise. He was most kind to us, ordered dinner for us and gave up some of the beds in the Mess house for our use. He seems to be a most amiable and kind hearted man. We remained 5 days at Waterloo or Fort Erie, where we were kindly entertained at the Mess of the Niagara Fencibles commanded by Col. the Honble Kerby who is a fine old fellow, full of energy and good fellowship. Our three Companies are distributed along the shore of Lake Erie, one commanded by Capt Grierson[1] about 9 miles above Fort Erie: another (my own) 12 miles above Fort Erie, and the third Capt Mitchell's[2] about 5 miles farther up at a place called Point Abino where there is a kind of harbour. Major Elliot our Commg Officer and his staff including *Wood* who is acting Quarter Master is about 1/2 mile from me at the house of a respectable Dutch farmer. Part of my Company is along with him, and the rest including *Hawthorn* who is my Lieutenant are with myself at the house of a Scotch Settler on the Lake Shore where we have our barracks. In the daytime we have little to do except to take a look at the Lake now and then. Our people catch plenty of large Salmon trout by cutting holes in the ice and baiting hooks for them. The lower part of Lake Erie is frozen over and our business is to prevent an invasion from the other side which was once attempted – but the rebels were dispersed by the *American forces*. At Point Abino there is a steep sand hill of difficult access to which the Company stationed there are to retire in case of an attack and they are to set fire to an [o]ld barn for an allarm fire which will bring my company to their assistance. This Point is almost insulated in the spring by a large swamp and will therefore be a desirable point for the enemy to gain possession of. I was roused out of bed last night by the Major who had just recieved an express from Col. Kerby stating that a body of about 400 were collected about 8 miles above Buffalo on the other side ready to cross. We were therefore kept on the look out all night, but the sca[m]ps did not venture to pay us a visit. If they do they may expect a warm reception from our back woods savages. In a few days more the ice will be unpassable as the weather is getting warm thro' the day and but little frost at night. I am next in Command under the Major. I hope we may have an opportunity of doing something. Our men are rough diamonds but I am sure they will stick to me in case of danger. Still all is quiet at Buffalo tho' a number of troops were seen by us at Fort Erie marching westward with flags flying. The good people (*the Sympathizers*) at Lewiston have been firing at our sentinels on this side. All this humbug must end in war sooner or later.

I have attempted to give you an idea of our position at present and I have nothing further to tell you at present. It is getting dark and Mr Forest[3] who will carry my letter will be here soon. Kiss my dear little ones for me and remember me affectionately to all our friends. God bless you my dearest Susie

> and believe me Ever Your
> Aff^te Husband
> *J.W. Dunbar Moodie*

P.S. I like my present quarters better than Toronto in many respects. Our mess there was very expensive – here we can live nearly upon our rations and will be able to save some money.

1 George H.H.E. Grierson, formerly of the 2d Durham Regiment and a member of the militia since 1832

2 Thomas Mitchell, formerly a captain in 2d Durham Regiment, was appointed to the Queen's Own on 15 January 1838 (MR, 1B1, 23, 26, 41).

3 Frederick Forest was a captain in the militia and parochial clerk for St John's Anglican Church in Peterborough. He was likely also the author of a satirical sketch criticizing the financial arrangements for the Peterborough court-house and jail, which appeared in the *Plainspeaker*, 'a small sheet then published at Cobourg,' in August 1838. See Elwood Jones, *St. John's Peterborough: The Sesquicentennial History of an Anglican Church* (Peterborough 1976), 30; and T.W. Poole, *A Sketch of the Early Settlement and Subsequent Progress of the Town of Peterborough* (Peterborough 1867), 46–8.

---

19 John Moodie to Susanna Moodie

Alexander's Bay
Near Point Abino
Niagara District

My Dearest Susie   17th April 1838

I have been waiting in vain for several weeks in hopes of hearing from you. I wrote you a few hurried lines from Toronto the evening before we started for this place; – and again from this place by Mr. Forest who was returning to Peterborough. I was glad to escape from Toronto, where we were harrassed beyond measure with unceasing drills, and every kind of annoyance which the ingenious tyranny of our Commanding Officer could invent. The expected attack from the Patriots was put down before we arrived so that we have had almost nothing to do but to keep a sharp look out on the Lake.[1] Our mess was so expensive at Toronto that it took most of my pay to keep me. Here however Hawthorn (who is my Lieut.) and I manage to live on little more than our rations, so that I expect to save a few pounds. We are domiciled at the house of a respectable kind hearted Scotchman (Alexander) where we have a couple of rooms at the rate of 2/6 each. We are close to the lake shore and have a fine view of the city of Buffalo which is only eight or nine miles from us and appears to be a very fine town – far superior to any thing in Canada. Alexander brings me any little thing I want from Buffalo at prime cost. I intend taking a trip over to that place with him in a few days, and shall try to get a few pounds of Tea smuggled for our use when I get home. I fear there is not much chance of the Reg.t being kept up after the term of service is expired viz the 15th of May – but others think differently. There is an order *for discontinuing the recruiting for the several Reg*ts.2 This does not look well. However it may be I am tolerably sick of *Militia Soldiering*, and shall be right glad to get back to my old woman and our dear brats again. We at first expected to have been recalled to Toronto, but have since heard that the remainder of the Regt will join us here. If it should be determined to continue the Regt and that we should be fixed on the frontier, I would let the farm and get you all up here with me. At all events I shall apply for leave soon and pay you a visit for a few days. I fear, my dearest, you are but poorly provided with the needful, but as we have recieved no pay as yet for March3 I can only send you £2.10 to help you on till I can get down. Some time ago Mr. Black4 who is only 12 miles from me at Port Colborne (the Western entrance to the Welland Canal), hearing of my being here wrote me a very kind invitation to pay him a visit and my kind landlord lent me a horse for that purpose. He is living in a comfortable cottage on the top of a sand hill with a fine view of the Lake. He is still employed by the Company and is Postmaster. He told me, by the way, that when you write to poor Mrs Welstead5 if you would direct the letter to his (Mr B's) care it would save postage. Mrs Black is still brisk and lively though she grumbles a little at the country. They had a daughter with them who is in bad health. She has a talented expression of countenance, tho' somewhat masculine and determined in [her] look. I *could prescribe for her*, but in their [remo]te situation I fear my nostrum could not be obtained very easily. When I left Toronto I left the subscription paper for poor Mrs Lloyd with my friend the Revd Mr Maynard and Col. Brown promised to assist in the matter – but I have not heard from either since. If the Regt is to be reduced most probably we will be marched to Toronto again in which case I can attend to the business. It was unfortunate that I was sent off so suddenly. Do write me soon, My dearest Susie and tell me all about my dear children. I could not live long without seeing you all. I am dying here for want of excitement and I have no inducement to take much exercise which I find is absolutely necessary to my constitution. The sudden change from the constant exercise we had at Toronto to half torpid life we lead here has had a very bad effect on my health. I am besides anxious and fretted from curious causes which I cannot explain at present. I am not sure but the bush is the best place for me after all. I am taking long walks *on principle* which I have always found a hard task but I am better in consequence for some days back. You need not be at all anxious on my account for my complaint is only my old friend Dyspepsia with a due seasoning of *Blue Devils.* Kiss my dear Katie, Aggy, Dunny and Donald for me and tell them to be good children and Papa will love them more and more. If I don't get away from this place soon I believe I shall take French leave and cut the concern altogether. Remember me most affectionately to Traill & Katie. I should have written him but really I have felt so unsettled in my mind [and] uncomfortable about my prospects that it has been out of my power to write a line.

> God Bless you, my dearest Susie
> & believe me ever your
> Aff^te Husband
> *J.W. Dunbar Moodie*

1 Cruikshank, 'Memoir,' 161–2
2 *Ibid.,* 165
3 On 6 May 1838 Kerby wrote to Bullock, 'I visited the Queen's Own at Point Abino and found them all quiet, they having received their Monthly pay a day or two before, which caused peace and quietness to be restored' (*ibid.,* 186).
4 James Black had emigrated from London to Darlington, Upper Canada, in the early 1820s. Connected with the Canada Company, he was postmaster of Darlington when Susanna's younger brother, Sam Strickland, emigrated in 1825. Black later moved his family to Port Colborne, where he served both as postmaster and as collector of customs. In 1844 James Kerby described Black both as 'an infirm and timid man' and as 'an old and feeble man' (*ibid.,* 319, 321; see also *LOL,* 216, 218n). Black died in Brockville in 1845.
5 Black's daughter, Mary, an old friend of Susanna Strickland (*LOL,* 346), had married another English emigrant, John Welstead. He was an officer in the 2d Northumberland Militia under his father-in-law's command but left the province in the late 1820s to try Lower Canada. By 1837 he was back, seeking to settle in the Western District (MR, 1B1, 23).

---

20 John Moodie to Susanna Moodie

My Dearest Susie,   Drummondville
                                     22nd June *1838*

You must not expect to see me home so soon as I expected when I left you. Our Regiment is to be kept up for another month, *until the 1st of Aug^t* and from present appearances I see little chance of its

being reduced *then*. Before this reaches you probably you will have
heard of the state of matters here. In fact we do not know what
moment we may be called out to meet the rebels and invaders –
domestic and foreign. The night before last a party of nine men of
the Lancers were attacked in a house they occupied in the Township of Pelham which is disaffected almost to a man. The strength
of the rebels is variously stated at from 60 to 200. They fired upon
the sentries and riddled the house with their balls, but the Lancers
made a gallant deffence with their pistols and swords hand to hand
while the rebels endeavoured to rush up stairs killing one and
wounding several. The rebels at last set fire to the house when the
Lancers were obliged to surrender. After taking their horses and
arms they were liberated after most of them were compelled to take
an oath not to take up arms against the rebels again. Fortunately
only two of them were wounded tho' the rascals fired up at them
thro' the ceiling on the room below. As soon as it was day light a
stronger party of the Lancers went in pursuit and killed another
rebel and brought in several prisoners two of them badly wounded.
One of them who is shot thro' the cheek bone the ball coming out
at his mouth, is an Englishman and the other a man from near *Port
Hope* called Warner is shot thro' the thigh. I went to see them in
our hospital and learned from one of them that they have several
hundred about this part of the country and more constantly coming
from the American side. People are coming in every two or three
hours with intelligence by which it appears nearly certain that there
are *now* from 1000 to 1200 already in our neighbourhood. I have
heard all the depositions of these people before the magistrates and
also those of a Patriot Captain – now employed as a spy by us and
their statements all nearly agree in the leading particulars. We are in
fact in a regular nest of rebels – not one in 50 is to be trusted. Major
Elliott yesterday while riding out with one of the Lancers, having
gone into a *public house* for a drop of *spiritual comfort* had his
horse shot thro' the neck by some one of the bystanders at the door
who took the Lancer's pistol out of the holster for the purpose but
he could not find out who had done it. Lieut. Kirchoffer[1] of our
Reg^t made a narrow escape yesterday. While he was bathing in the
river near Chippewa some one fired two shots with a rifle at him,
one of which *grased* his *side*. I am horr[ified in] these circumstances
that I did not bring my own four [shot] gun with me as I have to
go my rounds several miles at night when on duty, alone or with
only a man or two with me. Tell Evans that I have spoken to Col.

Kingsmill about him and impressed him much in his favor so that I have no doubt that he will soon be made a *Sergeant* by attending to his duty. Any thing better than this is out of the question at present as there are hundreds of applicants for Commissions. Our *officers* are to be reduced immediately to six Captains (I am the fifth from the head of the list) so that I shall probably escape the *break*. Two of *my seniors* will probably resign so that I will be then the third from the top. Major Elliott being *Second Major* will also go – *the sooner the better*. He and Dempsey[2] were *both drunk at Mess* yesterday. Col. Kingsmill sarcastically told Major Elliott to go to his bed, and when he ordered Dempsey to retire to his quarters and not disgrace the Corps, the latter refused and was extremely insolent and even refused several times to give up his sword when Col. K. put him under arrest. He had changed his mind and returned to the Reg[t] after he had agreed to go home. *He is now fairly dished.* If Evans should *come up let him come immediately.* If he brings a trunk I wish he would bring my gun with the *ball moulds* and *balls* powder flask &c. And also *my flute* to *kill time* when I am not better employed. All the papers talk of nothing but war war war: [I k]now my dearest you have too much sense and trust in Pro[vidence] to feel over anxious on my acct[t] for no circumstances can lessen [His] power to protect those who rely on God's Goodness. One thing appears certain, that we cannot expect any thing like peace, but thro' the means of a war to support the National honor. Our cause is a good one and we may be sure that it will ultimately prevail. If the things I want are locked up in my trunk you can break open the lock as I shall have no opportunity to send the Keys. If Evans could get hold of a pair of pistols they would be useful in the kind of service we are likely to have. The Governor is to be here tomorrow morning. The Indians are out from Brantford[3] and other troops are coming from Hamilton while we are to attack from this side. I believe the intention is to endeavour to surround the rebels and prevent their escape. I forgot to mention to you that a black man came over from Buffalo last night bringing information that he saw one waggon load of *cannon balls* and another waggon load of muskets proceeding to be embarked for Canada for the service of the Patriots – both the waggons belonged to General Whitney of the American Militia, and *they were driven by his sons.* This shews the feelings of the people on the borders. Lights were seen the whole of last night on the American Shore on Grand Island and on Navy Island and all accounts agree in stating that a body of about 300 intended to cross and *probably have crossed*. I must now finish my letter my own dearest wife for I am getting very sleepy having been up going my rounds till 2 o'clock last night or rather this morning and I should not be at all surprised if we should be turned out again before daylight by our *patriotic* friends who are not more than 10 or 15 miles from us and perhaps much nearer. I enclose you a ten Dollar Bill as a stop gap, and shall send more by & bye. Kiss my dear sweet children for me and tell them I am always thinking of them and of you my dear good wife, God bless you all. & believe me Ever Your Aff^te. husband

J.W. Dunbar Moodie

1 Lieutenant Nesbitt Kirchhoffer was a Port Hope barrister-at-law. He served in both the 1st Durham and, under Kingsmill, Queen's Own militia regiments. According to a Cavan patent map on file at the Archives of Ontario, he owned land in Cavan Township in the early 1830s.

2 Adjutant Francis Dempsey (late of the 21st Regiment) formally resigned from the Queen's Own by a letter to Colonel Kingsmill (24 June 1838), which the latter forwarded to Bullock (MR, 1B1, 23). But while Dempsey resigned, Elliott didn't. In fact, surviving Kingsmill correspondence is silent on the matter until 4 July, when he forwarded a letter to Bullock signed by many of the Queen's Own officers, including Lieutenant Colonel Robert Brown and Moodie, expressing 'surprise' and 'indignation' at the behaviour of Elliott, who had effectively prevented 'the men extending their services in compliance with the Militia General Order of the date June 18th' and who had introduced 'latterly' 'a party spirit among the men, subversive of discipline, and injurious to the future prospects of the country' (MR, 1B1, 23).

3 In response to Arthur's alarm, the 24th Regiment under Colonel Townsend came to Drummondville from Toronto. At the same time Samuel P. Jarvis, superintendent of Indian affairs, called out several detachments of natives from the Six Nations Reserve, one to guard the Grand River bridge, the other to bolster the frontier troops. As John suggests, the Indians under William Johnson Kerr moved east from Grand River to the Short Hills (Fryer, *Volunteers and Redcoats*, 89).

1838–1839

'Of exile and widowhood'

I N 'THE OUTBREAK' in *Roughing It in the Bush* Susanna tells
how, during the late stages of John's service on the Niagara frontier, she endeavoured to find a way to escape the backwoods life:

I rose from my bed, struck a light, sat down, and wrote a letter to the Lieutenant-Governor, Sir George Arthur, a simple statement of facts, leaving it to his
benevolence to pardon the liberty I had taken in addressing him.

I asked him to continue my husband in the militia service, in the same
regiment in which he now held the rank of captain, which, by enabling him
to pay our debts, would rescue us from our present misery. (*RIB*, 448)

John himself had petitioned Sir Francis Bond Head on 1 January
1837 (Letter 15). Whether or not Susanna's letter to Sir George Arthur
had any immediate effect,[1] Arthur's own respectful comments about
her in later letters to John Moodie imply special treatment, and John
was not long in receiving a second appointment, this time as 'Captain
and Paymaster to sixteen Companies of Militia, distributed along the
shore of Lake Ontario and [the] Bay of Quinte.'[2] Announced in the late
fall, and effective the beginning of 1839, the position was not likely to
last more than six months unless, as he hopes in Letter 21, 'something
more *permanent* is designed for me' in the 'New District of Hastings.'
Leaving Douro in early December, he stopped on the way to visit
his old friend William Brown and his family at Thorndale, their home
in Cavan Township, before proceeding via Brighton to the military
headquarters at Belleville. Lieutenant Colonel Robert Brown, a brother
of William, was formerly in Moodie's Scottish regiment and came to
Canada in 1830. Settling first in Peterborough, Robert Brown was a
prominent citizen, a neighbour of the Stewarts, and a member of the
St John's Church building committee. He was also a land agent working on contract for Alexander McDonnell. Brown, however, had a
serious drinking problem, which probably led to his leaving Peterborough for in the summer of 1837, according to the then-incumbent
minister, R.H. D'Olier, 'Col. Brown cut a shine in town for six days
from June 4th and sold the church bell to pay expenses.'[3] He eventually settled on Rice Lake near Gore's Landing,[4] having resigned his
militia position in the 4th Northumberland on 11 January 1840 (MR,
1B1, 38).
Moodie's letters home from Belleville consistently evince his admiration for his commanding officer, Lieutenant Colonel (also Baron)
George de Rottenburg (1807–94), whose job it was to coordinate the
operations of the militia companies assigned to guard the north

Colonel Robert Brown

shore of Lake Ontario. A young officer of distinguished lineage, de Rottenburg was the son of Major-General Francis de Rottenburg (1757–1832),[5] a Pole who, after an impressive military career on the continent, had joined the British army and come to Canada to command the forces in Lower Canada during the War of 1812. In 1813 he served briefly as president and administrator of Upper Canada. Moodie found young George de Rottenburg 'a delightful companion' and, as part of his team, was close to the centre of military intelligence for the area. De Rottenburg, who had previously served as Sir George Arthur's secretary, was 'the provincial government's chief representative and militia commander' for the area surrounding Belleville and as such he reported directly to and likely had the confidence of Arthur.[6]

Another notable member of the military command was Deputy Assistant Commissary General Henry Addington Bayley, a British officer who had originally been posted to Quebec. Bayley's wife, Diana, was the author of several juvenile works published in England, notably *Employment, the True Source of Happiness* (1825), *Tales of the Hearth* (1825), *Scenes at Home and Abroad* (1827), and *Improvement* (1832). Her 1836 book, *Henry; or, The Juvenile Traveller, a Faithful Delineation of a Voyage across the Atlantic in a New York Packet: A Description of a Part of the United States ... a Journey to Canada*, has given substance to the claim that she was the 'first resident of Canada to write for children.'[7] While living at Isle aux Noix in Lower Canada, she had contributed to the short-lived journal the *Museum* in Montreal, but her husband's military appointment brought her to Kingston. Susanna's letters do not provide us with her literary response to a juvenile work sent to her by Diana Bayley, but it is clear from Letter 31 that she was prepared to be complimentary, if only out of civility and kindness.

Functioning as paymaster for the district, Moodie was not only busy but also hard-pressed financially. Accounting for 'about 26 Companies' was onerous and exacting work which involved a great deal of travel, usually at his own expense. Duties and travel, however, had the advantage of fostering connections. Moodie's surviving letters from Belleville in 1839 reveal a growing network of personal contacts and an increasing awareness of the political and social tensions that characterized Belleville area life in the late 1830s.

Initially these contacts were consistent with his own loyal outlook. Among them was Dr George Neville Ridley (1794–1857), an Englishman and surgeon who came to Belleville in the 1820s and maintained a medical position with the 1st Hastings Regiment. A conservative in politics, Ridley was a Bellevillian of social prominence. His sixteen-year-old daughter, Louisa Mary, married George de Rottenburg in July 1839, though Moodie confidentially offered Susanna a somewhat low estimate of her worth. That Moodie would later find Ridley a problematical and prickly character in his unyielding conservatism is anticipated in Letter 36. Medical service, like everything else in Belleville, was highly charged and politicized.

Another prominent figure with interests both in Rawdon Township, northwest of Belleville, and the village River Trent (Trenton) was Sheldon Hawley (1795–1868). A militia commander and colonel during the post-rebellion period, Hawley, an Englishman, had held land east of the Trent River from early in the century. With John Strachan and on his own he had much to do with developing the River Trent area. He sought in particular to have River Trent designated the district town for the Victoria District in 1839 (he had helped to establish the town in 1834) and was a leader in early initiatives to develop the Trent Canal. In the late fall of 1839 his home was burnt; suspicions ran high that the fire, like several others in the area, was the work of 'reformists' or 'Americans.'

The wealthy Hawley and 'Major Meyers' – Adam Henry Meyers (1812–76) – whom Moodie termed 'one of the richest landholders in Canada,' served as Moodie's sureties upon his appointment as the first sheriff of Hastings County in November 1839. Of German descent, Meyers was a lawyer in River Trent and the owner of a well-located mill on the Trent River a mile north of Lake Ontario. His father of the same name had settled on the Trent in 1805 and by means of his mill and general store had becomed Trenton's most successful merchant.[8] Militia duties allowed Moodie and the young major to become 'pretty thick,' a friendship Moodie was forced to call upon when delays occurred concerning government approval of the initial sureties he had submitted to qualify him for service as sheriff.[9] Meyers and Hawley remained as Moodie's sureties until 1842, when, in his official capacity, Moodie felt it his duty to uphold a ruling that worked against and offended Meyers.[10] Meyers would later serve as a conservative member of Parliament for Northumberland and distinguish himself as a strong supporter and friend of John A. Macdonald.

Indeed, political conservatives held most of the prominent military and political positions along the front. While Meyers and Hawley stood out in what was to be the Trenton area, men like Thomas Parker, Benjamin Dougall, and Edmund Murney were leading figures in Belleville. It must have been military and social contact with such individuals that led Moodie as a newcomer to the area to worry increasingly about the implications of polarization of 'ultra selfish Toryism' on the one hand and 'Revolutionary Radicalism' on the other. He was comfortable with neither side, both of which seemed to him excessive. While conservatives were usually in positions of control, the area Moodie served as paymaster was *rather* very much dissaffected.' At the same time Moodie was much attracted to the region – at first near River Trent, then Belleville – seeing its settlers as 'far superior' in character to the men he had known in Hamilton Township, especially the land-dealers of Cobourg. Still, for all the attractiveness of the area, Moodie was struck by the intensity of factionalism in and about the Victoria District.

It is not clear from Moodie's Belleville letters what led him to adopt reformist sympathies, conservative as those sympathies would be. Perhaps it was less particular events and individuals than it was the opportunity to observe at close quarters the political attitudes, biases, and tensions that characterized not only the Belleville area but much of Upper Canada. In particular he must have been struck by the polar responses to Sir Francis Bond Head, who, by then back in England, had published his memoirs; and to Lord Durham (1792–1840),[11] whose controversial *Report* on colonial self-government[12] first appeared in the local press in April. A conservative paper like the Kingston *Chronicle and Gazette* published not only excerpts from Bond Head's *Narrative*, lauding the author's character and astuteness, but also the full text of Durham's *Report*, complaining of its 'confused notions as to the state of parties among us,' discrediting its attack upon the Family Compact as 'absurd,' and suggesting that the *Report* had been written less by Durham than by his aide Charles Buller,[13] who was closely associated with 'individuals whose private disappointments would lead them to paint our condition in jaundiced colouring, or whose political partialities were such as "assimilated" to those of the Radical M.P.'[14]

Moodie's own reaction to Durham's *Report* occurs in the form of an extended and spontaneous postscript to Letter 32. Aware of his own imminent discharge and thinking again about the possibility of emigration, perhaps to Texas, he launches into a tribute to Durham's work and sagacity and, more personally, to the 'stern unyielding spirit, and integrity of purpose' of the Scotch. Clearly Moodie was depressed by and resistant to what he saw, particularly of the ways in which politics, religion, and special societies (secret or otherwise) conspired to promote factionalism in the area. Thus, even in recognizing Durham's acuteness and his potential to be 'the best friend Canada ever had,' Moodie's exasperation is implicitly directed at the conservative party's power. Dr Strachan's 'half Radical letter,' which had in fact appeared in the Kingston *Chronicle and Gazette* (10 April 1839) and was itself dated 20 September 1838, fauningly praised Durham as 'the pacifier of the Canadas' and was written in apparent outrage at the 'shameful' action taken by the House of Lords in summoning Durham back to England. In this letter Strachan criticizes not only the British govern-ment but 'His Lordship's political opponents in Canada,' that 'factious opposition' which wished above all to undermine Durham's 'mission,' 'the most important, perhaps, that was ever entrusted to a British Subject.' Obsequious on the one hand and self-promoting on the other, Strachan's letter, which cleverly disguised his own conservatism, did not fool Moodie. Neither did it fool the *Chronicle and Gazette*'s conservative editor, who, in noting that the letter appeared to be a part of an appendix to the *Report*, added wryly, 'The Venerable Archdeacon appears to hold his Lordship in high esteem.'

The shrievalty and the grim factions of Belleville politics were, however, matters for the future. In the late winter and spring of 1839 Moodie's eye was largely on his paymaster duties and the continuing signs of unrest along the Lake Ontario and St Lawrence River border. Appointed in the wake of the Battle of the Windmill at Prescott (11–16 November 1838), Moodie was paymaster to a newly enlarged militia that remained alert to American invasion and the prospects of war. The activities of secret societies (Hunters' Lodges), reports of the amassing of arms south of the border, and continuing threat of border skirmishes had led Sir George Arthur to increase the contingent of citizen-soldiers along the Upper Canadian border to twelve thousand, offering six-month appointments. The Battle of Windsor in early December doubtless confirmed the validity of such preparation.[15]

While it was Moodie's job as part of the small Belleville branch of the Kingston commissariat to coordinate the payments to enlisted men and officers and to do so in an efficient, responsible manner, his activ-ities involved him in a good deal of correspondence, training of com-pany captains, and travel, in all of which he took workmanlike pride.

Moodie's references to his military activities, irregular as they are, suggest that an anxious state of affairs persisted well into the spring of 1839, even as militia units were being cut back. The activities of disaffected Patriots quickly degenerated into criminal acts during 1838–40. For example, William 'Bill' Johnston, originally from Trois Rivières, styled himself 'the Admiral of the Patriot Navy' and boldly attacked British shipping and settlements along the upper St Lawrence, including the steamship *'Sir Robert Peel*, which was burned about 2 a.m. on May 30, 1838, off Wells Island, the largest of the Thousand island group.' He was arrested near Ogdensburg and sentenced to jail for one year in Albany, but he escaped and returned to plunder in Upper Canada. The Toronto *Patriot* on 15 February 1839 reports that the *Upper Canada Gazette* contains a general militia order 'setting forth the names of 140 pirates who were tried at Kingston, four of whom were acquitted – and 136 condemned to death, 20 have been recommended to mercy, and 11 have been executed; and 44 who were tried at London, one of whom was acquitted and the remainder found guilty and received sentence of death – four being recommended to mercy, six only have been executed ...' Bill Johnston was eventually pardoned in 1841.[16]

Continued concern about the vulnerability of the region informs Moodie's letters even as he notes that his own position is part of a reduction of forces that summer. Whatever his disappointment, he was involved in numerous dinners to honour his commanding officer, de Rottenburg. Beyond the drunken affair celebrating de Rottenburg's marriage that he describes with some astringency in Letter 30, newspaper reports confirm his presence at several militia dinners given at Belleville, River Trent, and Brighton in late April and early May. At the Brighton dinner in de Rottenburg's honour, for instance, 'Capt. Moody' responded to the toast to the Duke of Wellington.[17] An 18 May editorial note in the Kingston *Chronicle and Gazette* praised the conduct and professionalism of de Rottenburg's militia units, which were now being 'suffered to depart for their homes, where their presence is required in the cultivation of their farms.' In particular, the paper commended

the effective state of discipline and soldierlike appearance they have obtained under that gallant and accomplished officer, the Baron de Rottenberg, during the last winter. It shows a heartiness and zeal on the part of the commander and commanded, highly creditable to both – it is a convincing proof, if any were wanting, that there is a 'naero me impune lacessit' spirit, a sort of 'touch-me-not' feeling in the country, in which our friends on the other side 45 may do well to note.

As one of the few acts of a whig government that we can approve of, we congratulate them upon their judicious selection of the officers generally, and of the gallant Baron in particular, chosen for the arduous and responsible duties of the Particular Service in this country.

George, Baron de Rottenburg

The festivities over, it is clear from their correspondence that Moodie took more than a month to extricate himself from his paymaster's duties, even though his position had formally ended. In *Roughing It in the Bush*, however, Susanna does not recall her 'dreadful state of uncertainty' about her husband's whereabouts through June and July. Rather she simply reports that 'he once more returned to help gather in our scanty harvest,' their overall condition 'much improved' because of the payment of old debts out of 'his hard-saved pay' (*RIB*, 500).

During the long period of his absence, John's letters were an essential source of consolation to Susanna, and her responses to him served as a way of coping with the exigencies of her 'state of widowhood' (Letter 31). He kept her posted on events, his own movements, and the people he met during 1838 and 1839; she provided him with detailed accounts of the trials and achievements of his family and the very different world of the bush. Overall the letters give expression to the tensions she was experiencing between her domestic obligations and her artistic inclinations, between the hardships of the pioneer farm and the attractions of other horizons. But through all the constant theme is her love for and devotion to her husband.

That affection is manifested in the opening and closing of each letter and in numerous expressions woven into the report of events. Perhaps there is no better example than the lengthy passage in Letter 33 in which she catalogues her riches and blessings, beginning with John's love for her and ending with the resolution that they will be 'firm friends through a happy eternity.' This passage is one of many indications that the letters are the product of narrative and dramatic talent. Although the letters often contain matters of local concern, like the disposal of their bush farm, there are also passages of extended narrative, such as her accounts of her own and the children's illnesses, which she renders in graphic and effective detail, retaining even the storyteller's manipulation of suspense.

At the same time her letters have particular application to *Roughing It in the Bush*. It is neither possible nor necessary to enumerate all of the connections here. Like the book, the letters, with their diversity and tonal variety, are susceptible to individual interpretation; however, certain facets of the relationship between letters and book may prove useful to the reader.

The letters are closely related to three chapters of *Roughing It in the Bush*: 'The Outbreak,' 'The Whirlwind,' and 'A Change in Our Prospects,' although there are incidental connections to other chapters, like

'The Walk to Dummer.' These are the chapters that reveal how, in John's absence, Susanna coped with the operation of the farm and with her poverty and illnesses. Her energetic management, outlined in 'The Outbreak' and 'The Walk to Dummer,' is alluded to in the extant letters, but a letter from Thomas Traill to John Moodie dated May 1838 confirms the accuracy of Susanna's account:

Your wife deserves all you say of her. She has commanded the esteem of every one. Your spring crops are nearly in. She was anxious to spare you every trouble when you came home. In fact she is farther advanced than her brother or me, or indeed any of the neighbours ... I am happy to say that all your children look fat fair and flourishing as do mine, and you will find on your return which I hope will be soon that every thing has been managed admirably in your absence and every difficulty met with energy constancy and courage. I am proud to do justice to the worth and value of your most excellent wife. She is indeed a treasure of which you may be proud. (PHEC, no. 154)

Both sources also reveal Susanna's willingness to assist neighbours in distress. The mission of mercy to Mrs. N—— recorded in 'The Walk to Dummer' was in fact to the Louisa Lloyd referred to in Letter 17; clearly, however, the walk took place in the winter of 1838, not 1839, as *Roughing It in the Bush* suggests. As a result of her account John raised a subscription of forty dollars from his fellow officers for the abandoned woman. Louisa was the wife of Lieutenant Frederick Lloyd, a discharged marine who had settled in Dummer in 1831. He initially held two and a half lots in the first concession and acquired another in the second, but undoubtedly these had been lost by 1838. Indeed, lot 20 in the second concession was yielded to Joseph Jory of Dummer in exchange for work done in April 1835. Nine years later, Samson Lukey, another person familiar to the Moodies, stated, in an affidavit supporting Jory's claim, that Lloyd and his son Albert had gone to the United States and that neither had 'been since heard of in this part nor is it known where they are.'[18] For her part, Mrs Lloyd did not forget the kindness done her and made a present of a fine cattle dog to Susanna in the spring of 1839 (Letter 33).

Susanna's care for her neighbours was rewarded in other ways; Letters 22 and 25 show how the social system of interdependence and mutual assistance depicted in 'The Walk to Dummer' applied in her own case. They vividly reveal the vulnerability of the settler in the bush when illness struck and medical assistance was required. When in late December Susanna suffered an infection of the breast resulting from the nursing of her third son, who had been born in October, Thomas Traill, responding to the seriousness of her condition, sought the help of Peterborough doctor John Hutchison. Dr Hutchison gave invaluable medical service to many Cavan Township and Peterborough area people during the thirty years of his practice. A Scot, he was a particular friend of the Traills, and on this occasion he made the emergency journey with Thomas, in the dead of night, from Peterborough to the Moodies' clearing, a distance of more than ten miles.[19]

That visit appears to have been an exceptional one in more than its emergency character. Dr Hutchison did not attend the births of any of the three Moodie children born in the bush. In contrast, his registry indicates that he was present at the delivery of five of the Traill children born between 1836 and 1844. By frequency of visits Hutchison's 'Account Books' suggest that the Traills, unlike the Moodies, who were treated only occasionally, were subscribers to the Hutchison Medical Insurance Policy. The account of his refusal to attend the Moodie children in March 1839, together with Dr Bird's comment on that refusal in Letter 25, may hint at some degree of antipathy between Moodie and Hutchison about which we shall probably not know more. More plausible is that the demands for treatment of the epidemic closer to home were such that neither Hutchison nor his young associate, Dr Dickson, could justify so time-consuming a trip.

Of Welsh background, Dr George Gwynne Bird had been in the Peterborough area for some years, trying his hand at farming and later pharmacy; only in 1838 did he obtain his licence to practise in Upper Canada. In 'The Whirlwind' chapter of *Roughing It in the Bush* he is cited as Dr B——, in reference to the visit described in Letter 25, while Dr Taylor (who was Hutchison's partner)[20] is erroneously substituted for Dr Hutchison as the doctor who did not come. Dr Bird closed his medical dispensary at Bird's Landing on the Otonabee River in 1841, moving to the Darlington area, where he died in 1863.[21]

Several of the letters show that even more valuable than medical aid was the assistance of neighbours, many of whom belonged to the class of military officers and their families. In settling near relatives and persons of similar social background, such people created a supportive community that would help to make pioneer life endurable in good times and bad.

When Susanna was in difficulty, her sister Catharine responded to her needs when she could, although the letters reveal that she had her own child-rearing cares, often simultaneously with Susanna's. The Traills' financial problems and their movements are repeatedly subjects of Susanna's reportage to John. It would seem that very early in his Canadian experience Thomas Traill realized, like John, the error of settling in the backwoods. Overwhelmed by debts, he began trying to sell his farm in 1835, placing advertisements in the Cobourg *Star*, and when the Traills went to visit the Rev. George Bridges in 1839 (Letter 24), it was probably in part an exploratory journey. Bridges was an eccentric Englishman who moved to Canada from Jamaica in 1837 after reading Catharine's *The Backwoods of Canada.* He built an unusual octagonal home on the south shore of Rice Lake, the house he offered to the Traills. Although Catharine named the house 'Wolf Tower' at the time of this visit, they did not accept Bridges's offer until 1846–7.[22]

In April 1839 Traill finally sold his farm, lot 19 in the 7th concession, to Henry Hulbert Wolseley (he is the Rev. W.W. —— in *Roughing It in the Bush*), an Anglican priest of somewhat advanced years for a settler (Letter 27). The Traills' removal from the woods in March was a severe loss to Susanna, making her 'doubly lonely.' Even though there are signs of occasional friction between the two families,[23] the importance of the proximity of the Traills is clearly realized in several of the letters and in 'The Walk to Dummer.'

Perhaps even more remarkable were the self-endangering journeys of young Cyprian Godard (1817–96), one of the eight children of newly widowed John Godard (1782–1862), who had recently settled his motherless family in Douro Township on lot 22, concession 4. While Cyprian appears to have been indispensible to Susanna as a messenger on more than one occasion, his brothers Alured and George rendered other kinds of assistance to her. Their aunt, Hannah Godard, was married to Colonel John Thomas Caddy and lived on lot 21 of the 4th concession, about two miles to the east of the Moodies.[24] She was one of the first to respond when Susanna became ill in December 1838. That they were a family of warm and generous hospitality is vividly revealed in 'The Walk to Dummer,' as well as in these letters.

Charlotte Emilia Shairp, so often referred to in *Roughing It in the Bush* as Susanna's cherished friend and her companion on the walk to Dummer to assist Mrs Lloyd, was likewise alert to her needs. Emilia had married her cousin, Lieutenant Alexander Mordaunt Shairp, in January 1834. Their son, Henry Easton Shairp, also mentioned in 'The Walk to Dummer,' was born in December of that year. Although the Shairps lived on their land, the west half of lot 21, concession 5, not far from the Moodies, they also spent long periods in Peterborough at Endsleigh Cottage,[25] the home of Emilia's father, who also owned property in Otonabee and Verulam townships.[26] When Emilia's husband returned to Britain to seek a naval position in 1839, she opened a school in Peterborough, thus depleting Susanna's neighbourly support.

While Emilia was obviously a key figure in the network of female assistance in Douro, she was but one of several. Mary Hague, the wife of James Hague and youngest daughter of Lieutenant Colonel Walter Crawford of the 4th Northumberland Militia Regiment, was the principal representative of yet another kin group important to the Moodies. They may have been known to the Moodies earlier when they lived in Hamilton Township, for Walter had a farm near Cobourg, known as Spring Vale, the north half of lots 19 and 20 in the 2d concession of Hamilton. James and Mary were married there in April 1837.[27]

Lieutenant Colonel Walter Crawford must have been a man of considerable financial resources. While he owned the land in Hamilton Township, he also purchased lot 9 in the 8th concession of Douro in 1831 from the Canada Company. In 1833 he was advertising in the Cobourg *Star* that, 'after having surmounted numerous difficulties,' he had rafted 'a large quantity of LUMBER to Peterborough' from his Douro Mills and had established a lumber yard there. By early 1837 he also owned lot 13 in the 8th concession of Douro, parts of lot 13 in the 7th, and lot 11 in the 8th, which he sold to his son-in-law, James Hague, in April 1837. When Mary gave birth to a child, Eliza Georgina, in October 1838, the Hagues were apparently living in Douro, and the child was baptized in Peterborough in June 1839. Documents reveal that the Crawfords, including Walter's father, George, the major referred to in Letters 22 and 24, also moved to Douro, leaving the management of the Spring Vale farm to Walter's son, Angus.

It is no wonder then that the Crawfords and Mary Crawford Hague were able to come to Susanna's assistance in a material way and to take care of the Moodies' daughter Agnes, furnishing her with 'shoes and nice clothes' (Letter 22). Mary is a key figure in the later chapters of *Roughing It in the Bush*, being the person who, in Susanna's opinion, spoils Agnes, and is reluctant to give her up even when the Moodies are on their way to Belleville. James Hague is also alluded to in the book as H——, one of the men at the Moodies' logging-bee who later drowned in the Otonabee, for James was a victim of the river in May 1843.[28]

Probably the delineation of Susanna's struggle with illness, so restrainedly dealt with in *Roughing It in the Bush*, is the most compelling feature of her letters. In them the reader witnesses the darkest period of her bush life. She notes in her first letter of 1839 that her spirit had been 'tamed down,' that she was 'no longer able to contend with [her] comfortless situation' and that '... the charity of [her] kind neighbors really distresses [her].' The observation is curious in the light of her own mission of charity to Mrs Lloyd and the readiness with which she lends vital help to her neighbour, Hannah Caddy, so soon after her own recovery in February. Although she had suffered great physical and emotional trials, in actions such as her assistance to Mrs Caddy, Susanna shows her own resilience and endurance.

Such qualities are revealed likewise in her dealing with another stratum of the bush society, that of the indispensible 'yeomen' who sought crop sharing arrangements, like the Garbutts and Godards, or who undertook onerous tasks for hire, like the Jorys. Many such people involved in these aspects of the Moodies' lives are also mentioned in her book.

Edward Sibbings or Sibbon, for example, lived north of the Moodies on lot 22, concession 5. He was the comic figure 'Old Wittals' of 'Our Logging Bee,' whose one-eyed son, Sol, told of his father's eating capacity and who later assisted Jenny Buchanan in the sugaring incidents reported in 'The Outbreak' and in these letters. Sibbon was 'a Suffolk settler of low degree' who had emigrated in 1830 with a wife and six children. He endeavoured to take advantage of John's absence in the way he dealt with the grist he took to the mill (Letter 22), but, because he was illiterate, he was very dependent on the good will of others. His own petition for patents to his land is supported by a host of the Moodies' neighbours, including Thomas Traill and Samuel Strickland, the Caddys, and Major Shairp.[29]

The Jorys are referred to in *Roughing It in the Bush* as the Y——ys. In both letters and book Susanna recounts the necessity of paying them off for work long since completed, and she is very concerned about that obligation, while appreciative of the Jorys' patience. That they remained on good terms is indicated by the fact that Susanna left her dog, Rover, presumably the one given to her by Mrs Lloyd, to James Jory. James had land in the 2d concession of Douro, but he probably lived with his father, Joseph, in Dummer Township, as indicated in *Roughing It in the Bush*. Another son, Stephen Jory, later married another near neighbour of the Moodies, Sarah Anne Copping, a daughter of Samuel Copping of lot 22 in the 5th concession, yet another Suffolk settler.[30]

The Isaac Garbutt family was another on whose services the Moodies had relied (Letters 22, 33, and 35). Isaac Garbutt senior arrived in Canada in 1832 and settled in Smith Township in 1835. Lake Katchewanook was not, however, a formidable barrier to labour and commerce with the township of Douro on the other side of the river. To promote their own prospects, people such as the Garbutts cleared land for the Moodies and others like them. Some of Garbutt's children eventually relocated in Douro on land near the Moodies' farm, and years afterward, on a nostalgic cruise to Stony Lake, reminiscent of the one she describes in *Roughing It in the Bush*, Susanna was to renew acquaintance with the elderly Isaac Garbutt (Letter 79).

Further connection with people of Smith Township is reflected in the search for a buyer for the Moodie farm. Norah Young's husband, James Carney (Kearny), was but one person interested in it. He was probably from Smith Township, and certainly Norah was, being one of the daughters of Francis Young, the owner of the mill at Young's Point, whose family the Moodies visited in 'A Trip to Stony Lake.'

Many other persons mentioned, such as Copperthwaite and Christy Wright, William Erskine, Joe Dunlop, Mrs Brown, Richard Birdsall,[31] and Robert Casement, concerning illnesses, marriages, land availability, and other matters, show that information was very effectively communicated through the backwoods by persons moving from place to place. The marriage and ensuing scandal involving H.R. [or H.H.] Copperthwaite and Christy Wright (Letters 24 and 33) is an excellent example. Although he was one of the original subscribers to St John's Church in Lakefield, there is good reason to think that Copperthwaite may have lived in the nearby township of Otonabee and that he is the same person as the 'Old Woodruff' revealed in 'Adieu to the Woods,' Susanna's final sketch in *Roughing It in the Bush*, about the journey she and her children made to Belleville to join her husband. Both men are identified as Yorkshiremen, the one in the letters designated as 'sly,' the one in the book as 'shrewd.' In an earlier version of the sketch first published in the *Literary Garland* (January 1847), Susanna gives a more elaborate description of the man, in which she seems to be pursuing her usual practice of slightly disguising the names of her characters, who were, after all, people whom she knew. Hence, it is observed of Old Woodruff that 'the aspect of his head [gives] you the idea of a copper pot with the head closely screwed down.' In Letter 33 she refers to him as 'Copperhead,' although his real name is Copperthwaite. A thwaite is 'wild land made arable,' but it would not be unlike Susanna to render such a meaning as 'Woodruff.' Furthermore, the notion of Copperthwaite as one who is 'outwitted by a woman after all' (Letter 33) is consistent with the rather callous attitude towards women conveyed in the portrayal of Old Woodruff.

William Erskine, alluded to in the same letter as Copperthwaite, was a respectable Scotsman who lived in Douro near the Crawfords. In 1835 he married Mary, the second daughter of James Wright of Monaghan, a union that Thomas Traill termed 'not a very good marriage.'[32] Traill's hint of disrepute in the Wrights seems to be borne out by the escapades of Mary's sisters, Christy and Ellen.

While local gossip as well as news of sickness and the interests of various persons obviously circulated quickly in the backwoods, these letters make clear that, in spite of the Moodies' isolated situation, they also maintained important contacts with the world beyond the bush and received news of matters occurring in distant places. The media for such information were, of cource, correspondence and newspapers, both foreign and domestic.

Information about John's relatives in South Africa was received in letters from his brother Donald (Letter 23), keeping the Moodies abreast of the domestic affairs of that far-off branch of the family and outlining the complexities of colonial politics there. Sir Andries Stockenstrom was a major figure in the conduct of British policy on the frontier of the Cape colony. His career was characterized by a number of personal feuds, and when he was appointed lieutenant-governor in February 1836, an attempt was made to discredit him by accusations that he had shot a 'caffre' or Xhosa in the back in 1813. In response, Stockenstrom brought a charge of libel against Captain Duncan Campbell, civil commissioner for Albany. That charge was not substantiated, and in a subsequent inquiry, Stockenstrom was exonerated of any wrong-doing. He remained as lieutenant-governor until August 1839, when he was dismissed by the colonial secretary, Lord Normanby.[33]

While the Moodies found such matters interesting, the fate of John's land near Grahamstown was of more concern. But, in spite of the expectations raised by the reported sale of Groote Valley, noted in Letter 23, later letters indicate that John received nothing from the sale until 1842 (PHEC, no. 50). At that time he was sent £234 through Patrick Lawrie of Lawristone near Cobourg. Lawrie and other persons in the Newcastle District of Upper Canada had connections in South Africa, and through those connections Donald Moodie, on more than one occasion, received news of his brother and his family. As early as October 1833, when the Moodies had been in Canada for only a year,

Donald wrote: 'I don't know what you have been doing to offend Rubidge or his relations in Canada but he has been attacking you in the Grahams Town paper for running down this colony – the charges are not very serious. *You are a moody* settler – Have married a bit of a blue and the cattle you sold were wild' (PHEC, no. 47). The Rubidge in Canada was Captain F.P. Rubidge,[34] brother of Charles, who was an early Otonabee Township settler. In later years Donald was to hear, probably through Lawrie, that the money John had invested 'in steam had evaporated.' The reference is to the steamboat *Cobourg*; in their letters to one another (Letters and 30 and 32), John and Susanna reiterate the hope that the investment of the proceeds from the sale of his military commission in 1834 would yet bring them some financial assistance.

George Hodson (Letter 24) was another of the Moodies' Old World correspondents. His letters brought them the stimulus of intellectual discussion of theological matters. Although only one of these letters, dated 23 October 1843, survives in the Patrick Hamilton Ewing Collection, it refers to earlier correspondence with both John and Susanna. Furthermore, these were rather long letters. Hodson makes reference to John's 'very long and friendly letter,' and his reply to John runs to nine foolscap pages.

Hodson was probably the assistant secretary of the London Missionary Society in the early 1830s, when the Moodies first knew him. John mentions seeing him in London in May 1832 (Letter 8), but in 1843 he was living in Upper Norwash, Surrey. The tone and substance of his letter indicate that he was a Church of England clergyman and a member of the evangelical movement who shared with the Moodies a relish for theological discussion. Such discussion was an important part of Susanna's life during the period of her conversion to Congregationalism in 1830 (*LOL*, 43–8), and clearly she did not forsake it when she emigrated.

Hodson's long letter to John, after friendly reference to their relationship and previous correspondence with both husband and wife, addresses two basic issues. The first is the validity of a National Church, which Hodson defends, even though he must reluctantly acknowledge that recent divisions in both the Church of Scotland and the Church of England seem to '*look like* verifications of [dissenters'] sentiments as to the essential opposition between genuine piety and Political Headship in all National Churches.' The subject was prompted by John's 'influence on Mrs M. as to Presbyterianism.'[35] On this matter Hodson is only concerned that John use 'such means of persuasion as were honorable in themselves, and suitable for you as her husband to employ.' Hodson's point is that Susanna ought to 'freely exercise her judgement on the arguments.'

The second point is that although John Moodie favours the 'Presbyterian System of Church Govt.,' he would be 'esteemed as defective in a Capital ... article of their faith, if you deny the doctrine of absolute Election, or predestination.' Hodson is again responding to one of John's statements from a previous letter, which he quotes: 'In these views my wife and I agree, and we hold in horror the doctrine of the rigid Calvinists and Presbyterians.'[36] Even though Hodson had addressed the subject 'last year' in a letter to Susanna, because she had introduced it in one of hers, he takes up the issue again in response to John. The remainder of his letter, some four foolscap pages, is an explanation and defence of the doctrine, with frequent biblical reference. That his argument had little effect on the Moodies' liberal spirits is suggested in Susanna's denunciation of John Calvin in the midst of her review of the churches of Belleville in *Life in the Clearings* (1853): 'To the soul-fettering doctrines of John Calvin I am myself no convert; nor do I think that the churches established on his views will very long exist in the world. Stern, uncompromising, unloveable and unloved, an object of fear rather than of affection, John Calvin stands out the incarnation of his own Diety ...' (*LC*, 16). Apparently John Moodie had expressed such sentiments to his friend, Hodson, along with assessments of Belleville, to which Hodson replied, 'I am grieved by the picture you present of the conflicting state of Society in your vicinity arising from differences as to religion.' His letter further reveals that John and, doubtless, Susanna remarked on such matters as the Temperance Society and the abuses of patronage, two more subjects that would be addressed in *Life in the Clearings*. Such parallels indicate once again the extent to which the groundwork for later books was laid in the Moodies' correspondence.

While the Moodies doubtless had many distant informants, it is evident that the principal one was Susanna's sister Agnes Strickland. The Patrick Hamilton Ewing Collection contains many letters from Agnes, the majority being sent in the two decades preceding the publication of *Roughing It in the Bush*. There were two main areas of news in Agnes's letters: the literary life of London which she experienced; and news of the family and Suffolk acquaintances. In the 1830s much of the family news had to do with the loss or sickness of aged relatives, including Jane Cotterell and Rebecca Leverton, but the inheritance anticipated and, indeed, apparently received by Susanna appears not to have come from these sources.[37] Agnes's letters express only disappointment of her expectations and annoyance at the interference of her mother and her sister, Jane Margaret, in the handling of such matters.

To counterbalance her grievances, Agnes often included a literary dimension in her letters and that may have been just as troubling to Susanna. Especially in the early days, when her sister reported at considerable length her attendance at the painter John Martin's 'soirees' and her meeting there and elsewhere with people who knew Susanna (*LOL*, 12, 56), pangs of regret at her distance from such affairs must have been sharp:

... went twice to Martin's *Soiree's* and enjoyed the thing much. I was introduced to your friend Mr Allcock whom I greatly admire as a philanthropist and general friend to society at large. He is plain and eccentric but I think possesses a beautiful mind. He enquired after you and Kate with the warmest interest and expressed himself in the highest terms of admiration of you both and said the moment he heard I was your sister he was anxious for an introduction.

I was there introduced to Godwin the Author of Caleb Williams whom I greatly admire – we were very friendly though Roundhead and Cavalier ... I saw Leitch Ritchie for a moment in Smith & Elder's shop – he enquired after you and Moodie. (PHEC, no. 111)

Furthermore, Agnes acted as a literary agent for both Susanna and John, whom she called 'the chief,' looking after their interests with the publishers Smith and Elder, and with Richard Bentley, and seeking items of poetry from Susanna for which she could and did find outlets. But Susanna sent only two Canadian-based poems to her sister for inclusion in the *Lady's Magazine*. 'There's Rest: Stanzas Written at Night on the St. Lawrence, North America' appeared in the February 1834 issue, and 'The Emigrant's Bride. A Canadian Song' in the January 1837 issue, although other items that she had written, probably before leaving England, appeared there as well. In the light of Agnes's encouragement (Letter 22), it is somewhat surprising, but also interesting, to find Susanna reticent about sending work to Britain. Her refusal is, perhaps, a reflection of the 'tamed down ... spirit' that she acknowledges in this letter. And yet her refusal of the trial of seeking popularity in Britain is, ironically, followed by the wish to 'be popular in the country of my adoption.' That wish is the beginning of another important theme in Susanna's correspondence with John.

Earlier literary activity by Susanna, apparently sparked by the discovery of New World outlets while she still lived in Hamilton Township (*LOL*, 73–7) and then again when her loyal enthusiasm issued in poetic outpourings against rebellious activity in the Canadas, had given way to her domestic burden and the management of the farm. But as the prospects grew brighter that they might be able to get out of the bush through John's attainment of a permanent appointment, her literary and artistic aspirations were stimulated once again and constitute a contrasting motif to her ongoing domestic concerns. By 6 March (Letter 25), having coped with the severe illness of her children, she is able to begin dreaming of collaboration with her husband in the editorship of a newspaper, and by April she is painting maple-sugar fungi for sale in Peterborough and in Britain. By June 1839 she has sent 'two small MSS. down to Mr Lovel, the Editor of the Garland,' which she hopes will 'open up a little fund for me' to assist in the economy of the family. It is likely that her patriotic poems for the *Palladium* had attracted the attention of John Lovell, who included some of them in his newspaper, the Montreal *Transcript*. In *Roughing It in the Bush* Susanna recalls, 'Just at this period I received a letter from a gentleman, requesting me to write for a magazine (the *Literary Garland*), just started in Montreal, with promise to remunerate me for my labours,' noting that the 'application was like a gleam of light springing up in the darkness,' one that 'opened up a new era in my existence' (*RIB*, 440–1). That optimism is confirmed in Letter 33, where she follows her comments on Lovell with an emotional statement of her blessings. Hence, she took up her writing again with renewed energy, and in her book she writes of how her servant, Jenny Buchanan, reproved her for the exhausting efforts she was making to produce literature. Given the close relationship of these very letters to some parts of *Roughing It in the Bush*, it is tempting to speculate that some of the sketches for the book originated at this time.[38]

Whether or not Susanna had prospects of re-entering the literary world in Canada, she nourished her intellect and spirit through the availability of Canadian newspapers. We know that she had access to the Cobourg *Star*, but the letters reveal that there was knowledge of others too. She was aware of the editorial roles of Adam Thom,[39] Thomas Rolph,[40] and Robert Hamilton,[41] and Charles Fothergill's *Palladium* was publishing poetry by both of the Moodies. By far the most valuable resource for her and John with respect to literary, political, scientific, and general news was the *Albion*, published in New York, edited by Dr Bartlett, and widely distributed throughout North America. Its pages kept the Moodies abreast of new scientific theories such as James Pollard Espy's philosophy of storms (Letter 35).[42]

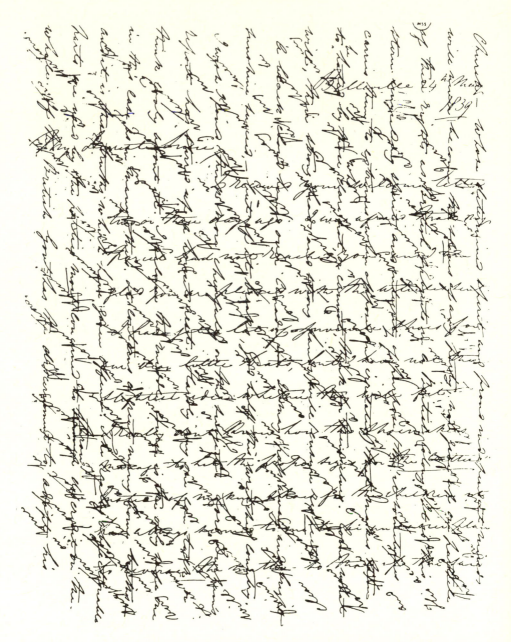

Facsimile of John Moodie's cross-written letter
of 24 May 1839 to Susanna

In July 1839, 'dispirited' by John's prolonged absence and by the cares of coping with the bush farm, Susanna is able to draw on her curious bit of knowledge by suggesting that Professor Espy had conjured up the stormy period that affected Douro Township. That stormy period is, perhaps, an apt symbol of the physical and emotional ordeals that are vividly recounted in many of these letters. She could not know, of course, in mid-summer of 1839 that her family's fortunes were about to be radically altered. In October John was appointed sheriff of Victoria District. He himself moved to Belleville later that month to prepared for his position, and his family left Douro on New Year's Day 1840 to join him there.[43]

1 Susanna apparently wrote two letters to Arthur in 1838, neither of which has been found, although one dated 18 December 1838 is listed in NA, Finding Aid 881, Upper Canada Sundries: Correspondence of the Civil Secretary, vol. 14.
2 In October 1838 a general militia order called into service four battalions of incorporated militia and numerous regiments of sedentary militia. Two of the four incorporated battalions were commanded by Moodie's former officers, Lieutenant Colonel Kenneth Cameron and Lieutenant Colonel William Kingsmill. On 7 November George de Rottenburg was elevated from captain to lieutenant colonel, particular service, and ordered to assume command of the militia force in active service in the Belleville-Presqu'ile area. Moodie's own description of the particulars of this office occurs in Scenes and Adventures, as a Soldier and Settler (Montreal 1866), x.
3 Elwood Jones, St. John's Peterborough: The Sesquicentennial History of an Anglican Church (Peterborough 1976), 27
4 For more information on Brown see T.W. Poole, A Sketch of the Early Settlement and Subsequent Progress of the Town of Peterborough (Peterborough 1867), 35; Norma Martin, Catherine Milne, and Donna S. McGillis, Gore's Landing and the Rice Lake Plains (Cobourg 1986), 227–8; and Lloyd J. Delaney, Small But Bountiful (Orillia 1983), 56–8.
5 See DCB, 6:660–2.
6 Gerald Boyce, Historic Hastings (Belleville 1967), 81
7 Marjorie McDowell, 'Children's Books,' in The Literary History of Canada, gen. ed. and introd. Carl F. Klinck (Toronto 1965), 624
8 Boyce, Historic Hastings, 239
9 Initially Thomas Traill and Samuel Strickland offered to serve as Moodie's sureties. However, when the inspector general of Upper Canada, John Macauley, raised questions about the names, neither man being known to him, Moodie sought further affidavits from Thomas A. Stewart and the Rev. Samuel Armour. Continued delays on Macauley's part then forced him, once in Belleville, to draw on Meyers and Hawley, who, contrary to Audrey Morris's description (Gentle Pioneers [Toronto 1973], 186), were indeed well known to him. Though Traill and Strickland were finally recognized as sureties by the government, Meyers and Hawley were accepted beforehand.
10 As staunch conservatives, Meyers and Hawley were likely uncomfortable to be the

backers of a sheriff whose reform sympathies were increasingly a matter of public note in the early 1840s. Moodie lost their support when, in temporarily frustrating Meyers's attempt to gain possession of a certain widow's property in Sidney, he aroused his backer's 'bitter animosity' (Morris, *Gentle Pioneers*, 186–7, and Letter 44).

11 See *DCB*, 7:476–81.

12 See Gerald M. Craig, *Upper Canada: The Formative Years 1784–1841* (Toronto 1963), 260–70.

13 See *DCB*, 7:117–19.

14 Because so few issues of Belleville's *Intelligencer* survive from this period, the Kingston *Chronicle and Gazette* is, like the Cobourg *Star*, a good barometer of conservative attitudes and opinions along the front. (See 10 April 1839 and subsequent issues for that month.)

15 Craig, *Upper Canada*, 258

16 See E.C. Guillet, 'The Cobourg Conspiracy,' in *Victorian Cobourg: A Nineteenth Century Profile* (Cobourg 1976), 108; and Mary Beacock Fryer, *Volunteers and Redcoats, Rebels and Raiders* (Toronto 1987), *passim*.

17 Kingston *Chronicle and Gazette*, 15 May 1839. Reporting on the dinner held 30 April 1839, the editor notes that Lieutenant Colonel Landon, the commander at Brighton, was in the chair, and toasts were given by, among others, the Honourable R.C. Wilkins, Lieutenant Colonel E.D.S. Wilkins, and Colonel Hawley.

18 AO, Township Papers, RG 1, C–IV, MS–658, Reel 112

19 Dr Hutchison's important service to the community is commemorated in the designation and maintenance of his house as a heritage site and museum. His records are now a valuable research tool for historians. See Jean Murray Cole, *Peterborough in the Hutchison-Fleming Era, 1845–1846* (Peterborough 1984), which contains a reprint of Hutchison's register of births for 1817–47. Hutchison was affectionately depicted by Catharine Parr Traill in *The Old Doctor, a Backwoods Sketch* (Peterborough 1985).

20 Dr Hutchison had two young associates, Dr William Henry Taylor and Dr John Robinson Dickson (1819–82). For further information on Dr Dickson see *DCB*, 11:263–4.

21 See William Canniff, *The Medical Profession in Upper Canada 1753–1850* (Toronto 1894), 254–5.

22 See Martin, Milne, and McGillis, *Gore's Landing and the Rice Lake Plains*, 130.

23 In his 24 May letter to John (PHEC, no. 154), Traill alludes to some disagreement between them: 'I again express my sincere and bitter regret at ever having given you any uneasiness, the more particularly at a time when you had more than enough to annoy you otherwise. I hope we shall hence forward live as friends and brothers.' There is also at least one reference to Traill, probably the Mr T——, owner of the sugar kettle in 'The Outbreak' (*RIB*, 442–3), that suggests the relationship between the two families could be characterized by a want of charity on occasion.

24 Colonel Caddy had served in the Royal Regiment of Artillery for thirty-three years, twenty-one of them at stations in Canada. In fact, the Caddys' first seven children were born in the Canadas, and another four in England, where Caddy finished his military career and retired in 1827. In 1834 he and his wife and their four youngest children emigrated to Canada and settled in Douro. Two other sons, George and Edward, had preceded them in 1833. (We are indebted to Professor

Gordon Roper's manuscript 'Chronicles of the Caddy Family' for much of this information.

25 Emilia's sister, Mary Ann Valentine, was married at Endsleigh Cottage on 19 April 1838 to George Caddy, fourth son of John and Hannah Caddy.

26 See Ontario Church Archives, 600 Jarvis St, Toronto, Records of St John's Anglican Church, Peterborough, mf, 78–3. In a letter to his sister-in-law, Barbara Fotheringhame, of Kirkwall, Scotland, dated 27 March 1836, Thomas Traill writes: 'We are remarkably well off for neighbours. One of them is a son of the Major Shairp who received his instructions at the Custom house at Leith, at the same time with your father. He is a good natured fellow, but too fond of his bottle, but his wife, a cousin of his own, also a daughter of a Major Shairp of the Marines, is a very kind friend to Mrs. T.' The letter is in the Scottish Record Office, Edinburgh.

27 Her elder sister Jane was also married at Spring Vale in 1835 to Edward Duffie (Duffy) of Peterborough, the would-be dueller with Colonel James Gifford Cowell, mentioned in Letter 25.

28 For information on the Hagues and Crawfords see William D. Reid, *Marriage Notices of Ontario* (Lambertville, NJ, 1980), *passim*; AO, Peterborough County, Township of Douro, Abstract Index 2, GS 4960; and Ontario Church Archives, Records of St John's Anglican Church, Peterborough, mf, 78–3, reel 1. James Hague's drowning is recorded in the *Cobourg Star*, 10 May 1840.

29 See NA, Upper Canada Land Petitions, 'S' bundle 22, 1839–41, RG 1, L 3, vol. 474, 171; and TFC, letter of 7 Jan. 1834 from Catharine Parr Traill to James Bird. Evidence in the letters and in *RIB* indicate that Sibbon is 'Old Wittals.'

30 AO, Municipal Records, RG 21, Douro Census and Assessment, MS 16; Records of St John's Anglican Church, Peterborough. Samuel Copping is mentioned in Samuel Strickland's *Twenty-Seven Years in Canada West*.

31 See *DCB*, 8:91–2.

32 See Traill's letter of 27 March 1836 to Barbara Fotheringhame, Scottish Record Office, Heddle Family Papers, GD263; and Reid, *Marriage Notices of Ontario*.

33 *DSAB*, 1:774–8

34 See *DCB*, 12:930–1; and for Robert Henry Rubidge of South Africa see *DSAB*, 4:526–7.

35 It is interesting to note that the Moodie children were baptized as Presbyterians.

36 On 8 April 1845 the Moodies were 'excommunicated' from the Church of the Congregational Faith and Order in Belleville 'for their disorderly walk and neglect of Christian fellowship.' (This information was kindly provided by Mr J. Rodney Holden, of Montreal; the minute book is now in the Hastings County Museum.)

37 See *RIB*, 263; and *LOL*, 71.

38 'At the period when the greatest portion of "Roughing It in the Bush" was written, I was totally ignorant of life in Canada, as it existed in the towns and villages' (*LC*, xxxi).

39 See *DCB*, 11:874–7.

40 See *DCB*, 8:764–5.

41 See *DCB*, 8:357–9. Susanna's linking of Hamilton with Rolph and Thom may imply that Hamilton held an editorial position with the *Palladium* in the post-rebellion period, when Fothergill was very ill.

42 Articles and reviews on the theory of storms were published in the *Albion* on 16 March and 14 September 1839.

43 The Kingston *Chronicle and Gazette* of 13 November 1839 announced the list of officers for the new Victoria District, formerly Hastings County. T.D. Moody [*sic*] was listed as sheriff. The announcement came from Government House, Toronto, on 7 November.

---

21 John Moodie to Susanna Moodie

My Dearest Susie,

Belleville
25 December *1838*

I need hardly tell you that I arrived here *safely* on the evening of the third day after I left you. I stopped all night with our kind friends at Thorndale. They were all quite well and Miss Brown seemed much pleased with your review of poor Pringle's Book.[1] I found our worthy Chief the Baron de Rottenburg at Brighton about 20 miles from Belleville, with D[r]. A Commissary General Bailey instructing a batch of volunteer Captains in the useful art of making up their Pay Lists. I found the Baron, what I expected from the style of his letters, a gentleman in every sense of the word. A more amiable and delightful companion I have never met with. He is full of wit and talent united with the soundest judgement and decission of character. He puts me very much in mind of James Traill, but much his superior in industry and application to bussiness. I met with every kindness and assistance from D[r] A. Com[y]. G[l]. Bailey, whose wife he tells me is an Authoress and F.W.N. Bailey[2] is his son. The Baron, Fleming the District Quarter Master[3] and I live by ourselves at one of the taverns very comfortably and quietly smoking our cigars, and never tasting anything stronger than water – this is something new in Militia service. The Baron at first thought it rather odd that I had not got an appointment under Kingsmill, but as soon as I showed him K's letters, his eyes were completely opened, and he now takes the greatest interest in my favor, and I am persuaded will do all in his power to serve me should he have an appointment. I have just recieved my appointment as Paymaster for Presqu'Isle, Trent, Belleville *Bath* and *Amherst Island*. The two last mentioned places the Baron thinks are put in by mistake (as they are close to Kingston) instead of the Prince Edward District which is under his Command or else the latter has been *omitted*. I shall have to pay about 26 Companies equal to three ordinary Regiments. I shall have plenty to do, but the business is much more simple than I expected requiring only great care in the calculations (to save myself from loss) and a good deal of correspondence with the Military Secretary and the Commissaries at Kingston. The different, independent Companies are only engaged for six months and I fear my appointment will terminate with them, unless I may get some other appointment in the mean while. There will be an opening in the New District of Hastings, of which Belleville is the Capital, if I could make sufficient interest to get an app^t in it. The New District will probably go into operation in the Spring as the Court-house is already built. I think it rather singular that I should have been appointed to this place instead of *Peterborough. Possibly* something more *permanent* is designed for me. The Baron asked me the other day 'if I was related to Col. Halkett's^4 wife, as he seemed to take so great an interest in me.' When I got here on the 17th I had to go thro' the calculations of 18 Pay Lists for broken periods, and sat up the whole of the following night making out an estimate for the pay of the Companies. The future work will be much easier. The worst of it is that a number of the Captains are so ignorant or careless that they are making continual mistakes, and I must trust entirely to myself to keep out of errors. I have no risk to run except in recieving and making payments as the Commissariat are also responsible for the calculations. So much for my own matters. I had a visit from Col. Brown the other night on his way to Kingston to try to obtain A Company in Col. Hill's reg^t. He told of Mrs. Traill's safe confinement on which I heartily congratulate all concerned, but he could not tell me whether it was a boy or a girl.^{5} I could not hear from Brown whether Traill had any chance of getting an appointment in McDonnell's reg^t. Indeed I do not think it would be any advantage to him unless in the event of selling his place. I hope and trust something will turn up for them when they least expect it, as has been the case with ourselves. I should have enclosed you some of the needful, but I have not yet recieved a penny as I cannot make out the Pay List for the Staff Officers until I can ascertain the dates of some of the appoint^{ts} from the Military Secretary.

Decr 30th I was interupted in my letter, and have [been so] much occupied with writing letters that I could not continue it till now. I trust you have been able to get a boy to chop wood for you, I fear My dear, that you are very uncomfortable, but we must be patient as I can see no help for it at present. Garbutt seems inclined to take the farm if he could get it for three years on *a clearing lease*. If I should get a permanent appointment, I should be glad to let him have it. I send you a 'Palladium' I carried off with me to file with the rest. Write me soon My love and tell me all about the dear children. Kiss them all for me and tell them papa does not forget them, and hopes they will be good children and learn their lessons well. The country here appears to be fine, and in the summer I believe it will be beautiful. The land is about the same price as in the neighbourhood of Cobourg but there are few British settlers, and the mass of the people are disaffected to the Gov[t]. They were all prepared for a rising had the Rebels obtained any footing at Prescott. Secret societies were organized and considerable quantities of arms were secreted by them, of which occasional discoveries are made. I met one of our fellow travellers from Montreal, '*Wilkins*'[6] the man with the lame leg and short-tailed coat, but he is now a *great man*, he has recovered from his lameness and his short tailed coat has grown to a superfine Surtout and he is now *Colonel Wilkins*, one of the richest men in this part of the country. Our other fellow travel- ler '*Cummins*'[7] drank himself to death, trying to poison the live oysters he swallowed at Quebec. I found three or four Orkneymen settled here – two of them 'Sinclair & Odie' from the parish of Holm have a Store in Belleville, and another Fidler[8] the son of a boat-builder in Stromness is one of our Six months Captains, and has Mills & a farm near the mouth of the Trent, he has been doing well, but like many others has burnt his fingers in the lumbering trade. Traill may know something about these people. I wish I could bring you down here though I do not yet know whether the society is particularly desirable. Still there are two or three very respectable families here, particularly our Surgeon Dr. Ridley's. I know you would be delighted with the Baron, who possesses the most extra- ordinary versatility of talent. He has a fine taste for poetry. He often asks me questions about you, and I am sorry you did not put a vol- ume of your 'Poems' in my trunk, as I think he might be gratified by recieving a Copy. He has read my Book on the Cape, but did not know that I was the Author. He was surprised when I told him that I had not got anything from it. He thought from its popularity that I should have got £400 for it. We are thinking of taking a house for ourselves in the village, which will be more pleasant than in a tav- ern as our occupations require greater quietness than we can get here, but I doubt whether it will be quite so cheap. We pay 3 1/2 dollars per week for our board. We all recieve a money allowance in lieu of rations of 9[d] a day and I am allowed a cap[t]'s lodging

Money £31 Sterling per Ann. Altogether my yearly pay amounts to £324.12.9 Currency which is good enough if it *would only last*. Now I must finish up my letter with my kind love to all our kind friends, and the dear children & believe me Ever

> Your Affectionate husband
> *J.W. Dunbar Moodie*

When you write Direct to me Capt Moodie District Paymaster Belleville

1 Leitch Ritchie had edited *The Collected Poems of Thomas Pringle* (London 1835) just after Pringle's death in 1834. Susanna may have reviewed it in the *Palladium*.
2 F.W.N. Bayley (1808–53), a minor British writer and first editor of the *Illustrated London News*, is described as 'improvident' and 'constantly in difficulties' in the *DNB*. Some of his work was published in the *Museum* of Montreal. Moodie mentions him again in Letter 30.
3 Thomas Fleming of River Trent was appointed captain and quartermaster in December 1838, having applied to Bullock for a position 12 November 1838 (MR, 1B1, 23, 24, 33).
4 Frederick Halkett (1813–40) accompanied Sir Francis Bond Head to Canada as aide-de-camp and remained when Head left in 1838. He married the daughter of Colonel Robert Moodie and served as military secretary to Sir George Arthur. By the time of Halkett's premature death from fever, he had reached the rank of colonel. See Colin Read and Ronald Stagg, *The Rebellion of 1837 in Upper Canada* (Ottawa 1985), 154.
5 The Traills' fourth child and second daughter, Anne Fotheringhame, was born in late 1838.
6 The Moodies had originally met Robert Charles Wilkins of Carrying Place, Prince Edward County, when they travelled from Montreal to Cobourg in September 1832. Susanna identified him as the fellow traveller and 'backwoodsman' who had been involved in an animated discussion about eating oysters (*RIB*, 48). Wilkins (1782–1866) was a successful storekeeper at the head of the Bay of Quinte who had done well in timber and importing. Born of Loyalist parents and an area resident since the 1790s, he had, as a military captain, made a significant contribution to the Canadian effort in the War of 1812, supplying rations to the soldiers and controlling boat routes in the Bay of Quinte even as the Americans dominated Lake Ontario. In 1839 he was appointed to the Legislative Council of Upper Canada and functioned as a vigilant Tory and Family Compact supporter. Not surprisingly, he was not reappointed to the Legislative Council of Canada after the union of the provinces in 1841. He served as a colonel in the 2d Prince Edward County Militia.
7 *RIB*, 48
8 Edward Fidlar, 'an enterprising Orkney man' who opened a flourishing mill in Rawdon Township northwest of Belleville, was another good friend (*LC*, 67). While he would later be first warden of Hastings County (1850) and a founder of Belleville's St Andrew's Church, in 1839 he was serving as captain of the 2d Regiment

of Hastings under the command of Major Thomas Parker and, at a higher level, Lieutenant Colonel De Rottenburg. His business energies were concentrated upon the village of Rawdon, later to be known as Stirling. His comings and goings occasionally provided Moodie with a welcome means of transportation.

22 Susanna Moodie to John Moodie

Melsetter, Douro
Jan. 11, 1839

The receipt of your long kind letter dearest Moodie gave me great joy, as it convinced me that you were well and likely to succeed in your new and arduous situation. God bless you dearest, the children, and poor Susy, send you a thousand kisses and hope you may enjoy many happy new years.

How sorry you will be to learn, that I have been ill ever since you left us, confined chiefly to my bed obliged to send for Dr. Hutchinson, and even to have a nurse. During the Christmas week I was in great agony, and did little else but cry and groan until the following Sunday night, when kind Traill went himself after dark and brought up the Dr. at three o clock in the bitter cold morning. He put the lancet immediately into my breast, and I was able to turn and move my left arm for the first time for ten days, for I lay like a crushed snake on my back unable to move or even to be raised forward without the most piteous cries. You may imagine what I suffered when I tell you that more than half a pint of matter must have followed the cut of the lancet, and the wound has continued to discharge ever since. I was often quite out of my senses, and only recovered to weep over the probability that I might never see my beloved husband again. Poor Jenny nursed me somewhat like a she bear, her tenderest mercies were neglect. She is however behaving better now. Dr. H. seemed greatly concerned for my situation. When he looked round the forlorn, cold, dirty room feebly lighted by the wretched lamp, he said with great emphasis, 'In the name of God! Mrs Moodie get out of this.' Well, I have got through it, and am once more able to crawl about the house, but I am very weak. I have great reason to be thankful for the disinterested kindness of my female neighbors. Mrs Caddy, when she heard I was so bad, came down through a heavy snow storm, and offered to stay and nurse me herself. This I would not consent to, but she took away my noisy merry Dunny, and has kept him ever since, and more than this, she has clothed him from head to foot, and he looks so smart and handsome, and behaves himself so well. She brought him to see me one Sunday, but he would go back with dear Mamma Caddy, and is quite a plaything for the old Colonel.

She sent me fresh beef and chicken for to make broth and has been quite a Mother to me. Dear Mrs Hague and Mrs Crawford came to see me twice, and both wept much at my miserable state. Mrs H. sent me a gallon of old port wine, and so many nice things, I could not help shedding tears when I received them. She took away my poor little Aggy, and insists on keeping her through the winter. Traill tells me that they have bought her shoes and nice clothes, that Mrs H. is so fond of her and teaches her to read herself, that A. looks happy and well, and behaves quite like a little lady minding every word Mrs Hague says to her. I have not seen her since the week after you left me, but she is coming to see me on tuesday, and my heart yearns for my poor noisy little pet. So much for Aggy and Dunnie. Sweet Katie has remained to be my kind little nurse. During the period I was so very ill, she sat crying by my bed side all day, and till late into the night. To add to my sorrows Donald got a dreadful fall on the stove and laid his skull bare above the right eye. Jenny called out that he was killed, and for a moment when I saw his ghastly face, the blood pouring in a torrent from the frightful wound I thought so too. The old woman in her despair uttered only frightful cries, and I sent her away for help and took my poor bleeding boy into my lap almost as terrified or more so than he. After sometime I succeeded in staunching the blood with very warm water, and then I examined carefully his head, and I felt convinced his skull was not fractured though I saw the bone plainly, and I bound it up and got him to sleep before Strickland and Mr Traill came and dressed the wound. I have suffered much anxiety about it, often having to poultice it, but thank God he is well now, and naught remains of his wound but the ugly scar, which I think will wear away in time. He still looks pale from the loss of blood, but he says, 'dear Papa is at Bellwill,' and I am to write two kisses for him.

When my dear Mrs Shairp heard from Dr H. how ill I was she came up on New Years day, and has been with me ever since, the kindest of all kind nurses to me and sweet little Johnnie,[1] who has suffered little from his poor Mothers illness. Surely my dear love I have bought this boy at a price. He ought to be my best child. You would not know him, he is grown such a fine creature, and laughs, and capers, and crows, and is the most lively babe I ever had. I have not weaned him, through all, but the milk has left my bad breast in all probability for ever. Mrs Traills is a very fine little girl, the prettiest babe she ever had. She is quite well again, has been twice to see me and is going down on Sunday to the front to visit Mr Bridges, and Mrs W. Brown. He has got no appointment in the Peterboro' regiment, not even a Lieutenantcy though he asked MacDonnel for the last. I think he has been treated very ill. He has not heard any further particulars about selling the place. I hope poor things they will get something soon. Kate had a letter from Agnes this week, dated Oct. They are all well at home. Agnes has backed out from the old man, she says so discreetly that she hopes that he will leave her a legacy after all, and she is going to marry a Mr. Kirby, sometime during the winter, who is much attached to her and is only 55, is very rich, and promises to make very handsome settlements upon her. She says that W. Shoberl,[2] told her again, that your book sells *well* & that you should get some friend in London to insist on a settlement from Bentley. She hopes to sell Kate's Journal to Smith and Elder, who are highly pleased with it, but want more matter for a Vol.[3] She has got several of her sketches into Chamber's Journal.[4] Sarah has left Reydon, and is living opposite to where the Wales's[5] lived in Southwold, is visited by all the genteel families near, and is slowly but surely recovering her health and spirits. Some Mr Turner, has set a song of mi[ne] to music, and A. wanted him to make me some remuneration, but this he declined. I quite forget the words myself. She wishes me to try him with Canadian songs, as *it might, 'perhaps bring my poetry a little into notice.'* I don't think it worth the trial and would rather now, be popular in the country of my adoption than at home. This is all the home news. Traill heard from Orkney Yesterday. Your brother Ben, is on a visit there, he and Mr Heddel mutually pleased with each other. Traill knows nothing of the Orkney people you mention in your letter. I was not a little disappointed in the prospect of your appointment only lasting 6 months. I had wished that I could have got out of the discomforts and miseries of Douro. Mrs Shairp had kindly offered to let me three rooms in the house she and Mrs Lloyd occupy which would have been cheap enough. The girls would have been taught by her gratis – and Dunnie could have been taught at Mr William's school[6] for a trifle a week. But I must try to be contented, but sickness has tamed down my spirit. I seem no longer able to contend with my comfortless situation and the charity of

my kind neighbors really distresses me. Garbut, talks very pompous-
ly about the clearing rent, being too high. I have a better offer I
think than his. Norah Youngs husband, Kearnie wants to take it on
the same terms you offered it to Garbutt, viz. to clear fence stake
and rider five acres of land yearly in what ever part of the land you
wished such clearing to be made. Garbutt objects to clearing any
swamp. The Youngs would all help and bang down the five acres in
a few days. I must think as clearing tenants we should find them
the best.

Mr Godard has written to me begging the first refusal of the farm
on the same terms should you let it, and he would put up two stone
chimnies to boot, so you see, we should not want for tenants. Jury's
have been dunning me, but very kindly & I was forced to promise
them the first money you sent me, which promise I will faithfully
perform. John Young, has finished the sleigh, and Sibbings took in a
grist of 12 bushels of wheat for me to Peterboro' yesterday.

The wheat yields but badly, but it is not half threshed yet. I was
obliged to let Sibbings have two bushels on Mr Erskines order. I
have tried in vain to get a boy to chop for us, either in Smith Town
or Dummer. There are no spare hands to be had. I am obliged to pay
Solomon Sibbings sixpence a day, two days in the week for chop-
ping and drawing us a little firewood and Jenny makes up the defi-
ciency and I owe Mrs Jury for one weeks nursing. I was sorry to put
you dearest to this expense, but I could not feed myself, and the
baby and I, might both have been lost for want of assistance as
somebody was obliged to sit up with me every night and Jenny was
not always the kindest. I have shed more tears since you have been
away, than during the whole period of our marriage. I rejoice, however, that my beloved's prospects are brighter. That you have found
a friend and companion in the kind Baron, what a comfort it must
be to you to meet with such a man among strangers. I think I can
manage to send you a volume of my book through kind Miss
Brown.

Your letter is ten days after date. I did not get it until last night. I
hope you will write directly there is any prospect of your situation
lasting for any length of time, that I might move the children and
goods before sleighing is over. The sleighing is at present excellent
inspite of the great thaw for the last four days. We had some dreadfully severe weather before and after Christmas. Poor old Mary
Preston is dying. Mrs Hague has taken her into her own house to
nurse her. What a kind dear she is. Mrs Crawford asked the loan of

your four shotted gun, the Major I believe wants to buy it. They brought a gun case to put it into for fear of injury. It would pay a good slice off the Jurys debt. Dear Mrs Shairp, sends her love to you and best wishes and dear Katy and Donald are not behind hand. As for me, you have my constant thoughts, prayers, and blessings, and I remain

Your faithfully attached wife
Susanna Moodie

P.S. The Traills beg to be affectionately remembered to you. If any opportunity should occur, I should be glad of a quire or two of paper, as I have only one or two sheets left to write you. Miss Brown would forward me any thing if you could get a parcel so far. Gentlemen are often going from Peterboro' to Belleville who would convey a small parcel for me to Mrs. Shairp's – Mrs Shairp, is very anxious for us to exchange some of our land for Joe Dunlops.[7] She says, we could make a deal of money off it. Fire wood alone would pay a man's wages. Shall I sound Sam about it. Henry Evans[8] came up to see me on Christmas Eve. I was very ill, but he begged a night's lodging, and behaved very well, being with the Duffields[9] has greatly improved his manners. He was going up to Toronto, with a letter for the Governor from Mr. Hickson.[10]

1 John Strickland Moodie was born on 16 October 1838.
2 Frederick W. Shoberl (1775–1853), English poet, translator, and editor of annuals and the *New Monthly Magazine*, encouraged and published the young Strickland sisters in the late 1820s (*LOL*, 13).
3 There are manuscript entries of this journal in the TFC. Catharine's proposed title for a sequel to *The Backwoods of Canada* was 'Under the Pines.'
4 By late 1838 *Chamber's Endiburgh Journal* had published Catharine's 'Canadian Gleanings' (27 Feb. 1836), 'Notions of a Fine Lady in Canada' (30 April 1836), 'The Mill of the Rapids, a Canadian Sketch' (3 Nov. 1838), and 'Canadian Lumberers' (22 Dec. 1838).
5 Tom Wilson of *Roughing It in the Bush* is based on Tom Wales, a member of this Southwold family.
6 The government school for the district including Peterborough had been run first by the Rev. Samuel Armour, then by R.J.C. Taylor beginning in 1832. When Taylor returned to Trinity College, Dublin, in 1837 to pursue a Masters degree, the Rev. M.H. Williamson likely took over. See J. George Hodgins, *Documentary History of Education in Upper Canada* (Toronto 1897), 215.
7 Possibly an elder brother of Andrew Charles Dunlop, Thomas Stewart's future son-in-law, who farmed in Otonabee Township (Frances Stewart, *Our Forest Home* [Toronto 1889], 134).

8 Henry may have been John Evans's brother.
9 The Duffields, an Anglo-Irish family, lived near Peterborough. In September 1835 the Cobourg *Star* noted the death of Henry Duffield, Esq.
10 Probably Edward S. Hickson, JP and Peterborough banker, who, along with Thomas Stewart and Robert Reid, was responsible for taking depositions regarding rebellion activity in Otonabee Township. See E.C. Guillet, ed., *The Valley of The Trent* (Toronto 1957), 297–300.

23 John Moodie to Susanna Moodie

My Dearest Susie,
Belleville
24 Jan'y *1839*

Your welcome letter reached me some days ago, but I have been so unceasingly absorbed in my employment that I have actually been unable to write until this morning. I am grieved My Dearest to hear of your sufferings, and God knows how anxious I am that it might be in my power to relieve you from your comfortless situation. Though I think our frontier disturbances must lead to *a War*, in which case my employment would become permanent; still, until there is some greater certainty of its continuance I fear it would be imprudent to leave the farm, – or at all events to put it out of our power to re-occupy it. I trust you have entirely recovered by this time from your severest bodily sufferings, but I feel miserable to think of your uncomfortable helpless situation during the late very severe weather. Be comforted, my own Susie, and rely implicitly on that Providence which has so often befriended us, and all will yet be well with us. In spite of all our *present* difficulties we have always had the consciousness of doing our duty, and have been supported by hope founded on a never failing experience of the goodness of God, when all our own efforts have been fruitless. I am sorry I can send you only £2 at present as all my spare money has been expended in my journeys to Kingston and Bath and other places, and I have not yet been allowed anything for travelling expenses. Some time ago I had to go to Kingston for money for the troops and had to remain there for more than a week waiting till the Pay Lists arrived from Toronto and could be examined by the Commissariat. My trip with coach hire cost me near £5 and if I am not allowed travelling expenses my situation will be anything but profitable. I have no doubt, however, that the Gov^t must make me some allowance in my peculiar situation. I have to go to Kingston at least once a month to get money which the Commercial Bank do not seem inclined to allow me to draw thro' their Agent here who is entitled to 1/4 Per Cent. so I have to carry my bundle of £4000 or £5000 under my wing. I have now no difficulty whatever in managing my business, and keep regular books myself without having any clerk, as I cannot afford to pay for one. My health suffered much at first from the constant confinement but I am now much better. The kind hearted Baron often volunteers to assist me himself when he sees me working away late and early, which, of course, I will not permit. He was very much pleased with your book and takes the warmest interest in our affairs. I really think he will yet be of great service to us as he has much influence with Sir George Arthur having former-ly acted as his Private Secretary. Last night I gave him a long his-tory of our settlement and difficulties as well as of some others when he was *actually* affected to tears. He asked me what I would like to have and promised to use all his influence with Sir George in our favor and I know from observation that he *never* forgets a prom-ise and is indefatiguable in whatever he undertakes. I really cannot help feeling a sort of brotherly affection for this man, – he has so much nobleness of soul. He never, or very seldom, gives me *an order*, but seems anxious to remove any feeling of dependance, leav-ing me to perform my duty in my own way. The greatest fault in his character is a very passionate temper and (what I have heard some ladies call them) certain *amiable* weaknesses, but he must in some measure be excused for these faults on account of the colour of his hair which is what his enemies would call red and his friends bright Auburn. When I tell you that he is slight and active in his make, and very handsome you will have a tollerably faithful picture of one of the best hearted men in the world. I must now tell you a piece of good news (I hope). I have just recieved a letter from my brother Donald. It is long and deeply interesting. He has been en-gaged with my friend Capt Campbell *Civil Commissioner* of Albany in an investigation respecting Stockenstroem the Lieut. Governor who was accused of *murdering a Caffre* several years ago. Just as the different witnesses had been examined and the proceedings trans-mitted to the Cape Town, Stockenstroem arrived as Lieut. Governor from England, where he had got the character of a philanthropist by affecting a feeling for the Caffres. He immediately [in]stituted an action against Campbell and Donald [   ] which ended in the fact of the murder being completely proved by old and respectable

witnesses who saw him shoot the Caffre thro' the back while he lay
concealed in a heap of brush wood. The proceedings have gone
home to England, and Stockenstroem *has resigned*. What a subject
for a tragedy! Donald has been engaged for a long time in publishing
a collection of translations from Dutch records and letters found by
him at Graff-Reynett which he says will throw *quite* a new light on
the Caffre and Dutch character in former times. It seems the Colony
is in a most deplorable state on the frontier in consequence of the
encouragement and unjust favor shewn by our imbecile and wrong
headed Ministry towards the Caffres. The Caffres (Donald says) now
instead of skulking in the bushes traverse the country in large
parties well mounted *and armed with guns*. Donald enjoys a salary
of £400 Per Ann. while engaged in his work at Cape Town. He says
he can hardly *live* on his salary as since the *emigration* of so many
of the Dutch graziers into the interior provisions have *trebled* in
Price in the Colony. Notwithstanding this he has succeeded in selling *Groote Valley* for 5000 Rix dollars or about £450 Halifax Currency payable in instalments bearing interest, but he has no security
except on the place itself. If we could get this it would be a season-
able mercy.

By the bye, you must send me down 25 or 30 Copies of your
Poems for which a Commission Salesman (Mr Calder a Caithness
man) at Kingston tells me there are many enquiries and that he
could sell 35 copies at once. I forget what price you put upon them.
I would not say less than *a Dollar*. I shall try if I cannot get an offer
for *a new volume of Poems with your Canadian poems added*. I am
going to Kingston tomorrow or next day for more money and shall
enquire about this matter. The country about the Bay of Quinte
seems to be very beautiful but the price is nearly as high as near
Cobourg. I have been thinking of trying to make an exchange of
wild land for a cleared farm near the mouth of the Trent. Major
Meyers one of the richest landholders in Canada I think not unlikely to make a trade with me – we are pretty *thick*, as they say, and I
think [he] would be glad to attract respectable settlers. The old loyal
settlers here are a fine honest respectable sett of fellows far superior
in character to the Cobourg folks who are demoralized by land
speculation and other causes. My country man Fidlar is a very kind
fellow. He sent his sleigh for [me] the other day to take me out to
his place which is fifteen miles from Belleville. He has given me a
beautiful *brown partridge dog* and offers to drive me up to Douro
any time I like. I gave him the other Copy of your book which

pleased him greatly. If you send your books to Miss Brown she will forward them to me and I can find plenty of opportunities of sending them *free gratis* to Kingston, as all the good people are very obliging to me in this way, my situation giving me considerable consequence in their eyes as holding the sinecure of War. I was at Bath & Amherst island the other day – at the former I met with another Country man a son of Gordon of Livineys in Caithness, who drove me to Amherst Island where the Capt Com^g was an Acquaintance. They were very kind to me and sent me, *on my way rejoicing.* My Dear you quite distress me with the accounts of the kindness of my neighbours. I hope I am not ungrateful but these things are enough to make me *bankrupt* in gratitude. How I am ever to return these acts of kindness I know not, but we must contrive some way when it is in our power. The only one I had any chance of serving is James Caddy. From the time I first came down here I tried to sound the Baron about him *at a distance,* for I then did not know him sufficiently, but he says he will never interfere in the appointment of *Subalterns* to the Independant Companies. Capt Murphy who was our senior Captain in the 'Queen's Own' Commands one of these Companies and he had no Lieut. or Ensign appointed. I spoke to him the other day while he was driving me out to Brighton but it seems he will only be allowed *one Lieutenant*, but he told me if it had not been that he wished to get *his own brother appointed*, he would have been most happy to recommend James Caddy for it. I shall not, however, lose sight of him if I can see any chance for him, but I fear there is but a slight one unless we have a *National War*[1], which from the tone of the English papers is becoming every day more probable. I am happy to hear M[rs Trai]ll is so well. Poor Traill has been very ill used in not getting even a Lieutenancy. [As for le]tting the farm I should certainly prefer James Carney who is a worthy honest quiet la[d to al]most any one I know, and if we do let the farm I should like him to have it. However Garbutt is likely to do it most justice as to farming. However my Dearest I am willing to leave this matter to your own judgement. If Mr Crawford wishes to buy the gun you may sell it at any thing like a reasonable price, say £10 or £8 or even less if you like. *I shall not find fault* after their great kindness to our dear brats and yourself, *even if you make him a present of it.* I should have no objection to make a trade with Joe Dunlop on anything like fair terms and I have no objection to your pumping Sam on the subject. *He* will be pleased with the job at all events for next to *bleeding* or drawing a tooth he delights in having a hand in a bargain. I shall leave it to you my Dear Old Woman to express my thanks for the kindness of our dear kind neighbours for it is out of my power to do so. May God bless them now and forever. If I can find an opportunity I shall send you some paper. Remember me most affectionately to the dear Traills and to all our kind and affectionate friends. Again My Dear I entreat you to be of good cheer and to hope for the best and I must now conclude by sending my love to my dear Katie and all the rest of our darling brats. Kiss them all for me and believe me ever

> Your Aff^{te} husband
> *J.W. Dunbar Moodie*

If you direct to me *Via* Cobourg, your letter would probably reach me sooner as the Post goes twice a week from Peterboro' to Cobourg, – but only *once* a week by the route thro' the back townships. Poor M^{rs} McLean (L.E.L.)[2] is dead. Col. Landon (a retired Capt of the Army settled in Seymour) Com^g at Brighton under the Baron, is a cousin of hers. He is a gentlemanly kind man, but much of Col. Brown's *calibre* in intellect. That unlucky and (I think) worthless wight has now I am told lost every thing, what his family are to do God only knows. He called on me twice lately while going to and returning from Kingston. The first time he gained his main object in getting a few glasses of grog – but the last time when he *came drunk* from Kingston and wished to play the same game *telling me to call for something to drink*, I fairly shewed [him] to the *bar-room*. I was thoroughly disgusted with his impudence and heartless levity when his family were in such circumstances.

J.W.D.M.

We might perhaps make a conditional bargain with James Carney to let him *the farm on shares* if we could not let it entirely. He is a good lad and I would be inclined to make the terms favorable for him.

1 American Patriot activities along the border, reported in the British press, generated public fears of another Anglo-American war. See Craig, *Upper Canada: The Formative Years*, 252; Edwin C. Guillet, 'The Cobourg Conspiracy,' in *Victorian Cobourg*, 122–3.
2 Laetitia Elizabeth Landon (1802–38) (*DNB*, 11:493–5) was a popular contributor to

English annuals and magazines such as the *Literary Gazette*. Her death was noticed in the Kingston *Chronicle and Gazette*, 20 February 1839.

---

24 Susanna Moodie to John Moodie

	Douro
Good morning to you Valentine!	Feb. 14, 1839

Dearest and best, I have been anxiously looking for an opportunity of writing to you with the books; but no such occurring, my heart is sore to write to you, and I can delay no longer. Your affectionate and welcome letter made me *very happy*, and has done more to restore me to health, than all the Doctors in Canada. God bless you for all your goodness to me. My breast is quite well now, and I am beginning to gather strength again. We have suffered dreadfully from cold, these heavy gales, not daring to put much fire into the stove on account of the bad pipes, but the worst is past, and I begin to look forward with hope to the spring. Your tenderness, reconciles me to every thing and while you continue to write me such kind letters, I could bear ten times more privations without a murmur.

The contents of your letter deeply interested me. I am glad that you have sold the Groote Valley. It will do more to reconcile you to Canada, than anything else, and I have no doubt that the hand of Providence guided us hither. I grieve for Stockingstrom's delinquency. When such men are found out to be villains, it lessens our respect for human nature. What will Miss Brown say to this? –

I am curious to know how you got Donald's letter. I suppose Ben was the bearer, whose presence in Scotland, I hope will expedite the settlement of the Dundass Business.[1] Courage, beloved one! God will yet redeem Israel out of all his troubles. Your letter has filled me with hope and excellent spirits.

Have you been able to settle the Bill at Cobourg, which came due on the 1st of Jan? The money you so kindly sent me, just came in time to pacify the Jorys for a little. I did not give them all, for I wanted to buy a little tea, and a couple of pails for the sugar making, and a few other absolute necessaries, which I could not do without. They wrote me the most curious note you ever read signed – 'So no more from *we* – James and Stephen Jory.' They are all sick it seems and greatly distressed. That pretty little boy of Joseph's

having broken his arm, in several pieces, and the girl her leg, by a
fall upon the ice over an iron pot. When you can spare them a few
pounds do, it will keep the poor creatures quiet. Their note was not
very civil, but I excuse them – they have waited a long time very
patiently. I gave them 4 dollars, and if I have any wheat to spare, I
will sell it, and give them the returns. And now I am talking of the
wheat, I must tell you, that old Sibbings behaved like an old rogue
and changed my good flour at the mill, for his own black trash,
though he sold a bushel of mine for cash, at the highest market
price. When I told him of it, He said the, 'flour *was changed*, but he
knew nothing about it – he was sure' – and very insolently threw up
the threshing. I took him at his word, and the Young Goddards are
threshing the rest. They are very kind and attentive, feed the cattle
and bring in wood for me, when they are at work. They have fixed
the shanty for the oxen, for Buck, began to look ill during the severe
weather. They chop and draw the wood for me, to work out their
debt, which they frankly own they cannot at present pay. I thought
it was better than giving ready money to Sibbings and Sol. As to
poor old Godard, he is nearly broken hearted, I sincerely pity him,
and if he never had paid me, I could not find it in my heart to distress him. He was for years in the Commisseriat, and he tells me,
that Goverment [*sic*] are *bound* to pay all your expences, but you
must always make an account of them every journey and lay before
the officer commanding the District, and he puts it in the proper
channel for payment. Colonel Caddy told me the same – and both
should know. Poor Mrs. Caddy has been alarmingly ill, supposed
dying. Agnes was out, and I went, to her, and staid two days, during
which period I thought she would die every moment, with spasms
and obstruction in the stomach. We sent off for a Doctor, but no
Doctor came. Her cries were dreadful and all remedies failed – no
medicine would stay a moment on her stomach the vomiting was
bloody the bowels unmoved and I thought her sufferings were drawing to a rapid termination when I remembered your instruments.
Henry went in the dead of the night for them and the use of these
and hot fomentations and a large mustard plaister over the pit of the
stomach at last relieved her from unutterable agony. I am sure I
made a good doctor, and the poor dear thanked me when she
recovered herself sufficiently to know me with tears in her eyes. 'If
you had not come,' she said in the morning, 'Where should I have
been now – ' I believe she must have died. I have left little Katie
with her to fetch her medicine, and little things and stay in her sick

room till she is better, and Katie is very proud of being little nurse. It will be a useful moral lesson to the child who I wish to consider kindness to the sick as an imperative duty. She begged me to return you her grateful thanks for your kindness in trying to serve James. She is really a most generous affectionate woman, and I begin to love her very much and to be very sorry that I ever suffered my prejudices to overlook her real merit. She has offered me Woods house, (which Edward is going to rent for seven years, that wight having got an appointment in the Hudsons bay Company) for as long a period as I like to stay, and an acre of land for a garden and potatoe ground, rent free and her boys to draw all my goods and chattels thither. I think the offer needs some consideration before I refuse it. The house tho' *small is good.* A comfortable fireplace, cellar and out houses and a good well if cleared out. I have wheat enough for this year and enough in the ground please God for the next and as the Oxen would have to be at the farm with who ever took it on shares I should only have the two cows and pigs to feed and our half of the hay would more than do that. Even if you were at home, I think we should be better off than working the farm, it would leave you time to write and the cultivation of a good large garden would feed pigs and give sufficient exercise to amuse till better days came and you could afford to build a house on Melsetter. We could likewise cut and save the Beaver Meadow hay. Mr Goddard is anxious to cultivate the farm on shares, or on a clearing lease, and he would do it justice in manuring, working, and fencing, and I am confident now, that the poor fellow has been unfortunate more than unconscientious. I shall look for your reply soon on this subject. It appears that Joe Dunlops place is not so elligible as I at first supposed. The land that is cleared is bad. The road so infamous that it is shut in for 9 months in the year, a perfect mor[ass] impassable for almost man and beast. At all events, I think it would be best to let the farm on shares for this summer, as you cannot return before the middle of June, too late for any spring crop. The frost has severely injured the potatoes. I fear we will hardly get enough for seed good. One of the sows pigged under the barn in the middle of January six beautiful pigs. We fed her well, and the pigs all throve well inspite of the dreadful weather, until the foe who comes every day, took away three, but the rest are alive and likely to live if he lets them remain. The other sow Traills big dog bit so severely that I was forced to have her killed to save her life. She was my little sow, and weighed eighty pounds, and was one of the fattest we have killed.

Traills have returned from their visit to the front. Mr Bridges
received them very kindly. Miss Brown is staying with him, as gov-
erness to the little boy, so I cannot send the books through her. He
offered the Traills his house during his stay in Jamaica rent free. I
do not know whether they will accept it. Mrs Traill was forced to
wean little Annie, who is a beautiful babe, before she went, as her
breasts were very sore. But the child was dying in consequence and
they have been obliged to hire Miss Sibbings as wet nurse to save
its life. Poor Traill was greatly distressed about the child. I am so
glad now, that I persevered in nursing my beautiful Johnie or I
might have lost the lamb, as I think it doubtful whether little Annie
ever recovers. I could fill, a whole page with the witching wiles, and
smiles of my rosy dimpled John, who is the prettiest baby I ever
had. A credit to you – and to my good nursing. The other dear
children are all well. I was forced to scrig your grey frock coat for to
make Donald a suit, and he looks such a funny quiz in a coatee and
trowsers. He says, 'I am a man now, me never wear girls pettiacoats
again.' I must tell you something droll about Donald. The other day,
he had a pain in his stomach. He came to me, and said with the
gravity of a judge, 'Mamma something hurts me here. But I will go
down and see what's the matter.' Katie and Dunnie have laughed at
Donald ever since, and Dunnie says, 'Donald how will you get your
feet down your throat dont do it, till I am there to see.' Aggy is still
with Mrs Hague, who brought her the other day to see me, with the
present of a nice pair of shoes for Katie. She stays with Mrs H. all
winter, who has dressed her very handsomely and teaches her to
read and work herself. George Crawford is perfectly terrified with
the gun which went off all charges at once whic[h] quite confounded
the brains of the silent gentleman. I do no[t] think they will venture
to purchase it. I gave Mr Crawford t[he] Japanese dagger, with which
he is greatly pleased, and means [to] brighten it up, and give it a
conspicuous place among his ar[ms.] He enquired most kindly after
you. Copperthawate is married to Miss Christy Wright, Mrs
Erskines sister – What a match – It has surprised all the gossips in
Douro. At the intercession of Bolton,[2] the Bank, has given Traills a
year longer to pay their debt, but he is in wretched spirits. The
corps containing Birdsall, Bill Shairp, and Tom Fortune have been
dismissed from the Peterboro' Battalion, their services not being
required. To them a great disappointment. The officers sent me a
very polite invitation to their subscription Ball. But I had enough to
do to dance about little Johnnie at home – Katie sends you plenty of

kisses and says you must give her the new brown dog, and she will
call his name Fidler, which she says will be a capital name for him.
I received a letter from Cobourg the other day, from a Mr Morze,
informing me that he had been the bearer of two parcels for me,
intrusted to his care by Mr Hodson. That they were at the Albion
Hotel, and could be procured at any time by an application from
me. The letter was very kind and polite, and he said he had taken
care that they should be free of all charge. You may be sure, that I
am rather on the *que vive* about them. Major and Mrs Shairp, have
gone down to Cobourg, and return to Peterboro' to night. They have
promised to bring them up for me, and I will let you know the
result in my next. Mrs Caddy and I, are going to make the sugar
this year on shares. She is to lend me two large sugar kettles and a
great iron pot and a large brass stew pan for sugaring off, a hundred
and forty troughs, and Cyprian to help Jenny while the season lasts.
James and Henry are to make the spiles and tap the trees, and all
this for only half the sugar. Tis a magnificent offer three times better than Traills. We hope to make 400 weight of sugar with four
kettles. Poor old Jenny is behaving better again and talks of nothing
but the sugar making. I have never received any answer from Mr
Lovel, about contributing to the Garland, but he sends me the mag –
tis a wretched performance, but the typography and paper is good. I
must say, I do not much like being the lioness of it. I am delighted
with your portrait of the excellent Baron, whom I quite love for his
goodness to you. May God bless him for it. It gives me the most
heartfelt pleasure that you are so comfortably situated. How differently last winter. I shall rejoice to see you up here once more, but
parting with you again would be dreadful. I will be patient and of
good cheer, you have inspired me with hope, but do my precious
one take care of your health, remember how dear you are to poor
Susy and the wee things.

I should be very glad to sell the books, could I get them sent
down but the roads are so bad with drift snow that they are almost
impassable. Could you make any engagement, for the hundred
copies that are unbound I would sell them cheap for cash and transmit them by coach to Bellville. You could lay out the money in
necessaries for the house, and the children which could be procured
cheaper and better at Kingston. And now dearest love I must conclude this long rambling letter, in which I have left unsaid, a thousand things I wanted to say. The darling children all unite with me
in fondest love. Particularly Katie who wishes you were here to

spend her birthday with her tomorrow. The Traills desire most affectionate regards and I remain Your faithfully attached and loving wife,

Susanna Moodie

1 The Dundas business was the long-drawn-out litigation over the settlement of the Melsetter estate of the Moodie family in Orkney. Letters from John Phin, John Moodie's lawyer in Edinburgh, reveal that in that settlement Lord Dundas was overpaid £2,000 in February 1819. The Moodie family claimed that Dundas was obligated to repay that sum plus interest, a total of £3,700 by 1835. In spite of legal judgments on the account in the Moodies' favour, Dundas used avoidance tactics at his disposal, and in September 1835 Phin feared that 'by an appeal to the House of Lords etc. he may still put off the day of payment for years.' Before the death of Major Moodie, John's father, there was another claim initiated by him against the owner of Toftingall, Sir Patrick Murray Threpland Rudge. In the winter of 1838–9 John's eldest brother, Ben, was in Britain trying to settle these two claims. In an 1845 letter to John, Phin recalled that when Ben returned to South Africa, he expected Phin to carry on the lawsuit and act on behalf of the absentees, but since there was no guarantee against loss, in the event that the defendants won the case, Phin refused the undertaking. In fact, Ben left Britain without paying Phin even the money owing him for time devoted to the investigation of the Moodies' claim. It would appear, then, that the Melsetter estate was never settled to the satisfaction of the Moodie family. (See PHEC, nos. 98, 99, 100.)

2 George Strange Boulton (1797–1869), brother of D'Arcy Boulton, a prominent member of the family Compact, was a Cobourg lawyer and registrar of deeds for Northumberland County. A son of a wealthy family, George Boulton was 'active in business affairs and took part in various phases of Cobourg developments, including construction of the harbour' (Percy L. Climo, *Early Cobourg* [Cobourg 1985], 57–8). Boulton was connected with the Moodies through the sale of their farm in Hamilton Township and John Moodie's purchase of shares in the *Cobourg* steamboat venture.

---

25 Susanna Moodie to John Moodie

Douro

My dearest Husband   March 6, 1839

I have been anxiously looking for a letter from you for some days past, and I can no longer repress the strong desire I feel to write to you. Since the date of my last, I have been occupied incessantly at the sick bed of two of our dear children, whom I expected every hour to breathe their last. You may imagine the anguish of your poor Susy, and you so far away. Poor little Donald, was first taken, with sudden inflamation on the lungs, attended with violent fever and every symptom of croup. I had to put him in a warm bath, force castor oil down his throat and apply a large blister to his chest. Poor little fellow his cries were dreadful and his entreaties for me to take all the pins out of his belly which was the violent pains in his chest and at the pit of his stomach. Dear Mrs Traill came to me at the break of day, and Traill went down to get advice from the Doctor if the could not bring him up. That night my beloved baby was struck in the same manner. Only he was to all appearance dead. It was about five in the afternoon. He had been in a heavy dose all day. I was busy doing something for Donald when I saw Johnnie throw up his hands in an unusual way. I hastened to take him up. But all sense appeared to have fled. His jaws were relaxed the foam was running from his mouth and my lovely dear's beautiful limbs fell over my arms a dead weight. I burst into an agony of tears in which I was joined by poor Katey, and putting my insensible lamb into her arms, I ran and called Jenny who was with the two young Godards in the sugar bush. Thank God she came directly, and there happened to be warm water on. We got him into the bath but it was a long time before he gave any signs of returning to life. In the mean time kind Cyprian Godard ran off for the doctor, sending up in his way Mrs Strickland and dear Catharine who was at tea at Crawfords. Neither could give me any hopes of my darlings recovery. But we did all we could for him, we put on a blister, on his white tender chest and forced some tartar emetic down his throat and put hot flannels to his cold feet, and sat down to watch through the dreary night the faint heavings of his innocent breast. In the mean time my messenger sped on to Peterboro', and met Mr. Traill who was bringing up medicines for Donald, and dear Mrs A Shairp who would come up when she heard my dear child was so ill.

Oh what a comfort this warm hearted friend was to me in my dire distress for though she could not stop my streaming tears, she helped me nurse my poor suffering children, and shared my grief. It was four o'clock in the morning before Cyprian returned faint and tired. Dr H. would not come, but said, that he would send up Dr Dixon in the morning.

The next was a dreadfully severe day of wind, frost, and drifting snow. The dear babe was apparently worse and no Dr came, when Cyprian, again volunteered to go down for a Dr. But Dr H. would not be entreated. 'If you do not come,' Cyprian said, 'the sweet babe will die.' 'I cant help that,' was the unfeeling reply. 'The roads are too bad, and I cant leave Peterboro'.' Cyprian then went to old Dr Bird, who came up inspite of the bad roads and the dreadful night. Good old dear how kind he was – He told me, that without medical aid the child must have died. That he was still in great danger, though the remidies we had applied had prolonged his life – 'I am an old man,' he said 'to come thus far, through such weather, but I did it to serve Mr. Moodie, when I heard Hutchison would not come, I was determined that the child should not be lost if I could save it.' He told me Donald was out of danger, but that I was very ill myself. I had not even felt the effects of this horrible influenza – so great was my anxiety about my children. Numbers of children have died with it. Holland, Benton, Humphreys, Wein, and a host of other people have each a child dead with it. Oh how thankful ought we to be, that he who smote, in mercy has deigned to spare – My dear Donald is out of his bed, but looks thin and pale, the dear baby is only rising as it were from the very grasp of death and I have still to sit up with him all night. Katie is well, Aggy with kind Mrs Hague, Dunbar at mamma Caddy's – I have been ill myself, but have followed Dr Birds receipts and am better. In this time of universal sickness, how anxiously my thoughts turn to you. I hope my dear one is well. Do write me on the receipt of this, if only a few lines to dissipate my fears –

I have much news of various kinds to tell you, in which you will feel interested. 1st Traill, has sold his farm to the Wolsleys, for 400£ a hundred and seventy to be paid down, the rest in instalments of 40£ yearly – They leave us in a week, and have taken the house which Stevenson,[1] left near Mr Stewarts, for a month, till they can look about them. Bridges, has written to offer them the use of the tower, during his absence in Jamaica. He goes in April, and will not return before the fall. They are to have the use of the live and dead stock, and the crops in the ground. Their ill luck appears, poor things upon the turn. There has been a challenge between Col. Cowell, and Duffy. But the latter got his wife to apprize the magistrates of the meeting and the duel, did not take place. The gallant Col. and his second were on the ground – Mr Stewart called the other day with Mr & Mrs Haycock.[2] He advised an exchange with Joe Dunlop, whose land he says is excellent. His house the best log in Douro, and the place must rise in value. Joe, however seems not inclined to change, by what I can learn. Willy Rae was here to day, (and indeed this is the principal object of my letter). A Mr Drury, who has a capital cleared farm in Clarke, on the Toronto Road about 14 miles from Port Hope, wants to exchange it for one on these back waters. Rae says, he is sure that could you see Drury's farm you would be anxious for to get it. The lot is on the front road, contains 100 acre 60 of which is under cultivation. The house is new, cost 200£ and has good cellars and every convenience. There is an excellent barn and stables, a young orchard, and a good well of water at the door. It is 3 miles from the lake in a very respectable neighbourhood consisting of English and Scotch settlers. I was to write to you, and if you were willing to make any exchange Drury would communicate his terms, and you would name yours – and this is all I know on the subject. Bolton has sold to another person the land Rae wanted. So that negociation is at an end. Mr Casements friends are coming out in the Spring, and Sam says, that he wants to buy a part of this land. I would exchange on fair terms if I were you, for a cleared farm, or – sell, all but Cambells lot, which I should like to reserve for one of our dear boys. Mrs Shairp wants to sell hers. Godards have finished thrashing the wheat. It only yielded 36 and 1/2 bushels in which we were all greatly disappointed. The upper field contained whole sheaves of little else than smut. The wheat crop has yielded in all 61 1/2 bushels. The lads have been very kind and attentive. Have fed the cattle for me during the winter and done a hundred odd jobs – They take a third in the sugar making, have drawn wood to put up a shanty in the bush, and we hope to make about 200 [cwt] for each family. Mr Godard takes the spring cro[ps on] shares. Traill has given them his oxen for their keep [until] the fall. Rae told me to tell you, that if we left this place he would trade with you the pretty grey mare you liked for cattle or farm stock. The young lads here, are all greatly excited by the proposed expidition, to take possession of the Origon Territory. Captain Fraser, they say is to head it in behalf of government, to find the source of the Columbia river.[3] The expidition is to consist of 1000 active young men from this country. Alured Godard, Cyprian and their cousins George and James Caddy, talk of volunteering. It is for five years. Each private individual to be given 1200 acres of land, and all their expences paid by government. I am glad you are already engaged another way, or I fear your love of adventure would tempt you to join the perilous, but certainly interesting band of pioneers – Of those who go out full of hope and vigorous life, how few, if any may ever return –

Sam was here on Sunday last. He brought me a letter from home to read. No news, but what will grieve you to hear. Poor Bird is dying of a broken blood vessel. James is engaged with a party of surveyors who are surveying the parishes in Great Britain for Government, and is not likely to return to Canada.[4] Mamma has gone to law with the Norwich corporation, and lost her suit – and of course a good deal of money with it. Miss Acton, is dead, and left Agnes a beautiful old family ring as a legacy. They were all well at Reydon. No news of the marriage between Agnes and Mr Kirby. Tom Wales, has lost his wife and child, and poor Rachel Wales, Mrs Wood, died in childbed of twins greatly to the grief of all her friends. The other night as I was lying thinking of our affairs a thought struck me which I think might be of use to us. What if you and I were to edit a Newspaper in some large town on conservative principles and endeavor to make it a valuable vehicle for conveying intelligence respecting the Colony to the old country as well as this. I am sure we should get a multitude of subscribers, and I should enjoy the thing amazingly. Mrs Shairp thinks, that such a paper would be taken by all the Peterboro' folks. Think over it a wee bit. The successful Editors of papers like Adam Thom, T Rolph and Dr Hamilton find it a sure step to preferment – I could take all the light reading Tales, poetry &c. and you the political and statistical details. Without much effort I think our paper would soon be the first in the Provinces. Perhaps some wealthy bookseller might start such a thing paying us a salary for the first year, and giving us two thirds of the profits afterwards.[5] You have not told me what your Baron's christian name is. But remember my beautiful baby is to be called Johnny. You may add De Rottenburg if you like. Do dearest write to me to cheer me up a bit directly you get this. Katey and Donald send their best love and many kisses. I wish you were here dearest to receive them, together with affectionate love from your truly attached wife

Susanna Moodie

March 7. Poor little Johnnie is worse again to day. I shall be obliged to send for advice to the Dr – Adieu God bless you.

1 Frances Stewart mentions a Mr Stephenson who was in partnership with Thomas Stewart in 1834 (*Our Forest Home*, 83).
2 The Haycocks were neighbours of the Stewarts near Ashburnham (*Our Forest Home*, 104).

3 'Capt. A.S. Fraser, Esq. half-pay Lieut. 42 Reg't 1st Dec'ber, 1828' (Poole, *A Sketch*, 34). Apparently Archibald Fraser, who owned a barley mill in Cobourg, did not undertake the Columbia River exploration as he appears in Peterborough as a returning officer in the 1841 election and subsequently became a JP for Peterborough (Poole, 48, 121).

4 Susanna's old friend James Bird died in Suffolk in 1839. His son, however, returned to Upper Canada (see Letter 69).

5 Susanna's plan was eventually realized, though less successfully than she hoped, when she and John edited the *Victoria Magazine* for Joseph Wilson in Belleville from September 1847 to August 1848.

---

26 John Moodie to Susanna Moodie

Cobourg
My dearest Susie,   16th March 1839

I have been so busy lately, that anxious as I was, I have been quite unable to write you before now. I had just returned from Kingston when I recieved your letter and since then my time has been entirely occupied in paying the different companies. I came this morning to Brighton for this purpose, and took advantage of the opportunity to come here to pay the £13 to Bethune,[1] I have also payed £10 on the Note from the Commercial Bank and got it renewed for 3 months (to the 1st of July). My Dearest Susie your letter has made me most anxious about you, and our sweet children. God grant that they are now doing well. I could not sleep, after recieving your letter, thinking of the poor children and you. Whenever I fell into a doze some horrid vision of sickness or death presented itself. A kind of foreboding has haunted me since, – but I trust all is well as yet. Write me dearest whenever you have an opportunity and relieve me from my anxiety. Not having your letter with me I cannot reply to any of your queries just now. I took your books down to Kingston and left them with Mr Calder there who will do his best to dispose of them, – but he has *not purchased* them. I have given a Copy to Mrs. Bayley who is a most unaffected and agreeable woman. She gave me one of her juvenile books for you or our eldest daughter, which I shall send up to you. Bayley pressed me to bring you down to Kingston in case of *war* as a secure place of abode. Mrs B's society would be a very great inducement – (and she is very anxious to become acquainted with you) – but I fear Kingston would be too dear a place for our means. I have bought you a very nice shawl at

Kingston for 6 Dollars, – but I think of getting another of a commoner description – of worstead for every day wear. I have run
myself rather low in funds by the two payments I have made, – but
I shall buy the other articles you want at Belleville, and send them
up all together. I shall greatly regret the loss of the Traills from our
neighbourhood, tho' I rejoice in the prospect of their being relieved
from their difficulties. I send you *Ten Dollars* which is all I can
spare at present. I should be glad to repay Mr. Crawford the five dollars he so kindly lent me, if you can spare it. (I have paid
Kirkpatrick.²) I commenced a letter to him but was interrupted and
have not been able to continue it since. Give my kinds regards to
him, and to our kind friends the Hagues. I had a prospect the other
day of selling my Steam boat Stock to a gentleman at Kingston, but
he seems to have changed his mind for the present. Lawrie has
handed over my note for my debt to him to the farmers Bank, who
have demanded payment:³ – but you need not make yourself uneasy
about this as they cannot compel payment for several months, by
which time in all probability there will be a war, and the Govᵗ will
be glad to purchase Steam Boats on any terms. I think it not unlikely that my kind friend the Baron may get some high situation at
Toronto if a war takes place, as besides being in great favor with Sir
John & Sir George, it *is the general feeling among all classes* that
he should hold a higher situation. Bullock is unfit for his situation –
he is a bladder – another situation could be found for *him* which
would be more advantagious to himself and the public.⁴ I have left
the Tavern where I lodged in consequence of the insolence of the
Owner who is one of the Militia Captains –the Quarter Master has
followed my example and lodges with me at another tavern. The
Baron has taken a private house, and I believe intends getting a wife
soon to keep it for him. I have been the means, I believe *of hasten-
ing* this event, as he would not continue any longer at the tavern,
and wished us to join him in taking a house which however we
thought would not be *a cheap arrangement.* I think the Baron has
acted wisely. *He is rather too combustible* to be trusted in a state of
single blessedness. At all events he is a man with whom to think
and to act is almost simultaneous. I tr[us]t he will be as happy as he
deserves to be for a warmer hearted and more steady friend never
existed. I must now close my letter. I send this by Capt Boswell
who will put in the Post Office for me at Peterborough. There is
some talk of *a new draft of militia.* If this should take place my
situation may become more permanent and it may be advisable to

move you down to Belleville & let the farm. By the bye I do not much fancy a farm in Clarke *during a war*. It is too exposed. The Bay of Quinte would be a safer situation tho' the population is disaffected. Remember me most kindly to the Traills. Do write me soon dearest love and tell me that my dear children are all safe. I remain

> My Dearest Susie
> Your Affectionate husband
> *J.W. Dunbar Moodie*

P.S. I have sent the note of the Commercial Bank to Strickland for his and Traill's signature.

1 Donald Bethune (1802–69), lawyer, banker, shipowner, and politician. He launched his first steamboat in 1833 and ultimately had an interest in ten steamboats. His headquarters were in Cobourg between 1840 and 1843. He went bankrupt in 1848 and again in 1851, and by 1855 all his steamboats were sold (*DCB*, 9:48).
2 Sanford Kirkpatrick (1809–58) was one of Peterborough's first lawyers, arriving from Kingston in 1834. He played an influential role in Peterborough business, particularly in the building and development of St John's Church, heading the building committee and serving as one of the original wardens during 1836–8. His home, 'Consilla,' reflected his relative wealth and stature. During the rebellion he was a captain in the 2d Northumberland Regiment.
3 Lawrie, himself in debt at this time, went into bankruptcy with the Farmers' Bank in October 1841.
4 Richard Bullock (d. 1857) had been sheriff of Prince Edward District during 1834–7. In 1837 he became a colonel in the militia and was appointed adjutant-general of Upper Canada. In spite of Arthur's view of him as incompetent, Bullock held his post until 1846 (Read and Stagg, *The Rebellion of 1837*, 262).

---

27 Susanna Moodie to John Moodie

	Melsetter
My Dearest Husband,	March 20, 1839

Banish all your gloomy forbodings, our dear children are *quite* out of danger, though a cough hangs on both of them, especially my lovely Johnnie, but I do not feel uneasy about it; as the spring advances I hope they will lose it entirely. I cannot keep Donald indoors, and the poor moccasins that I can manufacture out of old cloth, keep his feet constantly wet, which is one cause of the obstinacy of his cough. Dunbar, who is no better off, is quite stout and well, and

grows a very noble looking boy. His love for Agnes Caddy, is almost
a passion, and he is always there. You would laugh to hear the little
creature talking to her, just like a man desperately in love. He
always sleeps with her, and says that he can't sleep if his head is
not on his dear Addy's bosom. 'Oh my dear little Addy; I love you
better than any sing in the world.' Addy is very kind to her wee pet,
and makes him so docile and obedient, that he is quite a pattern to
all the rest. Your kind letter was a great comfort to me. To know,
that you love us, and think of us in all our sickness and privations
atones for them all. How precious that love and sympathy is to your
poor Susy no written language can tell. In it, is concentrated every
better thought and feeling of heart and mind. Oh, that I were indeed
deserving of the love and esteem I so much covet. But, then, I
should be too happy, and perfect happiness is no denizen of earth. I
rejoice, in your having paid that miserable M'Donald dun, and so
much off the bank debt, you are an excellent Johnnie. I shall send
Jenny down to Crawfords with the 5 dollars and a note, some day
this week. The other 5 dollars I must give to Jurys as I promised and
I am glad to have something to stop their clamours for they grow
very impatient, and pay me a visit about once a month. An annoyance which I am forced to bear patiently, and treat the inflicters
with civility. I must thank you very much for the shawl, which will
be doubly prized, as a present from the beloved. I long to be with
you – to see, to speak to you, to hold you to my heart once more –
three of the long months are passed. They have been months of
sickness anxiety and sorrow, and worse than all, of absence from
you. There are times when I almost wish I could love you less. This
weary longing after you makes my life pass away like a dream. My
whole mind is so occupied with thinking about you that I forget
every thing else. I should not wish to live in a town, but near one.
If we are to join you, get a little place with a few acres of ground
within a ride of you, where we could keep a cow or two a few fowls
and cultivate a nice garden. Like you, I do not relish the idea of
living in Clark. Besides, 'tis an inauspicious name. Let us have none
of it.

The dear Traills are gone – I am doubly lonely now. Many tears
have I shed for their removal, we have been on such happy terms all
winter. They have been so kind to me especially poor Traill. One
knows not the value of a friend till one is left alone in this weary
world. The poor children quite fret after their good Aunt. On Monday, Donald and Katie went up to Stricklands in the ox Sleigh with

George Godard to return the wheat we borrowed of Sam in the fall.
They did not come home untill three o clock in the afternoon. Old
Jenny asked Donald if he had had his dinner – 'Oh no Jenny,' said
the poor innocent. 'Dear Auntie Traill gone so we got no bread –'
'Yes Mamma,' said Katey, 'Aunt Strickland never gave us a bit of
bread, but we went to see dear Aunt Traills desolate house to console us, but it was cold and empty. Every thing was gone but the
clock, and that was striking hours for nobody to listen to, and
when I thought of dear Aunt I could not help crying to think she
was gone –'

It was strange, Katey noticing the striking of the clock in the
empty house. It was a feeling connected with the highest range of
poetry. Yet she has not the least idea of rhymes, and seldom remembers them in her little hymns correctly –

Poor Traill, with many tears begged me to remember them most
affectionately to you. He left me his stove for the parlor, which has
made the house warmer and more comfortable, and has given me a
small pit of potatoes. Jenny has picked the whole cellar over, an
awful job. There were about sixty bushels of rotting frosty potatoes
to remove. I doubt whether we shall have enough good for seed.
Well, I trust it will be the last year we shall have to stow them in
that cellar – I begin to get tired o[f] the woods, and now the dear
Traills and Mrs Sha[irp] are gone, I care not how soon we follow –

Mary Ann Shairp (Caddy) has a fine little girl greatly to the joy of
all parties, and Maria Sowden Mrs Jones, a fine boy, and this is all
the news I have to tell you. Stop – Sam is going to take the Selby
Mills on a 20 year lease, and rebuild them in conjunction with three
others, but I dont know the parties. He has let his farm, or means to
let it on shares to old Billy Pine. He will either make, or mar his
fortune in less than half the term of the lease. The Wolsleys have
not as yet taken possession of Traills house, and I shall not be able
to call upon them till I get a pair of shoes. By the by, dearest when
you are in funds, if you could buy me a pair of Indian Rubbers it
would save shoe leather in the bad roads, and they would last for
some time. Mr Crawford tells me, that he fears you will not be able
from the nature of your situation to come and see me. I have a
strange longing to come and see you. But perhaps you would not
think it prudent. Mrs Caddy would take Katey and Dunnie during
my absence. Aggy remains with the dear Hagues, and Mrs Traill
would take Donald and I should bring my wee darling Johnnie to
put into his dear fathers arms. Ah this is one of my day dreams. But

it amuses my loneliness. The coach hire would be the sole expence as I have friends at Peterboro and Cobourg who would give me house room.

My health is better than could have been expected, having had to sit up so many nights, with anxiety and want of rest. Do not therefore make yourself unhappy my dearest love. Had the poor little dears died, I should not have told you. It would have done no good only made you suffer. Thank God, I can speak of their danger with calmness now. Do dearest write me soon and believe you live ever in the prayers and affectionate thoughts of your faithfully attached and grateful Susanna – all the little dears unite in kindest love to dear Papa. Poor old Jenny is behaving better. We have had no run of sap, worth gathering yet –

March 25
Dearest Moodie

The Sheriffs Officer is here and has seized our cattle for the sum of 23£ on the account which you have just paid – viz – Macdonalds or Askews. It seems the writ was issued before you made payment. Why did not Bethune inform you of this. They will give you a fortnight or so to settle it up before the creatures are taken away. This alas – has doubled the original debt, but it cannot be helped. I feel so agitated I can scarely hold my pen. The officer will be the bearer of this. Adieu, God bless thee ever.

                    S.M.

Do not buy anything for us till these horrid debts are paid. You can pay Askew himself he lives at Kingston – Is a storekeeper there.

---

28 Susanna Moodie to John Moodie

Melsetter Douro
My dearest Love   April 4, 1839

To day is such a lovely spring day, and moreover it is the anniversary of our wedding day, that I must try and console myself for your absence by writing to you if only a few lines to tell you how dear you are and how fondly I remember you – My last, ended with an ugly postscript, and I have some doubts as to whether the Constable posted it for you. Strickland, to whom I afterwårds applied, did not give him a bill for the cattle, and he told me, that if the debt was paid before the warrant was served upon the property, that they can claim nothing for the expences. But this you will learn better where you are. The thing flurried me much. I only regretted that I did not put the execution behind the fire when I had it so conveniently in my hand and I declare I will serve the next so. They would only say that Mrs M was a very eccentric woman. But supposing that you did not get my last letter, I must tell you that Cotter Lane the Con-stable[1] seized my cattle in virtue of a writ against you out of the Sheriff's court on that Cobourg account which you wrote me word that you had paid Bethune the 16th of March. The warrant was not served until the 22^d – or third I forget which now – The sum for 23£ – The constable did not take the cattle, but would not leave the house until I wrote a note to Strickland to give a receipt for them so that they might be forthcoming when required. Fortunately S was from home and the receipt has not been given. But I hope you will lose no time in setting the affair to rights and write me as soon as possible to alleviate my anxiety –

The dear children are all now *quite well* and looking charmingly. Though rather ragged and bare. Little Johnnie is the sweetest fellow in the world, full of engaging frolic and fun. He is very much like Dunbar, with the same sunny smile, but your own blue eyes, and lofty brow. I daresay he will cry, when he sees you, for he is very much afraid of strangers. Donald, is always going to *Bellwill* to see dear Papa, and Dunnie is still at Colonel Caddys, as fat, and as happy as a prince. I sent Jenny for little Aggy. But Mrs Hague sent word back, that when she was tired of her she would bring her home. She is so kind to her, and takes such pains in learning her to read and work, that I know it is greatly to Aggy's advantage to stay with so kind a friend. I sent Jenny with a note to Mr Crawford, and returned him the 5 dollars. He wrote me a most kind note back. I fear I shall be obliged to take some of the other note to buy Katie, some clothes for she is not fit to be seen, however, if I can sell some fungusses I have been painting, at Peterboro' I can manage without. These fungusses come off the dead maple trees and all Peterboro' are mad with engraving upon them birds and beasts, and monkeys, which is done with a large stocking needle. The idea struck me, that they might be painted, and I tried some birds and flowers and but-

terflies, which really look capitally at a distance and Sam thinks he
can sell them for me at Peterboro'. How glad I shall be for they take
but little time and look very splendid. I wish I could send you a few
specimens. How they would sell at home particularly if you wrote
at the bottom of each, Sugar Maple funguss, from such a wood in
Canada Birch Beech, &c. You must send me a pair of Indian Rubber
shoes, to garden in for I am without – I have no news to tell you. I
have not seen Traill since he left, but expect him every day – poor
Mr. Godard has been relieved from all his difficulties by his eldest
son, who has made several thousand pounds in the timber trade, and
is coming over to buy his father a farm. In the mean time he has
sent him money to pay up all his old arrears. The boys have nearly
worked out their debt to us, and their kindness and attention all
winter to my comfort has been great. The more I see of these lads,
the better I like them. While I may say, I owe the life of my baby to
Cyprian sparing neither time nor fatigue in going so often through
such impassable roads to fetch the Dr for him. They have rather a
fancy to buy the Clergy reserve, and to farm this on shares what
should you ask for it. The money down. They would likewise buy
our oxen and farm implements if we left. I have given them the
land on shares for this summer, reserving the lake field for the pigs
and c[ow]s. They begin ploughing for oats a[nd] peas next week. The
frost being quite out of the gro[und]. Till you have freed yourself
dearest from some of your difficulties, I think it would be prudent
for us to remain on the farm, though I should rejoice greatly at any
thing which united us again. I dreampt you returned last night, and
I was so glad, but you pushed me away, and said you had taken a
vow of celebacy and meant to live alone, and I burst into such fits
of laughing that I awoke. I have suffered tortures of toothache for
the last week, but Sam, who is very kind since Traills removed, has
promised to bring up Dr Hutchinsons instrument and extract the
two which rob me of rest, by night and day. We are in all the heat
and muddle of sugar making – The Godards, Caddys and us. We
made 100 cwt last week, but the weather has changed so suddenly
hot that the trees have ceased running for the present. We are afraid
that the season will be short – or we expect to make 100 cwt each.
Our three little pigs are perfect beauties though pigged in the
coldest weather under the barn – The oxen are quite well, and the
cows fat, but Mayflower is not in calf. Donald was so angry with
the sheriffs officer for wanting to take his cows, that he said he
would kill him with the Tomahawk for he must have me me – He

still says La for yes, and is a very clever little creature, but that ugly scar on his fine brow spoils the light of his countenance. He is so fond of George Godard, that he calls him brother George, and goes up very often to see him. They all send a kiss and their best love to dear Papa, in which I unite, and with the most affectionate wishes for your health happiness and safe return remain your own attached wife

Susanna Moodie

I hope you may meet with a good customer for the Steam Boat Stock, and pay up all our debts –

1 Cotter Lane was also a shoemaker who lived on Charlotte Street in Peterborough (Poole, *A Sketch*, 17).

29 Susanna Moodie to John Moodie

[23 April 1839]

... You would have laughed to have seen Donald hugging and kissing Aggy and begging her to come home in Ox cart. Mr Crawford was very kind to the little Scotchman, and fed him at dinner himself. Donald, had turkey and veal cutlets, and ham, which rareties he called chicken, and amused every one by his funny prattle. I have put him into trowsers. The manly little creature becomes them well; and is so proud of his pockets. Agnes sent many loves and kisses to dear Papa. Hagues begged to be most affectionately remembered to you. I have been greatly relieved, by the extraction of two teeth, which Sam pulled very dextriously. I expect my dear Dunbar home this week. I shall spoil my droll Donald, if Dunbar remains longer away. The latter is grown tall and handsome. You will hardly know him. If any body offends him, his greatest term of wrath is calling him or her a – 'live saw log' – The bugs, bit me and poor Johnnie to death – he can begin to sit alone, and is the delight of Donald's heart, who calls him, 'dear *wee* Johnnie' – Donald, still talks of going to *Belwill* to see dear Papa. There is a report, that poor Mrs Easton is dead. I hope it may not be true. I expect Alured Godard up from Peterboro' to day, so I will not close this till I see whether he has a letter for me –

April 24. Cyprian is waiting for my letter I must say Goodbye. No letter yet, but A G, is not home from Peterboro. Do dearest write me on the receipt of this. I have had another slight fit of ague and the pain in my back is almost insupportable. God bless you the little ones unite with me in kindest love –

Yours with the truest
affection. Susanna Moodie

---

30 John Moodie to Susanna Moodie

My Dearest Susie,

Belleville,
24th April *1839*

You will think me unkind in not writing you before now. – The fact is my Dearest I have been sadly bothered lately with various matters connected with my duty so that I could find no time to attend to my private matters. As soon as I recieved your letter respecting the seizure of the cattle I wrote to Bethune who promised to stop the proceedings telling me at the same time that the expenses would be very trifling. I have sent you my beloved Susie a box containing various articles of wearing apparel by the stage – directed to Traill at Peterborough.

		£	s	d	
viz.	12 Yards striped Ginham at 1/1	-	13-	-	⎫
	12 do. Check trousering at 1/4	"	16	"	⎬ Bought at
	1 *Dress* Mouseline de laine	1.	3.	6	⎬ Belleville
	(a new article here)				⎬
	1 Crape Hankf		7.	6	⎭

Turn over

	£	s	d	
9 yards light Chintz 1/3	"	11	3	⎫ Bought at
10 Do. Dark Do. 1/-	"	10.	"	⎬ Kingston
8 Do. Muslin 1/2		9.	4	⎭

I have also sent you two pair of boots, one pair such as are now worn, and a *strong pair*. I could get no shoes for the dear children, God bless them, but have ordered some to be made of different sizes. You should have *sent their measures and your own*, silly old woman perhaps you thought I should know the length of your foot by this time. If they do not fit send them back and I will send others. Now, My poor old widow in the bush, don't scold me if I have not made a good choice of the articles, for you know I am no great judge of these matters, and I had no female at hand to choose for me. I have put Mrs Bayley's little book in the box – I think she would be pleased if you gave her a little 'Soft Sawder' as Sam Slick calls it,[1] or wrote her a few lines. She is a very lady li[ke] kind unaffected woman, and very sensible – she doats on F. W. N. Did you know him? *Verb. Sat.* &c. The Baron is about to be married to a young lady of *Sixteen* Miss Ridley our doctor's daughter. I think he might have done better every way but he is not *in very good health* and wants a young person to nurse him. We have just been giving him a dinner – it was a queer scene a fine subject for a sketch which might be called 'The Rival Presidents' for we had two presidents, and one at each end of the table, speechifying both at once for about an hour and a half, – one a Militia Colonel *on half pay* and the other a Major on full: as the wine began to operate sundry missiles such as decanters, candlesticks glasses &c were discharged – I passed safely thro' the ordeal with the exception of getting a little wine in my face from a bottle *on its passage* to another head. We had some splendid transparencies. There was Sir Francis Head riding in a state of primitive nudity in the character of St George with a very vulgar looking Dragon clawing at him. And there was St Patrick honest man!, kicking the snakes out of Ireland. And last not least St Andrew scratching himself on a rather clumsily made cross while a whole forest of thistles were growing up in irksome contiguity with his bare legs. Orders have come for discharging one half of each company, and further orders will be given before the remainder of the six months has expired Viz. the 12th of May. I believe there is little doubt that some companies will be kept up in which case I shall of course be continued but I shall know more after the 12th of May. The officers have been required to give in the names of men desirous of extending their period of service. This does not look like peace tho' the good folks in England take matters cooly with regard to this Colony. If I see any chance of being retained on duty I shall take a small house and get you down here. I should not wonder if we were removed to Presqu' Isle harbour, where it is believed two *forts* will be built immediately. *If I possibly can* manage it I shall take a run up and see you my Dearest love, for I long to see you and my sweet babes again. I sometimes wish I had my *flute* with me, as I might amuse myself more rationally with a little music in the evening than among a parcel of vulgar minded animals who have no way of passing their time but in drinking. Send me my flute therefore and all the music you can find. There is *one lady* here (they are rather scarce here) who plays the piano very sweetly and I could spend an evening now and then very pleasantly there. I wish you would send me also some of the 'Palladiums' with articles of Yours & mine such as lines on the 'Caroline' and the Essay of Gynerocracy &c.

Now my Dearest I must wish you good bye for the present. Write me soon and kiss my dear Katie Aggy Dunbar Donald and little Jack for me.

Remember me most kindly to the Traills &c &c I remain, My Dearest Susie

> Your ever affectionate husband
> *J.W. Dunbar Moodie*

P.S. I shall be much bothered for some time till the men are discharged, and settling with the Commissariat. I find the business easy now, and I have not yet made a single mistake of any consequence. Lawrie has been dunning me a little but he cannot do anything for many months by which time I hope to be able to sell some shares of the Cobourg. She is paying now at the rate of 18 Per Cent on the original stock. I have been thinking of buying a farm in this quarter. I think it not unlikely that I may be able to make an exchange of Melsetter for a beautiful farm here on the Bay Shore of 200 acres with about 100 cleared if not more. The buildings and Offices are excellent with a capital orchard and every bit of the land excellent. The country is beautiful along the Bay of Quinte with excellent fishing and sailing &c. &c. The farm I allude to is worth £1000. I think I might offer a good deal of wild land to boot for it besides Melsetter. This is the most desirable situation in Upper Canada in my opinion in every respect excepting the population which *is* very much disaffected but the *worst* are clearing out as fast as they can get rid of their farms. Now is the time particularly if there should *be war*, to get farms cheap here as all the Radical Republicans will leave the Colony. I believe Clark told us a —— when he said this part of the country was *unhealthy*. Every one denies this, – and *their looks* confirm what they say of the healthiness of the country.

I send you 5 Dollars dear it is as much as I can spare. God bless you My love

J.W.D.M.

1 A reference to Thomas Chandler Haliburton's *The Clockmaker; or, The Sayings and Doings of Samuel Slick, of Slickville* (Halifax 1836)

---

31 Susanna Moodie to John Moodie

	Douro
My dearest Husband,	[May] 6th 1839.

I received your dear letter, last week, by the hand of brother T——and Jenny went down yesterday to Mr Crawford's, for the box, which Hague brought up for me from Cobourg. How shall I thank you my dear love for all the pretty things you sent me. They are all *very pretty*, and do great credit to your marketting and I hope I am *very* grateful for them. I think if you were here, Katie and I would give you so many kisses that you would cry out that you were paid to get rid of our caresses. I am particularly pleased with the sweet handkerchief, which is Katie's admiration. She says when she is a woman, Papa must buy her one like it. The brown gown is very handsome for a plain print, and it will be so useful. The *Mouseline de lain*, is *too* good for my fortunes. Katie says, I shall want such a grand cape and pretty belt to wear with it, that Papa had better not have bought it. So we sat down and laughed over the pretty gown, and wondered w[h]ere all the other pretty things were to come from – Don't you remember, in the memoirs of Benvenuto Cellini,[1] where he dressed up his boy Diego, in a grand lady's court dress, and took him to a mirror, and how delighted the boy was at the metamorphosis, and exclaimed, 'Can that be Diego?' – so I think when I have your handsome present on, I shall be apt to exclaim, 'Can that be Susie, the poor bush wacker?' –

You guessed the length of my foot *exactly*. No wonder – you know it so well, for surely if any man ever knew how to please a poor silly women 'tis yourself. The stuff for the boys dresses is very cheap. Bless me, how my fingers will ache before I have made up all the things for them, but *nil desperandum*, the very sight of the good cloth has put me into good spirits inspite of the ague, which I have had a slight fit of every day, for the last fortnight, not enough to confine me to my bed, but bad enough to render me very weak, and to turn me as yellow as a piece of parchment. I shall commence taking Quinine for it tomorrow. I had no means of getting up a little calomel from Peterboro', or it should not have run on so long. Now T—— is gone, I have few chances of sending into town.

Katie, returns you many thanks for the gingham for her and Aggy's best frock – she says, it is very pretty, and Mamma thinks it very neat and genteel looking. The black Muslin is very cheap, and very handsome, but can only be worn in the deepest mourning. I hope I may not want it. The pretty chintz I shall make up directly. I sent you dearest, a wee parcel by Cyprian Godard, with a painted fungus, did you receive it? – had I known, that you wanted the flute C. would have left it at Kingston for you, but I think you had better fetch it yourself, for without I carried it myself as far as Peterboro', I fear it would get broke – or spoilt. I have an order to paint some fungii for Mrs Hazlewood, but I have been too ill to hold down my head to do it, though I am sure of the money, the moment she gets the paintings. I sent the five dollars, to Joseph Jory by Mrs Jory, & she gave me a receipt for it. I hope this will quiet him for a few days.

I could have sold the oxen to the Godards a little ago for 18£, and had I been sure of your leaving Melsetter, I would have sold them and paid up the Jorys, for I fear I shall get no such chance again. They have bought a good yoke since for 19£ in Cavan. I hope you will be continued, and that we shall join you – these long separations, are most painful to me. A state of widowhood does not suit my ardent affections. Anxiety destroys my health. I have not suffered so much from sickness since I have been in Canada as this winter. If you could effect the exchange for Melsetter, you mention in your letter, I think it would be for the better even, if you parted with all your wild land. Every year convinces me of the madness of gentlemen attempting to farm in the bush, wasting their education, mind, manners, and property in drudging as pioneers. It is quite reversing the general order of things. I am not at all afraid of the Yankees, a strange cow or ox frightens me more than these bugbears that scare so many.

If we go from here, poor old Jenny petitions with tears to go with
us. Perhaps, in the troubled state of the country, a faithful honest
woman with all her faults, might be safer to trust as you would unavoidably be much from home, than a stranger – she promised to be
very clean and obedient if you would but take her and she certainly
has waited patiently for her wages and we now owe her 15£, a formidable sum. If your place should be retained, we might yet be very
comfortable and happy. I rejoice in the addition to your pay. How I
enjoyed your description of the dinner. Do write a sketch on it.
How Sir F. B. Head would laugh at the honor conferred upon him –
by the by, he had a strange fancy of riding about naked with the
indians.

You do not seem much to admire the good Barons choice. I hope
he may be happy for his kindness to you. He must be a very nice
creature. I have just glanced into Mrs Bayleys book – it seems a very
dull pragmatical affair, but I will do my very best to like it. She was
very kind to send it, and it may be my want of taste. However, I
have not read it, and it is unfair to judge of a work at first sight – I
will write a complimentary letter, when I send a parcel to you and
leave it unsealed for your approval. I have forgot to thank you for
the beautiful shawl. It will be a sweet summer shawl. The dear
children are all quite well. I have got my dear Dunbar home again.
He and the little Scotchman live rather turbulently together. Dunbar tells him he is his elder brother and he must mind him, which
piece of information Katie and Donald treat with peals of laughter,
to the great indignation of Mr Dunbar, whilst Mamma tries to convince him that eldership is only a greater claim upon him to be
kind to the younger ones. He shews a jealousy of disposition, I
never noticed in him before. He told me with flashing eyes, the
other day – That I did not love him so well as Donald for [I] had
only kissed him twice a day since he came home and I was always
kissing Donald. Where does he get this irritable temper from – I am
not jealous – I never observed it in you. I am sorry to see it so
strongly marked in him. He grows very handsome – at times he
looks almost beautiful, but he is getting very proud and imperious
and wants a father's authority to keep him down. Little Jack grows
nicely, Jenny says there is not a baby in Douro to compare with
him. I hope he will soon put Donald out of her affections, for the
poor old woman grows very fond of him.

I had a kind note from dear Mrs Hague, yesterday, she says Aggy,
is a dear good child. It will grieve her much to part with her if you
take us down to Belleville. Hague bought her another pretty frock

last week at Cobourg, and the little dear is a general pet with both Crawfords and Hagues. It will be a pity to take her from Mrs H—— if she continues anxious to keep her. She has learned her to sew beautifully, to behave so well, and she looks such a darling. You must see her as you come up. Oh do come soon – my heart aches to see you once again my own beloved one. Do write after the 12th and let me know how you are to be situated. Traills do not go to the plains after all. He has taken Joe Dunlops house till after harvest. Mrs Traill has been ill for some time. Adieu my dearest husband believe me with the deepest truest affection your own

Susanna Moodie

Sell the books by all means

When you come dearest, bring with you a bit of good tea, that I may be able to give you a good cup –

1 Benvenuto Cellini (1500–71), sculptor, goldsmith, and writer, published his celebrated autobiography in 1562. Two translations of the memoirs appeared in the 1820s: *Memoirs of Benvenuto Cellini*, trans. Thomas Roscoe (London 1822); and *The Life of Benvenuto Cellini*, trans. Thomas Nugent (London 1828).

---

32 John Moodie to Susanna Moodie

Belleville
My Dearest Susie   24th May *1839*

I received your welcome letter two or three days ago. I was afraid that my parcel had not reached you, and I am glad you are pleased with the articles sent.

I have got a lot of juvenile shoes for our *dear* little brats, but I have not the slightest idea whether they will fit. I really *don't* know how the shoemakers manage to hit the proper sizes for *'the critters.'* Instead of making shoes for the children it has always seemed to me to be an easier plan to *reverse the matter*, so that if the said shoes should not happen to suit any of the existing generation, – a new generation may be raised to suit them. A similar practise among our ancestors must have given rise to the common phrase of 'stepping into a man's Shoes.' I want to buy you a bonnet (black and white straw is much worn and looks well for the country) if I can

manage to carry it without injury. I really cannot say when I shall
be able to get away from this place as it takes a long time to wind
up matters. Since the Militia here have been discharged a new
Company of 100 men have been raised for 6 months (or longer, if
required) under our late Adj^t Capt Richey – but I am sorry to say
that I am included in the reduction tho' I have been busy ever since.
The Baron has written to get me Pay while I continue on duty. I
cannot possibly get away before the end of this month and probably
not for two or three weeks longer still.

As *I must go* I cannot tell you how I long to be once more with
my dear Susie and our sweet brats. The Baron will do all in his
power to get me employed, and from present appearances there
seems to be no chance of our remaining long quiet. Disturbances are
re-commencing in the lower Province, and notice has been given
authorities at Kingston of a band of Pirates having established themselves in the Thousand Islands.

I am trying to get my Steam Boat stock sold on any terms even
for one half to get out of debt which paralyzes all energy and hope.

> God bless you my Dearest
> And believe me ever Your Aff^{te}
> Husband
> *J.W. Dunbar Moodie*

By a new Post Office arrangement, letters will be conveyed from
any part of this Colony to *any part* of Great Britain *Via Halifax*
for one shilling for a single letter – and the postage may be paid
either here or in England by the reciever. This will be a great benefit
to the Colony, and you should attend to it if you are writing home.

Remember me kindly to our kind neighbours the Caddys &
Crawfords. I had some hopes of getting James Caddy a commission
in the new Company raised here, – but the Baron had promised it to
another before I could see him. It is perhaps no great loss as the
Captain is not one of the most amiable persons. I have not been
able to get much information regarding Texas for Major Crawford
but I have bought him a very good pocket map of the whole territory. I sometimes wish I could clear out from this unhappy distracted country where I can see nothing but ultra selfish Toryism or
Revolutionary Radicalism. The people in this part of the country are
split into some three or four factions – The Catholics harbouring
dark designs under an hypocritical profession of loyalty and Orange-
men goading them on to rebellion by claiming all the loyalty in the

country to themselves, – while the native Canadians are hugging the loaves and fishes as their own peculiar perquisite, agreeing with the others on hardly any one point but in hatred of the Scotch and their Church – whose determined spirit and proud independent minds will never become the *slaves* of any party, nor give up one particle of their rights as British subjects in a British Colony. It is this stern unyielding spirit, and integrity of purpose (tho' it sometimes carries them to extremes when opposed and irritated) that makes them to be hated by those who dare not, or cannot, think for themselves. Come what will, their strong heads and strong hands will ensure *respect*. A black cloud hangs over Canada. It may pass away and bright sunshine succeed, – but if it breaks, God help this wretched country. I wish I could think more cheerfully on this subject. Lord Durham's report has stirred up a hornet's nest. Hardly any one can talk or think cooly about it. I believe the middle course is the only safe one in this case, as in many others. It contains a great many home truths – and it is these truths which have given offence. The *really* objectionable parts are used by the parties *most* concerned to throw discredit on the whole. If the British Gov^t has the discernment to adopt his suggestions on some very important points it is my firm belief that he will yet be regarded as the best friend Canada ever had. It is perfectly clear that Lord Durham saw through the hollow loyalty of a large portion of our population, and their selfish views. This is an unpardonable Offence. His accute mind enabled him to see the difference between hatred of the Americans – and sincere attachment to British Institutions. What a contemptible figure Dr Strachan cuts with his half Radical letter. I long to see the Appendix with all the letters; which Lord D—— will publish in support of his assertions. I have given you a longer letter than I intended when I began, but my notions ran away with me.

Farewell Dearest. Kiss my sweet brats for me. I hope I shall be with you about the beginning of June.   J.W.D.M.

---

33 Susanna Moodie to John Moodie

My dearest Love –   June 1st 1839–

I did not get your letter until this morning, more than a week after date. You cannot imagine how anxious I have been to hear from you – and I had really determined on bringing Johnnie down with me, and paying you a visit, to see whether you were still in the land of the living. I am so tired of living alone, that this must be the *last winter* of exile and widowhood, another long separation from you would almost break my heart – Oh how dearly welcome you will be to your home. How I shall count the '*leaden footed hours*'[1] until you come. If I knew but the day you would come up, I would be in Peterboro' to meet you. Poor Mrs Traill has been very ill for the last fortnight. Traill wrote me a long letter enclosing yours. He seems in wretched low spirits. Mr Bridges has left for the West Indies. He offered Traills his house rent free with all its ample stores of provision. The crops in the ground, the use of the cows and sheep &c. Traill has let it slip through his fingers, and now seems very desponding on the subject. I am sorry he left his old place. I fear they will be long before they settle again. He wrote to Dr. Bartlett about Texas. The answer he received was tolerably satisfactory but in conclusion the Dr throws cold water on the whole scheme by saying – 'Be pleased to give my kind regards to Mrs Traill, Mr and Mrs Moodie and family, and tell them to stick to John Bull, as long as they can for I find with all its faults, that he has more sterling honesty and good principle in him, than all the world beside –'

I am pretty much of the Dr'[s] opinion, and if you should desert poor Canada in her day of distress, let us go to the Cape at once, and have naught to do with brother Jonathan and his scampish progeny – But if our debts were all paid, we might live happily enough here and rear up our children in the fear and love of God –

I was right glad, to hear you talk of selling the Steamboat stock. It would be better policy to sell it, and pay our debts than to derive from it, a precarious income. The farm will feed us at any rate. I am at Issue with the Godards and have taken the farm out of their hands. Perhaps, I was rather severe, but on the whole I am not sorry for it. I cannot enter into particulars here.[2] I am not in their debt, but they clear off the old score this week when they have ploughed and put in half an acre of potatoes, which I think as many as we shall require. If you think otherwise you can plough a small piece more when you return and Jenny can get them in. Sam tells me, that if we summer fallow the fields at the head of the clearing this month and draw the quantity of straw out of the barn and burn it upon the ground, and drag in wheat early in September we should in all probability have a first rate wheat crop and as we have no wheat land for next year, I think it would be a good plan. Godards are still willing to do this on shares, ploughing it twice and burning the weeds. Shall I accept it, or will you do it yourself on your return? If your stay should be prolonged till the end of this month you must write and let me know – As to Jory's, you *must not return* without money for them. I have been obliged to stave them off with promises until their patience is exhausted, and their present distress renders them doubly urgent. Do not dearest buy any more things for me. I have a new straw bonnet, which will do well enough for the bush. A few yard of *towelling* to wipe your hands upon is a *greater necessary*. Ask for Huckebuck towelling. A dozen Yds. would last us for some years. Mrs Hague, begged me to request you to bring her 15 Yds. of the black checked boys trowsering 1/4 per Yd. You will remember the stuff. She will repay you on delivery. I should be glad to oblige her, she has been so good to our little Agnes. Hague bought her two pretty frocks, and they keep her very genteelly clad. If we remain in Douro, I believe Mrs H. will petition to keep her longer –

I hope to be able to pay Garbut myself, and to buy poor old Jenny, who is behaving very well, some necessary articles of clothing. I sent by Cyprian Godard two small MSS. down to Mr. Lovel the Editor of the Garland, for which I asked 5£. He has returned me a very kind gentlemanly answer, accepting the MSS and promising to transmit the money the first week in June. He likewise hopes that any papers I can spare I will send him putting upon each a price and if they can possibly afford to purchase them they will. Though they are not able to offer much, yet this will open up a little fund for me which may enable me to pay Jenny's wages and get a few necessaries for the children. How great is the goodness of God toward us. I hope I am grateful even for these seeming small mercies, but great, in our depressed circumstances. But I am a very rich woman. *You love me*, my friends are kind to me – my dear children are well and happy, and we have united hearts and interests. Can poverty, ever outweigh these blessings? No dearest no? – We will defy temporary evils, and still enjoy the existence given us to improve for a better state of being, and be firm friends through a happy eternity, though the endearing tie which now unites us should be severed by death –

I have got a present, of the finest cattle dog, I ever saw. Poor Mrs Lloyd sent him up to me – Not a beast can come near the place. He races and chases them. The pigs tremble in their very skins for him, and I dont think he would let you come up to the house at night without biting you. You must call him Rover and coax him, if you should come after we are in bed. A great bear haunts the top of the clearing. Jenny has met him twice. And he has roared upon her lustily. Mr Bruin is waiting upon you to send him after his wife – So says Katie and Dunbar, and they are *good* authority.

The whole township is ringing with poor Copperthwaites misfortune. The sly Yorkshireman has been outwitted by a woman after all. I told you of his marriage three months ago, with the charming Christie Wright – a fortnight ago, she was put to bed. The child undeserved by Copperhead who never suspected the matter till the babe was born. He is mad with rage, and sent away the child the day after it was born to its father a man that worked on her father's land. The same morning as her sister Miss Ellen was safely brought to bed in Cavan the child by a working wheelwright of the name of Luckie. He yesterday married her, and the wedding and the christening I suppose took place on the same day. Erskine is miserable. His wife and Mrs Savene, loud in their lamentations and all the world laughing at and pitying poor Copperhead by turns – So there's a choice bit of scandal and true to boot. George Caddy has brought up his little wife and very sweet baby. It is a far handsomer child than Mrs Hagues, and if it lives I think from its fine eyes and features will be a beauty, though a dark one. George doats upon Miss Elinor and Mary Ann, who often comes to see me looks very interesting as a Mother. Mrs Acton, left our dear Mary Gooding 100£ per annum for life. Are not you glad. Mrs Childs wrote a long letter to Catharine, it was full of kind enquiries respecting us. Poor Rachel Wales died in childbed of twins, a girl and boy. The children are well and thriving. Poor dear Rachel. I could not forget her for some days. All at Reydon were well –

Stricklands are very kind, quite affectionate. Mrs. S—— was saying she quite longed to see you again. Mrs. Wolsley is a nice lively kind creature. Very hospitable cheerful and intelligent. I am sure you will like her very much. She is making great improvements in the place. You will hardly know it again. Young Casement, is a quiet nice lad. He sings well, and plays upon the flute. On the whole I think them very good neighbours, and they are very friendly with me. You will come dearest to an empty house for we are out of meat, but we have plenty of good flour and oatmeal, and Brine ...

1 Possibly a reference to John Milton's 'leaden-stepping hours' from his sonnet 'On Time'

2 See *RIB*, 494.

---

34 John Moodie to Susanna Moodie

                                          Belleville,
My Dearest Susie,   5th July 1839[1]

You will wonder at not seeing me or hearing from me so long. The fact is, that I have been sadly bothered to get my business concluded. Some of our Pay Lists have not *yet* been recieved from Toronto, and I cannot settle with the *Staff* and pay myself among the rest till they come. A few days ago I found I should fall short about £65, and I cannot describe the anxiety and trouble I have had to ascertain, how this had happened. I laboured for three or four days incessantly and at last discovered that I had paid that sum *twice*. Fortunately it was to a rich man, from whom I shall have no difficulty in recovering it. The Baron was as usual extremely kind on the occasion and offered to assist me in going over the accounts, tho' he was just about to be *spliced*.

He is now married, and I have just been tasting the *Bride Cake*. I trust he will be happy, for there is not a kinder heart [in] existence than his. I think I told you that he had spoken to the Governor about me. I followed his advice to write to His Exc^y and ask for the *Sheriffalty* of this place, which is about to be created into a separate District viz the Dis^t of Hastings. Almost by return of post I recieved an answer from the Governor, which I copy for your comfort my love and you will perceive that *you* are neither unknown to or forgotten by our good and benevolent *Ruler*.

'Sir,   Gov^t House 26th June *1839*

The Lieut. Governor has directed me, in acknowledging your letter of the 24th ins^t to say, that not only on your own account, but from the esteem and respect he entertains for Mrs. Moodie, he has an earnest wish to be of service to you, and has felt the same wish for many months. His Excellency can make no promise of any particular office for fear of doing an act of injustice to others, but I am to assure you, that he will avail himself of the first possible opportun-

ity of complying with your desire for employment, and thereby gratifying his own anxiety to render some service to your interesting
family.'

'I have the honor & c.
J.B. Harrison
Private Sec^y'

Is not this a *kind* letter my beloved? The Baron is quite pleased
with it and assures me I may rely with entire confidence on his Exc^y
keeping his word. This will comfort your desolate heart my own
beloved wife, relying as I have long done on a Merciful Providence,
and as I know *you* do, still more perhaps; I trust in that Providence
that we will see an end to our troubles and again take our proper
place in Society, from which we have been so rudely jostled by our
adverse fortune.

I went to Cobourg the other day and paid the remainder of my
note at the Bank viz £33. I might have renewed it but I thought it
right to redeem it when I had it in my power and relieve my secur-
ities. It is necessary I might raise another and pay off some other
debts. I trust however that I shall be enabled to sell my stock in the
'Cobourg.' I have written to the Secretary of the Boat for a correct
statement of her affairs which is absolutely necessary before I can
effect a sale.

Another outbreak has been expected here about the *fourth of July*,
and three companies of the 93rd Regiment have just been sent down
to Presqu' Isle harbour where a landing is expected, – but I believe it
will all end in smoke. You must not say a *word to any one* of my
having applied for the Office of Sheriff of Hastings, as it would certainly be found out in Belleville where there are several expectants
and would excite great jealousy – and perhaps disappoint my views.
I think there is no doubt I shall get something worth while, as I am
sure that I stand well in the Governors opinion. Your letter I have
no doubt has had its full effect.

I really can hardly say when I shall be able to get away from this
place – so my dearest you must just do your best to manage matters
at home in the mean time. I cannot tell you how I long to embrace
you again my own beloved and affectionate wife and my dear little
children. I fear you have been badly off lately, and I have not been
able to assist you. I send you a few dollars which is all I can command at present. I have begun my letter to you with a wide margin
in the usual official style from habit, thinking that I was about to

write a letter to the Military Secretary, – so you must try and find
my continuation where there is a vacant space.

I would start off for home, but I have left myself so poor with
paying my debts that I have not the means to pay for my Board at
the tavern &c. I suppose it is now time for mowing as they have
begun here lately. Perhaps you will be able to get it done by some of
[the] neighbours – but I leave this to your own management as I
know you will do the best you can. I would rather live on bread and
water, or even on *potatoes* with a remote prospect of butter to them
than be so long away from you again, – however, I believe it as all
for the best and I rejoice in the prospect we now have of better
times, – chiefly on your account my dearest, for you know I can
bear any thing in the way of physical privation cheerfully. All *I* care
about is independence. I shall submit to any sacrifice to obtain this.
Kiss my dearest brats for me and tell them I never forget them. I
hope Dunbar has been a good boy and obedient to you in all things.
Tell him I cannot love him if he is not obedient to you and does not
love you and his sisters and little brothers. I am sure my own dear
Katie is a good girl and I hope and trust Agnes is the same. God
bless them all and keep them from harm. I suppose they will hardly
know me when I come back at least Donald and master Johny will
be considerably puzzled for a while. Birdsall (late of the Peterborough Reg^t) is here and has been telling me of wonderful doings at
that place. We have got one comp^y of militia here, – but they are a
miserable drunken set. I thought there was more drinking in our
neighbourhood but *here* 'it beats a.'

God bless you my Dearest love and believe me Ever Your Aff^{te}
and *dutiful* husband.

                                    J.W. Dunbar Moodie

1 Letter 35 suggests that this letter may have been very late in reaching Susanna,
  although it is postmarked 6 July 1839.

---

35 Susanna Moodie to John Moodie

                                    Melsetter Douro
My Dearest Moodie,   July 16, 1839

When I recal the date of your last letter written so many weeks ago,
I know not how to still the constant enquiries of my anxious heart

– 'What can keep him – why does he neither write nor send to us.'
Surely dearest, we cannot have become indifferent to you that you
should leave us, in this dreadful state of uncertainty as to your
plans and present situation. Your long absence and silence, paralizes
all exertion. I only live from day to day, in the hope of seeing you
before night, or hearing from you, but night comes and no word
from you, and I take poor little Johnnie into my arms and pray for
his absent father and bathe his innocent face with tears. Cruel
Moodie, one short sentence which would tell me you are well
would remove this miserable state of anxiety. Oh do write, if but
one line to me. You were to have been here, the first week in June.
Here is the middle of July, and no Moodie.[1] I will walk down to
Belleville if you do not come or send to me. The poor children have
ceased to talk now of your return. Katie says, 'Papa has forgotten
us.' Thank God the dear children are all well and send a kiss and
their best love to dear Papa. We have had six dreadful thunder-
storms during the last six days, and at this moment the lightning is
turning the night into day. On Monday, Stricklands house was
struck with lightning. It split the chimney from top to bottom
hurled the stones to a considerable distance and struck the baby on
Mrs Stricklands lap, so that it was stiff and senseless for a quarter of
an hour burnt the hair on James Fowlis head, his whiskers and eye-
brows – (He is to day confined to his bed) and set the house on fire,
which fortunately the heavy rain put out. Sam was at Peterboro' and
Mrs S. and the children were so paralized with terror they were
quite unconscious that the loft was burning over their heads – What
a providential escape. On Sunday, during the tempest, large pieces of
ice fell, that cracked several panes of glass. The storm was truly
awful – Again last night – It made us all tremble. I fear Professor de
Espy has been brewing one of his storms, and cannot put a stop to
his impious work.[2] What do you think of his theory?

I have been reading some Texas Newspapers that are published at
Houston, the capital, and was much interested in the accounts of
the country as described in them. Mr Crawford has given up all idea
of settling there.

I know not what to do about the farm, and I am so dispirited that
I care nothing about it. I have no money to hire labor to cut the
grain and the crop is but indifferent. I fear I cannot even let it on
shares. Sibbins, and Garbut have both declined taking it. I have been
disappointed in receiving the money I expected from Montreal, and
Jorys and Garbut dun me constantly. Oh heaven keep me from

being left in these miserable circumstances another year. Such another winter as the last will pile the turf over my head. I cannot help crying when I think, that such, may be in store for me. While I had you to comfort and support me all trials seemed light, but left to myself, in this solitude, with only old Jenny to speak to, and hearing so seldom of you makes my life a burden to me.

Dear Mrs Shairp has been staying a few days with me. She is in very poor health, I fear she will go into a decline.

I write in great haste, clinging to the last moment in hope of hearing from or seeing you.

God bless you dearest, I am very unhappy about you, do not quite forget your

poor Susie.

1 De Rottenburg reports that Captain George Fraser of the 3rd Hastings Militia had mismanaged his funds for April. The matter was not finally settled until September, at which time Fraser had either to resign or be court-martialled (MR, 1B1, 44). Moodie's delay may well have involved matters of this kind.
2 James Pollard Espy published *The Philosophy of Storms* in 1841. He had been chairman of the Joint Committee of the American Philosophical Society and Franklin Institute investigating data on storms. Annual reports were published from 1834 to 1838, and these led to references to the work of Espy in the *Albion* and in scientific literature produced by other persons.

---

36 John Moodie to Susanna Moodie

My dearest Susie

Belleville
24th Novr 1839

Yesterday I received your very welcome letter and am rejoiced to hear that you are all well. I wrote you several days ago telling you that I had got Meyers & Hawley for my Sureties, and that I had made a fair start in my business. Parties, as usual, run high here, and find some difficulty in steering a middle course, which I am determined to do. I now see my way pretty clearly, and I shall have less trouble (I expect) than in my last year's employment.

With regard to James Jory I have no objections to his having the farm, and I shall be glad to have him for a tennant. I think the terms so easy for him that I think he cannot object to paying the taxes as we did. You know the clearing is partly *on all* the lots. I wish the land along the lake to be cleared first, and have no objections to allow him anything reasonable for the *extra* difficulty of clearing the swamp, – but the *unlogged* land is in fact land, already *half cleared*, and an advantage to him. The chimnies he can easily put up as there are plenty of stones on the spot for a common chimny, and you can make a present of the parlour stove if you have not disposed of it.

The fences must be good and sufficient, that is to say of pine, oak, or cedar. There must also be a *proviso* that I shall not be prevented from selling the place, if I allow the am^t of one years clearing, *this*, however, is not likely to occur. Strickland I know, will be kind enough to draw up an agreement on these terms, which I will sign, or he can sign it as my agent. [With the] exception of the conditions I require as [noted above], I have no objection to leave the mino[r details] to be arranged by him and you, and [I will] ratify any agreement you may make. [Bring] poor Jenny by all means. She is a goo[d hearted] soul, and I should be sorry to disapp[oint her] when she is so anxious to remain [with us]. Bring my dear child Aggy Caddy wit[h you] and [pack] the little Gazelle careful[ly] [   ] with plenty of cotton rou[nd her]. [I will n]ot, however, promise to return her *as she comes*, unless she is uncommonly hard hearted to our Belleville swains. I believe I shall be obliged to take a small house in town. There is very little choice. The brick house with the orchard might be had, – but there is the hereditary nuisance of an old man and an old woman who live in a *vinegar bottle* on the ground floor. [   ] it you. The Baron's house [   ] it is rather cold and we could only have it for 3 months. The only other place is a small house near where the Baron is going to live, and where the best society is to be had. There [are] three or four rooms besides upstairs bed rooms kitchen stable and tollerable garden. &c. The rent about £15 or £17.10. Parker asked £30 per an. for the house the Baron inhabits. I should not object to the rent if I could have it for a longer period, and if he would give me a few acres of land with it on which there is an orchard. I shall buy the things you want in a day or two and send them by the stage to Traills care. I have a great mind to get some lady here to buy you the materials for a cloak also. [In the] mean time my love lose no time in getting all you w[ant, such a]s shoes for the children &c. And come down as soon as I let you know that I have got a house for you. I really long to kiss you all again, and I feel miserably out of my element in a tavern. The Baroness is looking *round* and plump, which is not to be

wondered at, as the Baron has little else to do, – and you know a
great deal is done in that way in a short time. But for this miserable
petty party and national feeling we might be very comfortable here,
– even as it is I hope we will be so. I am rather out of concert with
some of my countrymen here, – who would fain draw me into their
narrow notions. The two Doctors Ridley & Marshall both tollerably
well disposed men on other points are the two opposite extremes in
this way, and both are ready to give and take offence on every occasion. I am labouring to smooth the mutual prejudices of these differ-
ing Doctors, –. I go to both Churches, and most of my countrymen
go to the English Church when Mr. Ketcham[1] is absent. The Epis-
copalians, however, are not liberal enough to follow this laudable
example. Our worthy and truly Christian Minister (Ketcham) sup-
ports my views from the pulpit. I know you will love this man.
Tho' somewhat of a Calvinist he never alludes to their severe doctrines either in the pulpit or in Conversation, considering them as
doubtfull matters and not as essential to salvation.

We shall have a difficult part to perform here, but by steadily
pursuing a conciliatory course to all I trust by the blessing of God we
may be the means of doing much good. The 'Kingston Whig' has
thought proper to attack Sir G. Arthur for appointing me to the
Shrievalty, calling me an out and out advocate of *Responsible Gov*ᵗ.
That paper is held in such contempt that I have not thought it worth
while to answer it – but I see the 'Patriot'[2] has taken up the Cudgel
for me and called me a loyal trusty man and perfectly competent &c.
and says that these qualities had recommended me to Sir George.

Poor Parkers disappointment has made him half crazy – he has
thrown up his commission as a Magistrate, and when his resignation was accepted by the Governor he is like to bite the ends of his
fingers off. If you want money dearest write me and I will send you
some. I am very sorry to hear of poor Kates illness. I hope you will
be able to go to Peterboro and get the things you want. As soon as
you tell me that you are ready to start I will write to Bletcher[3] to
send his teams. Tell me how many loads you will have. Kiss all the
dear children for me and believe me ever your Affᵗᵉ husband

J.W. Dunbar Moodie

Bring all the bedsteads with you. I shall get some chairs tables &c.

---

1 Rev. James Ketcham (1797–1871), a Scot, was the Presbyterian minister in Belleville from 1831 to 1844.

2 These issues of the Kingston *Whig* and the *Patriot* are no longer available. However, on 28 November 1839 John Moodie wrote to S.B. Harrison, Arthur's civil secretary (*DCB*, 9:369–73), requesting a public announcement of his appointment, perhaps in an effort to quell the contention surrounding it in Belleville.

3 Barnabas Bletcher lived on the Rice Lake Road at Dale (three miles north of Port Hope) on lot 2, concession 3. He and his sons were important movers of freight in the Peterborough region. Poole says that at one time they moved 'eighty per cent of the freight that concerned Peterborough' and eventually they owned warehouses at Bewdley and Port Hope, and hotels at Dale and Bewdley. See Harold Reeve, *The History of the Township of Hope* (Cobourg 1967), 131–2, 228.

1840–1849

'Morals amidst a
vicious community'

WITH THE OUTBREAK of the rebellion the Moodies were united in their pro-British response. Indeed, the first of Susanna's loyal poems is dated in late November 1838 indicating that, while at a distance from Toronto, they kept a sharp eye upon the growing tensions in both the Canadas as described in newspapers available to them. For them there was no question but to support the British cause and to defy the republican clamour.

Loyalty to the crown was in no way at odds with the moderate progressivism of their shared outlook. They had first met, for instance, at the home of Thomas Pringle, the secretary of the Anti-Slavery League in London and shared with him a commitment to the abolition of that practice. Politically, however, they were loyal and conservative during their backwoods years, no doubt 'perfectly ignorant of the abuses that had led to the present position of things'; to them, as Susanna's poem 'On Reading the Proclamation Delivered by William Lyon Mackenzie, on Navy Island' indicates, the rebels were 'a set of monsters, for whom no punishment was too severe.'[1] Thus, it was perfectly consistent for Susanna to be attracted to Emilia Shairp's idea and to propose to her husband in 1839 that they undertake to run a newspaper in some town on 'conservative principles' (Letter 25).

It is not clear what factors changed – or perhaps better, modified – John Moodie's political outlook. His Letter 32 from Belleville does indicate a very fresh enthusiasm for Lord Durham's *Report*, which he had been reading in its full text in the papers and about which there was such disagreement and hostility in the Canadas in general and in Belleville in particular. He may have attended a Durham meeting out of curiosity and interest, or he may have been influenced by new acquaintances in Belleville or the various militia units he served. Whatever the case, he admired the middle course Durham recommended, seeing in his plan (part of which report Baldwin and his father had put forward to Durham) a safe course between the 'ultra selfish Toryism [and] Revolutionary Radicalism' that seemed to characterize Belleville's volatile politics.

From that date Moodie was quietly committed to the cause of moderate reform and responsible government. In moving to Belleville as the first sheriff of Hastings County, however, he confidently believed he could steer a safe middle course, if need be attending several churches, hiring deputies to represent both political persuasions, and even patronizing each of the politicized local doctors. But as his reactions to the domineering and conservative Dr Ridley suggest, he planned better than he was able in the long run to execute. How

long it took for the extremist tory faction, abetted by the strong local
Orange contingent, to brand Moodie a reformer is not clear from surviving records and correspondence. There was, after all, considerable
local hostility to his patronage appointment, despite his exemplary
military service. For instance, the temperamental tory Thomas Parker,
a former postmaster, was an influential Belleville figure whose business interests had fallen on hard times in the general economic depression of the period; he had banked heavily on gaining the shrievalty and
was beside himself with anger and disappointment at being denied a
position he desperately needed and assumed would be his by dint of
local achievements and loyal militia service.[2] As others shared that
anger, it is likely that Moodie was not long in being made to feel the
legal, economic, and social ramifications of such widespread vexation.
Still, it must be noted that it was Sheldon Hawley and Adam Henry
Meyers, two prominent tories from the River Trent (now Trenton) but
with strong Belleville connections, who came to Moodie's rescue late
in 1839 when his first attempt to establish his sureties for the
shrievalty was turned down by government officials. At that point his
politics could not have been a matter of question.

Steering a middle course in Belleville was more problematical than
Sheriff Moodie anticipated. The town was indeed a hotbed and
'hornet's nest' of factionalism at a time when factionalism was rife
throughout Upper Canada. In particular, tory sentiment in Belleville
proper was closely allied with the strongly politicized Orange contingent angry at the implementation of Durham's recommendations
regarding the Union of the Canadas.[3] As sheriff of Hastings County
Moodie also was growing increasingly aware of the split between the
large rural areas he served, which, though less organized, were more
reformist in their thinking than the tory-dominated and volatile town.
In such an environment it is not likely that he could have kept his
personal views under wraps for long, especially as friendships usually
went hand in hand with political persuasion. Much of his work and
income depended on court appearances and decisions, and as the great
majority of Belleville's magistrates were tories, Moodie could not have
been long in running afoul of their preferential agendas and vexatious
suits.

With respect to public policy, he began to express his reformist
views very soon after moving to Belleville. In gratitude for his appointment and with Sir George Arthur's encouragement, he wrote to the
lieutenant-governor in May 1840 offering a critique of existing land
policy, an issue that Arthur described to him as 'the most important

and the most difficult problem we have to deal with in Upper Canada.'[4] In Moodie's view settlement in Upper Canada had been too diffused because absentee, and largely tory, landlords had been allowed to accumulate large tracts of wild land. The result was the discouragement of settlement and a weakened economic infrastructure. To improve the system he recommends a greater degree of government planning, possibly to include higher taxes on wild lands held by absentee owners, the encouragement of British investment in cleared areas, repurchase and resale of wild lands by the government, and stronger control of settlement through the deployment of more official land agents. At the same time he tempers his critique by remarking on the suitability of labourers for opening up wild lands, and by advocating that educated gentlemen settle and invest in the cleared areas, thereby creating 'a truly British Aristocracy' for Canada.

In Life in the Clearings Susanna recalled the political atmosphere of Belleville in the early 1840s. The asperity of her comments reveals her lingering anger at the intolerance and violence of the factionalism they found there:

The Tory party, who arrogated the whole loyalty of the colony to themselves, branded, indiscriminately, the large body of Reformers as traitors and rebels. Every conscientious and thinking man who wished to see a change for the better in the management of public affairs was confounded with those discontented spirits who had raised the standard of revolt against the mother country. In justice even to them, it must be said, not without severe provocation; and their disaffection was more towards the colonial government, and the abuses it fostered, than any particular dislike to British supremacy or institutions ... But the odious term of rebel, applied to some of the most loyal and honourable men in the province because they could not give up their honest views on the state of the colony, gave rise to bitter and resentful feelings, which were ready, on all public occasions, to burst into flame. (LC, 35)

While Susanna felt the factionalism affecting her new social relationships, there can be no doubt that she was deeply disturbed by the treatment her husband and other prominent local reformers – William H. Ponton, William Hutton,[5] and John Ross,[6] for instance – received at the hands of local tories and the Belleville Intelligencer. The simmering antagonism of the Belleville and Hastings scene came to a head in the first two elections under the Union, in March–April 1841 and October 1842. In an atmosphere of grumbling and recrimination Moodie as sheriff was appointed to serve as returning officer. Political neutrality under such charged conditions was difficult at best; however much Moodie tried to maintain detachment, his reformist sympathies were likely too much a matter of personal principle for him to resist their expression on occasion. What was soon identified as his bias became a *cause célèbre* for the local tories, who found themselves faced by none other than the most prominent and important of Upper Canadian reformers, Robert Baldwin, who had just been appointed solicitor-general.[7] Responding to a petition signed by nearly six hundred freeholders of Hastings and on the recommendation of John Ross, then a young Belleville lawyer who served as his local ear, Baldwin decided to test this difficult constituency, where strong differences of opinion among the local reformers weakened the chance of an election victory.[8] Already sure of election in the fourth riding of York, Baldwin threw himself into the Hastings contest. He knew the power of the local tories and Orange organization, and he knew he would have to run against his cousin (by marriage), Edmund Murney. Perhaps the family rivalry added a flavour to the contest, for there was no love lost between Baldwin and Murney.

For all his long service as an elected representative, Edmund Murney (1812–61) has been a somewhat elusive figure in historical documentation. However, data in *History of Odd-Fellowship in Canada* (1879) provides a useful sketch of him. Born in Kingston, he was educated at Upper Canada College and trained as a lawyer in the office of Marshall Spring Bidwell, a long-standing reformer. Called to the bar in 1834, he set up practice in Belleville and in 1836 was elected to the Upper Canada Parliament for Hastings, while also serving as clerk of the peace and crown attorney at home. In 1835 he married Robert Baldwin's first cousin Maria Breakenridge, the eldest daughter of Mary Warren and the late John Breakenridge.

Murney's politics, like those of his father-in-law, were passionately tory. The Oddfellow history remembers him as 'a consistent Conservative of the extreme type,' using as an example his refusal in 1854 to support Sir Allan McNab when he associated himself in the government with 'some of the friends of Mr. Hincks.'[9] Otherwise sociable and genial, Murney was passionate in his desire to defeat Baldwin and the reform interests in the first Union election. Favoured by a wide body of support, particularly in Belleville, he ran an emotional, name-calling campaign, labelling Baldwin a rebel and papist.[10] Murney found support in the area among some members of Baldwin's own family, including two of his uncles, Captain Augustus Baldwin[11] and John Spread Baldwin.[12] The result was a close contest, characterized by near-violence at the hustings, where, under the worried eye of the returning officer and his deputies, both sides sought to out-shout and intimidate each other. Murney spent extravagantly in order to maintain his parliamentary seat.[13]

The 'Hustings' affair took place during the April voting. As returning officer, Moodie had the right to choose the location for the hustings, or platform, that would serve for the speech-making and voting. He also had the right to authorize and draw funds for its construction. Against the strong advice of Murney and the tories, who wished to hold the election in town (as had been done in the past), Moodie opted for a rural location. He may have been thinking of fairness to the Hastings farmers, who would by then be at work on the land. Likely too he was worried about the possibility of violence, since hostility was very much in the air. Indeed, in March with the election in mind, the governor general issued a general proclamation ordering all sheriffs, JPs, and magistrates to 'EFFECTIVELY REPRESS any turmoils, riots and breaches of the peace.'[14]

Having by statute £5 available for the hustings, Moodie contracted with Benjamin Ketcheson, a carpenter and one of the few local JPs who was a reformer, to build them. The high cost was required because of the depth of the March snow. Doubtless both the Ketcheson appointment and the choice of a rural locale served to inflame the local tories. In the wake of Murney's narrow defeat, they not only launched a formal appeal (in the name of Thomas Parker) regarding the conduct of the election and the actions of the returning officer, but at the next quarter sessions the dominant tory magistrates voted to allow Moodie only £2 10s. to pay Ketcheson.

In the subsequent name-calling and recrimination in the *Intelligencer* Moodie was attacked for his partisanship and cavalierly accused of trying to cheat Ketcheson by keeping the money to himself. While no Belleville papers survive, the *Upper Canada Herald*, a reform paper in Kingston, provides information on the 'affair' in its issues of 20 July and 3 August 1841.[15] A correspondent calling himself 'Reformer' responds in the latter issue to the earlier accusations of 'Fair Play.' Enclosing an affidavit from Ketcheson himself, which clarified Moodie's predicament and embarrassment, 'Reformer' sought to answer the falsehoods uttered about the sheriff and to identify the 'affair' as another 'link in the chain of petty persecution and MOSQUITE annoyance' systematically directed at Moodie since his appointment. In his 20 July letter 'Fair Play' even implied that Moodie himself might be the epistolary 'Reformer.'

With Baldwin victorious and the Parker petition dismissed by the Legislative Assembly as 'frivolous and vexatious,'[16] there was hope of a cessation of hostilities and a new tranquillity. For his part and in response to the active and pernicious role played in the election by what he called the 'Orange faction,' Moodie sought remedies. He was thus quick to launch his own petition to Parliament calling for a law to make all secret societies and secret meetings illegal.[17] While that concern would be actively debated in Parliament through a Baldwin initiative, the volatility in Belleville did not diminish. As Letters 40 and 41 indicate, the formal matter of presenting a welcoming address from the citizens of Hastings to incoming Governor Sir Charles Bagot[18] further exacerbated the charged political scene. Moodie described the nearly riotous meetings which led to two addresses being sent to Bagot, one from the tories under Murney's name and one from the loyal reformers under his own. Moreover, it is likely that it was Moodie's letter, dated 14 February 1842, that appeared in the *Upper Canada Herald* on the 22d of that month under the signature 'O.P.Q.' It replicates Letter 40 detail for detail.

At the same time he reveals his by now well-factionalized sense of friends and enemies. Among the former he includes William Hamilton Ponton, the second son of Dr Mungo Ponton, who came to Belleville in 1834 from his native Scotland. A lawyer and partner of John Ross, Ponton had been appointed clerk of the district in 1839. Despite Moodie's recommendation (Letter 38) to Baldwin there was no immediate change in the position of registrar; Ponton did become registrar, however, in 1854. He would also enjoy subsequent prominence as one of Belleville's earliest mayors (1851-3) and as one of the first Canadian directors of the Grand Trunk Railway. Other prominent reform-minded Bellevillians included rising businessman Billa Flint;[19] merchant Henry Yager, who had served as an MLA in the late 1830s; Nelson Gilbert Reynolds, a Methodist and a successful merchant, who had been arrested as a suspected traitor during the rebellion days and was to become president of the Marmora Iron Foundry in the late 1840s; young Lewis Wallbridge,[20] a prominent and well-connected Belleville native, who articled with Baldwin and son and was called to the bar in 1839; agriculturalist William Hutton (Moodie's replacement as returning officer after the 1842 election), who was warden of Hastings in the 1840s; Benjamin F. Davy, a businessman, who would become Belleville's first mayor in 1850, would run as a reform candidate in 1857 (even starting his own newspaper as a campaign vehicle), and who, with his wife, Louisa, joined the Moodies in spiritualist seances in the late 1850s; and John Ross, Irish-born but educated in Brockville, who trained under Andrew Norton Buell[21] and George Sherwood and would parlay his moderate and flexible reform interests and his close connection with Robert Baldwin (he married Baldwin's daughter, Augusta Elizabeth, in 1851) into a successful career both in business as president of the Grand Trunk Railway and in politics as receiver-general and minister of agriculture (and later senator) under John A. Macdonald and Etienne Cartier.

In addition to Murney, whose antics on the podium Moodie found startling in a gentleman, George Benjamin became increasingly the focus for Moodie's anxiety. One of the most fascinating characters in Belleville politics, Benjamin (1799–1864)[22] was an English Jew born in Brighton as Moses Cohen. Taking his mother's name, he came to Canada via the southern United States, where he married a very young New Orleans girl. In Belleville he worked as a teacher but was quick to draw on family experience in starting a newspaper, the *Intelligencer*, late in 1834. Well-educated and an accomplished linguist, he soon established himself as the tory voice and conscience of Belleville. Seeking as much preferment as possible, he sought to hide his Jewish background, though as the authors of *Burn This Gossip* have discovered, he did not always (or perhaps often) escape the sting of anti-Semitism. As a doggerel poem in the *British Whig* (Kingston) in 1836 and as Moodie's own comments make clear, Benjamin's Jewishness was publicly and privately recognized.[23]

By the early 1840s Benjamin had drawn together resources that constituted a major threat to reform interests and, from Moodie's point of view, to civil order in itself. He combined roles as the clerk of the Belleville Board of Police and grand secretary of the local Orange Lodge, which he had helped to found (indeed, he would soon become grand master for British North America). As newspaper editor and Murney's 'chief lieutenant,' he had a position of influence that led Moodie to mistrust virtually every move he made. The hostility between sheriff and police board clerk during these years would haunt both men throughout the remainder of their lives. Old wounds were to fester for decades.

Other leading tories included Charles Otis Benson, who married the widow of James Hunter Samson (Belleville's first lawyer and its conservative MLA from 1828 to 1835) and who in 1843 would launch what Audrey Morris calls a 'particularly vicious' suit against Moodie following the 1842 election;[25] the unpredictable Benjamin Dougall, who in his capacity as judge for Hastings made constant difficulty for

George Benjamin

Moodie, finally losing his position in 1843, on the recommendation of a government inquiry, for having used illegal practices in suits involving the sheriff;[26] Judge Christopher Alexander Hagerman,[27] a Queen's bencher and former solicitor-general of Upper Canada, who did not hesitate to use his considerable influence to draw out tory support; Peter O'Reilly, who as coroner colluded with Dougall to disadvantage Moodie in the courts;[28] the combative Dr George Neville Ridley; and the more moderate Dr William Hope (1815–94), who set up practice in Belleville in 1838 and would later become the town's mayor (1860) and sheriff (1881).

As tensions continued to build, it seemed but a matter of time before real violence broke out. That came, in fact, with the election of October 1842, when, with wounds still raw from Baldwin's disputed victory, the same candidates met at the hustings before the same returning officer. Baldwin feared the worst and was right. Both sides were ready and armed, and Moodie found himself with a potential riot on his hands. His conduct under these circumstances is the subject of Letters 44 and 45. 'The election turned out to be one of the most disorderly, at a time when disorderly elections were the rule.'[29] A count of the votes cast before Moodie closed the polls gave Murney the victory by a narrow margin. The sheriff, however, was loathe to report the incomplete results and was deeply upset when, after Murney signed a memorandum admitting 'that in consequence of the riots at the Election, it was impossible to take the sense of the County within the time allowed by law for polling votes,[30] it was wrestled away from John Ross by Adam Henry Meyers. Murney promised a copy to Baldwin the next day but, thinking better of it, decided to take the obvious advantage he had.

The results were many. Benson's petition against the sheriff was sent by government officials to the Home Office, and Moodie was soon after relieved of his position as returning officer.[31] For his part Baldwin thought better of contesting the ugly Hastings situation further, convinced that nothing worthwhile could be gained by continuing; moreover, he now realized that what was needed above all were improved and less confrontational regulations for the conducting of elections. Murney, however, did not have it all his way. Finding him in a conflict of interest in contesting an election while serving as a paid government employee, the government summarily stripped him of his comfortable income as clerk of the peace.

But perhaps the most lasting effect was on Moodie himself. He seems to have welcomed his removal from the eye of the storm. The vexatious treatment he had come to expect, particularly in the courts, did not cease, for the Belleville lawyers were a litigious lot and Moodie was a political and personal target for several of them. The Dougall fiasco over Moodie's sureties (Letter 43), instigated by a vengeful and hot-tempered A.H. Meyers, doubtless had its roots as much in the political arena as in Meyers's sense of betrayal at Moodie's hands. He had to live with such problems, as they were a part of his job as defined. Not one to accept the inevitable or the unfair, he fought back as best he could, using the courts when possible, currying favour such as he felt he had earned, and using his access to Baldwin to make suggestions, particularly about the ways in which the duties of a sheriff in Canada West might be effectively altered. This was the

Robert Baldwin

subject of serious debate throughout the decade, and Moodie, as he did in the matter of wild lands and secret societies, gave considerable thought to the issue.

It is difficult on the basis of these letters alone to measure the extent of the friendship between Moodie and Baldwin. Certainly they met with some frequency when Baldwin participated in the two elections. Moodie's great respect for him is evident in the letters; indeed, he seems to feel a confidence in reporting to him and in venturing suggestions and opinions, many of which Baldwin, with his concern for much larger issues, must have taken with a considerable grain of salt. But as comrades in a noble and heroic battle of principle, there must have been a strong sense of alliance between them, an alliance that extended from family and one in which the supportive 'war whoop' of a young son meant more than a convenient salutation.

1 *RIB*, 436. See also Carl Ballstadt, 'Secure in Conscious Worth: Susanna Moodie and the Rebellion of 1837,' *Canadian Poetry* 18 (Spring/Summer 1986), 88–98. Moodie's 'Mackenzie' poem appeared in the *Palladium* on 17 January 1838.
2 Audrey Morris, *Gentle Pioneers* (Toronto 1973), 171–2; and Betsy Dewar Boyce, *The Rebels of Hastings* (Toronto 1992), 126
3 Among the several issues affecting public opinion at this time was the growing temperance movement, which found strong opposition among the Orange order and many of the tory-conservatives. The Moodies supported temperance initiatives.
4 Morris, *Gentle Pioneers*, 177
5 *DCB*, 9:404–5
6 *DCB*, 10:631–3
7 *DCB*, 8:45–59
8 The response of the Belleville freeholders is printed in the *Upper Canada Herald*, 17 October 1843, appended to Robert Baldwin's letter in which he withdraws from the controversy surrounding the 1842 election and from future candidacy in the riding.
9 *A History of Odd-Fellowship in Canada under the Old Regime* (Brantford 1879), 12–13. This book is a reprint of the journals of the Grand Lodge from 1855 to 1875.
10 George E. Wilson, *The Life of Robert Baldwin: A Study in The Struggle for Responsible Government* (Toronto 1933), 101
11 *DCB*, 9:24–5
12 J.M.S. Careless, 'Robert Baldwin,' in *The Pre-Confederation Premiers: Ontario Government Leaders, 1841–1867* (Toronto 1980), 117
13 AO, William Wallbridge Papers, MS 93. In a letter to his sister (4 November 1841) William Wallbridge reported that Murney had spent £450 in losing the 1841 election.
14 The governor general's proclamation was reported in the *Upper Canada Herald* on 2 March 1841.
15 Issues of the *Upper Canada Herald* are missing from the microfilm for 9 March to 4 May 1841.
16 Morris, *Gentle Pioneers*, 195
17 *Ibid.*, 196. On 6 October 1840 Moodie sent a copy of the pamphlet *Proceedings of the Grand Lodge of British North America* (Toronto 1840) to Sir George Arthur 'for the information of His Excellency ... which I think it is my duty to communicate to the Governor General – being aware that His Excellency has expressed a desire to receive every information on this subject.'
18 *DCB*, 7:30–3
19 *DCB*, 12:321–3
20 *DCB*, 11:908–9
21 *DCB*, 10:109–10
22 *DCB*, 9:44–6
23 Sheldon and Judith Godfrey, *Burn This Gossip: The True Story of George Benjamin of Belleville, Canada's First Jewish Member of Parliament, 1857–1863* (Toronto 1991), 25–7
24 *Ibid.*, 50

25 Morris, *Gentle Pioneers*, 199
26 *Ibid.*, 191
27 *DCB*, 7:365–72
28 Morris, *Gentle Pioneers*, 191
29 Wilson, *Robert Baldwin*, 164
30 *Upper Canada Herald*, 15 Nov. 1842. The passage is italicized in the newspaper.
31 Morris, *Gentle Pioneers*, 199

37 John Moodie to Sir George Arthur

Belleville 28th May[1]

May it please Your Excellency,   *1840*

I herewith beg leave to inclose a few observations on the subject of Emigration etc.[2] in the sincere hope that you may find some of the suggestions I have ventured to submit to your consideration, of some practical utility. Should they prove so, Your Excellency may believe me, that I shall feel much more satisfaction than I could derive from any emolument arising from the Office Your Excellency has been pleased to confer on me. I have to thank Your Exc[y] for the kind feelings you have expressed to One so justly dear to myself; and I hope there is no egotism in my saying, that she is in every respect, truly worthy of your good opinion.

Though often brought to the verge of want, through unforeseen misfortunes, she has never ceased, even for a moment, to rely with confidence on a Merciful Providence which has so wonderfully befriended us in our greatest need.

Mrs. Moodie begs me to express her grateful sense of Your Excellency's Kindness in having so generously placed us in a situation of so much respectability and comfort.

I was very happy to learn from Your Excellency that I had been misinformed respecting Mr. Parker,[3] who I believe has no unfriendly feeling towards me.

With our united expressions of Gratitude and esteem –

I have the honor to be
Your Excellency's
Most Obedient &
Humble Servant
J.W. Dunbar Moodie

1 A handwritten note across the top of the first page reads: 'Answer, very much gratified. Many suggestions have been carried out.' Although dated 25 May and 28 May the letters were sent together.

2 Moodie enclosed a long letter on 'the state of the wild lands' in the new colony and how they might best be settled and developed. It is very similar in content to the letter he wrote to James Traill on 8 March 1836 (Letter 14).

3 According to Audrey Morris (*Gentle Pioneers*, 177), Moodie wrote Arthur in February in an effort to clear himself of derogatory remarks he believed Thomas Parker to have written to Arthur. The governor had replied: 'I am happy it is in my power to undeceive you – Mr. Parker has not made any communication of the kind directly or indirectly, of which I am aware' (*The Arthur Papers*, ed. Charles A. Sanderson [Toronto 1957–9], 2:437).

38 John Moodie to Samuel B. Harrison

Sheriffs Office
Belleville
Sir,   23rd Novr 1840

Having been informed that the Office of Registrar of the County of Hastings – (District of Victoria) is now vacant in consequence of the resignation of Mr. McLean,[1] – I hope you will excuse the liberty I take, – in requesting that you will have the kindness to call His Excellency the Lt Governor's attention to the application of Mr Ponton, the Clerk of Our District Court, – who is desirous of obtaining that Office, should it still be at his Excellency's disposal.

With the great esteem I entertain for Mr. Ponton's character – for moral integrity, strict honor and general correctness of conduct, – whatever weight His Excellency may attach to my recommendation, – I feel that I am only performing an act of duty in giving my humble testimony in favor of a gentleman, who I feel persuaded is in every way well qualified for the faithful discharge of the important duties of Registrar.

I trust that the terms which I use in speaking of Mr. Ponton will not be attributed merely to the partiality of friendship; – for independently of the interest I must necessarily feel for a person of his character, in a place where, – I am sorry to say, – highmindedness and integrity, – united with temperate habits, are so seldom to be found; – I also deeply feel the powerful influence, which the character and habits of such a man must have in raising the standard of morals amidst of vicious community.

> I have the honor to be
> Sir
> Your Most Obedient
> humble Servant
> *J.W. Dunbar Moodie*
> Sheriff, Victoria Dist[t]

1 It would seem that nothing was done about replacing Allan McLean in 1841, though he was in his late eighties. A lawyer who had been a founder of the Law Society of Upper Canada and who had served in the House of Assembly, he left the registry work in the hands of his son, Robert Charles. Whatever concerns there were in 1841, they had grown enormously by 1846, when the Victoria District Council petitioned for McLean's removal on the grounds that some three thousand documents were currently unregistered. McLean, then in his nineties, was dismissed. In his place George Benjamin was appointed over William Hutton by W.H. Draper. Interestingly, Benjamin himself 'forfeited the said office' in 1854 and was replaced by Moodie's friend, William Hamilton Ponton. See Godfrey and Godfrey, *Burn This Gossip*, 57–8.

---

39 John Moodie to Samuel B. Harrison

Private[1]   Belleville
                                              25 Octo[r], 1841

Sir,

It is with much reluctance I venture to address you, on my own account, – in the hope that should the office of Treasurer of this District, under the District Council Bill, be not already filled up; – you might be induced to use your influence with His Excellency in my favor.

Of course I could not for a moment expect, that you would recommend me for this appointment, should you concieve that there would be any inconsistency in my holding that office in Conjunction with my present one. At present I am hardly able to support my family with the most rigid economy: – and when the great responsibilities in pecuniary matters, attached to the Office of Sheriff, are duly considered, it seems only reasonable that the emoluments should be sufficient to cover any occasional loss, which, notwith-

standing the most careful circumspection, will sometimes occur.
The emoluments arising from my office have not only been greatly
reduced for some months back, in consequence of a considerable
decrease in the number of Suits, in the District Court; and from
several of the Attornies being in the habit of serving many of their
own *writs* and *notices* etc. – but I have always experienced the
greatest difficulty and delay in the payment of my accounts. My
office which certainly requires independence of mind, is thus rendered one of anxious dependence. After my long experience of the
toils and hardships of the back woods, you may readily suppose, my
desires as to *emolument* are of the most moderate description. I
merely desire to enjoy that degree of independence which I think
essential to the respectability of my office.

   Should you feel disposed to recommend me for the Treasurership,
I have no hesitation in saying that I have ample leisure to enable
me to attend to the duties of the office; – as my present duties seldom employ me more than two or three hours daily.

> With great respect
> I have the honor to be
> Sir
> Your Most Obedient
> humble Servant
> *J.W. Dunbar Moodie*
> Sheriff V.D.

1 Note in another hand at top of first page reads: 'Acknowledge, say offices incom-
  patible.'

---

40 John Moodie to Robert Baldwin

My Dear Sir,
Sheriff's Office – Belleville,
3rd Feby 1842

I have received your two letters the day before yesterday but have
not been able to write in reply till now.

   I have to thank you most sincerely for your kind intuition
respecting the 'Hustings' affair, which I am now sorry that I noticed
to you. The fact is, being rather sensitive on the subject, in conse-

quence of the manner in which I have generally been treated by the *Tories* here, – I took the refusal of the Magistrates to pay what I thought myself *legally* entitled to, as an *insult* which I had done nothing to deserve, – and I therefore continued to demand what I thought they had no right to withhold. As to the £2.10 – they are perfectly welcome to it, and I trust *you* will not be offended by the Sum being returned, as I cannot possibly recieve it in any manner but as a *right*. The Bill which the Bank call a forgery I recieved I believe from Mr Bouter the Innkeeper here, who tells me he recieved it from the Com¹ Bank at Kingston. On examining the Bill notwithstanding the high authority of the Bank, I cannot believe it to be a forgery, tho' it looks rather suspicious at first sight. No part of the Bill has been cut out, *secundem artem*, but the parts have been stuck over each other.

There has been a Meeting here a few nights ago, called by *Mr Benjamin* in the name of the Board of Police, at Young's Tavern, the house where the Orange Society meet for the purpose of Sending an Address to the Govʳ General. They fixed the night for the Meeting on the same night appointed for the annual Meeting of the Temperance Society. Great efforts were made and *successfully* to have a large majority of Tories. Ross and I intended at first to go to the Meeting but on after thoughts we considered it better to let them *show themselves* in their own way. The next day I was asked to sign the Address which of course, was exceedingly loyal. 'British Connexion' 'attachment to British Institutions,' and all the usual cant. There was one expression, however, which is perfectly understood by both parties, '*theoretical systems* of Government' or words to that effect, which his Excʸ is kindly advised to eschew, and to attend to the improvement of the country. The phrase w[as] cunningly introduced and many of the country[men] have been induced to sign the Address without [seeing] it. Davy was at the Meeting and objected to this mode of proceeding & Murney called him every thing but a rebel. The latter with your uncle & Benson went down yesterday with the Address. A requisition for a *District Meeting* will be handed to me in a day or two and I intend calling it for Saturday the 12ᵗʰ Insᵗ. I enclose a copy of the Address I have written for the occasion which I trust will be adopted.

Mrs Moodie is glad your children are pleased with the books and she will be delighted to hear from your dear Maria. So she must write without taking courage at all for Mʳˢ M. as you know is not so formidable a *blue* as many I have seen. Mʳˢ M. joins me in

kindest regards to yourself and them and believe me ever yours
Most Sincerely

J.W. Dunbar Moodie

---

41 John Moodie to Robert Baldwin

Belleville
My Dear Sir,   17th Feby 1842

On the other side you will find our proposed Address to His Exc^y
which I have altered in such a manner that I trust it will now meet
your views. I entirely concur in your observations in your last letter,
and feel greatly obliged by your frankness in stating your objections.
I would be the last person to compromise our claims by an incau-
tious admission, – but I have no doubt you will agree with me, that
the character and influence of the Reform party will greatly depend
on their *Moderation*, – particularly at the present moment, – and I
should be sorry to see anything introduced into any Address or
other document which might be interpreted into *grumbling* or still
less as pointing to changes inconsistent with the true principles of
the British Constitution. With these views I think temperance and
forebearance is our, true policy, for by pursuing this line of conduct
we shall array ourselves on the side of Good order and will thus
secure the good will and esteem of any Government or Governor,
whatever may be their politics: while the tories by pursuing their
present course of agitation and irritation must sink at last into a
discontented and disloyal action. I must now tell you how we got
along with our Meeting on Saturday last. The roads were bad and
the Reformers did not turn out as expected thinking that they
should meet with no opposition. The Meeting was called for 12
O Clock which was too early under the circumstances, so that
very few country people got in till 1 or 2 O Clock. The tories
with Murney at their head crowded up to the Court House about
20 minutes before the hour and insisted that the hour had arrived
producing three or four watchs in coroboration, which showed a
marvelous and *almost supernatural agreement*, – hardly to be
expected in Belleville watches, and in ordinary cases, you know that
tory watches go much *slower* than ours. It was intended that Our

Warden should adjourn the Council at 12 O Clock or as soon as the people should arrive, – unfortunately however he did so too soon and the tories having a large majority *at first* put Mr Hagerman J.P. into the chair with Mr Benjamin for Secretary. Mr Murney told me this was their intention just before the meeting when I assured him that we had no intention of getting up an Address of a party character. I suppose he considered me as insincere as himself, and anything like fairness or straight forwardness with him is out of the question. My Address was read by the Clerk and Murney moved his Address in Amendment. He objected to mine as a party one and with his usual low cunning attempted to misrepresent one part of it asserting that we told the Governor that we *did not* consider him as the Representative of Her Majesty. I immediately made him retract the falsehood which he did in the *lowest possible* voice amidst some cries of 'Shame.' The Address congratulated the Govr on the *change of ministry at home*, which would be the means of saving the Constitution of the Country there and here, or words to that effect. Before the Addresses were read I had spoken a few words, expressive of my anxiety that nothing of a party nature should be introduced and recommending unanimity. Mr Murney in reply sneered at the very idea of agreement between parties, and said that he knew but *two parties* one attached to British Institutions and the *other*, opposed to them and desiring a *seperation*. On a shew of hands being called for the Chairman gave it as his opinion and decided that the majority was for Murney's Address. This however was denied and he agreed at Murney's request that a division should take place. When this was done he could not decide, and at my request agreed that one of each party should be chosen to count the votes on each side. Dr Hope and Wallbridge were appointed by the Chairman for this purpose but finding that the Reformers were coming in pretty fast nothing was done and a riot was got up by the tories. Several people were pulled down who were standing on the tables and seats and the little Jew prudently crept under the table. Ponton was struck very violently without provocation by a person in Sidney and kicked. He however got a blow or two at the scoundrel and would have punished him to his heart's content had he been allowed. The Chairman in the mean time left the chair and was induced to sign Murney's Address though there was no doubt whatever that the majority *latterly* when he agreed to have the votes counted was for the other. When the disturbance had subsided, I was called to the chair by what appeared to be a majority but this being disputed on the other side and no appearance of an agreement, I adjourned the Meeting to Saturday next at 2 O'Clock. Murney has got 200 or 300 names to his Address, principally by trickery as they take especial care to shew the Address to as few as possible. We propose to embody the circumstances of the last Meeting in a number of resolutions to accompany the Address. The Warden and all the Counsellors sent an Address from themselves to the Governor which was much more of a Reform or party character than mine. It is not known whether Murney's Address will be sent by a deputation or by post but I suspect they are rather doubtful of the reception it may meet with. The Reformers are now *quite up* and I have no doubt there will be a large assemblage on Saturday. The tories keep all quiet but I suspect they are at work thro' their 'orange men.' I am determined as far as lies in my power to preserve the utmost moderation among our party and thus throw the other party into the shade. I firmly believe all things are working together for good for the tory violence and intollerance is certainly enough to disgust any Governor whig or tory.

Buel's Case[1] (the treasurer of the Johnston District) will show His Exc^y the true spirit of the party in pretty strong colours. I have now scribbled until my paper is nearly exhausted and I must therefore conclude. Mrs Moodie joins me in kindest regards to yourself and family. Donald often salutes our ears with his 'war whoop' 'Hurrah! for Baldwin.'

I have sent a Statement of the proceedings of the tories here to the Kingston Herald which you will see next N°. I suppose.

I remain
Yours Most Sincerely
J.W. Dunbar Moodie

P.S. I should have mentioned that two or three propositions were made by our party to appoint a Comt^{ee} of *two* of *each* party to adopt an Address which was rejected by Mr Murney – this will show his spirit – tho' I do not believe they would have agreed.

J.W.D.M.

1 The Buell controversy arose over accusations from tories that reformer Andrew Norton Buell had been an agent of William Lyon Mackenzie and a Patriot during the rebellion period, and was therefore unfit to hold the public office of treasurer

of Johnston District. The governor general refused to investigate the charges, and Buell served in that office from 1842 to 1847.

Address to Sir Charles Bagot[1]

To His Excellency Sir Charles Bagot
May it please Your Excellency

We the Inhabitants of the District of Victoria beg leave to approach Your Exc[y] with our sincere congratulations on your safe arrival in this Colony and on your assumption of the important duties of Your high Office.

It would be presumptuous in us to suggest the line of policy which we would desire Your Excellency to pursue in the administration of the Government of this Province.

We do not regard Your Excellency as the Representative of any party in the Mother Country: – but as the Representative of Our Gracious Sovereign; – commissioned to Govern this Colony in accordance with the well-understood principles of the British Constitution. The Inhabitants of this District have read with the most heartfelt satisfaction, Your Excellency's reply to the Address from the Inhabitants of the Gore District, and gratefully accept it as a pledge of that even handed justice and impartiality on the part of Your Exc[y] to all parties, without reference to past dissentions, which in the opinion of the present Meeting, is the true means of insuring the continued loyalty of the People and the future prosperity of the Province.

Deeply impressed with the conviction, that the interests of this Colony are identical with those of Great Britain, we cannot doubt that our *New Constitution*, – founded on those principles which alone can give efficiency to Representative Institutions, – must tend materially to strengthen the bonds of Attachment to the Mother Country: – and we beg leave to assure Your Exc[y] that we entertain no doubt, but that the wishes of the People as expressed through their Representatives, will meet with due attention from Your Excellency's Government.

With these views and feelings we sincerely trust that through the blessing of Divine Providence, Your Exc[y] may be enabled, by means of wise and just measures, to strengthen and confirm those sentiments of attachment to British Institutions, which we have ever cherished, as most conducive to the improvement and happiness of the People of this Province.

1 Sir Charles Bagot (1781–1843) was the first governor of the new unified colonies of Upper and Lower Canada from 1841 to 1843. This copy of the community's address is in Moodie's hand, enclosed with Letter 41 to Robert Baldwin.

42 John Moodie to Robert Baldwin

Belleville
My Dear Sir,   25th Feby 1842

My Dear Sir,   25th Feby 1842

I fear you have misunderstood my words respecting *Moderation*. I merely spoke of it to show you that I am anxious to be actuated by the same calm and forbearing spirit which, allow me to say, I have observed and admired in your own character and conduct, and which, I believe, most eminently fits you for a leader among those who believe they are contending for the *right*. I have no doubt that *your* character for Moderation and justice is not only duly estimated by your friends but also by your enemies. Hence the concentrated bitterness of their feelings towards you. It is bad enough for the Tories 'et *ho[c]* genus omni' to be thwarted by you, – but to think that you are *in the right also*, is almost too much for their gentle spirits to bear.

Our Meeting went off as might have been expected – or better. The people crowded into town and the Court Room was filled. The tories did not shew themselves, with the exception of two or three to watch the proceedings. The Address was adopted and the Warden[1] and myself with six farmers appointed to present it. I drew up two or three resolutions before the Meeting which were adopted with some additions and modifications. One of them reflected on the inflamatory language used by Murney at the last Meeting. The others on the irregularity of the said Meeting, &c. &c. The other party had sent down their Address by a deputation consisting of Hagerman, J.P. Appleby, J.P.[2] Wm Ketchison J.P.[3] and last but not least George Benjamin Esqr who I suppose acted as interpreter. They had not the honor of dining with his Exc^y. Mr Benjamin has opined a lot in fine style against me. The man wants tact. He ought not to shoot all his arrows at once. I hope he will not take it into his head to praise me. I could hardly stand *that*. I perceive he also abuses Mr Harrison in the same breath, by which I conclude that he has not met with as warm a reception as he expected.

Mrs Moodie was delighted with your daughter's letter, and trusts she will have the pleasure of becoming better acquainted with her. By the bye Mr Benson opened her letter by mistake thinking it was for himself. There was *no treason* however in it. Mrs M. unites with me in Kindest regards to Your father and Mother and all your family

> And believe me
> My Dear Sir
> Yours Most Sincerely
> *J.W. Dunbar Moodie*

P.S. Our friend Ponton has been disappointed in obtaining the office of Clerk of the Council tho' he had the majority of votes. It seems *Dougall* wrote down stating that he had a plurality of offices. He is Clerk of Dis^t Court with £90 per ann. and *Deputy* Clerk of the Crown which yields about £20 per ann. That scamp O'Reilly has been appointed Clerk of the Council.   J.W.D.M.

1 William Hutton (1801–61) was the warden.
2 Nathaniel Stephen Appleby (1820–91) was the influential tory reeve of Tyendinaga Township. After supporting George Benjamin for Warden of Hastings County in 1851, Appleby himself served as warden from 1857 to 1861.
3 Probably a son of Colonel William Ketcheson, an early settler in Thurlow Township

---

43 John Moodie to Samuel B. Harrison

Private   Sheriffs Office –
                                             Belleville
Sir,   18 April *1842*

It is with much reluctance that I send you the included *Statement*, which I am ready to verify upon oath, – and Mr Ross is ready to do the same as far as he is concerned in the matter. I had hoped that by a strict attention to my duties, and by patience under insults and injuries the attempts of my enemies in this place would have been frustrated: but though I am well aware that truth generally prevails *at last*, I am hardly able to contend with the low cunning and artful misrepresentations which have been so indefatigably employed against me from the time I was appointed to Shrievalty of this District. It is not my intention at present to trouble you with matters

which are long past: – but I shall at all times be most ready and
anxious to have my conduct subjected to the most rigid investigation on every point connected with my duties in the Office I hold. I
have been repeatedly informed, lately, that every means will be used
to get me deprived of my situation, and the request of my two
sureties to the District, Messrs Meyers and Hawley to be relieved
from their responsibility, and also the intimation lately given me by
my Deputy that he saw it was the intention of my enemies to ruin
me by bringing vexatious suits against me, – convince me that my
suspicions are not without foundation. In the present instance I
have been informed, that my enemies intend to avail themselves of
the circumstance of my sureties desiring to be relieved, to represent
my conduct to Government, as being of such a nature that they
were affraid to be any longer responsible for my acts; – and that I
could not find sufficient sureties. It is obvious, that being invested
by law with that power, – the Magistrates may easily give an appearance of truth to such a statement by pertinaciously refusing the
most unexceptionable sureties. To prevent any misrepresentation of
facts as to the *immediate* cause for my sureties desiring to be
relieved by me, – I shall state the circumstances. It appears that
M^r A H Meyers, one of my sureties, who is a Barrister, had some
years ago, purchased from a widow in the township of Sidney, her
life interest in a certain property, from which he ejected her son,
whose name is Reeves.[1] The consequence of the boundaries being
improperly described Reeves brought an action for trespass against
Mr Meyers and obtained heavy damages at one of the Assizes held
in this place. The case, however, was removed to be tried before the
Judges at Toronto. In the mean time Mr Meyers by purchasing notes
against Reeves had obtained an execution against his lands &c. The
writ was returnable on the 1st November 1841 but was not recieved
by me till the 20th Nov^r *184[1]*, so that I could not, *legally*, have
returned it till next Term (Easter) which commenced on 7th February
1842. The *lands* were advertised for sale on the 5th February 1842,
but the day before the sale should have taken place, Reeves called
on me, and begged that I would postpone the sale for a few days; –
giving as a reason, that his suit against Mr Meyers for trespass
would be decided during the Term, (Easter 1842) and, that in the
event of the said suit being given in his (Reeves') favor, – he could
easily raise the money, and thus prevent the property from falling
into Mr Meyers' hands. Under these peculiar circumstances I thought
it was my duty, in common humanity, to accede to his request;

though I well knew, from the knowledge I had acquired of Mr Meyers' character, – that I would become the object of his bitter animosity.

Lest I should commit myself with him in any way, I asked Mr Dougall's advice, and he advised me to postpone the sale to the 17th of February 1842; – the 19th Feby being the *last* of Easter Term. Mr Dougall told Mr Ross, who was employed by Reeves, that he had advised me to do so. On finding that I had postponed the sale Mr Meyers wrote me, that after the specimen I had given him of my good will towards him, he would not consent to remain any longer responsible for my acts; and requesting that I would find other sureties, as after stating the circumstances to Mr Hawley, – my other surety, – *he* also wished to be relieved.

I am now fully convinced, in my own mind, that the whole is a deep laid scheme to injure or ruin me. As to the sureties rejected by the Magistrates I have only to observe that Mr Reynolds[2] is generally believed to be the possessor of property or money to the amount of £5000 or £6000, and Mr Ross, besides the property he owns – which is considerable, has more business as a lawyer than any one in Belleville and has thus become the object of jealousy and hatred. I have been informed by one of the Magistrates, that Mr Davy, one of the other sureties offered, would also have been rejected on the same grounds that Mr Reynolds was objected to; – that of being engaged in mercantile business; – though he (Mr Davy) has been accepted as one of the sureties for the Treasurer of the District.

With respect to Mr Dougall: – he has publicly insulted me before several of the Magistrates of the District, and as I have no other means of redress, I think you will admit, that I have a right to claim the protection of Government.

Before concluding this communication, I beg leave to say, that the sureties offered by me to the District, are among the very best that can be obtained in the District, – and should the ones I have last offered be rejected, I must believe that the Magistrates can be actuated by no other feeling but that of violent party hostility.

I leave it to you to make such use of this communication as you may think proper and just to both parties, and

> I have the honor to be
> Sir
> Your Most Obedient
> Humble Servant
> *J W Dunbar Moodie*

1 Morris (*Gentle Pioneers*, 186–7) has a full discussion of the Isaac Reeves / Meyers case and its subsequent ramifications for Moodie.
2 Morris discusses the sureties matter in some detail (187–90).

Statement &c. &c.

On the 12th day of April 1842, the first day of the Quarter Sessions of the Peace for the District of Victoria, being desirous of giving new sureties to the said District, as Sheriff, in the place of Adam Henry Meyers and Sheldon Hawley Esquires, who desired to be relieved from their responsibility, – I presented to the chairman of the said Sessions, – Benjamin Dougall, Esquire, – a Bond in Duplicate duly executed and signed by myself and four sureties, to wit, by John Gilbert,[1] David Roblin,[2] Nelson Gilbert Reynolds, and John Ross, – which Bond was returned to me by the Chairman, stating that the magistrates would prefer a Bond from myself with two sureties only, which sureties the[y] wished should be David Roblin and John Gilbert, – two of the above named sureties already offered – and also stating that the Magistrates did not know anything of the circumstances of the above named Nelson Gilbert Reynolds and John Ross, the other two of the above named sureties, and from motives of delicacy did not wish to make enquiries respecting them. In consequence of this statement, I mentioned the matter to Mess[rs] Reynolds and Ross above named, and both of them requested me to state to Benjamin Dougall Esquire, the Chairman of the Quarter Sessions, their readiness to satisfy the Magistrates as to their eligibility as sureties for me as Sheriff. They also requested me to get a definite answer whether the Bond I offered would be accepted as sufficient or be rejected. On requesting a definite answer from M[r] Dougall on this head, he remarked that the only motive the Magistrates had in declining to recieve Mess[rs] Reynolds and Ross as sureties, was that they did not wish to be compelled to inquire into their circumstances, – which might be offensive to these Gentlemen. I then stated that the Gentlemen in question felt no delicacy *themselves*, on this point, and were ready, whenever they were called upon, to satisfy the Magistrates, that they were sufficient as sureties for a much larger amount. I also stated that Mess[rs] Reynolds and Ross felt hurt that their names should have been objected to: – on which M[r] Dougall remarked that they could only be influenced by party feeling. I replied that these Gentlemen had, at least, as good reason to suppose that the Magistrates were influenced by

party feeling in rejecting them as sureties, as it was well known that
Mr Reynolds, in particular, was one of the wealthiest inhabitants of
the District, or words to that effect. Mr Dougall then said, 'he did
not care what they thought.' Subsequently Mr Ross, one of the
above named Gentlemen and myself, spoke to Mr Dougall while
sitting on the Bench, when Mr Ross stated his readiness to make an
affidavit as to his property, and also stated that he owned property
in Brockville, which Mr Murney, the Clerk of the Peace then present well knew: and I also repeated Mr Reynolds expressions to the
same effect. On the meeting of the Sessions after an adjournment,
the Bond was returned to me by the Clerk of the Peace as insufficient: – without either Mr Ross or Mr Reynolds being called upon to
satisfy the Magistrates on the required points, – or any desire being
expressed by them that they wished to be satisfied as to their sufficiency. In consequence of this determination of the Magistrates
another Bond was prepared, with the names of John Reynolds[3] (the
father of the above named Nelson Gilbert Renolds, – who I was
informed would not be objected to) Caleb Gilbert,[4] David Roblin
and Benjamin Fairfield Davy as sureties, and the said Bond was
rejected in consequence of the omission of the name 'Davy' in one
of the Duplicates, – an error which Mr Dougall the Chairman of the
Sessions, stated could only be corrected in the presence of all the
paries to the Bond. I expressed my regret at the error, but before I
should take the trouble of having it corrected I begged that the
Magistrates would state, whether the persons I had given for
sureties would be accepted or not; – as they had already rejected
Messrs Reynolds and Ross as insufficient, without requiring them to
satisfy the Magistrates as to their circumstances. On this point the
Magistrates did not satisfy me, and showed no disposition to do so.
When I stated to Mr Dougall, the Chairman that I had told him that
Messrs Reynolds and Ross were willing and ready whenever an opportunity should be afforded them to satisfy the Magistrates as to
their sufficiency, Mr Dougall flatly denied my assertion, which I
repeated, and he denied it several times. I then told him, that not
only had *I* told him so – but that Mr Ross had also told him so in
my presence. Mr Dougall then stated that a very improper use had
been made of the facts already stated out of doors, which he had
heard from a person in whom he placed confidence. As these observations were evidently pointed at me, I told him whatever others
might have done, *I* had made no improper use of them, but had simply stated what he (Mr Dougall) had told me, to Messrs Reynolds and

Ross, respecting the request of the Magistrates to have the names of Messrs David Roblin and John Gilbert to the Bond without those of Messr^s Reynolds and Ross; – and I insisted that he would state what improper use I had made of the facts. Mr Dougall then said that I had accused the Magistrates *to him* of being influenced by party feeling. To this accusation I made no reply, not knowing what use might be made of my admission. The Sessions were then adjourned to the 14th of May, to afford me an opportunity of correcting the error, in consequence of which the Bond was refused. Still no information was given me, as to what names would be considered sufficient, and I left the Court under the strong impression, which I still feel, that no sureties, however unexceptionable will be deemed sufficient by the present Magistrates.

Belleville 18 April 1842.   *J W Dunbar Moodie*

1 John Gilbert (1801–76) of Sidney Township was a member of the first Hastings County Council (Gerald Boyce, *Historic Hastings* [Belleville 1976], 101]).
2 David Roblin (1812–63) was a lumber merchant and a reform politician. At the time this letter was written he was in an early stage of his political career, being the reeve of Richmond Township (*DCB*, 9:679–80).
3 John Reynolds, Father of Nelson Gilbert Reynolds, lived on the Trent Road three miles from Belleville. A Methodist circuit rider and founder of the Belleville Methodist Chapel, he later became bishop of the continuing Methodist Episcopal Church of Canada.
4 Caleb Gilbert (1800–72) of Sidney Township was John Gilbert's older brother. He married Adam Henry Meyers's daughter, Nancy, and eventually became reeve of Sidney in 1860.

---

44 John Moodie to Samuel B. Harrison

Belleville
Sir,   6th October *1842*

In consequence of the dangerous riots which have unfortunately taken place here, – I feel it to be my duty as Returning Officer to state, that I do not think it possible to Poll more than one half of the votes within the time allowed by the writ of Election. *Four* days of the six are now passed and only 410 votes have been polled not quite one third part of the number polled last Election, and I cannot state the probable number *now* under 1400. It is therefore obvious that the sense of the County cannot be fairly taken by the end of the week.

Under these circumstances I would therefore recommend that the period for holding this Election be extended to an indefinite time: – particularly as it is the obvious intention of one of the parties to create all the delay in their power by riotous manifestations and acts of violence.[1] One of the Magistrates of the District will send a communication which enter[s] more fully into details.

> I have the honor to be
> Sir
> Your Most ob^t
> humble Servant
> *J.W. Dunbar Moodie*
> Returning Officer & Sheriff

1 Appended to the letter is the reply, sent 7 October by special messenger, refusing to extend the election period because it could not legally be done.

---

45 John Moodie to Samuel B. Harrison

17th Oct 1842

By virtue of the annexed Writ to me directed, after having given due notice I proceeded to hold the Election for the within named County of *Hastings*, on Monday the third day of October instant, at the hour of ten o'clock, A.M.; but in consequence of the time occupied by the addresses of the two Candidates, several hours were lost before I could begin to take the votes of the Freeholders. About half an hour before the time fixed for opening the Poll on Tuesday, a collision took place between the two parties, which, is in consequence of the time occupied in swearing special Constables, delayed the opening of the Poll until nearly twelve o'clock. On Wednesday at three o'clock a general riot took place, which prevented further polling on that day, and I was under the necessity of adjourning the Poll until nine o'clock on Thursday morning. During this riot deadly weapons were used, endangering the lives of the freeholders, and towards the evening I felt it my duty to send a requisition for two Companies of Her Majesty's Regular Troops, which requisition was concurred in by all the Magistrates present, and in the meantime it was found necessary to call out a company of Militia, with such arms as they could obtain, to protect the property of the Inhabitants.

On Thursday, from the excited state of public feeling, it was obvious to all that it would be unsafe to proceed with the polling until the arrival of the Regular Troops, and at nine o'clock I adjourned the Poll until one o'clock, P.M., and at that hour, the troops not having arrived as expected, I again adjourned the Poll until four o'clock, P.M., at which hour the Troops arrived at the wharf, but it was nearly five o'clock before they could be brought on the ground. When preparing to proceed with the Poll, it was discovered that one of the parties had taken possession of the ground around the Husting and its entrances, when for the sake of preserving the peace, I made a proposal that each party should occupy half of the ground and of the enclosure in front of the Hustings, to which proposal the party in possession would not consent. So much time was occupied in endeavouring to effect some arrangement which would be fair to both parties, that it became too late to proceed with the Poll, which I accordingly adjourned to six o'clock on Friday morning, at which time the Poll was opened, and continued without adjournment until six o'clock, P.M., when there were evident symptoms of a riot, and I adjourned the Poll to six o'clock on Saturday morning.

At the hour of three o'clock, P.M., a memorandum was drawn up by the two Candidates, which was shown to me, distinctly admitting on both sides, that it had become wholly impossible to poll all the votes of the County within the time prescribed by law, and that therefore it was agreed between the parties that I should close the Poll at three o'clock, P.M., which was accordingly done. At the said hour of three o'clock, P.M., 915 votes only had been polled; while I have every reason to suppose that the whole number of votes, had there been sufficient time left for polling them, would have exceeded 1400 votes. From the above causes I have not been able to execute the annexed Writ as I am commanded; because I cannot consider the Candidate who had the greater number of votes at the said hour of three o'clock, as *freely and indifferently chosen*, according to the terms of the said Writ, and because the votes then taken were not sufficiently numerous, adequately to express the sense of the freeholders of the County.

At the time of closing the Poll, the numbers for each of the candidates stood as follows:

For *Edmund Murney*, Esq. 482
For the Honorable *Robert Baldwin* . . . . 433[1]

J.W. Dunbar Moodie,
Returning Officer

1 Following the Moodie letter in the *Legislative Assembly Journals*, 2:4, is a protest
  addressed to John Moodie, as returning officer for the County of Hastings, and
  signed by Robert Baldwin and several prominent Belleville citizens (Billa Flint, Jr,
  D.B. Sole, N.G. Reynolds, Lyman Dafoe). The protest endorses the returning
  officer's report of the riotous conduct at the hustings and requests him not to
  return Edmund Murney as duly elected, because the rioters had prevented Baldwin
  supporters from polling their votes. It is claimed that, had they been able to do so,
  Baldwin would have received a majority.

46 John Moodie to Robert Baldwin

Private   Belleville
                                                 6th Feby 1845
My Dear Sir,

Well knowing your kind feelings towards myself and your inclination when forming a part of the Ministry to do what you thought
just and consistent with the *Public good, for Sheriffs*, I am anxious
to call your attention to *one point* in the new Bill for enlarging the
jurisdiction of the District Courts. I percieve in the printed draught
of the Bill that, as formerly, writs only are required to be served by
'a *literate person*,' still leaving the Sheriffs at the mercy of the
Attorneys, who all seem to think it quite fair to avail themselves of
this omission when from party hostility or private enmity they wish
to injure the Sheriff. A year or two ago I was complaining of the
great loss I had suffered in consequence of this circumstance to our
friend Ross, – but he very cooly told me that the Attorneys were
quite right to act as they did, as the *law* did not prevent them from
doing so. As I told him at the time, – I think this may be *law*, – but
it is indifferent morality; as the *writs being directed* to the Sheriff,
the *law* evidently supposes that he serves them. For some time back
I have carefully abstained from taking any part whatever in politics
and did not even vote at the last election. While I still feel as
strongly as I always did towards the great principle of Responsible

Government and to those who have so nobly sacrificed office in defence of it: – still I cannot, after the selfish indifference I have experienced on the part of some of the leading Reformers here, and the base treachery of others of them who have been eagerly watching an opportunity to supplant me and step into my office – feel myself called on to ruin myself to please them. I have no doubt my conduct will be misrepresented to you on this head, but at the age of nearly 50 with a large family entirely dependant on the paltry office I hold for bread, and unable to cloth them as well as respectable mechanics can do – I think you can hardly blame me if I endeavour *at last* to take some care of myself. By employing a Tory bailiff to serve writs for the Tory Attorneys, and a *Reform* Bailiff to do the work for the Reform Attorneys I manage to escape vexatious and ruinous suits from both sides *on the Bailiffs account* not *mine*, – not entirely, indeed, but in a great measure. Still a great part of the services (as in Declarations, Notices, &c.) are still put past me as before, and lately a new device has been resorted to by the Tories, that of getting a *Bankrupt* to bring an action against me for not taking a person on a Capias. I employ an Attorney (Ross) to defend the suit, I gain it and shall have the pleasure of paying more than £26.0.0 for costs as the Plaintiff (Thomas Parker) *has nothing* though he holds the office of Inspector of Flour &c. under Gov^t. Surely, the law requires reform in this particular. Before a lawyer takes up a suit of this kind he should be required to get security from the Plaintiff for the costs in case he should lose it. I believe it is so in the U. States. I formerly mentioned to you the miserable condition in which Sheriffs are kept in consequence of the difficulty of collecting their fees from the attorneys when they are due. With me here, this is quite systematic on the part of the Tories. Could *nothing* be done for us in this respect? I formerly suggested to you that the Sheriffs should have the service of Summons &c. in *the Small Debt Court*, I mean of the *No. 1* or *principal* Division. This would give them some *ready money* and considerably increase their income in the *Small Districts* – for I suppose in the larger Districts the Sheriffs would not care to be troubled with it, – without taking anything from the people. It is often extremely inconvenient at present when going to levy on property to find that it is already in the hands of the Bailiff of the Small Debt Court. At present, besides, *these* Bailiffs make a general practice of buying goods at their own sales thro' the intervention of some coadjutor, – and there are a number of other abuses practised which could hardly take place were the business in the hands of the Sheriff whose responsibility would be so much greater. Should you approve of any of these suggestions I trust you will bear them in mind, for if they are *just in themselves* I cannot believe that even the Tories would offer any opposition to them. I have lately been informed that expecting that the Tory Ministry will turn me out, – the Baron de Rottenburg has been making interest with some leading person in the *liberal* interest at Quebec to be appointed in my place hoping to please both parties. I can hardly believe the story but shall ask him. I think it must be one of his father in laws Dr Ridley's schemes. Mrs M. joins me in affectionate rememberance and remain Yours Most Sincerely

J.W. Dunbar Moodie

---

47 John Moodie to Robert Baldwin

Private   Belleville
                                            15th February 1845

My Dear Sir,

I have just recieved your very kind letter of the 11th & 12th Inst. and most gratefully thank you for the feelings you express towards me and my family, – none of my children have forgotten you, – but still speak of you with great affection. Friends are *scarce* in *these* times, and we cannot afford to lose any. Perhaps Ross may have told you, – for I would not while you were in Office – that we have a Robert Baldwin.[1] My poor Johnny,[2] whose melancholy fate even our enemies felt, when the Chief Justice[3] called upon us during the Assizes here, overhearing some remarks we were making as to the effect *that dreaded name* might produce on his *conservative nerves*, on being asked the name of the baby, slyly replied, 'we *sometimes* call him *Robert*.' Notwithstanding your kind intentions respecting me, I sincerely rejoice as a friend to my adopted country and as a loyal subject to the land of our fathers, that you did resign, *when* you did. No honest or independant man could do less, – *posterity* at all events, will do you justice, – and I *still* trust your successors, unless they belong to that rather numerous class of Conservatives, whose only principle is 'to get all they can' and to keep it as long as possible. Such seed as you have sown must grow *a little*, even though it may have fallen on stony ground, and if the Reformers neglect to water it, – let them reap the *thistles* which is not bad food for *Asses*. I think it only just that *the Districts*, particularly the *smaller* ones, should aid in Supporting their Sheriffs, and if any means could be found of regulating an annual salary to be allowed them, which should be *inversely* in proportion to the population of the District or amount of business done in the Office, – it would be very desirable even on public grounds. I have thought a good deal on this subject, endeavouring to divest myself of any bias arising from personal interest, and I can think of no way, liable to so few objections of combining the interest of the Public with that of Sheriffs as by securing to them the service of writs in the *No I Division* of the *Small Debt Courts*. I know that in *this* District there has been a great deal of petty roguery and *shaving*, as it is called, practised by the Bailiffs, which would certainly be less likely to occur under the Sheriffs whose responsibilities are so much greater. When I first came here there were usually 18 or 20 causes tried at each of the Sessions of the District Court, *now* however, with more suing, there is rarely more than one or two causes tried. On referring to my books, I find that from the 23rd March to 22nd June 1844 – 3 months – *23 Summonses* were entered in the District Court, – while from 22 June 1844 to 9 Novr 1844 – about 4 1/2 months only *16* summonses were entered – about *one half less* in two consecutive Terms. This is without counting *capiases & cases* which have disappeared altogether or nearly so. The fact is, that the *Small Debt Courts by the practice of dividing notes* into 2 or more sums, is taking all the business of the District Courts. The effects of this, when the jurisdiction of the Dis^t Court is increased, whatever advantage the Public will derive from it – will be ruinous to Sheriffs. The natural and *just* remedy for this is to give them the service of summonses &c. in the *chief Division* of the Small Debt Courts, and this can be done without mixing up the Sheriff's other business with the Division Courts as he would merely have to keep a separate set of books.

You ask me what amount I would consider a reasonable remuneration for the duties of *my* Shrievalty? Before endeavouring to answer this question I should state that the amount of my income from all sources *including the charges against the District* for serving Juries &c. by my last annual Return to gov^t which was carefully made up from my books, – was about £200 but large deductions must be made from this sum for losses & I think £150 would not be much under the mark.

This is my *clear income* after paying my Bailiffs who recieve *one half* of the fees of services made by them, and on *the supposition* that my accounts are regularly paid by the Attorneys, which is never the case, – and several of their accounts are *never* paid. I consider that with an income of £100 a year on a farm and hiring labourers to work it I should be more independant than with £200 a year in a town, and were I *regularly paid* half yearly or quarterly, for the services performed in the Office I should save at least 25 per cent in the expense of living by having ready money to pay for what I wanted for my family. *As it is*, with a certain salary of £100 per annum paid regularly in addition to the fees of the Office, – or say £300 per Ann. *in all*, I could with due economy live respectably and feel tolerably independent, – no more. Before burdening the public, *however*, with the support of Sheriffs it seems to me most disgraceful, that so reasonable a request as that of having the service of all process secured to Sheriffs should be refused. Though I have not acted up to the principle on all occasions, I think a Sheriff should of all others keep clear of *party politics* in practice, whatever he may think, and to do his duty properly he should be quite independent in *his circumstances*: – but this system of leaving his remuneration at the mercy of the attorneys is discreditable to the profession and can only be prompted by some base or selfish motive – and is only calculated to make him the slave of the strongest party. I cannot help thinking that in most of the Districts if the Service of *all* law papers in the BR & DC were secured to Sheriffs and their regular payment also insured (by requiring payment to be made before a return of the writ could be required) the public would have but little to pay for their support. *£300* per annum, I think should be the *minimum* salary of Sheriffs & equal to about £250 *without their risks*.

I trust that in the New Dist' Court Bill the Sheriff's fees will be nearly equalized to those of the Queen's Bench, as most debts being between £40 & £50 little business will be left for them in the latter *Court*.

M⁷ˢ Moodie and my children desire to be most affectionately remembered to you &

> Believe me
> My Dear Sir
> Yours Most Sincerely &
> respectfully
> *J.W. Dunbar Moodie*

1 Robert Baldwin Moodie was born 8 July 1843.

2 John Strickland Moodie, age five, had drowned in the Moira River on 18 June 1844.

3 John Beverley Robinson (*DCB*, 9: 668–79)

---

48 John Moodie to James Hopkirk

Sheriff's Office
Belleville
21st August 1845

Sir,

It is with reluctance, all other means of obtaining my right from the party in question having failed; – that I am compelled to lay the following Statement before you, for the purpose of being communicated to His Excellency the Governor General, in the hope that he will be pleased to exert the influence,[1] which as Head of the Government he possesses over every individual holding office under him in this Colony – in order that I may obtain a sum of money which is justly due to me by the Officer alluded to. The facts of the case are simply as follow: – Some time ago Mr Thomas Parker of Belleville, who holds the Office of Inspector of Potashes – which Office I am informed by my attorney yields him about £250 per annum – brought an action against me as Sheriff of the Victoria District for not taking a person named Walter Todd[2] under a writ of *Capias ad Satisfaciendum*. Mr Parker's attorney was defeated in his pleadings and he relinquished his suit which never went to trial. The Costs of my Defence, which should be paid by Mr Parker now amount in all to the sum of £27.3.10 including the costs of an execution against his goods and chattels. This Execution was returned by the Coroner '*no goods*' and it appears that the whole of the goods and chattels and lands of Mr Parker are in the hands of the Honble Peter McGill,[3] as I have been informed by M^r McCutcheon the agent of the latter Gentleman. Under these circumstances, it might be said that I should take out a *Capias ad Satisfaciendum*, against Mr Parker, – but the total inutility of such a proceeding is at once apparent from the fact that Mr Parker holds an office which necessarily confines him constantly within '*The Limits*' of the town. Before laying the matter before His Excellency I directed the Bailiff employed by the Coroner to inform Mr Parker how I intended to proceed if he did not pay the amount of the execution, but without producing any effect but the simple reply that 'I might do as I liked.'

One of the greatest hardships attending the Office of Sheriff, is that he is constantly liable to actions of this kind, on the part of individuals, who despairing of obtaining anything from the proper Debtor, hope to render that officer liable for the debt, which he would be, could any neglect on his part be proved. I have no hesitation in declaring my firm belief that the present case is one of that description, – with the further aggravation, as I am affected, that Mr Parker the Prosecutor has nothing to lose.

In making this statement I have no intention of saying anything to injure Mr Parker, who I have every reason to believe performs the duties of his Office in a zealous and efficient manner: – But holding an office of far inferior emolument in every respect and involving the most painful responsibility, I indulge the hope that His Excellency will be pleased to think my case one in which his interference would be just and proper.[4]

I have the honor to be
Sir
Your Most Obedient
humble Servant
J.W. Dunbar Moodie
Sheriff Victoria District

1 Sir Charles Metcalfe (1785–1846), the second governor general of the united colonies, was about leave office in 1845 (*DCB*, 7:603–8).
2 See Morris, *Gentle Pioneers*, 202.
3 Peter McGill (1789–1860) was born Peter McCutcheon but inherited a wealthy uncle's estate in 1821 on condition that he change his name to McGill. He had emigrated from Scotland in 1809 and from 1827 to 1830 owned and improved the Marmora Iron Works. It is conceivable that the Mr McCutcheon mentioned here is one of his brothers, though they are not named in the entry (8:540–4).
4 The attached reply to Moodie's petition turns down his request for the governor general's interference in the case.

---

49 John Moodie to Robert Baldwin

Private   Belleville
                                             4th May 1848

My Dear Sir,

I have just learned from Mr Reynolds that in a letter of your's, to him, you mentioned that there is a vacancy in the Office of Registrar in one of the Counties in the neighbourhood of Niagara, which M^r R says, you stated to be worth from £200 to £250 per ann.

I can only say, that I should most gladly accept such an appointment, and shall feel ever most grateful for your kindness if you can bestow it on me.

In such case, I should of course, send in my resignation of my present Office as soon as my appointment is made known to me. I only fear, that being but little acquainted with the inhabitants of that neighbourhood I might have some difficulty in obtaining the sureties required by the statute, as I am aware of the *objection* to *strangers* in this country. Mr Reynolds says that Drummondville is the place where the Registrar's office is held. If so, I am not entirely unknown to the people there having resided there and at Chippewa for several months with the militia reg^t under Col. Kingsmill, and where I believe my temperate habits procured me some degree of respect by a comparison with some other officers of our Corps, who were by no means distinguished by their temperance or consideration for the feelings of the quiet inhabitants. Mrs Moodie and my daughters desire to be most affectionately remembered to you, and believe me ever your's most sincerely and gratefully

J.W. Dunbar Moodie

---

50 John Moodie to Robert Baldwin

	Belleville
My Dear Sir,	5th May 1848

Since writing to you yesterday, I have seen Mr Ross, who informs me that you stated the probable income of the Office of Registrar of the County of Welland at £200 per ann. And that he (Mr Ross) thought from the improvement of the surrounding country that it was likely to improve. I think I stated in my letter that I was informed by Mr Reynolds that the income was from £200 to £250. I now trouble you with another letter to prevent misapprehension and to state *decidedly* that if *you* think it worth £200 per ann. *now*, and likely to improve I shall most gladly and gratefully accept the appointment. I consider £200 as about sufficient to support my family respectably. Of course I cannot leave this place without a considerable sacrifice of property, as though I have a valuable property, as I have many debts principally arising out of my Office. I am anxious to secure something like a small certainty and relief from overwhelming anxiety. Knowing how particular you are in your statements in these matters, Mr Ross advised me to write you again today. I should have liked to have seen your letter or that part of it which related to me as you must be aware that I must feel some anxiety about a matter of so much importance to me and mine, – particularly as I am aware that several persons will be desirous of obtaining the Shrievalty here, – which *should be* profitable.

I remain
My Dear Sir
Your's most sincerely
J.W. Dunbar Moodie

---

51 John Moodie to Robert Baldwin

Private   Belleville 17th June
                                            1848

My Dear Sir,

I recieved your kind letter of the 9th June a few days ago, and I assure you I feel much less disappointed regarding the Office referred to, than regret that the matter should have caused you a moment's pain on my account. Feeling assured that you will not forget me when any favorable opportunity arrives, I shall not blame *you*, if it should be out of your power to serve me in this respect, – for I can well understand the difficulty of your position in these matters, – and I am well aware of the number and importunity of applicants for various offices. The office I now hold *should be* a good one if the practitioners of the law here would treat me with common justice and humanity. I do not believe it is *the same* in all places. I went down to Kingston two or three days with a prisoner for the Penitentiary taking a number of accounts with me against the Lawyers there, intending simply to go through the usual formality of *presenting* them. Every one of them with *one triffling exception*, payed me at once in the most gentlemanly manner, hardly looking at the accounts. This is the second time I have been treated in this manner *in Kingston*. I am sorry that I wrote you about the office in Niagara Dis^t, but the matter was pressed upon me in such an urgent manner by Mr Reynolds that contrary to my own inclination I thought I was bound to write you at once as he told me that you said the office would be kept open only a few days – as there were several anxious applicants. It was not Mr Ross, but Mr Reynolds who first mentioned the matter to me, and I think it necessary that you should know the whole truth in order to excuse *myself* for prematurely troubling you on the occasion. Reynolds came into my office one morning and informed me that he had the day before recieved a letter from you on some *law business* of his in the conclusion of which letter you requested him to mention the office which had become vacant, *to me*, and begging that *I* would write immediately to say whether I would accept the appointment which you stated could only be kept open a few days as there was an anxious applicant for the office who resided near the spot. I told Mr Reynolds that I thought it odd *you* had not written to me yourself about the matter. What particularly raised a doubt in my mind as to his sincerity, – was that he very kindly suggested the kind of terms I should use in writing you on the subject, – *in which all allusion to your letter to Reynolds was carefully avoided* though you had requested him to ask me if I would accept the office, which he further said you stated to be worth (I think) from £250 to £300 a year.

I determined not to write you until I saw the part of your letter to Reynolds referring to this matter, and Reynolds went down with me to Mr Ross' office with whom, he said, he had left the letter. He soon came out of Ross' office and told me Mr Ross informed him that his brother James Ross had sent the letter off to their Agent in Toronto. In a few minutes afterwards I met James Ross and on asking him about the letter he utterly denied all knowledge of it or having sent any such letter to Toronto. I then went to Mr John Ross who gave no satisfaction about the letter, but told me of a conversation he had with you respecting the office in which you stated it to be worth what I mentioned in my letter to you. But for Mr Ross' urgent request that I should apply for the office at once I should not then have written you until I should have seen *your own handwriting*. The whole matter, from my intimate knowledge of the character of the men, seems very plain to me. They have got up a little intrigue to gain their own objects, – founded on your kind feelings and intentions regarding me. They evidently wished me to apply for the Office in question blindfolded, – and thus having shipped me off, Mr Reynolds would have applied *for my Office*. I suspected *this* when Reynolds first mentioned the matter to me – from his circuitous and foxy manner, and told I supposed he would get my office. He did not deny it after a while and *wished me to suggest it to you. I said nothing.* As far as *I am individually* concerned I care little who succeeds me, but though I am habitually unsuspicious it is impossible that I could be decieved by such shallow arts. In future I shall pay no attention whatever to such indirect or pretended communications but shall trust that you will write me a few lines yourself on any matter of this kind. I shall always tell you what *I believe* to be the plain truth, and you may put implicit confidence in my secrecy in any matter by which *you* might be compromised in any manner.

You will, I know, be pleased to learn that I have got a verdict in my favor in a second trial at the Assizes here (Eccles vs Moodie and Barry).[1] This was a cruel action brought against me *in particular*, as the other party had no property. The action was for *'false imprisonment'* and the *real parties* concerned were Def^t Barry & Mr John Ross his attorny, I was intended to be *the victim*.

The whole matter arose out of this: – that James Ross in John Ross' absence put *a Discharge* in a slit in my office door while I was absent, and some time afterwards *gave a new Capias* to my Deputy against the same party (Eccles). They contended that I had recieved the Discharge before I got the new writ.

On the *former* trial which went against me Mr Henderson[2] the p^ffs Att^y employed his father in law Mr P. O'Reilly as Coroner, and he would have summoned the same jurors again for the new trial if he had been allowed. I merely mention this matter to suggest the advisability of requiring Coroners either to give security as well as *Sheriffs* and *Magistrates*, or at least to be possessed of property. M^r O'Reilly you will remember was the worthy who assisted Dougall in packing a jury on a former occasion. Of the two though he escaped dismissal, he was certainly by far the most guilty by his double treachery. M^r O'R has gone to reside at Kingston I understand, so this District will be rid of him. This is the *second* if not the *third* suit against me I have gained, – in which I must pay the costs of the Defence as the plaintiff has nothing.

In a former case *Mr Thomas Parker*, who holds the office of Inspector of Potashes – brought an action against me in which he *was beaten*, but I had to pay more than £30 for the costs of the

Defence to Mr Ross though it never went to trial. I applied to the *then Gov^t* requesting that Mr Parker might be *directed* to pay the amount of my execution against him as he held an office which could well enable him to do so, though his goods were conveyed into other hands, – but the Gov^t would not interfere.

I know there is some difference of opinion as to whether it would be just in all cases for the law to require security to be given for the costs in such cases but I think it would be just that *public officers* who are so much more open to this kind of persecution should be protected by requiring surity to be given for the costs of the defense of actions brought against them.

Mrs Moodie and my children including the *'Young Crusader'* who is a prodigious pet, – send their most affectionate regards to you and believe me

> My Dear Sir
> Your's Ever Most Sincerely
> and Respectfully
> *J.W. Dunbar Moodie*

1 Morris (*Gentle Pioneers*, 190–1) discusses the Eccles vs. Barry case, which resulted in Dougall being forced to step down from the bench and a severe reprimand for O'Reilly.

2 G.E. Henderson was O'Reilly's son-in-law and partner in their law firm.

---

52 John Moodie to Robert Baldwin

Private   Belleville
                                            8th October 1848

My Dear Sir,

On returning from a journey to the 'Backwoods' Mrs Moodie handed me your kind note of 26 Septr respecting the Office of Inspector in this place. I have again to return you my best thanks for your kind attention to my wishes & I have long considered the matter before making up my mind on the subject.

As I formerly stated I should certainly prefer a small income without much risk or anxiety to a larger one *with both*, – provided that income was sufficient to support my family. On the whole I think it will be more prudent to hold on to my present office until something better may turn up, when I have no doubt you will not forget me. Thank God I have as yet escaped most of the snares of my enemies and I shall continue to endeavor to do what is right and thus to merit the continuance of that protection which we all require. If, however, any office should become vacant which would afford an income of £200, £250 or £300 per ann. without the risk of my present office I should consider it imprudent to refuse it – if offered to me. Were I to follow my own individual inclinations I should not like to hold an *inferior* office, – but on account of my *family* I should prefer security to honor.

I trust you may be enabled to fulfil your promise of visiting the *ladies* here before long, and I may add, without flattery, to rejoice the hearts of those among the men who love and honor you & I Remain

> My Dear Sir
> Your's ever most sincerely
> *J.W. Dunbar Moodie*

53 John Moodie to Robert Baldwin

Private   Belleville 25th August
                                                      1849

My Dear Sir,

The Trustees for the Grammar School of this District have lately recieved a letter from the Secretary's Office, stating that the sum of £112.10.0 has been apportioned by Government to the Victoria District for the Current year, from the 'Grammar School Fund' under the 4th & 5th Victoria chap.19 and requesting the said Trustees (of whom I am one) to report as to the best means of distributing the same. Now it so happens that instead of *five* members of the Board, there are at present *only four* of us, and as we shall probably be equally divided as to the appropriation of this sum, it becomes very desirable that a fifth Member should be added to the Board of Trustees. The names of the Trustees are:

The Revd John Reynolds
The Revd Michael Brennan[1]
Dr George N. Ridley

J.W. Dunbar Moodie
      &
The Rev^d – *James Ketchan* the *fifth* member who has left the Province. Allow me to suggest that the name of Dr William Hope be added to our number, as a person likely to be useful in such a situation from his general knowledge of the Inhabitants of the District.

> I remain
> My Dear Sir
> Your's ever very Sincerely
> *J.W. Dunbar Moodie*

1 Since 1829 Michael Brennan had been the Catholic priest in Belleville. Susanna refers to him (*LC*, 13–14) when he offers the Moodies his home after their first fire there.

1850–1860

'These mysterious sciences'

THE CONTROVERSY IN POLITICS that characterized Belleville life and so often affected the public role of John Moodie had its parallel in other family pursuits. Susanna encountered it in the literary arena and showed, as she had in the rebellion days, her own fighting spirit. Her letter of 1 March 1851 to John Lovell, for example, recalls her long and prominent role as a contributor to the *Literary Garland* and reveals her sensitivity to the public reception of her work.[1]

In February 1851 Susanna's sketch of 'Michael Macbride' first appeared in the *Garland*. It tells the story of a poor Irish emigrant who dies in peace after his wish to have the Protestant Bible read to him on his deathbed is granted. In other words, it hints strongly at Macbride's deathbed conversion from Catholicism to Protestantism. On 21 February 1851 the Montreal *True Witness and Catholic Chronicle* attacked Susanna as follows:

No doubt Mrs. Moodie is a good Bible Christian, and may probably find consolation herself in reading the sacred volume; but we tell her that if it were read over from end to end to a dying Catholic – one trained in the Church of Christ – it would afford him small comfort, unless he could at the same time confess his sins to Christ's minister, who has received the power of loosening and binding here on earth ... For shame! Bible-reading authoress! – how could you get an unfortunate scape-grace who had been a Catholic, to believe that your reading of some select chapters could supply to his soul these tremendous wants?

In her defence (Letter 54) Susanna focuses on the accusation of racism, not on religious controversy, citing her treatment of other Irish characters in her writing, such as the servants Jenny Buchanan and John Monaghan, whom she depicted in other sketches published in the *Garland*,[2] and noting her promotion of Irish authors. Her sense that she is the victim of criticism based on contemporary mores, which differ from those at the time of composition, is a familiar dilemma: 'The sketch was written years ago, without a thought that it could give offence to any party. Nor would it now, have done so; had it not appeared at this unfortunate crisis, when Catholics and Protestants stand in strong opposition to each other.' The 'unfortunate crisis' that precipitated the criticism is probably the 'papal aggression' of September 1850 when Pope Pius IX appointed Nicholas Wiseman archbishop of Westminster and metropolitan of the Roman Catholic Church in England. The appointment was seen as a hostile attempt on the part of the Roman Catholic hierarchy in Rome to regain power in Britain.[3] The ensuing uproar in the British Parliament and anti-Catholic reaction in the British press occasioned much comment in the British North American provinces. Susanna concludes her apology by promising, in future, to leave the examination of the Irish character to Charles James Lever (1806–72), who by 1851 had revealed himself as a somewhat dilettantish Irish-born novelist. A brief visit to Canada in 1829 had resulted in his anonymous publication in 1849 of the novel *Con-Cregan, the Irish Gil Blas: His Confessions and Experiences*, a picaresque tale of Irish immigrant life in Quebec.

If Letter 54 shows the continuation of controversy, in many respects it also marks the beginning of a new phase in the Moodies' lives. Although Susanna notes that she is sending yet another tale for publication in the *Garland*, undoubtedly 'Noah Cotton: A Tale of Conscience' (September–December 1851), the magazine was in financial difficulty and the December 1851 issue was in fact its last.[4] Perhaps anticipating the demise of her major literary outlet, Susanna had been preparing an account of her life in Canada, some of which had appeared in the *Garland* as 'Canadian Sketches,' for submission to a publisher. That work, *Roughing It in the Bush*, may already have been sent, for 'Michael Macbride' was a part of that submission. Subsequently she requested John Bruce, her London literary agent, to suppress it 'on account of the Catholics, who considered that story as written against them, although in every particular, *it was strictly true*' (*LOL*, 124).

The story of the publication and success of *Roughing It in the Bush* and the degree to which Susanna's literary career prospered internationally has been told in *Letters of a Lifetime* and in the Carleton edition of her famous book. The former contains her rich correspondence to her publisher, Richard Bentley, keeping him abreast of her literary interests and her family's affairs and movements.

The current collection enlarges our knowledge of the changes and new interests of the Moodie family in the 1850s. The oldest Moodie children, Catherine and Agnes, married and began to raise the first grandchildren. On 21 August 1850 Agnes Dunbar Moodie (b. 1833) married Charles Thomas Fitzgibbon. The young couple settled down in Toronto, where Charles practised law and became registrar of the court of probate. The Moodies' first grandchild, Mary Agnes (Maime), was born on 18 June 1851. Evidently John took Susanna, recovering from an illness, to visit Agnes and the baby in September 1852 and returned alone to prepare for the fall assizes. Letter 55 gives an interesting comparison of the two available modes of transportation from

Masthead of the *Spiritual Telegraph*

Toronto – steamboat from Toronto to Kingston, followed by a short voyage to Belleville in the *George Frederick*, or steamboat to Cobourg completed by a long stagecoach ride – and looks forward to even better transportation with the planned Grand Trunk Railroad between Toronto and Montreal, with a proposed link to Peterborough. He also records the expansion of Hastings County, requiring increased representation for the newly annexed areas.

Apart from Susanna's literary successes the most remarkable development in the Moodies' lives during the decade was in the private sphere of their 'spiritual investigations,' a detailed record of which was kept by John Moodie in a large album. Ultimately, many of those investigations were made public by him in the form of letters to the editor and publisher of the New York *Spiritual Telegraph*, Charles Partridge.

This facet of the Moodies' lives is partially revealed in some of Susanna's letters to Richard Bentley, published in *Letters of a Lifetime*. It is also hinted at in many of Susanna's works,[5] but the astonishing extent of their fascination with spiritualism only became apparent with the discovery of the 'Spiritualist Album' and the examination of copies of the *Spiritual Telegraph*. The newspaper was published in eight volumes from 1852 to 1860, but extant issues of it are very rare and fragile. More readily available is a nine-volume series of selections, from the parent publication, called *The Telegraph Papers 1853–7*, edited by S.B. Brittan, but these contain none of Moodie's submissions. His contributions apparently began with the 'Letter to Professor Gregory' on 1 May 1858; it is possible that other items were published after 9 July 1859 in volume 8, but a complete run of that volume has not been located. Copies of the successor to the *Spiritual Telegraph*, the *Herald of Progress*, have been examined, but they contain nothing by either of the Moodies.

Exactly when the Moodies began their spiritual investigations is not known. John, at least, had begun his experiments before the summer of 1855, when, at his expressed wish, they were visited by Kate Fox, 'the celebrated Spirit Rapper,' on one of her return visits to her Belleville area relatives (*LOL*, 157). In the letter of 22 June 1857 to Professor William Gregory, which is included in his communication of 2 December 1857 to the editor of the *Spiritual Telegraph*, he notes that the table-tapping sessions with Mrs Davy began 'about three years ago,' which would mean that the sessions were as early as 1854.

The 'Spiritualist Album' itself commences his record-keeping with the letter to Gregory, extending from pages 1 to 46, and that portion of the album is duplicated almost fully in the 'Record of Spiritual Investigations' published in the *Spiritual Telegraph* in May 1858. Gregory, a professor of chemistry at the University of Edinburgh, had written a book entitled *Letters to a Candid Enquirer, on Animal Magnetism* (London: Taylor, Watters and Maberly; Edinburgh: Maclachlan and Stewart 1851). The work consists of nineteen letters, the first fourteen inquiring into numerous related parapsychological issues including sympathy, clairvoyance, prevision, mesmerism, phrenology, thought-reading, and visions. The second part, letters 15–19, offers a consideration of facts and cases. John Moodie's letter was prompted by this book as well as by a more recent letter by Gregory to Mr Brittan, probably published in the *Spiritual Telegraph*. Brittan was Partridge's partner in the newspaper, at least until 1857, and in several other spiritualist ventures.

The sheer bulk and length of John's 'Spiritualist Album' indicates how important the spiritualist experiment was to the Moodies as an expression of religious conviction, as a social activity, and as a means to self-examination and self-justification. Moodie's index to the album indicates that pages 47 to 236 contained entries for more than two hundred sessions dated from 30 June 1857 to 19 June 1863. Not all of these pages are extant because his eldest daughter, Catherine Vickers, removed pages 182 to 235. Her written explanation for doing so, dated 2 April 1871, indicates that those pages contained 'communications

Agnes (Moodie) Chamberlain

written by my sister Agnes Dunbar Moodie ... relating to private family matters, advice regarding Father's office difficulties' as well as 'Homeopathic medical prescriptions & all of which my dear Father lived to see the fallacy of.' She further indicates that she cut the pages for the sake of all family members because, in her view, the 'censures ... of one alone' should not stand.[6]

Catherine's sensitivity concerning some of the content is one reason for republishing most of the material that appeared as letters to the editor of the *Spiritual Telegraph*; it is autobiographical writing and hence of importance to a fuller understanding of the Moodies' works as well as their lives and times. Regrettably, it has not been deemed feasible to reprint all of John Moodie's submissions. On 29 May and 19 June 1858 the *Spiritual Telegraph* carried additional long entries. Although they are called continuations of the record published on the 1st, 8th, and 15th of May, they are clearly not part of the letter to Professor Gregory, nor are they expressly addressed to Charles Partridge as succeeding pieces are. Their album entry dates are 24 June 1857 and 23 January 1858, and the second piece carries a closing date of 7 June 1858, presumably the day it was sent to Partridge.

As noted at the end of the 15 May item in the *Spiritual Telegraph*, these entries mostly concern Susanna's communications with the Anglo-Saxon spirit who was born in London in 1025 A.D. They begin, however, with reports of the development of Agnes Fitzgibbon as a writing medium and of some strange events at the Moodie home while John and Susanna were vacationing in Portland, Maine, that 'almost, if not altogether' convince Donald Moodie, their second son, of the 'truth of spiritualism.' The communications of the eleventh-century spirit that follow Donald's report are directed to overcoming the doubts of Susanna. She is questioned and admonished:

February 4, 1858. *Mrs. M.* – What can I say more to convince you of the truth of Spiritualism? When time shall have further developed your understanding, I will speak to you again ...

February 13, 1858. *Mrs. M.* – At a wonderful manifestation of Spirit-power, you are astonished. Why not at the words that Spirits spell out to you at this Board? Your own want of faith casts a shadow on the brow of truth. Believe, and the darkness will disappear and be lost in the effulgence of spiritual light, which flow from glorified intelligences into your soul, as the uprising sun dispels the gloom of the darkest night. How long will my instructions fall upon a closed ear, alike deaf to the voice of wisdom and truth. Arise, for the light now shines which must lead your Spirit to the endless day ...

These passages are characteristic of the style of such communications. It is an aphoristic and metaphorical wisdom literature, repeatedly invoking the abstract watchwords – truth, faith, and eternity, as well as their opposites – and offering numerous variations on the metaphorical possibilities of light and darkness, harmony and discord. The themes are not many. God is perfection, and it is man's proper condition to move towards that perfection, though he may never attain it, by struggling against the bondage of evil spirits, the snares of animal, worldly pleasures, and the limitations of reason. And yet, it is right to take delight in the works of God in his creation, because 'there is no waste in the divine economy. He gathers up the fragments so that nothing is lost, but renews them in other forms to suit his own purpose.' Not surprisingly, these themes are often found articulated in Susanna's earlier works, such as *Enthusiasm* (1831), or sections of *Roughing It in the Bush*, as well as in works by her husband or by her sister, Catharine Parr Traill.[7]

Such religious themes reverberating through the records show that for the Moodies spiritualism was an expression of religious belief. That is why John's poem 'Religion – a Fragment,' first published in the *Literary Garland* (March 1840), was sent to the *Spiritual Telegraph* and published there on 4 September 1858. It too develops the theme that contemplation of nature leads to God.[8] But his history of spiritualism in 'Spiritualism and Its Teachings' (Letter 61) most clearly sets out their conception of it as a new Reformation, 'a great instrument ordained by God to harmonize the human race' (25 June 1859), prepared for by such prophets as Emanuel Swedenborg (1688–1722), Friederich Anton Mesmer (1734–1815), and Prince Hohenlohe (1787–1841). For Susanna it was a triumph of faith, but for John it was the attainment of a new level of human reason and a victory over sectarianism and superstition as each individual could realize a spirit-power.

Because of this belief that spiritualism indicated progress in human development, John, in yet another letter to the *Spiritual Telegraph* (14 May 1859), disagreed with the author of *The Apocatastasis; or, Progress Backwards: A New 'Tract for the Times'*.[9] The letter, essentially a review of the book, reiterates points made by John in other contributions, and is, therefore, omitted from this book. The author of *The Apocatastasis* endeavours to discredit spiritualism as 'The New Dispensation,' seeing it as yet another infidelity 'nibbling at the heal of Christianity, like its thousand and one equally boastful predecessors and allies to be crushed in its turn' (202). His claim that the Bible says all that could or need be said about spiritual communion is, clearly, rejected by John Moodie.

In three more contributions Moodie dealt with the antecedents of spiritualism in yet another way, but these too have been omitted from this collection, largely because both form and content make them rather tangential to a volume of letters. On 24 July 1858 the paper carried a poem by J.W.D. Moodie, 'Brodir's Fleet in Clontarf Bay.' The poem, which had first appeared in the *Victoria Magazine* in December 1847, is Moodie's rendition of an episode from the Icelandic 'Niala Saga' that has as its subject strange visions and premonitions experienced by Brodir and created by the 'magic arts' of Ospac, who is about to forsake his pagan gods and become a Christian. The poem anticipates the publication of two prose pieces by John entitled 'Spiritualism among the Norsemen.' The first, 'Brian's Battle (Battle of Clontarf), A.D. 1014,' appeared on 7 May 1859, and the second, 'St. Kevin's Apples,' on 11 June 1859. They are 'translations from the Icelandic historians' that, in Moodie's view, reveal numerous incidents of clairvoyance and miracle healing. The rather disjointed narratives are interspersed with his brief commentaries, drawing attention to their value as examples of spirit communication that complement those contained in the Bible. The conclusion to 'Brian's Battle' suitably reflects his purpose in these submissions:

Every reasonable man will, I think, believe the purely historical portions of the Old Testament, as he will similar portions of the Norse histories, for the very same reason that they are both natural and probable. As to the miraculous, he will believe as much as can be confirmed in kind, if not in degree, by the facts of modern Spiritualism. Little do the jealous and narrow-minded Churchmen, and Christians generally, of the present day, know what a powerful support is afforded to the 'miracles' of the Bible by modern 'Spiritualism.' The proofs derived from the modern miracles are of a kind which can not be gainsaid. They appeal to the senses; and the inference is obvious, that if such things are done now, why may not similar and still more stupendous 'miracles' have been performed under the requisite conditions in former times.

Excepting the omissions cited above, all other available letters by Moodie to the editor of the *Spiritual Telegraph* are included in this collection. In addition to their expression of the Moodies' themes and interests, they have value as a reflection of social activity both in Belleville and elsewhere. They indicate frequent sessions with families in the community, such as those of the first Belleville mayor, Benjamin Davy, and the Moodies' neighbour, J.W. Tait, a civil engineer with the Grand Trunk Railway, or Frederick Rous, a member of the Society of Friends; and, indeed, with one of the famous Fox sisters, as well as members of their own family.

In addition, the records provide details of the Moodies' lives that are not available in any other source. One need only cite the account contained in the letter to Gregory of the manner in which their third son, 'Johny,' died in the Moira River, or of the premonition of that death as told in the curious pre-Freudian letter on dreams that was published on 11 September 1858. Such messages from family members and from deceased friends seem to have provided consolation for losses sustained long ago or justification for actions taken by the medium or others present. In still other communications, more immediate tribulations were addressed. Repeatedly in the 1850s Moodie's shrievalty was subject to the harassments of his enemies, and it was in this context that charges such as the following from 'Johny' were especially meaningful: 'Tell my dear father that I love him, and am ever at his side trying to overthrow the evil influence of bad men, who presumptuously deny the divinity of my Lord.'

It was a consequence of the harassments of his enemies that John was in Toronto on 16 December 1860, the date of Letter 62. He was awaiting a hearing of his appeal of the verdict handed down at the Belleville assizes in December 1859 that he was guilty of the 'farming of offices' in his capacity as sheriff (*LOL*, 121–2). As the letter indicates, the occasion offered an opportunity for him to affirm his belief in spiritualism by his assertion that 'the spirit' of his old friend Thomas Pringle '*was* in court at the time though invisible to mortal eyes.' Pringle's spirit was invoked by John because of their shared opposition to slavery. Moodie's own hearing was delayed by the trial of John Anderson, and he watched the proceedings with great interest. While attempting to flee his slavery in Missouri, Anderson had stabbed and killed a man who was attempting to arrest him. He escaped to Canada and was eventually arrested in Brantford, Ontario. At issue in the trial was whether or not Anderson ought to be extradited to the United States to be tried as a murderer. The case extended through many months and phases, drawing widespread legal, journalistic, and public debate and eventually bringing about British interference in colonial legal affairs. Ultimately, Anderson was freed and left Canada for England.[10] The sequel to John Moodie's own hearing was not so favourable; there were no miraculous, spiritual interventions or cures.

1 In this letter the subject is a professional matter, but it is important to remember that Susanna and Lovell also maintained a long and warm personal contact. Lovell's publication of John's *Scenes and Adventures, as a Soldier and Settler* in 1866, which occasioned the only extant photographic portrait of John Moodie and the shocking last photograph of Susanna at age sixty-three (see *LOL*, 86, 258), taken by the celebrated Montreal photographer William Notman during the Moodies' visit to Lovell's home in Montreal in November 1866, no doubt came about as a result of this sustained professional and personal relationship as literary compatriots in a pragmatic, new world. For more information about Lovell see *DCB*, 12:569–74.

2 'The Walk to Dummer' (March 1847) and 'Uncle Joe and His Family' (Aug. and Sept. 1847)

3 See Desmond Bowen, *The Protestant Crusade in Ireland, 1800–70* (Montreal 1978), 231–2; and J.M.S. Careless, *The Union of the Canadas: The Growth of Canadian Institutions, 1841–1857* (Toronto 1967), 177.

4 The undermining of the *Garland*'s patronage by the infiltration of cheaper American periodicals was the subject of the editorial for December 1850. Susanna was to write about the demise of the *Garland* in her introduction to *Mark Hurdlestone*.

5 See Carl Ballstadt, Elizabeth Hopkins, and Michael Peterman, 'A Glorious Madness,' *Journal of Canadian Studies* 17 (Winter 1982–3), 88–100. Susanna often, apparently, proclaimed scepticism of spiritual experience. Hence, it is additionally interesting that in the tale of 'Noah Cotton,' to which Susanna refers in her letter to John Lovell, Susanna describes an experience very similar to that of Alice

Crane, as reported in the excerpt from her letter that appeared in the *Spiritual Telegraph* on 31 July 1858. The passage from 'Noah Cotton' is: 'And, lo! in the black darkness of that dreary room, she thought she saw a bright shining light. It spread and brightened, and flowed all around her like the purest moonlight, and in the centre she beheld a female form, smiling and beautiful, which advanced and laid a soft hand upon her shoulder, and whispered in a tone of ineffable sweetness ...' (*Literary Garland*, 9 Oct. 1851, 447).

6 The 'Spiritualist Album' is a bound manuscript in PHEC.

7 The title poem of *Enthusiasm* dismisses all human enthusiasms except devotion to God, although it allows for one's delight in the natural world because of the meditation that it inspires. In *Roughing It in the Bush* Susanna writes on the theme of human spiritual progress in a style that closely parallels that of the 'Anglo-Saxon spirit': 'Man still remains a half-reclaimed savage; the leaven of Christianity is slowly and surely working its way, but it has not yet changed the whole lump, or transformed the deformed into the beauteous child of God. Oh, for that glorious day! It is coming. The dark clouds of humanity are already tinged with the golden radiance of the dawn, but the sun of righteousness has not yet arisen upon the world with healing on his wings; the light of truth still struggles in the womb of darkness, and man stumbles on to the fulfilment of his sublime and mysterious destiny' (*RIB*, 494).

Catharine addresses the theme that 'something gathers up the fragments' in such essays as 'A Glance within the Forest,' published in *Canadian Monthly and National Review*, 6:48–53, as well as in several pieces in *Pearls and Pebbles* (Toronto: Briggs 1894).

8 The poem stands apart from any letter and has been omitted from this collection.

9 *The Apocatastasis* (Burlington: Chauncey Goodrich 1854) is attributed by the British Library to Leonard Marsh, a professor of theology at the University of Vermont. It is, as John notes, a seemingly very learned monograph.

10 See Patrick Brode, *The Odyssey of John Anderson* (Toronto 1989).

---

54 Susanna Moodie to John Lovell

My Dear Sir,

Belleville
March 1, – 1851.

I received by yesterday's mail, two copies of the Montreal True Witness, and I hasten to write to you, to assure you of my unfeigned regret, that any article of mine, should have drawn upon you, the illiberal threat, with which that paper, is pleased to close its remarks upon me. As far as *I am* concerned – neither the review in the Transcript, nor that in the True Witness gives me the least uneasiness. The deathbed scene of Michael Macbride is strictly true – for the subsequent portion of the narrative, I was indebted to a person whose veracity I never heard doubted –

The sketch was written years ago, without a thought that it could give offence to any party. Nor would it now, have done so; had it not appeared at this unfortunate crisis, when Catholics and Protestants stand in strong opposition to each other. The Sketch, was transmitted to you, as you well know, long before the papal aggression had taken place.

I do not lack protestant friends who would defend me against the attacks of these Catholic papers, did I think their observations worthy of notice but in all religious contests, both parties suffer because the two great essentials to *real* Christianity *charity* and *mutual forbearance* are often lost sight of in the heat of argument. If these two papers think that they have atchieved [*sic*] a great victory they are perfectly welcome to enjoy it.

The True Witness, however, accuses me of *hatred to the Irish*, because in one of my stories – One, out of a very many – I happened to make several Irishmen bad characters. Surely it is very absurd, to accuse an author of such a crime as hatred to a large class on this score – ? If I have drawn one or two bad characters from Ireland, my own Country has fared still worse. Oh, barbarous, and unpatriotic Mrs Moodie! how came you not to believe in the perfectability of the English character, when you dared to draw portraits of such wretches, as Robert Moncton and his son, of Geoffrey Hurdlestone and his accomplice William Mathews, and style them Englishmen. *Whisperers* – I have always understood to be synonimous with *Backbiters* – and these same whisperers to the *True Witness* – have certainly borne false witness against me. Is Jenny Buchannan, a bad Irish character – Or John Monaghan – ? Both these persons lived for years in my husband's employ. Aye, and loved us well, English and Scotch though we be –

In common justice, these same whisperers to the *True Witness*, should have set the good Irish characters drawn by Mrs Moodie against the bad. But the *True Witness*, or wolf in lambs' clothing, had another object in view when he held me up to the public as a hater of the Irish. This assertion could be refuted by Irish Catholics who have lived in our service and by those who still live in it, who have ever received kindness from our hands. Who imagines Lever to be an enemy to his country. Yet had Mrs Moodie drawn such a picture of the Irish, in the Lower town of Quebec, as he has done, in his Con-Cregan, I suppose, that my home stead would long ere this, have been burnt over my head. Yet, I never heard the fidelity of the picture questioned –

I do not allow myself to indulge in National prejudices. A good man belongs to the world at large. His influence is not confined to his own country, and his precepts and example form a standard for the conduct of mankind. So, a true Christian belongs to the church of Christ, by whatever name he may be known on earth, whether as Catholic or protestant, and will only be acknowledged as such here-after, by his love, and the likeness he bears to his divine Master.

But I have said enough upon this subject, and I again repeat, that in your account alone, do I feel the least regret at this Catholic cru-sade against me. If, as a body they are capable of the meanness of persecuting you on my account, they are not worthy of the respect with which I have hitherto regarded them.

Let us hope, that Miss Murray's beautiful story, and Michael Ryan's fine poems,[1] will open a new era for the Garland of fame and emolument. These two persons in whose success I feel the deepest interest are both Irish, and one – will the True Witness give me credit for the assertion – A *poor Catholic* –! Mrs Moodie where is your consistency – Are you a good hater? –

Now my dear friend if you dare venture upon publishing any thing of mine in the Garland after this Newspaper Tirade against me, I assure you that the characters in my next tale, good and bad, are all English and protestant. I will leave Lever to do justice to the Irish in future –

Let me hear from you at your leisure and do with this letter what you please. I enclose one from Miss Murray, and will write a notice of her fine tale when it appears for some of our papers. Mr Moodie unites with me in compliments and best good wishes, to yourself and Mrs. Cushing,[2] and believe me dear Sir,

Ever Yours Most Faithfully
Susanna Moodie

My friends here, think highly of Michael Macbride – so we have the for – as well as the against.

1 Louisa May Murray, a new contributor to the *Literary Garland*, whose story 'Fauna; or, The Flower of Leafy Hollow' appeared in 1851 (see *LOL*, 80, 99–100). Michael Ryan's poetry appeared in the *Literary Garland* in March, July, and August of 1851.
2 Elizabeth L. Cushing, a Montreal contributor, became editor of the *Literary Gar-land*, succeeding John Gibson in 1850, during its last year of publication. See *LOL*, 81, 96, and *DCB*, 11: 321–2.

55 John Moodie to Susanna Moodie

Belleville
My Dearest Old Woman   3rd October 1852

I would have written you long ago but you know how busy I have
been. I recieved your letter of the 26th September on my return from
summon[ing] the Jury for the Assizes last Thursday evening. I got
through my journey much sooner than I expected and the roads
were not so much injured by the rains as might be supposed. I am
rejoiced to hear that you feel so much better. I believe all you
require now is *strength*, and I have no doubt the shower baths[1] will
do you good service. *I* have felt much better since I have used
[them] having been less troubled with bile. On the wharf at Toronto
I met our friend Colonel Crutchley.[2] He did not remember me at
first when I spoke to him, an[d I] should not have remembered him
but for Char[ ]. The reason is obvious. We are both several years
older than we were. He has lost much of the freshness of youth. He
introduced me to a very pretty and elegant looking woman, a Mrs
Pears, a sister of Mrs Crutchley. My time in the boat of course
passed very pleasantly. Had I been a few years *younger* and *single* I
think I should hav[e] fallen in love with her for she is a very sweet
creature. She is one of the Misses Harris of London C.W. She is
decidedly the handsomest *Canadian* I have seen. I got to Kingston
about 6 O'clock and went up the Bay by the 'George Frederick'
which leaves Kingston for Belleville every *Wed*n and Saturday Morning. I think you would like this mode of travelling better than going
to Cobourg and taking the stage from thence. However, you must
please yourself. If you start on Tuesday the day you recieve this you
would get to Kingston in time for the 'George Frederick' on Wednesday morning. But I suppose you will not get my letter from the Post
Office until it is too late to start. In that case you will have to wait
until Friday following. Telegraph me and I or Donald will meet you
at Kingston. I am glad you saw the 'Fair.'[3] The articles you describe
I saw both at Kingston and Brockville. I am sorry poor Ruttan had
to leave his Stoves.[4] I suppose he must have heard of the annexation
of the Trent village to my County which I know he regarded with
pious horror and only inferior in attrocity to the partition of Poland.
The Proclamation is out in the Gazette and I am ordered to hold the
first election for Councellors there on the 3rd of January next. The

annexation of the township of Murray must soon follow. Ruttan
will lose more in the shape of mileage (36 miles from Cobourg) than
I will gain by the change. I find that the Season is so late that I
cannot put in 'wheat in the land with any chance of a crop.' I am
advised to plow it, however, and put in Barley in the Spring. Perhaps
you have heard that the Rail Road business is all Settled. The front
line to Toronto is fixed with [a] loop from Belleville to Peterborough
and thence on to the main line near Toronto. Poor Katie's arms are
better but they have annoyed her very much since we left. What an
amusing creature Mrs Dewe's is. She would kill me outright, she is
such a lively absurd creature. I have no doubt she keeps *Jack busy*
in one way or other.

I gave Mrs Mary a blowing up this morning for allowing the cats
to take every thing off the table after breakfast, and she was very
saucy and told me she would leave in the morning. I told her she
might go when she liked as I had borne her impudence long enough.
She is becoming quite intolerable and I think she will be no great
loss.

It is getting dark, and I have a shock[ing] bad pen, so must conclude abruptly.

Give my love to my dearest Aggie and the sweetest of babies, kiss
them both for me.

I remain My dearest Susie

Your's every affectionately
J.W. Dunbar Moodie

P.S. I forgot to say that the furniture came safe is fixed up and looks
first rate. I wish you could get a box for holding music of a good
size to stand in the drawing room and bring it with you.

JWDM

Charlie, (who is sound asleep on the sofa) sends love
Katie (reading) do do
Donald & Rob (up stairs) do do

P.S. I have bought a stove for the sitting room. It is one like that at
the 'Falls' 2 feet long and it looks very handsome. It cost £4. It saves
a great deal of wood as being self acting the damper or draft hole
closes as the heat increases. The shape is oval and it is made of Rus-
sian sheet iron all except the top and bottom and the inner sheet
iron can be replaced when it is used up. JWDM

1 Hydrotherapy, or water cure, was a popular medical technique at the time; its principal proponent was Dr R.T. Trall, who edited the *Water Cure Journal* from 1849 to 1861. That publication and many others by Trall were based on the principle that all curative power is resident in the living organism and that all remedial agents can do is to provide favourable conditions for the exercise of that power. Trall and his school did not believe in the administration of drugs.

2 Lieutenant Colonel Crutchley, formerly of the 23rd British Fusiliers, had married Eliza Bayfield of London, Ontario.

3 See *LC*, 229–39.

4 Henry Ruttan (1792–1871) was in business in Cobourg from 1815, elected to the House of Assembly in 1820, and was sheriff of the Newcastle District from 1827 to 1857. He designed air heaters and ventilation systems which were widely used. His son, Henry, carried on the business and was also editor of the Cobourg *Star* from 1846 to 1855 (*DCB*, 10:636–7).

---

56 John Moodie to Sir Edmund Walker Head

Belleville
30 Ap^r 1855

His Excellency, Sir Edmund Walker Head, Baronet[1]
Governor General of British North America, etc. etc. etc.

The Petition of John Wedderburn Dunbar Moodie of the town of Belleville in the County of Hastings Sheriff of said County –
Humbly Sheweth,

That your Petitioner in 1833 being then a Settler in the backwoods of Upper Canada purchased a *Clergy Reserve* lot viz. *No. 20 in the 6th* Concession of Douro from Mr. Ephraim Sanford, a merchant in Peterborough U.C. (since deceased) who had purchased the same at the Government sale in Peterborough in Sep^t 1833.

In fulfillment of the agreement made with Mr Sanford, as shown in the accompanying document, (No 1) Your Petitioner afterwards repaid him the instalments paid by him on the day of sale as appears by Document No. 2 inclosed herewith and afterwards the sum of £100 in cash (his receipt for which sum has been lost or destroyed by fire) being a sum far exceeding the intrinsic value of the land in question but which Petitioner was induced to give in consequence of the very limited extent of his military Grant of land adjoining thereto.

That subsequently, your Petitioner paid at the Crown Lands Office in Toronto the Second instalment on the said Clergy Reserve in the name of Mr Sanford whose name still remains on the lot as the original purchaser thereof. That Your Petitioner from various losses after wards became unable to pay any of the remaining instalments until the accumulated instalments with interest had put it out of his power to redeem the land in question.

Your Petitioner further begs leave to state that he built a large frame barn and cleared some 8 or 10 acres on said lot so that your Petitioner has expended the following sums (at the least) on said lot,

Cash paid to Mr Sanford	£100.0.0
2 Instalments to Govt.	20.0.0
(without counting interest)	
Cost of Barn in cash	50.0.0
Paid for Clearing by contract	30.0.0
Making a sum of	£200.0.0

which will be utterly lost to your Petitioner if the lot should be sold to another.

As the lot is now liable to be forfeited to Government in consequence of the non-fulfillment of the conditions of sale – Your Petitioner therefore *prays* that Your Excellency will be pleased to authorize the *re-sale* of the said lot to your Petitioner on as easy terms of payment as Your Excellency may, under the circumstances of the case, deem right and proper, and Your Petitioner as in duty bound will ever pray,[2]

J.W. Dunbar Moodie

1 Sir Edmund Walker Head (1805–68) served as governor general of the Canadas from 1854 to 1861 (*DCB*, 9:381–6).
2 'A committee of council on 2 August 1855 found in favour of Moodie's petition and offered the land to him at 10s per acre, because, according to the surveyor, Thomas J. Dennaby, the land had been plundered of its white pine and was worth no more than that' (note appended to letter).

57 John Moodie to Charles Partridge

Belleville, U. CANADA,
December 2, 1857.

TO THE EDITOR OF THE SPIRITUAL TELEGRAPH:

Sir: On the 22d of June, 1857, I addressed the following letter to Professor Gregory of Edinburgh, Scotland, but up to the present moment have not received in reply, even a simple acknowledgement of the receipt of my letter. I carefully posted and postpaid the packet, and I can therefore hardly doubt that it reached its destination. Still, though personally unknown to Dr. Gregory, I can not bring myself to believe that he could be wanting in the common courtesy usually observed in such matters. I therefore conclude that my communication must have been mislaid or overlooked by him, in the midst of other matters of a more pressing, if not more interesting, nature. Attracted by the noble and truly philosophical candor of his character, I was desirous of furnishing him with a simple, unvarnished statement of my experience in 'Spiritualism,' with my own observations on the subject. I am well aware of the very limited opportunities I have enjoyed in British America of witnessing many of the higher and more startling manifestations of 'Spirit-power,' but I thought that a communication, coming from one who had been but little 'mixed up' with Spiritualists, might have had a good effect in drawing attention to the subject.

In order to give a full account of my experience in Spiritualism generally with media but imperfectly developed, it is necessary that I should go into a few details, which I trust you and your readers will not consider altogether unimportant, if they tend in any degree to place the manifestation in a true light. I do not hold myself in any degree responsible for the incongruities and contradictions that occasionally manifest themselves in spiritual communications, still less for what may be called *false* communications. I give them just as I received them, and when in any of them opinions are given on certain commonly received religious dogmas or doctrines, I leave the reader to take the same course as I do myself – to accept or reject the statements of the Spirits, in accordance with the dictates of his own judgment. As no being, be he 'Spirit' or man in this world, is perfect, so the graduations from man in his highest developments in this world up to the greater Creator himself, must be infinite. Therefore, none but God himself is infallible.

In the following copy of my letter to Professor Gregory, I have omitted many details which would not possess any particular novelty in this continent:

LETTER TO PROFESSOR GREGORY
BELLEVILLE, U. CANADA, June 22, 1857

Dear Sir: My only motive for venturing to address you, is the deep-

ly-engrossing interest attached to the subject of this communication: the Modern Spiritual Manifestations. I can well remember the
time when the subjects of 'Animal Magnetism,' 'Mesmerism,' and
'Clairvoyance,' to say nothing of 'Phrenology,' were held in unmiti-
gated contempt by all who had any pretensions to science. These
days have gone by; and it now begins to be perceived that, strange
as these things are, they are not the less true – because with our
limited capacities, we are unable to comprehend them. There is
obviously a point, to which human reason, in tracing back the chain
of causes of natural phenomena, can reach, and no farther. Our
knowledge may be compared to a beautiful structure. We can
describe every part of the superstructure, but we can tell but little
of our solid foundation upon which the whole edifice rests. Every
science must have a solid foundation of this kind, and it is worse
than useless to quote great names and scientific theories against
what the common sense of mankind, founded on the evidence of the
senses, is compelled to recognize as *facts*. A number of these facts I
propose to submit to you in this letter; and not professing to possess
more than a very limited amount of scientific knowledge, I am
anxious to communicate the fruits of my own limited experience, in
order to contribute in some degree to the formation of a rational and
intelligible theory of the manifestations.

Though the facts given by you in your letters on 'Animal Magnetism,' may, very possibly, weaken the position I have been compelled to take, as to the origin of the spiritual manifestations, I
must candidly admit the strong analogy that is observable between
the two sets of facts; and I can not help thinking that this similarity
is attributable to a *common origin*. When we first heard of the 'Fox
Girls,' and the 'Rochester Knockings' in 1848, the thing appeared so
utterly ridiculous and puerile, that I only looked upon it as a
money-making scheme. Afterward, however, I heard accounts from
several intelligent persons who had visited the 'Fox Family,' which
induced me to modify my first opinion; as I could not believe that
any such skillful mechanical contrivances could be devised by inex-
perienced girls, or rather, children, as any imposture of this kind
would require. Even admitting the mechanical skill, where or how
they could obtain the extraordinary 'intelligence' on matters only
known to their visitors themselves, or to the Spirits with whom
they profess to communicate? Taking a wide view of these mysterious sciences, it seems to me that a kind of gradual development and
progression is observable in them all, and that they are all linked in

a manner together. Thus the discovery of the properties of the magnet has naturally led to 'animal magnetism' or 'clairvoyance,' and
'clairvoyance' to 'Spiritualism.' A few years ago, Professor Faraday's
explanation of 'table-turning'[1] satisfied the minds of most people,
particularly of those who are influenced by great names, without
taking the trouble to reason or investigate for themselves. Having
seen something of 'table-turning,' my first impression was, that it
was a delusion produced by the involuntary action of the mind and
muscles together, as supposed by Professor Faraday; but still I could
not think his experiments conclusive; and therefore, Mrs. M. and I
set to work to endeavor to turn a little round table at our own
house. At last it began to turn, *almost invariably with the sun*. At
this time I could not perceive that I exercised any power in the
matter, as I found that it moved under her hands after mine were
removed. But what convinced me that there was no self-deception
or 'volition' in producing the motion was, that I observed that on
some occasions the table would *not* move under her hands, though
she was naturally anxious to get it to move. By degrees, however,
her power increased, so that she could move it with one hand, or
even with one finger placed in the center. One evening a neighbor,
Mr. T, a civil engineer employed on the Grand Trunk Railway,
spent the evening with us. After seeing the little round table turning about all over the floor, he proposed to test the power by sitting
on the table. In this position he was turned round several times by
Mrs. M. Afterward I got on the table and was turned round with
equal freedom, though my weight is about two hundred pounds.
Mrs. M. merely touched the table with the points of her fingers.
This little experiment fully satisfied me that there was something
more in 'table-turning' than merely the involuntary action of the
muscles. There is now nothing new in this part of the subject and I
merely allude to 'table-turning' as an introductory process which led
me to investigate further.

I now come to what I will call Spiritualism Proper. I am glad to
find that you take a generous view of the character of the 'media.'
Of course, in Spiritualism, as in religion, we may expect to meet
with hypocrites and imposters, but it is equally absurd and unchari-
table to suppose that such a numerous body of individuals would
join in a continuous attempt to impose upon mankind, with nothing to gain, and often a great deal to lose, by such imposture. I have
seen many, mostly unprofessional ones, and in only one instance
have I detected imposture. Even in the instance referred to, I have

great reason to believe that the trick practiced arose out of a failure
to procure the genuine 'raps.' From the observations I have made on
this subject, I have long been fully satisfied that the *will* of the
'medium' has nothing whatever to do with the manifestations,
whether physical or mental. Before going into this part of the subject, I should premise that I was quite skeptical to say the least; and
that it was only after long and close observation, that I began to
believe in their spiritual origin.

As I proceed with my narrative, I will state the means I adopted
to satisfy my doubts. About three years ago I met the mayor of the
town in the street, and knowing my curiosity on the subject of
Spiritualism, he stopped me to say that his wife, Mrs. D, had
become developed as a 'tipping medium,' and had received several
communications through the alphabet from her father, and he
invited me to his house, that I might be able to judge for myself.
Mrs. D. is a very intelligent and sincere woman, and having been
intimately acquainted with her for seventeen or eighteen years, I
knew her to be incapable of deception of any kind.

On my first visit to Mrs. D., after her husband's invitation, sitting
round a light work-table with Mrs. D., her husband and one of her
daughters, hoping to obtain a communication from my father's Spirit
the table began to tip, or rise, on the side opposite the medium, as a
signal that Spirits were present, and wished to communicate with us.
I took the alphabet, and pointing with my finger to the letters in succession, the table tipped at the letters J.A. Of course I expected that
my father's name – ' James ' – was coming. But the table would not
rise at the letter M., though Mrs. D. was also anxious that the desired
name might be given. I went back to the beginning of the alphabet,
when my eldest sister's maiden name, Janet D. M., was spelled out.
Her name was quite unknown to Mrs. D., who knew nothing of my
family. I then asked aloud, 'When did you die?' but I got no answer
until I wrote down a number of different years on a piece of paper,
and on pointing to each of them in succession, the table tipped at
1855, which I afterward found to be correct, as I did not remember
the exact year of her death. I then asked, 'Of what disease did you
die?' 'Consumption,' was the answer. 'Did you die before or after
your sister?' 'After.' All these answers were perfectly correct, and I
took every precaution to avoid anything like suggesting or assisting
the process. I had nothing more from my sister on that occasion, but
several short communications were spelled out from deceased relatives of Mrs. D.'s, chiefly of a religious or moral character.

On another occasion, while Mrs. D., her husband, a chancery
lawyer from Toronto, and Mrs. D.'s daughter 'Nelly,' a young girl of
fourteen or fifteen, and I, were sitting round the table, Mrs. D.
found fault with Nelly for sitting at the table in a manner which
might excite suspicion. Immediately the table began to rock violently. I took the alphabet, when the following words were spelled out,
'You are too suspicious.' Mrs. D. had been communicating with her
father, and she inquired, 'What does my father mean?' 'Of Nelly.'
'Why, are we suspicious of Nelly?' 'Because you think Nelly makes
the raps.' Whenever the table began to rise and strike the floor with
two legs, Mrs. D. could at once tell by the strength or energy of the
raps whether communication was coming from a strong or weak
man, a woman, or a child. When my father desired to communicate
with me, she at once said: 'Your father must have been a large and
strong man,' which was true.

One evening my friend Mr. T., already mentioned, accompanied
me to Mrs. D.'s house, when, as a test, he said he would ask a
mental question, and requested any Spirit present to give a certain
number he wanted, by so many tippings of the table. Thirty-six raps
were immediately given, which we all counted separately, and
agreed in the number. Mr. T., after making a slight calculation with
his pencil, told us the number was quite correct. As he and I were
returning home together, he told me what his question had been
'how many years is it since my father left England for the United
States?'

In the summer of 1855, Kate Fox, one of the mediums in the
'Rochester knockings,' came to Belleville with her mother, on a
visit to a relative in the town. The Fox family, before they removed
to the United States, lived on a farm in the county of Prince
Edward, a few miles from Belleville. Since 1848, leaving the neighborhood of Rochester, they removed to New York. I was glad to
have an opportunity of testing the manifestations in a situation
where there could be no possible facilities for mechanical contrivance or deception of any kind. I found Kate a simple, artless girl,
with an intelligent and ingenuous expression of countenance, and
elegant and refined in her manners. I called on her several times at
the house where she was residing in Belleville. I had a ring which
belonged to my father. It was a mourning ring for my grandmother,
and the name 'Henrietta M., of M., ob. 6 September, 1806.' was en-
graved on it. Having entirely forgotten the dates, not having looked
at the ring for several years, I placed it on my finger without
looking at the inscription. Having often heard it asserted that noth-

ing is ever communicated by the Spirits but what is already known to the inquirer, I asked Kate if she could tell me the name inscribed on the ring? She said she could not, but if I would write any number of names on a piece of paper, at a side table, so that she could not see it, the Spirit, if present, would knock on the table when I pointed to it. I did as directed, and three knocks came on the table when I pointed to the name. In the same manner, the month and year of her death were given correctly. The sounds on the table were such as to preclude any probability of their being produced by mechanical means. They sounded almost exactly like knocks produced by human knuckles. I looked below the table, but could discover no possible means of producing the sounds. In order to satisfy me still further on this point, Kate opened the room door, and on gently touching one of the panels with the points of her fingers, loud and distinct knocks came all around and near her hand. I held my ear to the door and distinctly felt the vibration. She then took me out into the street, in front of the house, where the sidewalk was formed of large limestone flags, and the knocks came under and near our feet, like taps of a hammer on the stone, the sounds invariably corresponding with the nature of the substance on which they were produced.

I did not pursue my investigation further at this time, but invited Mrs. Fox and her daughter to spend the evening at my house. After tea, we seated ourselves round a large center-table in the drawing-room, with a large lamp standing on it. Our party consisted of Mrs. Fox and her daughter, Mr. T., a medical student, and also a stranger to the Fox family, Mrs. M., and myself. The mediums inquired if any Spirits were present who would communicate with us, and she began to call the letters of the alphabet. Three raps came on the top of the table at the letters J A M E S M, and two other letters of my father's surname, and the following communication was spelled out letter by letter:

'I have much to say to you. It is joy for me to speak with you through echo. I wish you to investigate this subject, and I will convince you beyond a doubt. Do not let your mind be influenced by idle and thoughtless words, but investigate for yourself, and your Spirit friends will all gather in groups around you and aid you in your efforts. I still hover over you, my dear son, and protect you from evil
'JAMES ——'

Next came a communication to Mrs. M., from her father, which, with the accompanying remarks, I copy from a memorandum of these communications I made at the time 8th Sept., 1855:

THOMAS S——D: *Dear Child*: I am still living; I take an interest in your welfare and weave your heart with many bright dreams. You must not doubt my presence. There are many beautiful truths in this subject which can not fail to find a echo in your mind. The time will soon come when you can hold converse with us alone.

At the word 'us' a shower of raps like those of large and small knuckles came all over the table. Now the table itself was lifted and shaken with some violence first at one corner then at the others, in succession, and turned partly round each time. During these movements the large lamp, with a glass shade, was burning in the center of the table; but it never moved from the spot, as if it were held fast by some invisible power. Otherwise, it must have been overturned. Mrs. M. then asked the Spirit of her father the following questions, which were all correctly answered. 'When were you born?' '8th December.' 'When did you die?' '18th May, 1818.' 'Your age?' 'Fifty-eight.' 'Of what disease did you die?' 'Gout in the stomach.' 'Where did you die?' 'At Norwich, England.'

At Kate Fox's request, Mrs. M. wrote down a number of names of dead and living persons intermixed, at a side table where she could not see them, and on pointing to them we heard *five* raps for the dead, and *three* for the living. We tried the experiment again and again, and the raps were given correctly each time. Among the names of the dead, she wrote that of Anna Laura H.,[2] the daughter of the editor of a London magazine, to whom she was much attached, and with whom she made an agreement, that whichever of the friends should die first, would appear to the other, if permitted. Mrs. M. wrote on a slip of paper, 'Why did you not keep your promise?' 'I often endeavored to make my presence known to you,' was instantly spelled out by the alphabet, 'In order to convince me that you are really the Spirit of my friend, spell out your name by the alphabet.' 'Anna Laura' was instantly spelled out. I had an Irish servant, who was expecting his wife and children out from Ireland, and as Kate Fox was standing on the floor, he asked the Spirits how many weeks it would be before his family would reach Belleville? Six raps were immediately given on the floor, three or four feet from where we were standing. *Six weeks* from that night the wife and family *did* arrive in Belleville. In the same manner he was told how many of his children were dead and how many living. At this the old man was fairly frightened, and telling Kate, in a tone of mingled fear and respect, 'You're a witch ma'am,' took himself off in double quick time.

After the departure of Mrs. Fox and her daughter, I followed up my investigations at Mrs. D.'s, where I received several remarkable communications, a number of them indeed absolutely and uselessly false, but still exhibiting extraordinary intelligence and knowledge of matters only known to myself. What the motives of these false Spirits could be, I can not conjecture, as the falsity of several of them could be detected in a few hours or days. I am fully satisfied, however, that neither my mind nor that of Mrs. D. had anything to do with them, for often when we desired a communication from some particular Spirit, one would be spelled out from some Spirit neither of us had thought of. I will just give one other example of this fact, where the name of my wife's sister, a lady well known in the literary world, and *still living*, was spelled out by the alphabet, under circumstances which rendered it highly improbable that our minds at the time had influenced the communication, unless the Spirit had read my mind, as the medium, Mrs. D., knew nothing of the facts so obscurely hinted.

October 23, 1854. The table began to rock, and the following words were spelled out when we requested the Spirit, as usual, to spell its name: 'Do not ask my name; you are not prepared to hear it.' Mrs. D. asked if we would be alarmed? 'Yes.' My mind instantly suggested the name of a very dear daughter at Toronto, who was near her confinement at the time, and I asked, Is your name Agnes? 'Yes.' I then thought of my wife's sister in England, and I asked, Is your name Agnes S.? 'Yes.' Where did you die? 'Do not ask.' Did you die in Scotland? No answer. In England? 'Yes.' At R——? 'Yes. Do not be alarmed at my appearance here, although you may be indeed surprised to hear from Agnes S. Dear brother, did I not love you all better than you gave me credit for? Every cause I gave Susan (as my wife was generally called by her sister in England) for reasons' (here there was some confusion in the communication, as if some words had been omitted) ... 'after I had put all my works into print ... but I hope Susan will forgive me.'

[To be Continued]

RECORD OF SPIRITUAL INVESTIGATIONS.
LETTER TO PROFESSOR GREGORY
(Continued from Page 9, last week)

Before proceeding farther, in order to convince you that I have not adopted my opinions on this subject without due caution and close observation, I will describe a few of the many contrivances I have resorted to in order to facilitate the communications. The process of tipping a table for each letter indicated, being exceedingly tedious, and liable to the suspicion of deception, I contrived the machines referred to, in order, as far as possible, to obviate these objections. But first, the question arose in my mind, whether, on the supposition that the communications really came from the Spirits of the dead, the Spirit moved the table by acting indirectly on the nervous system and muscle of the mediums, or directly, by moving the table itself. When I first witnessed these manifestations, I had not yet seen tables moved without actual contact. It therefore appeared as if the tables were actually moved by muscular action. I had soon an opportunity of satisfying myself on this point at Mrs. D.'s house. I candidly stated my doubts to Mrs. D., and she at once entered into my views. We seated ourselves opposite each other, at the two ends of the little work-table, which was about three feet long and about eighteen inches wide. After taking our places keeping my hands on the table as lightly as possible, I requested the Spirits, in order to convince me that they acted on the table *directly*, to raise it as high as possible under Mrs. D.'s hands. The table immediately rose about a foot from the floor, at her end of it, and remained a few seconds in that position, until I had time fully to satisfy my mind of the fact. I shall not here enter into the question whether the 'will-power' of the medium had any influence in moving the table. I shall simply state my conviction arising from the distinct statements of all the media I have seen, as well as from close observation on my own part, that volition has no influence whatever in these manifestations. I shall describe only two or three of the machines I contrived for obtaining communications from the Spirits. The first is a board with a raised edge, two inches high, twenty-seven inches in length, and ten inches in breadth. On the edge farthest from the medium, the letters of the alphabet are pasted. A little board, about nine inches square, mounted on four little wheels or rollers, with grooved edges, runs upon brass rods fixed parallel to each other longitudinally on the board. A pointer is fixed in the center of the little hand-board, to indicate the letters as they are required to spell out the sentences. At first Mrs. D. obtained a short communication with this machine, but strange to say, at subsequent trials she could obtain nothing intelligible, unless the hand of another person, along with her own, was placed on the hand-board. Whenever we desire a communication, Mrs. D. places her right hand on the board, and I my left hand, leaving my right free to write down the communications as we receive them. For a long time, also, we never could get any intelligible communication, unless Mrs. D. kept her eyes on the letters. Within these last few weeks, however, for the first time, I obtained one while she was purposely looking out of the window. Observing this, I sat down with her husband at the board, and we received a communication, though neither of us could ever before this time get the board to move, unless Mrs. D.'s hand was on it along with ours. In order still farther to satisfy my mind that the Spirits, at least in Mrs. D.'s case, did not act on the muscles of the medium, I contrived another machine, the movements of which, requiring more power, would depend, as may be supposed, chiefly on the muscle power of the mediums. This machine is simply an upright stand, with a spiral brass spring in the center, and with a transverse handle sliding over it, and placed horizontally, for the hands of the medium to rest upon. On the top of the stand is placed a dial, with letters of the alphabet. A string is tied to the upper end of the spiral spring, and then passes over a pulley which carries a hand to point to the letters, and the other end is tied to the cross handle. When the hands of the medium press this handle downward, extending the spring, the hand turns round to the different letters, and when the hands are raised the spring contracts, and turns the hand round in the opposite direction. This machine, however, *was not moved at all*, though, on the supposition of any deception being attempted, there would be as little chance of detection as in the other.

While speaking of these machines, I may mention another one I contrived on a somewhat different principle, having the object of portability chiefly in view at the time, as my wife and I were starting for a bathing place near Portland, where, as she had recently become a medium, we expected to have many communications from the Spirits. This machine was simply a piece of pine wood, twenty inches long, with two wheels placed one before the other, in a mortice in it, the wheels being nearly five inches in diameter. The letters of the alphabet were pasted on the edge of the right-hand wheel, so that when the machine rolled from side to side on the table, the communication would be spelled out by a fixed finger hand or pointer. So little power was required to move this very simple machine, that I did not entertain the slightest doubt of its performances when held in my wife's hands, or in hers and mine

together. As it turned out, however, we were utterly disappointed in
our expectations, as the machine would not even begin to move
under Spirit-influence. This I consider an almost unanswerable argument for the spiritual origin of the communications received in a
similar manner. The non-compliance with certain necessary conditions, was probably the cause of the failure. Perhaps the hands were
removed too far from the table, in consequence of the large diameter
of the wheels. I intend, however, to make further experiments, to
illustrate the mechanical difficulty in this case, if it be mechanical.

As in your late letter to Mr. Brittan, of New York, you make no
mention of a book entitled, 'Spiritualism Scientifically Demon-
strated,' by Dr. Hare, Professor of Chemistry in the University of
Philadelphia, I suppose you have not yet seen it.[3] Among a number
of ingenious machines invented by the Professor, he gives an engraving of one which, from the principle on which it is constructed, is
well calculated to show that the medium could not produce any
motion in the machine, even did she desire to do so. He had a light,
narrow table, running upon four wheels or castors. A pulley turning
on an axis, with a hand to point to the letters arranged on a circular
card or dial, was secured by a thumb-screw to the edge of the table.
A band was passed round a grooved wheel on one of the feet of the
table, and round the pulley on the edge of the table. Thus, as the
light table rolled along the floor, under the hands of the medium,
the index hand turned round, and pointed to the letters. The Professor first got communications while the eyes of the medium could
perceive the letters. Then he turned the card round, so that she
could not see them. Still he obtained communications as before; but
the objection remained, that by means of clairvoyance the medium
might see the letters. In order to meet this objection, he had a little
carriage made, which ran upon castors and placed it on the table.
Upon this little carriage the hands of the medium were placed. Thus
she could not see the letters, and could only move the little carriage, but could not move the table on which it rolled, by any muscular power she could exert. In spite of all these difficulties, the
table was moved, and communications spelled out as before, which
could only have been done by some other power or intelligence than
that of the medium.

The argument derived from these experiments, appears to be unanswerable. The spirit in which I entered on my investigations into
this subject, has been, invariably to comply with all known conditions, and in doing so, to be sure about the *facts*. In this way I have

obtained manifestations, when, by pursuing a different course, I would probably have obtained few or none. I have seen too much of the Spirits to believe that we can command or control them. On the contrary, I have often found that we were perfectly powerless in obtaining even some of the common physical manifestations, when, in order to convince skeptics, we were most anxious to obtain them.

Though, as already stated, several of the communications are false or unreliable, a number of those we received were of a very different character, and we could generally know the source from which they came, by their peculiar style. The Spirits often assume the names of other Spirits, and give us communications, generally of a religious or moral character, in the character of the Spirit personated, displaying considerable knowledge of our family matters, and feelings of the moment, obtained, no doubt, by reading our own thoughts. However, their ignorance on some matters, which must be well known to the individual personated, soon betrays them. When communications come unexpectedly, from persons you may not be thinking of at the time, and at places where you are not known, they may generally be considered more reliable.

As an instance of this, I will give you a short communication I received through a medium, Mrs. Swain, at Toronto, where I was very little known at the time. In 1844 I lost a very dear and promising boy, who was drowned at Belleville. He was not quite six years of age. I often expressed an anxious desire to Mrs. D. to receive some communication from him, but without success. Had Mrs. D.'s mind or will had any power in the matter, I should certainly have been gratified in my desire, as she loved the child, and was anxious to assist me in procuring the communication. Two of my poor boy's elder brothers had been fishing from a wharf in Belleville, and had caught a great many fish, when their younger brother Johnny strang them on a twig, and ran off with the prize, to show to his mother, while his brothers were busying winding up their lines. They suddenly missed him, and giving the alarm, after a long search I found his body in a hole in the wooden wharf, from which two or three planks had been removed. He had no doubt gone down to a crossbeam to wash the bundle of fish, and had lost his balance.

While on a visit to a married daughter in Toronto, November 29, 1856, I accompanied a friend, Mr. B., to the house of Mrs. Swain, the spiritual medium. We sat down at a square table, Mr. B. and I on one side, Mrs. Swain on our left, and her husband opposite to her – the fourth side, opposite to Mr. B. and me, being occupied by a gentleman who was a stranger to us. I had never seen the medium or her husband before to my knowledge. Mrs. Swain is a tipping and writing medium. The strange gentleman first took the card containing the alphabet as soon as the tipping commenced, expecting to get a communication from some deceased relative, when the following words were spelled out, as he pointed to the letters on the card:

'My dear father, I am here; talk to me.'

The tipping suddenly ceasing, the gentleman asked the Spirit if some other person should take the alphabet? Three tips for 'yes.' On pointing to each of us in succession, one tip for 'no' was given, until my turn came, when the table tipped three times for 'yes.' I took the card, when the communication was immediately continued.

'Don't you remember when I went down into the water? I am your little boy. D——d (his next elder brother, the other being in California) must remember. Tell my dear mother that I am often with her.
                                                    JOHNY.'

This was the way he used to spell his name, as he was just beginning to write when he died. After receiving this communication, I mentioned the circumstances attending his death, and when I stated my belief that he had 'gone down' to wash the fish, the table tipped violently three times for 'yes.'

From a number of communications received at different times through Mrs. D. and myself, I select a few which seem best calculated to illustrate the subject, and to remove the doubts of skeptics, and not from containing anything remarkable in themselves.

One day 'Henry W——s' was spelled out. He was a fine boy, who lived a few doors from my house. He was very like a boy of mine, Robert; and I remembered speaking to him as he was driving past my house in a carriage like mine, but did not recollect what I had said to him. I asked the Spirit: 'Henry, do you remember my calling to you when you were driving toward Belleville; and what did I say to you?' 'Yes; you told me dear M——, that the door of the stable was locked.' 'Who did I take you for?' 'You took me for Robert.' 'Did any of my family go to your funeral?' 'Robert.' I had quite forgotten the conversation on the road, and Mrs. D. knew nothing of it. On going home I met Robert, and asked him if Henry W——s had ever mentioned what I said to him when he was driving into town?

'Yes, papa, he laughed about your mistaking him for me, and said
you told him something about the stable door being locked; for you
remember we had no man-servant at the time?'

'Robert W——s' (a cousin of the above H. W——s) was spelled out a
few days afterward. Not knowing well what to ask as test, I said,
'Who did you meet first in the Spirit-world?' 'Sophia, my grandmother.' This short communication is particularly remarkable, because neither Mrs. D., the medium, nor I, knew his grandmother's
name, nor anything about her. We afterward ascertained from Mrs.
W——s, the mother of Henry W——s, that the name was correct. On
the 24th March, 1857, we received the following from a very worthy
Methodist minister, a relative of Mrs. D.

'Avail yourselves of every opportunity to communicate with the Spirits.
You ought to all make yourselves sure before you yield to your convictions.
You are among those who will be your friends. Fear not what is coming.
Inquire of my father, ye to whom I speak. You will trust in him.' (We were
talking of forming a spiritual circle.) 'Coming together, my dear friends,
convince yourselves before you begin any circle. Commence with communications when I advise you.' (To me:) 'You are a medium. You begin to
be developed, and you will be awakened to the truth of Spiritualism.
Acquire all the knowledge you can, and be certain about circles being regular in their attendance. You are among good Spirits. Fear, dear friends,
always gives your communications doubt, and bad Spirits will always endeavor to control you, and make you doubtful about the truth. Dear friends,
you are being guided by good Spirits. You never ought to despair. You desire
to learn God in reality, dear friends. You are children of Nature, and God's
own children. Christ was the best of men, and he died for you all, that all
might believe in the immortality of the soul, and be saved; and you are your
own judge concerning punishment. It all depends upon your own conduct.'

'Was Christ equal to God?' 'No.'
'Was he then a mere man, born of a human father and mother?'
'Yes.'
'Was he capable of commiting sin?' 'Prayer and watching saved
him from being tempted.'

I was making some remarks on this subject to Mrs. D., when the
Spirit continued:

'You are right about Christ and God, and you are right about the Bible. It
was not inspired altogether. You are safe in your belief. You are beyond all

danger of being laughed at by common people, and very soon it will be believed by all. Be your own lantern, and your own guide. You must be guided by the laws of Nature.   D.P.'

March, 1857. – Communication to me at Mrs. D.'s. I was express-ing an ardent desire to become developed as a medium.

'Few can at all times be your guide. You are too energetic. I will wait you hopefully, and you must live in hope. You, by giving proper attention to it, will make converts to Spiritualism. With your desire, communications will be made to convince your friends that Spiritualism is true. You will not convince your friend, Mr. R.' (a friend I had just been talking of to Mrs. D.), 'until you see him and converse with him.   J.H.'

As I do not wish to be tiresome, I shall pass over a number of communications I have received at different times, which are chief-ly of a personal nature, and therefore uninteresting to others. I shall in this place merely give one short communication which *professed* to come from a brother who died in India more than thirty years ago, and whom I had not seen since I was a boy.

'Thomas M.' When did you die? 'In 1830.'

'At what place?' 'Cawnpore.'

Both of these answers were wrong; but though otherwise unworthy of attention, there is this remarkable about the answers, viz.: that at the time I was under the impression that he had died at Cawnpore, where he long held an important civil office under the Colonial Government. But on referring to an Indian newspaper, giv-ing a long account of his death and services, I found that he died, not at Cawnpore, but at Calpee, on the 27th April, 1824. Now, as Spirits often answer *mental* questions correctly, it is obvious that in this case some deceiving Spirit simply read my mind as to the *place, and guessed* at the *date*, which I did not recollect at the time.

I shall now proceed to give an account of several remarkable phy-sical manifestations I have witnessed in different places.

During a short tour in the United States during the summer of 1856, I visited Mrs. Fox and her daughters Kate and Margaretta, who have resided in New York since 1848. I met Kate at the office of the *Christian Spiritualist*[4] in Broadway, and she invited me to spend the evening with the family at their private residence in the eastern part of the city. Margaretta, like Kate, is a rapping medium. While con-versing with Kate before tea, the Spirits frequently rapped on the floor all round us in approval of what either of us happened to say on the subject of Spiritualism. These raps came at uncertain points on all sides – on the floor, and on the partitions of the room, as if to defy all suspicion of mechanical contrivance. After several ladies and a gentleman came in by appointment, in order to form a circle for the physical manifestations, as they are called – though it is hard to draw the line between the different manifestations of Spirit-power, as all the physical ones I have witnessed, table-turning per-haps excepted, are accompanied by intelligence of some kind – we took our places at a large oval table, on which we placed our hands. Our circle consisted of nine persons. One of the ladies was Mrs. Sweet, the speaking medium; so there were three mediums present. A large hand-bell, weighing several pounds, was placed directly under the center of the table upon the floor. Kate Fox sat down beside me, and placed both here feet on my right foot, where they remained during the sitting. The gas-lights were burning brightly, and I could see no possibility of deception, had such been attempted. After sitting about two or three minutes with all our hands on the table, one of the company requested the Spirits to strike the bell-handle against the center of the table, which was im-mediately done with a blow that made the table jump. I then requested the Spirits to place the bell in my left hand, while I held it under the edge of the table. The handle of the bell was immedi-ately and gently introduced into the palm of my hand. Holding it thus, I thrust it down below the table as far as I could reach, and pulled it up again several times; and I distinctly felt the bell taken from me by something like the power of a human hand with human intelligence, as it instantly yielded to me when I wished to draw the bell up to the edge of the table, and obviously assisted in raising it. Lastly, I pulled it up to the edge of the table, and suddenly opening my fingers, fully expected that the heavy bell would fall to the floor; but it did not. During these motions I did not say a word of my intentions.

The bell was then handed under the table to each of the party in succession, no hand being below the table but the one which received it. It then occurred to me to ask for one more test. I asked if the Spirits would unbutton the leather strap which held my trow-sers under my boot. Something like human fingers tried again and again to undo the buttons, but without success. Something feeling like a finger and thumb were then thrust between the strap and the boot, and once my foot and leg were pulled violently by the lower part of the trowers, several inches to the right side, in order to favor the operation. The oval shape of the large and broad table was quite unfavorable to any deception, as well as the bright light of the gas. No *foot* could have done what I felt, and every hand was on the table. I am certain I was not deceived; nor do I believe that deception was ever thought of, or necessary, in order to do what was done.

I regret that I could not prolong my stay at New York in order to witness some more manifestations of this description. Strange to say, I found an extraordinary amount of incredulity on this subject even in New York, where any one may witness what I did, and much more.

The following remarkable manifestations came under my own immediate notice during several months in this town. My friend, Mr. T——, already mentioned, was a believer in Spiritualism from his knowledge of the respectability of many of the Spiritualists of the United States, though at the time I now refer to he had seen but little of the manifestations. Being both equally interested in the subject, we often wished to have a good medium in our immediate vicinity, where we could investigate the matter in a more satisfactory manner. As chance would have it, Mrs. T. had hired two Scotch girls, sisters, as house-servants, neither of whom knew anything about Spiritualism, having been only twelve months in the colony. Much of what I have now to relate is upon the authority of Mr. and Mrs. T., both of whom are persons of unquestionable veracity. A large portion of the manifestations at their house were, however, witnessed by my wife and myself and several others of my family – as Mrs. T. invariably dispatched a servant for me when anything notable took place.

One morning about daybreak, Mr. T. was awakened by three distinct raps on the partition of his bed-room, which in a few minutes were repeated. This was the first intimation the family had of there being a medium in their house. A few nights afterward, Mr. and Mrs. T. were alarmed by a loud scream from the bed-room occupied by the two sisters, and the exclamation, 'In the name of God, what do you want?' Lighting a candle Mr. T. went to the girl's room, where he found Mary, the elder sister, in violent convulsions, supported in the bed by her sister Annie. When she came to herself, she said that she saw a pale light, resembling that of the moon, spreading from one corner of the room, in the midst of which she saw the figure of a man, whose appearance she minutely described as being of the same height as Mr. T., but stouter. But she only saw the upper part of the figure distinctly. The figure seemed to float forward toward her, which occasioned her fright and exclamation of alarm. Annie said she saw the light before her sister observed it, but no figure, and knowing how nervous her sister was, she did not call her attention to it, until Mary asked here if she did not see a man standing in the corner, and Mary's description of the figure suggested the idea of Mr. R., the former owner of the house, who died a few months previously, in Scotland, but whom neither of the sisters have ever seen.

From this time the taps followed Mary through the house, and wherever she went. Still she had not the slightest idea that she was a medium, and only thought the house was haunted by some unquiet Spirit. I should mention that Mary, as I learned from her sister, is one of those persons who are continually seeing visions; that, in short, she possesses the 'second-sight.' In two instances Mary told us she saw large funerals passing along the road from Belleville past our houses, which literally came to pass within a week or two afterward. I have no personal knowledge of 'second-sight,' but you will no doubt recollect what is said respecting it in the Highlands of Scotland, that a person in company with a seer does not see the vision until the seer touch him. Now, in the physical manifestations, contact, such as joining hands, or laying the hands on the table, is in most cases essential to their exhibition. I am therefore the more inclined to think that 'animal-magnetism,' 'table-turning,' 'Spirit-rapping,' 'second-sight,' and 'Spirit-seeing,' etc., etc., are only portions of one great science, still in its early infancy, and which will yet establish the connecting link between spirit and what is called matter.

Be this as it may, the Spirits in Mrs. T.'s house were determined to attract attention. One morning, just after the breakfast-things had been removed, after shutting the doors of the room, Mrs. T. went up stairs with her children. Mr. T. had just left the house to go to his office in town, and Mary was washing the dishes in the next room, and singing, as usual, when Mrs. T. heard a loud crash in the breakfast-room. She ran down stairs and met Mary also in great alarm, coming from the room where she was at work. On entering the breakfast-room together, they found the large heavy dining-table thrown behind the stove, with its legs in the air, in a manner that could not have been done so instantaneously by any two men. It was done so suddenly that Mrs. T. was able to call back Mr. T., who had not got a hundred yards from the house. There was no person but Mary in the room next to the breakfast-room at the time.

It would be an endless task to relate all the cantraps of the Spirits. I shall merely mention a few of them. Mrs. T. showed me a billet of wood which was conveyed from the yard into a cupboard, the key of which she always kept in her pocket. Small articles were frequently conveyed through the air in the sight of the whole family, from one part of the sitting room to another, without any visible agency. The handles of the doors would be returned in rapid succession, and doors would be violently shut after Mrs. T. had just passed through them. On one occasion going into the dining-room with Mary, they saw the large dining-table rise up about two feet in the air without contact of any kind. On another occasion, when my family were invited to Mrs. T.'s, we sat round the dining-table with Mary, the medium. While her hands were on it, the table would slide along the carpeted floor five or six feet backward or forward as requested. Mr. T. got on the top of the table with his son, a boy of twelve years of age. Still it moved along the floor as easily as before, and would sometimes jump up on one side, the additional weight seemingly making the difference in the freedom of the motion. To satisfy myself still farther, I proposed that we should all stand up several inches back from the table, and I stood beside Mary to see that she did not shove the table with her hands. I then placed my hands on the table, and told Mary to place her hands on mine. I barely felt the touch of her hands, yet the table moved about and jumped up as before. I then placed the little finger of my right hand on the table, and brought the little finger of my left hand into contact with the thumb of my right hand. Mr. and Mrs. T. applied their extended hands in the same manner to mine, thus forming a connected chain of hands rising above the table. I then told Mary to touch the uppermost hand, when the side of the table under our hands jumped up violently, several inches above the floor. I then requested the whole party, the medium included, to join hands over the table for a minute or two; then separating our hands, and holding them about six inches above the table, it jumped up several times, without any contact whatever. We repeated this experiment several times, with the same result. Several times afterward, however, we failed in obtaining this manifestation, when we were most anxious to do so, in order to satisfy some of our skeptical friends. After the arrival of some relatives of Mr. and Mrs. T.'s, on a visit, the disturbances were renewed with increased violence, as if there were an accession of power. One evening, after dinner, the family had retired to the drawing-room, leaving a candle burning on the dining-table which had been lengthened out by two end pieces. They had left the room only a minute or two, when, hearing a loud noise, they ran to ascertain the cause of the disturbance, when they found the long table standing on one of its ends, and the candle, still burning, standing on one of the legs near the ceiling. A day or two afterward, they found it standing on its end in the same manner, with two chairs suspended on the legs. It was left standing in this position for Mr. T. to see it when he should come home from his office. A little while afterward, while Mrs. T.'s son was playing on the verandah, opposite the window of the room, he happened to look through the window at the table, when it suddenly came down on its legs, and the two chairs at the same instant flew to their places against the wall. In the room next to the dining-room, a narrow table was placed across the chimney-board, where Mary generally washed the dishes and tea-things, and here the raps were louder than in any other part of the house. At first we used to hold communion with the Spirits, standing, with our hands on this table. The raps that came through Mary's mediumship were somewhat different from those of the 'Fox girls,' which sounded exactly as if the top of the table were struck by human knuckles. With Mary they seldom came on the table, but on the bricks of the chimney, in the ground below our feet, or on the chimney-board. The remarkable variety of the sounds produced by the Spirits, is, indeed, strong proof of their being genuine. Sometimes such violent blows were struck on the chimney-board, even when we stood some feet back from it, that the medium and her sister Annie would run away in a fright. As it might be supposed that the chimney afforded an opportunity for imposition, I always removed the table in front of it, and examined the chimney, though it was too shallow to conceal any human creature. It is remarkable that, at first, a certain degree of darkness seemed to favor these demonstrations, as the raps were louder and the movements of heavy tables were more violent when the room was partially darkened. We found also that there was something in Mr. T.'s organization or presence, which interfered with the rapping, for as he approached the table or the medium, the sounds became gradually fainter, and became louder again when he left the room. At this chimney-board I received the first intelligent communication form what professed to be the Spirit of Mr. R., the former owner of the house, with whom I was well acquainted. We were told by the raps that it was Mr. R. who appeared to Mary when she went into convulsions. After getting some communications in the back room, partially darkened, I asked the Spirit if he would not communicate with us in the dining-room, with the candles lit? 'Yes,' was rapped out. When we moved into the dining-room, the Spirit communicated quite freely. The raps in this room generally came first on the partition wall, and then sounded as if they were produced deep in the ground below the house, and seemed constantly to change their locality. All the communications we received from this Spirit, were intelligent, and showed an intimate knowledge of his family matters, and of the character of various persons known to us both. A few evenings before the departure of Mr. T.'s visitors, it had been arranged that they would have a sitting with the Spirits and Mary, the next evening. But something came in the way, and the engagement was forgotten until the ladies were retiring for the night. A bell wire passed through the room in which the visitors slept, connected with the bell which hung in Mary's room. The ladies saw the wire pulled down, as if by an invisible hand in their room, where there was no bell-pull. At the same time they heard the bell ring in Mary's room, which was next to theirs. Mary was already in bed, where she was annoyed with loud raps and the ringing of the bell. The whole family were now assembled in Mary's room, where they saw the bed raised up several times under her. Calling the alphabet, on being asked what they wanted, the Spirits told Mary to get up, for she had not kept her promise, and to go down stairs to receive a communication. Mary immediately got up, and went down stairs with the family. On sitting down at the table, the Spirits rapped out, 'Now, Mary, go to bed, but don't deceive us in this way again.'

(To be Continued)

RECORD OF SPIRITUAL INVESTIGATIONS
LETTER TO PROFESSOR GREGORY
(Continued from page 13, last week)

These strange disturbances will not fail to recall to your memory the account of similar ones which took place in the Parsonage House in Epworth, as given by various members of the Wesley family in their letters to each other.[5] *A few years ago*, I should hardly have taken the trouble to read the account of these disturbances in 'Clarke's Memoirs of the Wesley Family.' The exact correspondence between these disturbances of 1716 and those I have myself witnessed or related on the most unquestionable authority, in 1856 and 1857, is indeed most remarkable. I have never perused the history of the celebrated 'Cock Lane Ghost,' the supposed actors in which alleged imposture were punished by being made to stand in the pillory, but I am now inclined to believe that they were the innocent victims of an unreasoning and bigoted incredulity.

When at the High School in Edinburgh, in 1810 or 1811, I can recollect the newspapers being filled with the accounts of similar disturbances in a certain 'close' in Leith, and I well remember going down there with a crowd of schoolboys to see 'the ghosts!' but all we could see, beside the crowd, was the outside of the house with all the windows broken. It was said that bricks and stones were thrown in at the windows at all hours; but though the disturbances continued for several days together, no plausible conjecture as to their origin was ever suggested, excepting the vague suspicion that it was done by a blacksmith *with a cross-bow!!* Such manifestations of Spirit-power have taken place at different times, and in various localities; but the world, dreading a renewal of what was called 'witchcraft,' and of witch-burning, was determined to believe nothing of the kind any more, and to make martyrs of those who did. The spiritual communications generally partake, more or less, of the character of the medium. The language, forms of expression, and even the orthography, if they be illiterate, resemble those of the medium. I believe this to be a general rule; but it is not without remarkable exceptions, as in many of those Mrs. M. and I have received, where the *style* was neither like that of the medium, nor like mine. There are, moreover, many well-authenticated instances of communications having been obtained in languages entirely unknown to the medium. Of this, however, I can not yet speak from personal knowledge. It is highly probable that the Spirits, acting by simple impression from a higher sphere of intelligence, where our modes of intellectual intercourse through bodily organs are unnecessary, may use the organs and language, and even the orthography of the medium as the readiest mode of communicating their ideas. As to the intelligence or knowledge displayed in such communications, it is a perfectly gratuitous supposition that in passing from this world to the next, all Spirits, however unequal in natural capacity or in educational acquirements, would at once stand on the same plane of intelligence. Such a supposition would, of necessity, at once annihilate individuality, and put an end to progression,

which is obviously a part of the law of Nature. In a moral point of
view, there *may* be less disparity between the philosopher and the
man of uncultivated mind; but is it rational to suppose that all the
knowledge we have acquired during a lifetime of study and observation, must be cast off and left behind us like Elijah's cloak; or that
there should be no farther use for those acquirements which have
been stored up in the soul of man – in a word, where all is spiritual?
So great is the real or apparent change from this material world to a
more advanced stage in our existence, that we imagine that all
traces of our individual character must at once disappear. Therefore,
when in these spiritual communications we observe the use of
familiar and ordinary expressions, we are shocked, because the language and ideas of the Spirit do not attain to our ideal standard of
perfection. Admitting that a great change will take place, it is not
probable that such change will be instantaneous; for it is impossible
for us to conceive that any improvement in our natural faculties can
take place without the consumption of *a certain portion of time*. I
shall not, however, enlarge on this part of the subject, as my business is now with facts.

A few months ago I again paid a visit to Mrs. Swain, the medium
in Toronto, where, for the first time, I had a communication in
writing through her hand. I will, however, first describe the physical
manifestations I witnessed on this occasion. Her husband, Mr.
Swain, placed a large hand-bell and a speaking-trumpet below the
center of the table, the room being well lighted with two candles. In
a few minutes the bell was moved about and rung repeatedly, and
the speaking-trumpet was also moved about in all directions, and
slapped against my feet and legs, and against those of my friend, an
old lawyer, who accompanied me; and in such a manner, that it was
impossible to have been done with anything but hands guided by
intelligence. At my request, the trumpet was presented to me under
the table. I took it by the mouth-piece, which was held in a sloping
direction toward me, so that it must have fallen on the floor if it
had not been supported in some manner, and placed it on the table.
I then presented it to the Spirit under the table, when it was literally snatched out of my hand. No *foot* could have done this, and
all the hands of the party, which consisted of only four, were on the
table at the time. But what chiefly surprised me was, that something which felt like human fingers kept feeling about the knee-pan
of my left leg, which I had broken by a fall some nine or ten years
ago, and more particularly where the separated portions of the knee-

pan were united by a ligament. The cure of the fracture had been so
perfect that no one could know by my walk that I had met with
such an accident; and I had not mentioned the subject to any one.
Being satisfied that there was evident design or intelligence in these
manipulations, I quietly slipped my hand below the table, and made
an attempt to seize the object in question. I grasped a part of what
felt like a human hand, between the thumb and the wrist. I felt at
the same time the small end of the speaking-trumpet, but they were
both quietly withdrawn from me, and slipped through my fingers. I
then took the trumpet and bell, and placed them on the floor below
the corner of the table, between my friend and me, where I knew it
was impossible for any other one of the party to reach them with
their feet without coming in contact with our legs. Still the bell was
rung, and the trumpet slapped against our legs, and sometimes
straight across both my feet. When these movements had been continued for about an hour, Mrs. Swain's left hand and arm began to
shake violently, so that she seemed to have no control over it,
though she held it with her right hand. She then suddenly seized a
pencil which was lying on the table, and her husband throwing her
a quire of large printer's paper, she dashed off the following communication with great rapidity, and threw it across the table to me:

'The old chief's papoose will make his father write. Me help him.'
                              'JIM.'

   The Spirit communicating was an Indian chief who calls himself
'Jim Black.' The Spirit of the Indian meant to tell me that my
'papoose' or child would make a writing-medium, and that he would
help him. Whenever this Spirit comes, Mrs. Swain grasps the pencil
in her *left hand*, just as a stone-mason handles his chisel, and the
writing is performed by a spasmodic action of the whole arm, which
spreads the writing over the whole page, occasionally tearing it with
the point of the pencil. When other Spirits communicate through
Mrs. Swain, she writes quietly in the usual manner, with the right
hand.
   A friend in Toronto showed me a number of communications
written by a medium at Buffalo, in the same rapid manner. They
were written upside down, and back foremost, so that to read them
they must be held between the eye and a light. Yet the letters and
words are as distinct and well formed as any ordinary manuscript.
In the family of my friend, Mrs. D——, of Belleville, we have been

continually witnessing fresh manifestations of Spirit-power, which were exhibited as if for the purpose of removing any latent doubt which might still exist in our minds. Some time ago I read in one of the New York spiritual papers an account of some extraordinary performances, in Germany, of a miniature table with three legs, one of which was a pointed pencil. I thought the story a hoax, but as the machine was so simple, I determined to satisfy myself of the fact. I sawed out a bit of an old table in a circular form, nine inches in diameter. I made three little legs for it, five inches long, one of them being a pointed pencil, as before stated. I left the little table with Mrs. D., to try what could be done with it. Meeting Mr. D. next day, he told me that on Mrs. D. putting her hands on it and placing it on a sheet of paper, it immediately wrote the name of a niece of his, 'Maria Miller,' who died some years ago. On hearing this, I went to see Mrs. D., when putting each of us one hand on the little table, it immediately began to move about rapidly. At first it described a number of circles, and regularly formed spirals. I asked the Spirit if it could not write. It answered by lifting up one side of the little table, and striking the large table on which it stood once, for 'no.' I then wrote a number of manuscript capital letters, and requested the Spirit to imitate them. The Spirit was an apt scholar, for before it reached the letters *J* and *K*, the characters were better formed and written with much more freedom and symmetry, than I myself could have written them. I then wrote the word 'man,' which was imitated exactly, on a larger scale. I then asked the Spirit to write 'God,' which was instantly done, in large well-formed letters, about an inch high. The machine then, without suggestion of any kind on our part, or even thinking that such a thing could be done, drew some large plant of the palm species, while we kept the points of our fingers of one of our hands lightly touching the machine, holding the paper down with the other. I then asked the Spirit to draw a human face. It immediately drew a female face, with a large comb in the hair. After drawing the *eye*, it went back, slipping and turning under our fingers, and drew the *eye lashes*. Seeing that the eye-brow, as well as the ears, were forgotten, on remarking the omission, it went deliberately back, and drew them in their proper places. All these operations were concealed from our eyes by the top of the little machine, which was an inch thick. After completing the picture, which was rough enough, the name of 'Maria Miller' was written under it in a large hand. Mrs. D. observed a strong resemblance in the outline of the side-face to those of the

deceased Maria Miller. We have never since been able to get any
Spirit to draw another human face. It now generally draws representations of hands with the fingers and thumbs extended, of large and
small sizes, and writes different names of deceased friends upon or
under them. The motions of the little table are almost entirely independent of our hands, as it will often slip from under them, the
motion instantly ceasing when the *contact* is broken. The name of
Mrs. D.'s father was frequently written in the same large hand, and
when I compared it with his signature to private letters in his lifetime, the imitation, if such it may be called, was perfect.

One evening, Mrs. D. requested me to place my hand on the little
table along with hers, when, on turning it upside down, and holding
it above us, it came down on the top of my hand, with a power
which I was compelled to evade by getting from below it. The performances of this little machine has suggested the idea to my mind
that some simple machine, furnished with a pencil, and moving
freely in all directions, like the pantograph, might be contrived, and
which might be operated by the Spirits with the aid of the hands of
the medium lying passively on its surface. It might easily be so constructed that the medium could not see the letters or words as they
were formed, and could not, therefore, influence the communications by any direct action of her mind. Such a machine would furnish an unquestionable test of their spiritual origin, to those who
still doubt. There are so many *kinds* and *degrees* of mediumship,
that any simple machine which would facilitate and shorten the
time occupied in the communications, would be a real satisfaction
to intelligent inquirers, while it would extend the benefits of mediumship to a numerous class of mediums, possessed of very limited
powers, whom the Spirits are unable to influence more directly.

In a short time afterward, one of Mrs. D's daughters began to
write short communications, under Spirit-influence. By simple contact I find that this power can be exercised through my own hand,
on which the hand of the little medium is placed, when my hand
grasping the pencil is compelled to write. One of Mrs. D.'s daughters, a child of 12 years of age, lays her hand upon mine, without
sensibly grasping it, and it immediately begins to write away at a
rate which I can hardly restrain. The action of her arm was spasmodic while her hand rested on mine, but she assured me that she
was not sensible of the slightest effort on her part.

I now come to the latest manifestations at Mrs. D.'s. A few
weeks ago Mrs. D. told me that the Spirits had promised to make

two of her daughters play a duet on the piano. I knew exactly what they could perform on that instrument in their normal state. They could play simple airs and dancing tunes in good time, but they had not the slightest pretensions to execution, and they could not play any long piece without the music book being before them. At first Mary D. and her cousin, H—— P——, sat down to the instrument. They were both seized at the same instant with spasms in the arms, which became quite uncontrollable, and they struck the keys in well-measured time together, but the spasms were so painful to Mary D., that she left the piano and retired with her mother to another room. Nelly D. then sat down to the instrument, when the music became more regular, and for nearly a whole hour the two girls played a long piece of music, beautifully and singularly original in its character, quite unlike anything I had ever before heard, and in which the most extraordinary execution was displayed. During this performance there was no music before the young ladies, and for the greater part of the time it lasted, the principal performer purposely kept her eyes closed. I have witnessed similar performances again and again, and I do not remember a repetition of the same piece of music. Sometimes we turn off the gas, when they perform for an hour together in total darkness. (At this part of my letter I offered a number of observations on the conditions requisite for obtaining spiritual communications, but I shall here merely insert the concluding remarks.) I shall now make a few observations on a theory advanced by several of the opponents of Spiritualism, viz., the involuntary action of a portion of the brain, while the remaining portion is at rest, or passive. The idea on which this theory seems to rest, is, that the medium is in the 'somnambulic' or 'clairvoyant' state when communications are received.

Now, as in most cases, the answers are instantaneous, we must suppose that the medium is never in any other state than the one referred to, and that she is both asleep and awake at the same instant; that she answers questions she has neither heard nor read; and without being conscious that she knew them in any manner, or that she has answered them; and all the while may be conversing with those around her on ordinary subjects, apparently in her normal condition. The improbability of this supposition, coupled with the long array of facts which have come under my own notice, seems to me like taking the most difficult and circuitous route, in order to attempt to elucidate facts which we are unable to comprehend or appreciate. It, in fact, sets at defiance the evidence of our own senses, which after all is, perhaps, the very best evidence we can obtain on such subjects. If we once admit, that we can be thus *systematically* deceived by our senses, it is hard to say what we may safely believe on any subject; we may be deceived by our best friends – innocent all the while of any such intention – without their knowledge of the words, even, in which the deception is conveyed.

While admitting the great candor and freedom from prejudice, displayed in your letter to Mr. Brittain, I trust you will pardon me for saying, that your explanation of the spiritual manifestations only *looks* more like the truth than any other one; while nothing short of the admission of the fact of spiritual intercourse will reconcile all difficulties, and explain, in a satisfactory manner, the astonishing array of facts, which are accumulating from day to day in endless variety. Indeed, when we take a comprehensive view of *all* the phenomena of Spiritualism, we may well ask what more the Spirits can do to remove our skepticism. In this vast mass of evidence we see the obvious anxiety on the part of the Spirits to convince us of its truth, by acting on our minds through every available avenue. First, we have the physical manifestations to attract our attention, in such a manner as not to alarm the mind or injure the body – gradually preparing our minds for more startling manifestations of Spirit power. Then we have communications which are obviously intended to convince us of the immortality of the soul, and a life of endless progression hereafter. It is not for us to ask: Why do the Spirits take such indirect and uncertain modes of communicating with mortals, and so little in conformity with our conventional ideas of dignity? The question is a question of *fact*, and at this stage of the investigation *reasoning* is altogether out of place. But instead of appealing to our hearts in private, by raps or other sounds, or movements of tables, let us suppose that the Spirits of the deceased should appear to us in the shapes they bore on earth, how could the unpracticed nerves of some of us sustain the shock? Would not many be driven into absolute insanity, by such apparitions coming suddenly before their eyes, without the gradual preparation so wisely adopted by the Spirits themselves? It should be remembered, besides, that our ideas of propriety and dignity are in a great degree influenced by external circumstances. In modern times, for instance, riding on an ass would be deemed a somewhat undignified mode of progression, simply because the horse, a superior animal, is in common use. What is language, itself, but a mechanical contrivance, in which our natural organs are used by the Spirit within us to communicate its ideas to other Spirits 'in the flesh.' Keeping in view, therefore, the obvious intention of the Spirits to convince us of the immortality of the soul, it matters little by what agency the great fact is brought home to our minds; and where can this be done with more propriety than at the family board in our own quiet homes? The little insect we carelessly crush beneath our feet, shows the power of the Creator as unmistakeably as the earthquake, or the trumpets that proclaimed his presence to the assembled hosts of Israel! As we communicate our thoughts by means of bodily organs, obedient to the will of the internal soul, we may naturally believe that disembodied Spirits, in order to convey *their* thoughts to us, must necessarily avail themselves of the properties of matter. As by volition the Spirit acts on the material organs of the body, so, when the spirit at death is set free from an association which limits its powers, it will soar aloft, or move through space unobstructed by the resistance of matter. In this state of freedom the spirit, being superior to matter, will obtain dominion over it, and may move inanimate substances, or, by overpowering our will act on our nerves and muscles, when our minds are in a passive state. In order to obtain certain results in natural science, certain conditions must be observed. On this consideration I found one of my chief arguments for the truth of Spiritualism; for with regard to Spiritualism, the observation of *certain conditions* does not insure *certain results.* When we see the ordinary laws of nature suspended, when heavy bodies are raised in the air without actual contact of the hands of the media, or the hands of others present, when, as in several instances within my own limited experience, a table has been held down to the floor, so that we could hardly raise it; when we see tables move about or jump up at the request of those present; when we see such things, we are compelled to admit that some power is present that can control gravitation – and what can this be but Spirit-power?

When a magnet is held near a piece of iron or steel, it attracts or repels it, as the south or north pole is presented to the object. The condition being complied with, the same result invariable follows. With the spiritual manifestations, on the contrary, there is no invariable conformity between the conditions and results. We are frequently disappointed when we are most anxious to have an exhibition of Spirit-power, in order, doubtless, to convince us, that Spirits, by virtue of a superior law, can control or suspend the ordinary laws of nature. In admitting the facts now so widely proclaimed throughout the world, and at the same time attributing the phenomena to the ordinary laws of nature, we, in fact, admit the truth of Spiritualism, and we simply bring the whole host of manifestations within the domain or nature. This, I confess, is my own opinion, as I can set no bounds or limits to the laws of nature, which must pervade the spiritual as they do the material world.

I had tried the 'rolling board' with Mrs. M., at my own house, but until the 18th of June, 1857, without effect. On the evening of that day we were by ourselves, and sat down, Mrs. M. with her right hand, and I with my left hand on the board. For the first time it moved freely with us from side to side, but without giving any intelligible communication, until Mrs. M. closed her eyes, which she kept shut during the whole sitting. The first communication came from an honest neighbor of ours in the back woods, who died more than 20 years ago, and certainly neither of us had thought of the poor man for years. The communication was intelligent, and showed an intimate knowledge of his domestic concerns, but was otherwise unimportant. After receiving this short communication, I asked, 'Are there any other Spirits present who wish to communicate with me.' Answered by the board – 'Yes, many.' Then the following communication was spelled out:

'NEIL S——, Have you forgot me?' 'No, my dear Neil. How, and where did you die?' 'A bad end makes me unhappy. No man should despair of mercy, for God is always near to help him. I did, and must suffer for my sin, at least until the debt I owe to God and my own conscience is paid. Think kindly of your old friend Neil S' 'Will you speak to me again?' 'Not to night; but fear God, and be strong in faith, for the blood of Jesus atones for all sin. Lay this to heart, for this is truth. Good night.'

Neil S. was a captain in the army, whom I knew when he was stationed on the frontier in South Africa, having served with him in Holland in 1813 and 1814. He was a kind and warm-hearted Highlander. Since I emigrated to Canada, I learned from a brother-officer that poor Neil had got into some pecuniary difficulty in India, and had destroyed himself in a fit of despair.

The next communication was from my friend Thomas Pringle, the devoted and talented Secretary of the London Anti-Slavery Society under Wilberforce.[6] The first communication was short and pithy, just in my friend's natural style.

'I served an oppressed race, and have my reward in heaven. Do thou likewise, and be happy in the approval of God and your own conscience, my dear friend.

THOMAS PRINGLE'

On the 21st June, 1857, while arguing with Mrs. M., who was still strangely skeptical as to the *source* of the intelligence, on laying our hands on the board, the following short sentence was spelled out by our friend Pringle, at whose house my wife and I first met each other:

'Thomas Pringle. You are, dear Susanna, too doubtful. You have no faith.'

This was all we could get this night; but on the following, after sitting a few minutes at the board, the following was spelled out. I should state that *Kansas* at this time was very far from our thoughts:

'Thomas Pringle. You will not live to see the abolition of slavery in the States. It will end in blood, and great political changes must take place. The corruption of the Government will bring about a great moral reform, and people will see the necessity of getting rid of the cause of so much crime; but it will not be in your day. A long struggle between the North and South, with the defection of California, Texas and Kansas, will set the poor negro free; but this will take years to accomplish. God will prepare the mind of the slave for the great moral change that awaits his condition. When God brings about a great national reform, he works slowly and uses many instruments, because many changes are effected by one. No more. Good night.'

On the 23d June, 1857, I received the following communication from a brother who died in India in 1824. He held a high civil appointment at Cawnpore:

'Thomas M. Many years have passed since I passed into the Spirit-land. The time, though short to me, has been long to you, and marked by much sorrow and care. Never fear; the next life will bring much joy. You will be united to those you loved and esteemed on earth, and all high and intellectual Spirits who find their chief enjoyment in studying the wonderful works of the Creator. You are one of the inquiring Spirits, to whom life would be a blank without increase of knowledge. We shall yet meet and take sweet counsel together. Though long parted, I am often with you in Spirit. Though I have not often been in your thoughts, we shall know each other better there, and love as Spirit-brothers love, without rivalry or fear. The love of God that fills the hearts of purified Spirits makes a perfect harmony to exist among all his children. They are only emulous of doing his will, and increasing in purity and knowledge. Take brother's blessing, and good night.'

In my next communication, I will give some farther experiences in Spiritualism in my own family, together with a number of beautiful communications Mrs. M. and I have received at different times from a Spirit of a high order of intelligence, who steadily refuses to give his earthly name. All the information we have been able to elicit, is, that he was born in London in A.D. 1025, and suffered for 'indulging in freedom of thought.'

J.W.D.M.

BELLEVILLE, UPPER CANADA, Feb. 21, 1858

1 Professor Faraday's letter on table-turning was published in the *Times* on 30 June 1853 and in the *Athenaeum* on 2 July 1853. Faraday, 'aghast at the hold which the table-turning mania had gained on all classes of society, and at the loose thinking and presumptuous ignorance which the popular explanations revealed,' performed and wrote about experiments that revealed that the table movements were due to muscular action. See Frank Podmore, *Mediums of the Nineteenth Century* (New York 1963), 2:9.
2 See *LOL*, 8–9.
3 Robert Hare, *Experimental Investigation of Spirit Manifestations, Demonstrating the Existence of Spirits and Their Communion with Mortals* (New York 1855)
4 The *Christian Spiritualist* was published in three volumes from 1854 to 1856, according to the *Union List of Serials*. The American Antiquarian Society library has some of this series, but it is unlikely that a complete run exists anywhere.
5 The disturbances at the Parsonage House in Epworth in December 1716 and January 1717 are recorded in *Original Letters by the Rev. John Wesley and His Friends*, edited by Joseph Priestley in 1791, and in Adam Clarke's *Memoirs of the Wesley Family* (London 1823). See Podmore, 1:32–9.
6 *DNB*, 21:208–17

---

58 John Moodie to Charles Partridge

New York
July 9, 1858[1]

PHENOMENA AT BELLEVILLE, C.W.

MR. PARTRIDGE:

A few days after my arrival in this city, I received a letter from Mrs.

M., containing an account of a very remarkable spiritual appearance which took place in my house at Belleville, C.W. The following are a few extracts from her letter:

'You can not leave the house without some strange occurrence taking place, and I will endeavor to describe to you, as nearly as possible, what happened last night (July 1, 1858). I was very sleepy and went to bed, Agnes and A.[2] remaining talking in the parlor. I heard the Toronto down train pass, and fell asleep. I was awakened soon after by Agnes opening my door and saying:

' "Mother, are you awake? Come here." – "Is anything wrong?" "We want you; come." I got up and found A. lying upon the sofa; her large eyes wide open, her face deadly pale. She asked me in a very faint voice, "If I saw the hand surrounded with blue light, under the table?" I knelt down by her and looked; I saw nothing. The lamp was unusually brilliant. She seemed astonished. "Oh!" she cried. "It is moving. It is coming nearer. It is almost on your shoulder." Agnes laid her hand on A. —— seeing her tremble so – and said, "Don't be frightened, dear A.; it won't harm you." "Oh! my God," she cried, looking up, "there is a figure by the window all encircled in blue light. O heavens! it is Mr. R." Her eyes now became extended, and tears ran in a stream over her face. "Don't you see him," she cried; "Oh! don't you see him? How natural he looks; he is smiling at me!"

'The vision continued five minutes, and she remained with clasped hands, eyes upraised, and lips apart; but she seemed no longer to suffer from fear. Neither Agnes nor I could see anything, but we certainly heard a sound like faint, low raps. To look into poor A.'s earnest, pale, tearful face, and doubt her sincerity, was impossible. Soon after I went to bed she said, as the phantom disappeared, "It is fading away like a pale light cloud – it is gone." Shortly after Agnes came into my room and lighted my lamp. A. came with her, and sat and shivered on my bed, and cried. "She has seen something dreadful, she said, in the corner," and while sitting upon my bed *two baby fingers came upon the wall* quite transparent. With more courage than I thought she possessed, the poor dear kissed me and went to bed.

'In the morning early, James[3] and I went down to market. Coming out of the Post Office, a young man ran across to me from the Telegraph-office with an open telegraph in his hand, "This is very important," he said, "for Miss C. I had not time to seal it. I was afraid of missing you." I looked at it. Poor A.! It only contained these words – "Your father dying. Come as soon as possible." '

J.W.D.M.

1 Printed in the *Spiritual Telegraph*, 31 July 1858
2 John Moodie's 'Spiritualist Album' identifies this person as Alice Crane, who was romantically involved with Donald Moodie at this time.
3 Her nephew James Traill, age twenty-five

---

59 John Moodie to Charles Partridge

Belleville, C.W.
Aug. 6, 1858[1]

SPIRITUAL PHENOMENA AND THEIR SIGNIFICANCE
RECORD OF SPIRITUAL INVESTIGATIONS

CHARLES PARTRIDGE, ESQ. – Since I had the pleasure of seeing you in New York, my experience in Spiritualism has been considerably enlarged, and I feel anxious to give you the results of my late investigations. I shall make no apology for reiterating facts which have so often been witnessed and related by other investigators; because your paper, having a wide circulation in Canada, as well as in the United States, the truth and correctness of each narrative of facts will be judged of by the character for intelligence and veracity which the observer enjoys in his own particular locality. Still less need I feel any reluctance to relate what I witnessed in your great city itself, where so many are utterly ignorant of the existence of the remarkable phenomena which may be witnessed any day at the residences of your numerous mediums.

Accompanied by a friend from Canada, I first paid a visit to Mr. J.B. Conklin, Test Medium, 469 Broadway. We were both unknown to Mr. Conklin, having never seen him before. Giving me a number of blank slips of paper, Mr. Conklin directed me to write on a number of them the names of relationships. I wrote, 'Father,' 'Brother,' 'Sister,' &c. While I was in the act of writing *Father* and *Brother*, the little table at which the medium sat tipped three times respectively. The medium could not see what I wrote, and I folded up all the slips of paper without taking any notice of the circumstance.

Then separating each folded paper, the contents of each of which I could not tell, being alike invisible to the medium and myself – the table again tipped at two of them. On opening the papers thus indicated, I found *Father* and *Brother* on each of them respectively.

I laid these two papers open on the table, and after writing a number of family Christian names on other blank slips of paper, and folding them carefully, so that no one but myself could see what I wrote, I again separated them, one by one, as before, and the names *James* and *Benjamin*, for the names of my father and brother, were indicated by the tipping of the table.

I then asked my father to make the table tip a number of times, corresponding to his age when he died. The table tipped 67 times. I remarked that I thought he died at 65 years of age. The medium snatched up a pencil and paper which lay on the table, and wrote the following communication with extraordinary rapidity, from right to left, with his right hand. In order to read it I had to hold the paper between my eye and the gas light.

'MY SON – I was near 67 when I departed from the earthly form. I am happy to see you, my son, seeking to realize this truth. I have tried on several occasions to impress your mind with my presence. Your mother and brother are with me. Your father,

JAMES ——.'

The hand of the medium was immediately influenced again, and he wrote as follows, from right to left, as before:

'BROTHER – I also welcome you with a few words.
BENJAMIN.'

'Have you anything to communicate with me?'

'No, nothing to-night. I merely wished to indicate my presence.
BENJAMIN.'

Nothing could be more satisfactory to me as a test, than these short communications, in a place where I was almost entirely unknown. The statement of my father that my mother was with him is particularly remarkable, as even through my wife's mediumship I could never obtain any communication from her, though I had several communications from two of my brothers. My mother having died when I was only a few months old, I naturally imagined that there might be less affinity between here spirit and mine. It would also appear, from my own experience, that the Spirits prefer some mediums to others. In this view of the subject I felt sure, from former experience of her reliability as a medium, that I would get more satisfaction from my amiable friend, Kate Fox. Accompanied by my friend, I called on her in the forenoon of the 6th July last, and after sitting a few minutes at the table, I was repeatedly strongly touched on the leg and foot, and my mother's maiden name was spelled out by the raps, which are now much louder than they formerly were.

ELIZABETH D——. 'My son, you must be faithful to your new vocation, and great Spirits will aid you.'

'What vocation does the Spirit mean?'
'Healing in every form.'
'Will you guide or direct me in healing?'
'You will be guided while in the act of healing.'
One remarkable manifestation as a 'test' of Spirit power occurred on this occasion. *I had several answers to questions rapped out on the sole of my boot, while it was held flat on the floor.* The raps were quite distinctly felt by me, and as distinctly heard by all present, viz., by Kate Fox, my friend, and myself. Pursuant to an appointment I made with Kate Fox, I paid her a visit one evening afterward, (9th July), when she said she would be disengaged. In jumping from the omnibus at Nineteenth street, before it fully stopped, I had a severe fall. On reaching Kate Fox's residence, I missed my spectacles, and supposed they had been lost out of my pocket when I fell. Mrs. Fox told me that I should advertise them, and she was sure I would get them again. As she said this, three loud raps, for 'yes,' came on the floor. However, having little faith in advertising for missing articles, I gave up my gold spectacles for lost; but on returning to my lodgings I found them lying in my bedroom. I have not the slightest recollection of removing them from the pocket in which I usually carried them.

On sitting down at the table with Kate Fox and a gentlemen in whose presence, as she told me, many remarkable manifestations took place, we heard three very loud raps on the floor, as if it had been struck violently with the handle of a pitchfork. On asking Kate how such unusual raps could be produced, I was directed by the ordinary raps on the table to put my left hand under the table. I felt something moving about under my fingers, and then a round piece of wood was placed gently in my hand. I brought the object to the light, and found that I held in my hand by the leg a large heavy footstool, by which, no doubt, the loud raps were produced. I was then repeatedly touched on the legs and knees by what felt like human hands, and received the following communication:

'DEAR JOHN —— You have a great duty to fulfill, and if you are faithful, great and high Spirits will wholly assist you. Call always upon us to aid you. God has heard your prayer and has answered it. Have confidence in your power.

YOUR MOTHER AND OTHERS'

'How shall I be enabled to cure?'
'You will be able to cure by touch.'
I here remarked, 'How strange it seems that God, who gave power in former ages to work miracles, should withhold it from mankind in modern times! Has the power of working miracles really ceased?'

'It has not ceased. There is now revival in heaven among Spirits. Miracles have again commenced. Dear John, with the aid of this gentlemen's Spirit friends, I shall be able to give you a powerful test.

ELIZABETH'

I was then directed by the raps to put paper and a pen under the table. One of the gas-burners was lit, affording sufficient light to read or write on the table, but *not beneath it*. On placing the paper below the table, by Kate's direction, I examined it minutely, to be sure that there was no writing on it. In a little while we heard the rapid scratching of the pencil on the paper; and then the folding up of the paper into a small size. Putting my hand below the table, the folded letter was placed in it.

'MY DEAR SON —— God bless you. A mother never forgets her son. God bless you! Your path is filled with blessings from heaven. You are a good healing medium.

ELIZABETH M——'

For some two months previous to the receipt of this communication, I had been receiving one communication after another from my Spirit friends, through different mediums, telling me to prepare myself for becoming 'a healing medium,' and was directed to be abstemious in my diet, to drink no tea or coffee, &c. But I was still very skeptical about my healing powers. I remembered, however, about three months ago relieving Mrs. T., my wife's sister, from a very severe attack of hereditary gout in the knee, by merely making a few passes with my hands from the knee downward. This encouraged me to try my healing powers in other cases, and I have been successful beyond my most sanguine expectations. In one instance I relieved severe rheumatism in the shoulder and arm, of six weeks' continuance, by merely laying my left hand on the bare shoulder, while I held the patient's hand in my right hand. The whole time occupied in this operation was only 30 minutes, and the rheumatism has not returned. One of my first cases was that of a near neighbor, who had suffered several years from chronic rheumatism, neuralgia, and sore eyes. The first trial I made in this case enabled me to bring the rheumatism down from the elbow to the wrist, and the next evening I removed the pain altogether. Having succeeded so well with his arm, my friend asked me if I could not do something for his eyes, which had been sore for four years, so that his eyesight was much impaired. I laughed and said I would try, but did not expect to do any good. Drawing the points of my fingers from the center of the brow backward, along the eye-brows for a few minutes, his eyes began to stream with water, and he told me that the pain and irritation were gone. The next morning, on awaking, he could open his eyes freely, which he could not do for a long time previously. By continuing these manipulations for two or three nights for about an hour at a time, his eyes were nearly healed, so that he could read by candle light for several hours in the evening.

I can hardly tell how many cases of bilious and nervous headache I have relieved by similar means, in a few minutes. A daughter, Mrs. F., who resides in Toronto, had come down to Belleville on a visit to us. She had been suffering with inflammation of the lungs in consequence of a severe cold. Following the directions I had received through a medium at New York, I drew my hands from her ears downward to her stomach, and passed them off outward several times. She felt as if warm water were running down one side of her lungs. On the other side she experienced no particular sensation. She soon felt much better. The next day I repeated these passes with my hands, and she felt no particular sensation on either side. It would thus appear that the passes had the effect of equalizing the circulation throughout the lungs.

A few days after her return to Toronto, my daughter, in writing to her mother and giving an account of her state of health, was suddenly influenced by the spirit of her husband's brother, who constantly writes through her hand, to write a few words, which, as usual, were in his exact handwriting. The following passage occurs in my daughter's letter:

'It could not be possible when I felt that heat like hot water running down when papa mesmerized – [here the Spirit seized her hand] – *Did her very much good – I knew that all the time. She is trying to stop my hand, but I won't let her.* [My daughter continues in her own natural hand.] You see my query was satisfactorily answered without your opinion on the subject.'

This Spirit and some other Spirits constantly communicate with my daughter by what appears to her like an audible voice. If she is at a loss for a quotation or some text in Scripture, it is thus instantly supplied to her, either by the voice in her ear, or by moving her hand in writing.

In the course of my experiments in curing rheumatism, I find that the diseased member is generally quite susceptible to the influence of the mesmeric passes – although the patient is quite insensible to the influence of mesmerism generally. This is a happy provision of nature. My experience as yet is so limited, however, that I can not easily distinguish between the natural and ordinary powers inherent in my physical organization, and that power which the Spirits have so often promised to convey to me.

With reference to a short communication which appeared above my initials in the SPIRITUAL TELEGRAPH of the 31st July last, being an extract from a letter from Mrs. M. received by me while in New York, I wish to state a few additional particulars. On the 30th June last, before I left home, while sitting at the Spirit Board with the young lady referred to, who is so near-sighted that she can not read the large printed letters on the Board, we received the following communication, which I now suppose came from the Spirit who afterward appeared to her:

'A——, you will see to-night something that will convince you that you are to become a trance-medium, at two o'clock. So you are not to touch the Board after to-night. If you do, no good will come of it. You must not be frightened at what you see this night, as it will not harm you, but hereafter do you good. You must not miss going to church every Sunday, while you are in Belleville. Now, A——, leave the Board for a short time.'

We asked some questions about the health of A——'s father, and received the following reply from some other Spirit, as it was somewhat inconsistent with what preceded it:

'Your father is not so well, and you must go home to-morrow by the early train. As me no questions. He was taken worse this morning at two o'clock. The same hour you will have a manifestation this night. Go not asleep this night. Your father will give up the ghost at that hour.'

Here my daughter tried to relieve A——'s anxiety occasioned by this communication, which we thought must come from a *bad* – I beg its pardon – *undeveloped* Spirit.

'Hold your tongue, Agnes; you know nothing about this matter.'

I remarked, 'it must be a bad Spirit, trying to alarm A——.'

'No, it is not; I am a good Spirit, that wishes to warn A—— of her approaching loss.'

I paid no attention to these communications at the time, but now perceive their significance, though she saw nothing at the time promised. On the night of the first of July, after I started for New York, or rather at two o'clock on the morning of the second of July, A—— saw the apparition of Mr. R——, as related in my communication to the SPIRITUAL TELEGRAPH. Since seeing this apparition, A——, who was previously so timid and nervous that she could not sleep alone, has lost all fear. After she reached home the Spirits communicated with her a whole night by distinct raps on the head of her bed, and occasionally afterward. It is hard to account for the inconsistency or falsehood of some of this communication, but there is one leading motive in them which is sufficiently obvious, viz., a desire to prepare her mind gradually for the bad news she was to receive so soon thereafter.

In reading the account of the apparition, your readers will observe the cautious manner in which her mind was guarded against the sudden shock of seeing the Spirit at once, by the hand being first exhibited to her under the table. If some of the objectors to the spiritual theory would reflect a little more on the subject, they would easily understand the reason for the various indirect and undignified modes by which the Spirits choose to communicate with their friends in the present infancy of the science.

This last spiritual manifestation has obliterated the last traces of doubt or skepticism from my wife's mind. On the 12th July, 1858, she received the following communication from her guardian spirit, who often reproached her for her obstinate skepticism:

'Your dear friend is here, and greets you. Attend to my words. Your wish is granted. Even now, Spiritualism has taken a firm hold of your mind. Time will strengthen the impression. Letters cast on iron are not easily obliterated. You will never again doubt our ministration. Try and prepare your mind for the reception of divine truth, by becoming truthful in word, thought and deed; for the mind where truth dwells, cannot long be the recipient of error. For as light dispels the darkness, so truth dissipates the clouds of ignorance and falsehood. No one can entertain an angelic guest in an impure mansion, lest both should be defiled. Make your heart clean, my daughter, so we may rejoice to garnish it with flowers of heavenly growth. Now read your son's letter.

A letter from the post-office had just been laid on the table by our man-servant.

J.W. DUNBAR MOODIE

1 Printed in the *Spiritual Telegraph*, 28 August 1858

---

60 John Moodie to Charles Partridge

Belleville, C.W.
August 29, 1858[1]

SPIRITUAL PHENOMENA AND THEIR SIGNIFICANCE
DREAMS
BY J.W.D. MOODIE

EDS. SPIRITUAL TELEGRAPH: — A great deal has been written on the philosophy of dreams, and I can hardly hope to be able to advance anything new on the subject. But still, each individual, having his own personal experience and observation to direct him, may be expected, in some measure, to confirm or modify the opinions already entertained on this prolific theme.

There are two prominent aspects in which dreams may be viewed. They are either to be regarded as the simple reflex of the mind of the sleeper, or they are *from without*, and may thus be clairvoyant, or even prophetic in their character. As to the first, or more common description of dreams, a great deal may be said; but not having any work which treats expressly on this subject, such as

that of Macnish,[2] which I have never read, I must trust exclusively
to my own observations. In the first place, let us consider whether
any of such dreams are altogether independent of the will of the
sleeper, or if he is altogether or absolutely unconscious of them
at the time. As I can not consider that any mental operation can
possibly take place without the consciousness or will of *some
entity*, be it man or 'Spirit,' the question naturally arises, whether
the dream, with all its details, reasonings and refections on the current or apparent facts, springs directly from the mind of the dreamer
– or whether his mind becomes a mere automaton, and is played
upon like a musical instrument in the hands of a stranger?

I have heard many ingenious theories to account for common
dreaming, but most of them are more or less inconsistent with common sense and common observation, though they may have been
adopted and persistently maintained by philosophers, for want of
better. Among these theories the 'reflex' action of the back brain is
most prominent. According to this theory, if I understand it aright,
one portion of the brain is 'wide awake' – reasons and sits in judgment on the matters presented to it, just as wisely as if the whole
court or brain were present – while the more intellectual portion,
the front brain, is taking a quiet snooze, like the Lord Chancellor on
the woolsack in the House of Lords. An unlearned person would be
apt to think that the sleepy portion of the brain would be that
which is usually laid on the pillow when dreams occur, viz., the
animal, or back brain. As it seems to be a system of watch and
watch about, it is to be hoped that the intellectual, or front brain
duly takes its turn, and does not selfishly doze on like a fat million-
aire, while his bull-dog keeps watch in the back yard.

Now let us seriously examine the back-brain theory for one minute. Then, as no intelligence can emanate from an unintelligent
source, the back brain, as it reasons as soundly as the whole 'wide-
awake' brain on the subjects submitted to its notice or decision,
must be intelligent; and if so, it must possess an individual existence. Thus a part would be as great as the whole; for the front brain
being for the time defunct, the posterior portion has succeeded to
the whole property possessed by it. Is it not more rational to suppose that the effect of sleep is to benumb or partially paralyze the
sensibility of the whole mass of the brain? In this state it is in some
measure reduced to an automatic state, and may be played on by the
involuntary stimulus of the animal organs, which act and re-act on
the intellectual or voluntary organs.

A dreamer is much in the same condition as a psychologic

patient. To either of them an idea has but to be suggested, and the mind or imagination fills in all the details. The reason is still present, and performs its part probably as well as if the dreamer were awake. Dreamers are never sound sleepers, and therefore dreaming may be considered a state of imperfect sleep, with an intermingling of external consciousness. The dreamer is not deprived of his reasoning powers; he is merely passive, good-natured, without will of his own, child-like, impulsive and credulous. Is it not the same with any weak man in his waking state? – the *animal* is strong, the *man* feeble.

In the class of common dreams we are now considering, I have alluded to those which naturally arise, like the playful freaks of the imagination in the waking mind. They are almost invariably founded on facts previously known to the sleeper. The *dramatis personae* are persons well known, or persons like them in their leading features. The scenery is such in kind as we have seen in nature, or depicted in the landscapes of the artist. So far as my own experience goes, I can not say that the imagination, in dreaming, absolutely *creates* anything, as it seems merely to *intensify* and embellish. I never dreamed of more beautifully picturesque scenery than I have witnessed in some countries I have visited; nor have I dreamed of more lovely women than I have seen on *terra firma* – but my sleeping imagination has thrown an unspeakable spiritual charm around both that has spread a dreamy happiness over my every day life for weeks afterward.

I have dreamed of music and poetry which gave me exquisite pleasure in my sleep, and portions of both I have sometimes remembered when I awoke; and of these I preserved precious samples with much care to delight the 'outer world.' The music was simple, but tasteless; and the poetry namby-pamby, not very unlike some of the same dreamy commodity which some 'unprogressed' spirits have palmed out upon the world under the assumed names of Felicia Hemans[3] and Robert Burns. The fact is, that in dreams our senses are intensified, so that a very little beauty of any kind produces a most lively sensation.

Let us now turn to that class of dreams which are not created by our own imagination in its semi-conscious state, or suggested by some living person present, who by whispering to us when asleep, gives a subject which is carried forward in our minds while the busy fancy fills up the blanks. *Here*, it becomes hard to distinguish between a species of 'clairvoyance,' with which the mind is for the time possessed, and the action of disembodied Spirits *from without*. If 'clairvoyance,' in ordinary cases, is dependent upon the action of our own minds under certain known conditions, still I feel convinced that in other extraordinary cases our Spirit friends often adopt this mode of making *us* acquainted with facts taking place at a distance, by presenting them in the form of a picture to our minds during sleep. I will give a remarkable instance of this kind of dream.

In the year 1852, my wife had a most dangerous illness, arising from hemorrhage, and for a long time her life seemed to hang upon a thread. She however at length recovered, and I thought all danger past. Tired of the sedentary life I had been leading, I took it into my head to summon the grand and petit jurors for one of the next courts, *myself*; instead of handing the summons, as usual, to my deputy. I had travelled some four or five hundred miles without coming home, when I arrived late one evening at a village tavern about eleven miles from Belleville. I had still two or three jurors in that neighborhood to summon, but the heavy rain compelled me to seek shelter. I was awakened, after midnight, by a dreadful dream and a violent palpitation of the heart. I thought I saw my wife lying at the point of death. I saw no one but herself, lying in her bed, deadly pale, and breathing with extreme difficulty. I awoke with the violent palpitation of my heart, and sat up in bed, trying to drive the horrid vision from my mind; but I still saw the bed and my wife, until the picture gradually faded away. But long after it had disappeared, I continued to hear distinctly *the long-drawn breathings*. At that time I had no faith in dreams, but do what I would, there was no rest for me. I groped about for a match, and lighted the candle. On looking at my watch I found it was half past one. I read a book until sunrise, started to finish my work as quickly as possible, and hurried home. My eldest daughter ran out to meet me at the gate, and told me that her mother had been at death's door at the very hour when I had the horrible dream. Not expecting for hours to see the light of morning, my poor wife had been intently listening to the sound of the wheels of each carriage that passed our door, in the hope of seeing me once more before she died. My daughter described the very sound of the long-drawn breathings which I had heard so distinctly in my dream, and even, after I awoke. Happily the hemorrhage was arrested before life was extinct.

This was obviously an instance of temporary clairvoyance, produced by Spirits on one not naturally in the smallest degree susceptible of mesmeric influence, much less of clairvoyance.

I will relate another dream, which my wife had the night before my youngest boy was drowned, in 1844. She thought she had gone home to England, to show our dear boy to her aged mother before she died. The appearance of the family residence, R—— Hall, seemed quite altered. A number of ornamental trees that concealed the front of the old house had been removed, and the ground was laid out as a green plot and carriage road. Leading Johnny by the hand, she entered by the hall-door; but all the windows were open, and the house seemed deserted. At length her sister Jane made her appearance. She was, when we last saw her, very tall and thin, but now she seemed to have grown exceedingly stout. She told my wife that her mother had been dead several years, but that they did not wish to distress her by telling her when she had so many other sorrows of her own. My wife awoke from this miserable dream with her pillow absolutely drenched with tears. The whole day afterward a heavy cloud hung over her mind, believing that her mother was dead; but instead of this, before night our poor boy was drowned. Some weeks afterward all the local changes observed by my wife in her dream were confirmed by a letter from her mother (who still lives,) particularly the alterations about the house, and Jane's stoutness, a fact that seemed quite incredible to those who knew her.

At this communication has taken somewhat of a melancholy turn, it may in some degree remove its saddening influence to transcribe a few verses written in the backwoods of Canada many years ago, when my wife and I had our full share of anxieties, but as yet no sorrow for the loss of those dear to our hearts. Thanks to the Almighty Giver of all good, we can now, without the flickering aid of dreams, realize the presence of these dear ones who unceasingly watch over us and protect us from evil.

I may, possibly, make some further observations on the subject of dreams, in a future communication.
Belleville, C.W., *Aug.* 29. 1858.

O, LET ME SLEEP!

O, let me sleep! nor wake to sadness
The heart that, sleeping, dreams of gladness;
For sleep is death without the pain –
Then wake me not to life again.

O, let me sleep! nor break the spell

That soothes the captive in his cell;
That bursts his chains, and sets him free
To revel in his liberty.

Loved scenes, arrayed in tenderest hue,
Now rise in beauty to my view;
And long-lost friends around me stand,
Or, smiling, grasp my willing hand.

Again, I seek my island home –
Along the silent bays I roam;
Or, seated on the rocky shore,
I hear the angry surges roar.

And ah, how sweet the music seems
I've heard amid by blissful dreams!
But of the sadly pleasing strains
Nought but the thrilling sense remains.

Those sounds so loved in scenes so dear,
Still – still they murmur in my ear;
But sleep alone can bless the sight
With forms that fade with morning's light.

1 This letter was published on 11 September 1858.
1 Robert McNish (1802–37), author of *Philosophy of Sleep* (1830)
3 *DNB*, 9:482–3

---

61 John Moodie to Charles Partridge

Belleville, C.W.
[29 January 1859][1]

SPIRITUALISM AND ITS TEACHINGS

[The following interesting communication should have been
inserted before; but it has been unavoidably delayed. Its esteemed
author has our thanks, and we hope he will continue to remember
us, Ed.]

CHARLES PARTRIDGE, ESQ., Editor of Spiritual Telegraph: In your number of 18th December, 1858, I was very sorry to perceive an account of a fire in your printing office, by which an article of mine, among several others, was consumed. I do not suppose you meant to make 'light' of our valuable lucubrations, as your notice of the calamity would seem to imply. However, as I had kept no copy of mine, I must just try to supply the loss as well as I can. As it is now so near the conclusion of the year, I shall endeavor to give a rapid retrospective glance at the progress of Spiritualism up to the present time.

There was a time when Spiritualism, with its accompanying miracles, was received by all Christians, as well all Jews, with unswerving faith. This faith might be blind and unreasoning, but still it *was* faith. In an age when science had made but little progress, the minds of men were only receptive to what appealed to their senses, particularly to the senses of hearing and seeing. All men could meet on this plane – the learned and the unlearned. The simple-minded fishermen, the first followers of our blessed Lord, were just as capable of judging of what is called 'a miracle,' as the learned doctors of the law. They saw works done, which, as they believed, far transcended human power, and with undoubting faith they trusted to the evidence of their senses. The learned, on the contrary, in their pride of knowledge, doubted the very best evidence which can ever be furnished to the human race. For if we doubt the evidence of our senses, where can we obtain better? No amount of proof will convince one whose mind is not by nature receptive of reason. What was understood as 'miracle,' appeared alike to all minds. If their senses did not deceive them, or if they did not think that they did, all would be compelled to believe.

I would here say a few words on the subject of 'miracles.' The meaning of the word miracle is simply, a wonderful work. It would be well if it still could be regarded in this plain and more intelligible sense. The blind love of the wonderful, so natural to men, led them to consider a miracle as something supernatural, instead of looking on it as a higher development of natural powers. *Supernatural* is only another word for impossible. Miracle may be more correctly defined as 'a wonderful work of nature, *under certain conditions.*' Were you to give a piece of steel to one who never heard of magnetism, and tell him that it would attract or draw to itself another piece of steel, he would very naturally say, 'The thing is impossible.' But take a magnet; and magnetize a piece of steel; he would then find that by virtue of the power communicated to it, it would attract it. This is a very simple illustration, but it is not the worse on that account. Things are very simple and very obvious when they are known, and it would be well if the unbelievers in Spiritualism would only think of the magnet when, contrary to the evidence of thousands, they say it is impossible for a table to rise from the floor without being touched by human hands. This also is a miracle, in its correct sense; but it is not supernatural. All that is required is a good medium for the physical manifestations, and other favorable conditions, and the thing will be done.

There is a tendency in scientific men to think that because they know a great deal more than others, they know every thing. In a truly philosophic mind, like that of Newton, (for his deep insight into the eternal laws of nature, as well as his profound veneration of its great Author, taught him how very little he did know of all that was yet to be learned by man,) this shallow and presumptuous idea could never be entertained. But all scientific men are not Newtons. His was one of the great original minds, and the mind of your great Franklin was another of the same stamp of originality. Such men cut out the work for their successors in the same line of discovery, and each succeeding philosopher, with less originality of mind, walks in the footsteps of his master, and almost worships him as a god, as if nothing yet remained to be discovered. Their ideas become stereotyped, and they become bigots to science. Need we be surprised that the learned and scientific at the commencement of the Christian era should have in general been the last to embrace its doctrines? After performing unheard of miracles, Christ said to his Apostles, 'Verily, verily, I say unto you, he that believeth on me, the works that I do shall he do also; and greater works than those shall he do; because I go to my Father.' – (John xiii.12.) And the New Testament tells us what works or miracles the Apostles did perform. But was the power of working miracles confined to his Apostles? Certainly not; for in St. Mark, ch. xvi., Christ says, 'Go ye into all the world, and preach the Gospel to every creature.' * * * *'And these signs shall follow them that believe*: In my name shall they cast out devils; they shall speak with new tongues; they shall take up serpents, and if they drink any deadly thing, it shall not hurt them; they shall lay hands on the sick, and they shall recover.'

Now, these *ancient* miracles being admitted by all Christians, as well as by Christian 'Spiritualists,' the question naturally arises, when did these miracles cease? All 'Protestant' teachers will say,

'With the lives of the first disciples.' But how do they know this? The early history of the Christian Church (for it was not then divided into Roman Catholic and Protestant, &c.) tells us of numerous miracles wrought by saints and martyrs. The 'Protestants' may call these pretended miracles, or priestly fabrications; but what right have they to do so? Can they disprove them? They may try to throw the 'onus probandi' on the Catholic Church, but that will not answer their purpose – for have not the Roman Catholics their histories to appeal to respecting these early miracles, as we have our history to appeal to respecting the miracles of the Apostles and their first disciples. 'But,' say they, 'our miracles are recorded in the writings of "inspired" writers.' Here, again, they beg the question. Those whom they call 'inspired' writers, or historians, could only record such miracles as were wrought before or during their own life time. After *their* death, if any miracles were wrought, they could only be recorded by those whom the Protestants would denominate 'uninspired' historians. Again, supposing them to have been 'uninspired,' why should they be considered as *untruthful* historians? According to this theory, all historians would have to be inspired, in order to be believed. And what, then, will become of all our profane historians, in whose veracity we have trusted for ages? Verily, it seems to me, that in getting rid of much superstition by what is called the Reformation, we have lost much of the '*Spirituality*' of the Christian religion. In this respect the Roman Catholics, whom we reproach for their superstition, are far superior to us, because they have retained much more of the faith they derived from the Apostolic ages. Once diverge from the true path, and we stray farther and farther from our starting point. From the time of the Reformation this loss of spirituality has been progressive in the wrong direction, until in the natural course of our retrogression, we would, no doubt, have ended in infidelity, had not reason and philosophy come to our aid, and taught us that there is a God.

As the Reformation *overdid* its work, by blotting out much of the faith and spirituality of the first fathers of the Christian Church, along with the superstitions and external ceremonies of their immediate successors, a *new* Reformation is sternly demanded by the men of the present age, who dare to think for themselves. The belief in spiritual influence has been cherished by men in all ages, and in every form of religion. This ennobling faith is inborn in our hearts, and grows with our growth when left to itself; and though it may be smothered for a time by materialistic ideas, it will some time give proofs that it still survives. It is instinctive, and the clergy know full well how vain are all their endeavors to suppress the popular belief in spiritual intercourse. The 'ghosts' and 'haunted houses' of the present day are still to be recognized as the traditional Spiritualism of a former age, still cherished by the peasantry of Europe, and localized from father to son around certain old castles and domiciles, to which they adhere with a tenacity that defies the inroads of modern science and skepticism. The more educated classes, and the men of science, may sneer at the vulgar credulity of the people, but can they utterly destroy their superstitions without destroying ultimately the belief in the immortality of the soul, of which spiritual appearances are the very best evidence which we possess?

In all ages down to Protestantism, spiritual power and influence have been exhibited in one or more localities, in order to keep alive this faith in a spiritual world for the soul after it has parted company with the body. But a new and accursed superstition took possession of the minds of men, which raged for a time like a devouring flame, carefully fanned by malignant and narrow-minded priests, who had long ceased to be fitting mediums for spiritual communications by their grasping selfishness and intractable prejudices. I allude to the real or pretended belief in 'witchcraft.' When we compare some of the accounts of witchcraft with the modern Spiritualism of our own day, we can hardly help admitting the striking similarity of the manifestations of Spirit-power; but the minds of men were still unprepared for the reception of their spiritual guests, and *they* despaired of finding a resting-place on earth. No doubt many attempts had been made by 'Spirits' to hold converse with men, but the accounts of their manifestations have been lost through the general incredulity of the higher classes of society, and many more of them have never been recorded for the same reason.

In the year 1716, the family of Mr. Samuel Wesley, in the parsonage-house of Epworth, in Lincolnshire, England, were disturbed with extraordinary noises, which were deemed supernatural by all who heard them. These noises continued for many years, and bore so exact a resemblance to the recent spiritual manifestations, that there can be no doubt of the identity of their origin; but, strange to say, though there was evident '*intelligence*' connected with these 'raps' and other sounds, no one thought of the alphabet as a means of communicating with the Spirits. In this instance, however, the conditions being otherwise favorable, it was fortunate that the witnesses to the manifestations were persons of the highest character for intelligence and integrity. Still most men at the time, and ever since, altogether disbelieved their statements, and even considered some of the family as insane.

Then in 1762 came the 'Cock Lane Ghost,' the facts connected with which Dr. Johnson,[2] who was possessed of great candor and independence of mind, openly acknowledged to rest on evidence to which he could not withhold his assent. The manifestations in this case were again exactly similar to those witnessed by the Wesley family forty years before. The supposed actors in the manifestations were not indeed burned for witchcraft, as at a somewhat earlier period they would certainly have been; but they were only punished by placing Parsons, the chief offender, in the pillory three times in one month, and then to be imprisoned for two years, his wife Elizabeth to be imprisoned one year, and Mary Fraser, who acted only as interpreter between the 'ghost' and those who examined her, was sentenced to Bridewell for six months, and to be there kept at hard labor. I need not enlarge on the subject of the 'Cock Lane Ghost' (the particulars of which 'supposed' imposture are fully given in the SPIRITUAL TELEGRAPH of June 5, 1858).

In 1743, that great, holy and learned man, Emanuel Swedenborg, received his first communications from the Spirit world, which continued for nearly thirty years, up to the day of his death. It is not my intention to say much of this very extraordinary man. I would merely observe that what has been written of him rests on precisely the same evidence as all other similar histories of so-called supernatural intelligence. The remarkable general agreement of the intelligence from the Spirit-world received through Swedenborg, with the spiritual communications received through various mediums of the present day who have never seen his writings, or heard anything about them, deserves especial notice.

Something was still wanting to prepare the unbelieving minds of men for the reception of Spiritualism; and this was the great discovery of Mesmer, who first made his doctrines known to the world in 1766, hardly one year after the discharge of Parsons from the King's Bench Prison. We can all remember the ridicule with which mesmerism was formerly treated. The general admission of its most prominent facts and phenomena by all possessing any degree of intelligence, has formed a most important link in the chain of evidence by which common-place minds are generally brought to trace the influence of mind upon mind, and mind upon matter. Mesmerism, with its farther development, clairvoyance, merges so imperceptibly into Spiritualism, that it is impossible to determine the exact boundary lines between them.

About forty-five or forty-six years later, the Seeress of Prevorst[3] made her appearance in Germany, exhibiting many of the same manifestations that we now witness almost everywhere in North America. She formed an intermediate link between the magnetized subject of 1766 and the 'Spirit-rappers' of 1848. The science of mesmerism, or animal magnetism, as it is more properly called, led directly to the investigation of all the mental phenomena, while phrenology, if unattended with any remarkable *practical* results in the knowledge of individual character, greatly aided inquiring minds in the arrangement of their ideas in the classification of the diverse mental operations or physical propensities. The science of 'Spiritualism' is but the natural outgrowth of animal magnetism; but the first effect of animal magnetism was to direct the attention of speculative and benevolent minds to the cure of disease. In 1820, Prince Hohenlohe, having been struck with the cures performed by the prayers of Martin Michel, a peasant of Baden, was induced to adopt similar means, and became famous throughout Europe for the cures he performed. This benevolent man has been represented as the dupe of his credulity, and at length relinquished the practice of his gratuitous *'healing mediumship.'* Still the facts remain to prove that such a power still exists.

I might be here tempted to go into the philosophy of healing by the 'laying on of hands,' but I will merely observe that in most of the cures performed by our blessed Lord and greatest of all 'Healing Mediums,' *faith* was an essential ingredient. I believe it to be the same still. Jesus said to the blind man, 'Receive thy sight! thy faith hath saved thee.' The faith of the blind man was great, and the faith of the 'great medium' was boundless, for he knew all that was required for healing. Prince Hohenlohe possesses great benevolence and faith, but he wanted firmness, and allowed himself to be influenced by the fear of ridicule, which ultimately destroyed his usefulness. Had the *'Spirit-Rappings,'* through the mediumship of the Fox girls, in 1848, occurred in any other country than the United States, they would have excited but little attention. In Germany the way was prepared by the Seeress of Prevorst, and in France by Angelique Cottin,[4] but the manifestations through the latter seem to have been merely of a physical character.

Numerous instances of spiritual appearances and of 'Spirit-Rappings' no doubt occurred in various localities in all ages, but in the earlier ages they were looked upon by the ignorant as supernatural, but now, therefore, disbelieved by the learned, and soon forgotten; or the unfortunate mediums were persecuted as witches. After witchcraft ceased to be believed by the learned, unfortunately the belief in the possibility of Spirit communion ceased also; though in our church services we do profess to believe *'in the communion of saints.'* This expression is, indeed, an ancient monument of what our simple-hearted auditors did believe, but we, without becoming much wiser, have in a great measure smothered up this faith. A very little observation and attention to the progress of science generally, and of animal magnetism and Spiritualism in particular, will show very clearly the anxious desire of the Spirits to hold communion with men in their rudimental condition. Receptivity alone was wanting to enable them to gain their object. The power of the priest's prejudices, and hereditary conventionalism and conservatism was in England as strong as ribbed iron. Enjoying as free a government as any in the world, and liberty of conscience in perfection, the mass of the people allow their minds to be enslaved by the influence of the aristocracy and the Church. In Germany, with less general freedom, the people were allowed the most unrestricted freedom of thought on religious and speculative subjects, and therefore the first buds of Spiritualism began to germinate in Germany quietly and unostentatiously. Were it possible, therefore, to represent the two hemispheres in the same pictures, in common fairness, I think, you should have spared a ray or two of light to fall on our 'Faderland' in your ingenious engraving on the first page of the SPIRITUAL TELEGRAPH.

In Britain we claim little more than reflected rays of Spiritualism; our condition was not a very receptive one, from various causes, on spiritual subjects. No country in the world could compare with the United States in this respect. The absence of conservatism and established churches have left their people free from such unprogressive influences, and they freely use the reason which God has given them. If they often abuse this reason, and form erroneous opinions, they can not cast the exclusive blame on their priestly advisers. When, therefore, the 'Spirit-rappings' through the Fox girls in 1848 became known, the minds of the people, or of a large portion of them, were in a peculiarly receptive condition. They had freely indulged in speculations on religious subjects, trusting to their own reason, until, as might naturally be expected from the absence of that proof which was necessary fully to satisfy reasoning minds, a very large proportion of the people had become extremely skeptical on the subject of Divine revelation; and, strange as it seems, many had ceased to believe in the immortality of the soul. These, however, are natural results of freedom of thought in a free country; it is, in fact, a step in advance, though at first sight it appears to be a retrograde movement. Men doubt, or disbelieve, in order that they may investigate for themselves, with the aid of their own natural reason; and human reason, which is our only guide as to what we should believe, never fails to bring us to the truth at last. In the meanwhile, we are distracted with doubts and fears, for we are but men, and are ready to grasp at anything which promises to enlighten our darkness. The advent of the Spirit-rappings and communications through the Fox girls at Hydesville, near Rochester, was therefore hailed with boundless curiosity and joy by the first believers, and from that time there has been a succession of manifestations of Spirit-power and intelligence, becoming more and more wonderful as curiosity began to flag, until no rational person who has carefully investigated the subject, can doubt the reality of Spirit-communion.

So far, the mere fact of the Spirits of the deceased being able to hold converse with men in this world seems to be established beyond a doubt. There is no sound reason for the objection that these communications come from our own minds, or the minds of those present, for it has been shown over and over again that facts are communicated which are entirely unknown to any one present. We can not reasonably expect to be able to communicate with none but good and truthful Spirits. Some communications are true, and others false; but this by no means affects the *general* facts of Spirit-communion. The communications received by certain mediums, or by certain 'circles,' are generally reliable, and those received by others, false or unreliable. It has been observed for years that mediums and circles naturally attract Spirits of a similar character to their own, as to intelligence and moral feeling. The same takes place in this world. Spirit good or bad, intelligent or ignorant, are drawn toward each other by sympathy. This is a universal law of Nature. Men who have not studied this subject are prone to judge Spiritualism not by reason, but by their own unfounded or ignorant prejudices; they fancy the Spirits of the deceased know everything, not reflecting that such boundless knowledge would produce a universal equality, and would thus destroy individuality and the hope of future progression in future holiness and intelligence, for which we have good authority from several texts of Scripture.

The question still remains, and it is a very important one, Why do we receive so many false communications? I will endeavor to illustrate this part of the subject as well as I can, premising that it is extremely difficult to account for everything quite satisfactorily in the infant states of this science. If good and bad Spirits are alike permitted to communicate with men, the former retaining much of the individual character they bore on earth, there is little difficulty about the matter; the good Spirits will tell the truth, and the bad Spirits will often tell what is false. But I will take another view of the subject: In order to understand the motives of so many apparently uselessly false communications, we should endeavor to fancy ourselves in the particular position of the Spirits in relation to men in this world. Now let us suppose ourselves as a highly-developed Spirit desiring to impress an ignorant and illiterate man with some great truth; is it not obvious that being unreceptive from want of cultivation, his mind would be unapproachable to such a Spirit?

A Spirit of an inferior order would be required in such a case – one who with a great deal of ignorance, and even erroneous views on important subjects, might still communicate some thoughts to this unreceptive mortal which he could comprehend, and thus gradually expand his mind, until it became receptive to a higher order of intelligence. The Holy Scriptures clearly show that it must have been so. The whole tone of the Old Testament, compared with the New Testament, shows the complete barbarism of the Jewish nation. The Jews could understand the cruel justice of 'an eye for an eye, and a tooth for a tooth;' and we need not wonder that they committed acts of cold-blooded and vindictive barbarity quite parallel with the detestable acts of a Nena Sahib[5] of our own times. It is blasphemy to suppose that a forgiving and merciful God ever commanded such acts of merciless cruelty as are related in the Old Testament. The Prophets, like the people, were *then* unreceptive of what in a more advanced age was called Christian morality. Mankind had greatly advanced in knowledge and morality; the soil was prepared for the blessed seed, and Christ appeared, filled with the Holy Spirit, as soon as they had become sufficiently receptive to appreciate a purer and more Godlike religion. It is said by John the Baptist of Jesus: 'For he whom God hath sent speaketh the words of God: for God giveth not the Spirit *by measure* unto him.' (John iii.34.) This clearly implies that all the Prophets before Jesus had been gifted with the Spirit of God in only a *limited degree*; and that as 'mediums,' they were not entirely to be relied upon; and probably, like modern mediums, often unconsciously allowed their own thoughts and opinions to mingle with the spiritual communications they received. It may thus readily be conceived that bad or undeveloped Spirits may often be used by the higher Spirits to hold converse with men who are unbelievers, and it is not improbable that they often personate great Spirits, or the Spirits of those who were great on earth, in order to flatter the pride or vanity of the recipients of their communications. Of course there is no reason why the Spirits of the mighty dead may not communicate with the great or little people of this world; but really 'Franklin,' 'Washington,' 'Swedenborg,' 'Lord Bacon,' &c., must be kept pretty busy in answering all the calls that have been made on them of late, to say nothing of having often to be *in two or three places at the same time* – which is, certainly, a little too much even for a Spirit.

I am afraid, Mr. Editor, there is too much of a leveling spirit among your republican mediums and investigators, and I would, therefore, seriously entreat them not to bother these great Spirits so often, but allow them to rest on their laurels, until each investigator of Spiritualism can be regularly introduced by some mutual friend.

These observations have been extended to such a length that I must conclude by wishing you and all my Spiritual friends in New York a happy New Year.

J.W. DUNBAR MOODIE

1 The letter's date of publication in the *Spiritual Telegraph*
2 James Boswell, *The Life of Samuel Johnson*, 3 vols (London 1924), 1:250 and 2:280
3 The Seeress of Prevorst was Frau Frederica Hauffe. An account of her trances was published in 1829, the year of her death. See Podmore, *Mediums of the Nineteenth Century*, 1:99–105.
4 Angelique Cottin, an 'electric girl,' born in Normandy about 1834. An account of magnetic phenomena and the mysterious movement of objects in her presence was published by Dr Tanchou in Paris 1846. See Podmore, 1:41–2.
5 Nana-Sahib (1820–59), leader of Sepoy Mutiny (see *Encyclopaedia Britannica*, 14th ed. [1972])

---

62 John Moodie to Susanna Moodie

My Dear Old Woman,	Toronto 16 December 1860

I thought you would be anxious to hear the result of the trial yesterday. Nothing is yet decided. I went to Osgood Hall yesterday

morning, and on examining a list of the causes to be decided by the
Judges for that day did not find that mine was among them.
Consequently it will stand over to Saturday next. I am inclined to
think that the Judges will not decide the matter *then* unless they
grant a new trial. When it comes on if the decision is against me
and a new trial is *not* granted I will *appeal* which will give me *more*
time say to 28 February next. Mr. Adam Wilson[1] says that I may
again appeal to England by paying some money and thus the matter
may remain undecided for a year or two.

When I found that *my cause* was not to come on, the next interesting case was that of the negro Anderson who freed himself by
stabbing his pursuer. The Chief Justice[2] read his decision which was
admirably written though cold and rigid as the statue of Justice with
her scales that hang rather uncomfortably over the Bench of Judges.
The document was quite lengthy and shows no doubt his judgement
was sound according to strict *law*, though unfavorable to the
prisoner. Judge McLean[3] next gave his decision which was against
giving up the prisoner to *Southern Justice.* You could see the warm
blood of the Highlander mantle in the cheeks of the honest old man
while descanting on the horrible injustice of Slavery. His remarks in
fact somewhat resembled *at times*, an Antislavery address. He may
have been influenced by the spirit of Thomas Pringle whose works I
lent him some years ago. I have no doubt Pringle *was* in court at
the time though invisible to mortal eyes.

Dear old Burns[4] gave his views next supporting those of the Chief
Justice. Of course there were two Judges to one in favor of giving
the prisoner up. However an Appeal to the Court of Appeal is
entered so there is still a chance of the decision being reversed by
that Court, – if not there is still an appeal to England – or the Governor may not give him up. I do not believe he will ever be given up
to the tender mercies of the cold calculating anti-slavery politicians
of the *North* or the more consistent despots of the *South*. The audi-
ence in Court was somewhat *pepper* and *salt* in complexion from a
considerable sprinkling of kind hearted Niggers who watched the
proceeding with eager interest. Judge McLeans speech which he
made with tears in his eyes was loudly applauded in spite of Judges
and Sheriff showing clearly what the people, including the lawyers
who were in the majority, felt in the matter.

By the bye – the statue. or rather bas relief of Justice in the Court
Room, to which I have alluded, seems to have been designed for
some court room in the United States for one of the scales is tucked

up and nearly kicks the beam, and Miss Justice herself seems to be squinting under the loose bandage over her eyes, – while her left hand hangs over the descending scale as if she had just dropped a heavy coin into it. After all I think a blindfolded statue is but a poor emblem of manly impartial Justice. It seems to me better suited to a 'State lottery.'

I hardly know whether to return home in a day or two and return to Toronto by Saturday next, or to remain here till that time.

Tell Bob to get Anson Northrup's[5] advice as to any return called for, or to ask Wallbridge about such matters before acting. There were two or three *rules* served on me a few days ago. I think neither Wallbridge nor Dean[6] will press us hard under present circumstances until Bob can get the returns from the Bailiffs. I spoke to D[r] Arnoldi[7] about Bob. He says he thinks the sensation of *running* in his side to be occasioned by *dyspepsia* and entirely nervous in its character and common in such complaints. He thinks some simple anti-bilious medicine would relieve him at once. He says he should not *smoke much* as his ailments are most probably caused thereby.

Give my love to Donald, Bob and the dear girls. I conveyed Julia's kiss with the books to dear Nancy and will bring back kisses a piece for them. I like to carry such small parcels as they are easily carried and agreeable withall.

> I remain
> My Dear Old Woman
> Your's Every truly
> *J.W. Dunbar Moodie*

Katie is looking jolly as usual and Agnes is furnishing as they call it and looking as well in spite of a bad cold.

My *shaky* patient has had no return of *pain* since I laid my hands on him.

I suppose it was the good feeding oysters as gave me a horrible Nightmare last night. I dreamt that a tall man had got into my Office at the Court House. I clenched him and tried to shout loudly to Dafoe[8] for help. Dreams are not always to be despised. I think Bob should put my Office books every evening in the Debtors room and keep the Key as I know Frank or Ockerman[9] would like to get possession of them *Verb. Sat Sap.*

> *JWDM*

1 *DCB*, 12:1107–9
2 Chief Justice John Beverley Robinson
3 Archibald McLean (1791–1865), a judge who dissented in the John Anderson case on the grounds that he could 'never feel bound to recognize as law any enactment which can convert into chattels a very large number of the human race' (*DCB*, 9:512–13)
4 Robert Easton Burns (1805–63). See *DCB*, 9:108–9.
5 Anson G.N. Northrup, who served as deputy clerk of the Crown and pleas for Hastings County in Belleville at this time, is mentioned in Morgan's *Canadian Men* (1912) in connection with another entry.
6 W.W. Dean, a partner in the Belleville legal firm of Dean and Diamond
7 This Dr Arnoldi, practising in Toronto, was likely a son of Dr Daniel Arnoldi (d. 1849) of Montreal. See *DCB*, 7:25–7.
8 Zenas Dafoe was Belleville's gaoler and chief constable from 1851 to 1860.
9 Moodie's hiring of Dunham Ockerman as his deputy had resulted in the charges of 'farming of office' that occasioned this visit to Toronto. See Audrey Morris, *Gentle Pioneers* (Toronto 1973), 228–31; and *LOL*, 122–3.

1861–1885

'This beautiful but mournful world'

JOHN MOODIE'S TWENTY-THREE-YEAR CAREER as sheriff of the County of Hastings ended with his resignation on 15 January 1863. The story of the lengthy and complicated litigation and negotiations, with their personal, partisan, and political background, which led to Moodie's departure has been told several times.[1] In these letters we see more fully the impact of the events on John Moodie himself. Letter 63, for example, written in a shaking hand a scant two weeks after the stroke he suffered on 28 July 1861, reveals his emotional as well as physical resilience in the face of the anxiety and illness occasioned by the drawn-out legal action and his continuing burdens as returning officer for the 1861 general election.

Moodie resigned his office, rather than cause the legal and political authorities the embarassment of dismissing a loyal public servant on technical grounds, in hopes of remaining eligible for some other public position, in spite of his ill health at sixty-five years of age. But as Letters 64 and 65 indicate, his hopes remained unfulfilled, and by 1864 he seems to have abandoned them and accepted his retirement from public life. Late that year the fear of losing his property to creditors, along with his concerns for the future of Susanna and his grown children, persuaded him to divide his remaining property among the latter. This was to prove the last in a series of unfortunate decisions with respect to his finances. But if the 'too hasty' sale of his commission[2] in 1834 to purchase the ultimately worthless shares in the Cobourg Steamboat Company and all the Moodies' subsequent financial difficulties were a continuing source of concern, the decision to divide his one solid asset, his land holdings, was to lead to family division and deep personal pain.

In these late letters we gather a picture of his land holdings and mortgage arrangements, in Douro and in the Belleville area, which suggests that the couple's destitution at the outset of John's retirement was not as complete as they professed. For example, in the spring of 1855 (Letter 56) John sought reasonable terms on which to repurchase land adjoining his military grant (lot 20, concession 6) on which stood his old barn, but which he had failed to maintain according to the original terms of purchase. In the twenty-five years since his departure from the backwoods the white pine had been logged from the land, rendering it of little commercial value. In response to his petition to Sir Edmund Walker Head a committee of council offered him the opportunity to repurchase the property at 10 shillings an acre. Apparently John Moodie took advantage of this offer since in Letter 68 he arranges to give this lot as partial payment of legal expenses to R.A.

John and Catherine Vickers and their children, c.1875

Harrison. Indeed, several of Moodie's letters to his eldest daughter and his son-in-law, John Vickers, concern the protection of property he owns from seizure as payment for legal bills resulting from his lengthy and unsuccessful struggle to clear his name and retain his office.

Catherine, the Moodies' eldest child, had married John Joseph Vickers on 1 August 1855. Vickers was a successful Toronto businessman, whose Vickers Northern Express Company was involved in the development of rail transportation, mining, and land in northern Ontario. From 1864 to 1869 he served as alderman for St George's Ward in Toronto. Katie herself seems to have possessed business instincts and acted with her husband to look after the interests of her aging parents in their retirement.

In Letter 64, written to his daughter one week after his resignation as sheriff of Hastings, Moodie thanks her for the offer of 'asylum' but remains confident that he will soon be offered another position in spite of the fact that the government on which he depended had fallen, to be replaced by an administration committed to reducing patronage. Nevertheless, he reassures Katie, 'I have very few debts so I think I can save most of my land.' He asks only that John Vickers help him to redeem six acres which he had mortgaged for £125 some time earlier. Twenty months later, however, his hopes for a new office had dimmed considerably, and he was still struggling with the payment of legal bills for his defence in Belleville, although John Vickers had covered the costs of his Toronto appeal in November 1862. In Letter 67 Moodie reports to John Vickers that he has asked Attorney General Lewis Wallbridge (who had defended him in court in 1862) to assist in having his court costs reduced or cancelled. It seems, however, that Wallbridge was again unable to assist because on 20 November 1864 Moodie, writing to Katie, describes a scheme for dividing up his property among his children in order to save it from being seized by his creditors. Faced with sacrificing two lots to cover his debts to R.A. Harrison, he asks Katie to attend to separating the deeds to this land from the six acres Vickers held as surety on the £125 mortgage he took over for Moodie in early 1863. 'I am very sorry that Necessity compelled me to give you all so much trouble out of which I have been relieved by Vickers generous kindness.'

The relationship between John Moodie and his eldest daughter was close. In August 1861 John writes what must have been one of his first letters after the stroke of 31 July 1861, which paralysed his left side. In it he mentions Julia Russell, who, with her sister Eliza, boarded with the Moodies in Belleville at the time. In fact, both would become daughters-in-law, Eliza marrying Dunbar Moodie in Belleville in March 1862 and Julia marrying Donald Moodie in New York in February 1866. The first hint of trouble in these matters arises in Letter 68 when John Moodie reports Eliza's concern over Donald's attentions to Julia. Donald was hardly a promising match as even his father recognized: 'Poor boy he is so lazy that I fear there is little chance of his helping himself much.'[3] In the end, though, it was Eliza and Dunbar who would cause the greatest family trouble and create a rift between John Moodie and his beloved Katie Vickers that lasted from 1866 until his death in 1869.

In the meantime Susanna had kept her old friend and publisher Richard Bentley aware of the Moodies' circumstances in her correspon-

THE REWARD OF VALOUR

J. W. Dunbar Moodie.

J.W.D. Moodie's bookplate
showing the Moodie family crest

dence with him (*LOL*, 211), and it was perhaps by this route that she came to the notice of the Royal Literary Fund for impoverished British writers in the spring of 1865. In her application to the Fund she emphasizes the patriotism and public service of their writing and careers. Clearly, Bentley's encouragement and the act of reminiscing in response to the Literary Fund's application prompted John to write his long autobiographical letter to Bentley on 6 May 1865.

The financial anxiety that caused John Moodie to add in his postscript to Richard Bentley, 'You are perfectly at liberty to use this letter in any manner you may think likely to be beneficial to me or my closest family,' is a constant theme of his later correspondence. Though he still held much of the land he had invested in over the years, he was eventually compelled to mortgage most of it to provide 'the bare necessaries or life,' in spite of the assistance of the Vickers and the $600 he gradually realized from the sale of *Scenes and Adventures, as a Soldier and Settler during Half a Century* (*LOL*, 245), a collection of autobiographical essays from his early years with an introduction on his own family background and Canadian experiences, which John Lovell published for him on subscription in 1866: 'I may as well plainly state the fact at once, that I look to this little book as a means of support for my wife, now advanced in years, and myself' (i).

The Introduction to *Scenes and Adventures* provides a synopsis of the subjects which interested Moodie in his final years, expanded versions of which he submitted to other publications. For example, his interest in the historic link between the Orkney Islands and Scandinavia is reflected in his study of the origins of Orkney names (Letters 73 and 74) which the Orkney *Herald* printed in 1866 and 1867. His colourful family history, summarized in *Scenes and Adventures*, is expounded at length in Letter 74. At the same time the Introduction to his book offers some moving glimpses of his assessment of his long life and adventures: 'This was my *first* mistake – viz., in going to Canada instead of returning to South Africa; but, I suppose, the love of adventure, so powerful an impulse with Scotchmen generally, and more particularly with Orkneymen, was too strong for me' (ix).

Apart from their efforts to provide for their own modest needs, the Moodies worried constantly about the independence and success of their three sons. John Moodie's letter of 23 May 1865 to John Vickers seeks the latter's help in keeping an iron foundry at the mouth of the Trent operating because the Moodie's youngest son, Robert, is in danger of losing his investment and employment in it. 'Bob is honest steady and temperate and I know will do his best for the concern. It is really too bad that the poor boy after working like a horse to start the concern – should be chisselled out of it by an ungrateful rascal!' Whether or not John Vickers helped Robert Moodie on this occasion, he may have been responsible for Robert's accepting employment with the Grand Trunk Railroad in 1866, which lasted until 1872, when Vickers hired him as office manager for the Vickers Express Company in Toronto (*LOL*, 304).

The estrangement between the Moodies and the Vickerses took place early in 1866 when John Moodie decided to give their stone house on Sinclair Street in Belleville to his son Dunbar, 'in hope of securing a home for us, in our old age' (*LOL*, 223). Instead of settling there and looking after the elder Moodies, Eliza and Dunbar sold the property and moved to Delaware to farm. It is perhaps not surprising that the Vickerses, after all their care and assistance, should be upset with Moodie's precipitate actions. As Susanna later recalled, 'The two children who could have helped us, were so enraged at their Father's unfortunate disposal of his property, that they have withdrawn themselves entirely from us' (*LOL*, 231).

Left to their own resources, the Moodies rented a small frame cottage on lot 3 on the south side of Dundas Street, near the Bay of Quinte in Belleville:[4]

So here we are – living in a little cottage with just room enough to hold us, but beautifully situated on the edge of our lovely bay, with a fine common in front covered with noble trees through which we see the spires of Belleville about a mile distant, and for which we pay a rent of 12 pounds per annum and the rates 10 dollars. My servant Margaret's wages 12 pounds more for I am too old, now 65, for hard work and am able to earn the money that pays her wages ... Then I have a faithful Skye terrier who is known by the name of Quiz, very ugly and small, but full of almost human intelligence and much more love than generally belongs to the dominant human race. A steel kitten Grim, who is dear M[oodie]'s especial pet. A perfect incarnation of mischief very common to the Maltese race. 24 hens who help furnish our larder, who come to me to be fed at the sound of a small handbell. (*LOL*, 245–6)

In contented retirement at last, John Moodie spent his final three years, nursed lovingly by Susanna as his health gradually deteriorated. His peaceful death on 22 October 1869 is movingly described in Susanna's letter of 11 November to Daniel Ricketson (1813–98). A Quaker poet, historian, and fellow Abolitionist with whom the Moodies had apparently corresponded for some time,[5] Ricketson, who had inherited a large personal fortune, developed his estates, 'Brooklawn,' in New Bedford, Massachusetts, as a pastoral retreat for his literary pursuits and a quiet haven for such notable friends and acquaintances as Emerson, Thoreau, and the Alcotts. It is possible that John Moodie had visited 'Brooklawn' on his trip to New York and Boston in 1856 (*LOL*, 170, 176–7).

Susanna's description of John's death in Letter 76 is more detailed than the version she had written two days earlier to another old Quaker friend, Allen Ransome of Ipswich, England (*LOL*, 251–4). She clearly spent many hours in the weeks immediately following her husband's death, sitting in her cramped new surroundings in Robert Moodie's Seaforth Station home, composing these moving accounts of

John Moodie's last hours. In the letter to Ricketson she includes details such as wakening her neighbour Lawrence Wilkinson to summon Dr Hope and regretting her own inability to be present at John's well-attended funeral.

Among those who came to her support was John Vickers. Katie, who was expecting a baby in a few months, remained in Toronto, but John persuaded his mother-in-law to accompany him back to the Vickerses' home at 152 Adelaide Street in Toronto. There, while John Vickers closed the Belleville cottage and arranged Susanna's affairs, a reconciliation between mother and daughter took place (*LOL*, 271–2).

But Susanna did not remain in Toronto for many days. She had promised her youngest son that she would live with him and his young family in Seaforth, just west of Stratford, Ontario, where Robert was station master for the Grand Trunk Railroad. During the next year there were several visits to Toronto, including one to witness the marriage of her daughter Agnes, who had been widowed in 1865, to Lieutenant Colonel Brown Chamberlin (1827–97), the Queen's Printer in Ottawa. However, Susanna missed Belleville and her independence. John Vickers, who had looked after her financial affairs from the time of Moodie's death, arranged an allowance for her that enabled her to take room and board first with the Rous family and subsequently with Mrs John Dougall in Belleville from early 1871 to the summer of 1872, when she visited her sister Catharine Parr Traill in Lakefield with a view to settling back in Douro.

Letters 77, 78, and 79 were written from Catharine's cottage in Lakefield to Katie Vickers in Toronto. Catharine's household at this time consisted of her daughter Katharine Agnes, age thirty-six, and her five-year-old granddaughter Katharine Parr, whose father, Henry Traill, had been murdered in 1870 in the course of his work as a prison guard at Kingston Penitentiary.

In her letters from Lakefield Susanna delights again in the natural surroundings and reports on her meetings with the Strickland relatives and old and new Lakefield friends. Samuel Strickland had died in 1867, but his widow, Katherine (Rackham) Strickland, stayed on at the Strickland home, 'The Homestead,' in Lakefield. Four of Sam's sons, Robert, George, Percy, and Roland, along with their families, remained in the Lakefield and Peterborough area, involved in mills, logging, and other family concerns. Walter Strickland apparently worked in Toronto but made frequent trips back to Lakefield. James Bird, who had accompanied the Moodies to Canada in 1832, after an early career as a surveyor, settled down to farm in Herriot's Falls and married Agnes

Sarah Caddy at St John's Church, Peterborough, in 1850. He recovered from his fever in 1872 (Letter 78) but died four years later at the age of fifty-eight. His father had died in England in 1839 at the age of fifty-one, but his mother, Emma Bird, lived to the ripe age of eighty. New acquaintances in Lakefield for Susanna included the Rev. Vincent Clementi, the minister of the new Anglican church, and his wife, Elizabeth.

A few days after writing her daughter on 2 June 1872, Susanna received word that John Vickers had suffered a stroke, evidently his second. On 7 June she wrote to her daughter expressing her concern and sympathy and offering to return to Toronto to give what assistance she could. Susanna was of the opinion that John worked too hard and suggested that he plan to take a rest and change of air on his recovery. Certainly a possible cause of the stroke could have been the sudden departure of Vickers's assistant, Fraser, and two weeks later Susanna is able to report to a young Belleville friend: 'One good thing has resulted from this domestic trouble. Mr. V. has induced Robert [Moodie] to give up the station at Seaforth, and take the situation of Superintendent of his office, on a salary of 100 dollars per month. This will place R. in a very comfortable position, without the hard drudgery of his present office, and he will be near his poor wife' (*LOL*, 304). Robert's young wife, Nellie, had suffered a mental collapse in 1871 and was confined to the Toronto Asylum until her recovery in 1874.

By 13 June John Vickers had recovered sufficiently for Susanna to write a cheering and entertaining letter directly to him. After a charming little description of 'Katie 3,' as Catharine's granddaughter was sometimes called, Susanna provides John with a lengthy description of an outing to Stony Lake arranged by her nephew Robert Strickland. Accompanied by Catharine and her daughter, the Strickland nephews and some of their families, Emma (née Strickland) Barlee and her husband, Frederick, the Clementis, and old Isaac Garbutt, the party set off by steamboat for Julian's Landing, sailing past the site of the Moodies' old homestead and revisiting a much-altered Young's Point, where Susanna renewed her acquaintance with Pat Young, the lock master and son of the original gristmill owner of 'A Trip to Stony Lake' in *Roughing It in the Bush*. Susanna wrote at least one other, much briefer, description of this 1872 outing in a letter of 22 June to her Belleville friend (*LOL*, 305–6).

By February 1878 Susanna was living permanently with Robert Moodie and his family in Weston, then a small town on the railway line a few miles northwest of Toronto. A visit to Katie Vickers meant a short train trip to the city, which Susanna, as she approached seventy-five years of age, often found too taxing to undertake. Letter 80 is a birthday greeting in lieu of a visit to her daughter.

Robert and his household moved several times in the next few years, each time a little closer to the Vickerses' residence on the north side of Adelaide Street West, between York and Bay streets. By the end of 1879 the Robert Moodie household had moved to 30 Baldwin Street, just south of Queen's Park, and Susanna was spending the holiday period with the Vickerses while she recovered from another respiratory illness. Among the Vickerses' callers on that New Year's Day was Dr Edward Chapman (1821–1904), a professor of science at the University of Toronto and author of several books of poetry. Susanna tells her sister that 'he asked me for a copy of a little poem of mine "The Canadian Herd Boy" as he wished to recite it at a lecture he was going to give next week' (*LOL*, 337). Letter 81 in this collection is clearly Susanna's response to Chapman.

Less than a year later Robert Moodie had moved again, this time to 14 Clarence Terrace in Wellington Square. On 6 December 1880, her birthday, Susanna wrote to her sister Catharine from the Vickerses' residence, where she was spending a quiet week after the excitement of fire breaking out in the house above 14 Clarence Terrace. In the spring of 1881 Susanna moved for the last time with Robert and his family to 17 Wilton Crescent, just south of the then new Horticultural Gardens east of Jarvis Street.

In the final years of her life Susanna's health was seldom good, and by 1884 her mind had deteriorated to such an extent that constant care was necessary. Katie Vickers became convinced that her mother required a full-time nurse and, because Robert's home lacked sufficient room for another resident, Susanna was moved to 152 Adelaide Street at the beginning of 1885. In March her sister Catharine came down from Lakefield to visit her:

... the nurse brings my poor sister in to sit with me till she gets restless and then she leads her back again to her own comfortable room where she has every comfort and every attention paid to her ... The case is when I go into my sister's room and when she comes into me she keeps talking and rambles so that I lose thought of any thing and every one else. What a strange change – what a wreck ... It is wonderful to see the patience and care that her dear daughter treats her with and the good clever way the nurse has of humouring her vagaries. (*LOL*, 354)

Late on the afternoon of 8 April 1885 Susanna Moodie died. She was buried in the Belleville Cemetery beside the remains of her husband and the son they had lost in the Moira River forty-three years earlier.

1 See J.W.D. Moodie, 'Introduction,' *Scenes and Adventures, as a Soldier and Settler during Half a Century* (Montreal 1866); Audrey Morris, *Gentle Pioneers* (Toronto 1973), 228–35; and *LOL*, 121–3.
2 *Scenes and Adventures*, ix
3 See *LOL*, 202, and Moodie's 'Spiritualist Album.'
4 The Belleville assessment roles list the Moodies as renting this cottage from James Meagher in 1867, 1868, and 1869.
5 On 4 September 1869 Susanna had written Ricketson's young daughter Anna, enclosing songs and poems written by herself and 'the dear old Norseman' (John Moodie). See Letter 68 and *LOL*, 247–50. Apparently Daniel Ricketson wrote back during October, including his letter with a reply from his daughter.

---

63 John Moodie to Katie Vickers

| | Belleville |
| My Dearest Katie | Aug 10/61 |

Yesterday I recieved your very kind letter which was very welcome. I have perfect confidence in Lister's[1] treatment though I still have great doubts about the *bleeding* system in *my case*. However there might have been some danger of appoplexy. Thank God, I have suffered no pain, and I am quite resigned to *go* when my time comes. Very possibly I may recover from *this* attack, but remember, my dear child, I am now *64* and should naturally expect such an event. I am *quite* cheerful though a little *cross* sometimes as poor Mother knows.

I drink nothing strong of any kind except sometimes a half a glass of cherry whisky or '*Cherry Rosody*'[2] as Mother calls it. Lister does not wish me to take any thing strong as I think he is afraid of *my head*. I have not any great appetite now tho' I think it is improving slowly. My general health is good however. You must not judge of it by my *writing* for I write under great difficulty from wanting the full support of my left arm. At first I could not move it from my side and could hardly move a finger. It is however gradually improving and I can now open and shut my hand, put it on the top of my head and take hold feebly of my right elbow and other gymnastic feats of the same kind.

I believe some of my *friends*? here expected I was used up. However I laugh at them and tell them I am going to join the Cricket Club in a few days. I have had a few visits of curiosity and a *few* of Kindness. The Wallbridges,[3] Lewis & Cam and Dean and Diamond have been very kind. Caroline Wallbridge excused herself for not coming to see me at first as she thought she would be in the way, – but promises to come and see me often. Poor dear Julia Russell has not touched the piano since my attack thinking it might annoy me. I had to compell her to sing and play to me this morning. Elizabeth started with Dunbar yesterday morning on a visit to the Tates. He Dunbar will return immediately as the office business requires his presence. Poor old Jenny sent Mamma a present of stockings by old Burke yesterday. She is living on his farm. *He* told me George Boulton had an attack of paralysis some time ago much worse than mine from which he recovered. He told me Boulton bathed his arm night and morning with beef brine with brandy in it. I do not however believe much in *local* applications though no doubt it may help a little. Lister says I am regaining the use of my arm rapidly. This shows that my constitution [is] still pretty good. Anxiety and hard work lately connected with this Election[4] are the causes of my illness just now.

You must not be anxious about me for I really think I am doing as well as may be expected. I take the Daily Globe so you need not send me that but if you could send me the *Leader*[5] after you have read it I should be glad as I cannot afford to take it too.

God bless you my dear Katie. Give my love to dear Agnes John and the children. Mother and all the rest send their love.

I remain Ever Your Affectionate
father
J.W. Dunbar Moodie

P.S. I hope to be able to write better next time. I cannot sit quite straight. I want longer practice.

1 Dr James Lister (1811–78) was the Moodies' regular physician in Belleville, where he was a prominent member of the community.
2 Possibly related to 'rosolio,' a sweet cordial made from spirits.
3 'Cam' is Thomas Cameron Wallbridge, youngest brother of Lewis Wallbridge and fellow MLA until his 1867 defeat in North Hastings by MacKenzie Bowell. Thomas Wallbridge was a barrister, mill owner, and local historian.

4 Campaigning for a national election was at its height in July 1861. John A. Macdonald's Conservatives were returned to power, defeating the Grit reformers.

5 The Toronto *Leader* was a conservative newspaper and party-organ until 1872, when it became independent, and somewhat quirky, in its last years. (It ended in 1878.) During the period in question it opposed George Brown's *Globe*, though not very successfully, judging by circulation. See Paul Rutherford, *A Victorian Authority* (Toronto 1982).

---

64 John Moodie to Katie Vickers

	Belleville
My Dearest Katie	Jany 22/63

I was anxious to reply to your letter at once, but somehow missed the mail. This is indeed a most unexpected blow after the change of *Ministry*, – but when I saw John Sandfield Macdonald[1] at Montreal in the summer I observed though his manner was kind that there was a certain reserve and seriousness in his manner which rather alarmed me. Wallbridge showed me his letter and also that of the Solicitor General in which they give their opinions fully on the matter in which they both agree – viz. That the neutering of a 'Nolle Prosequi' or abandoning the prosecution would be attended with the most serious consequences to the Country and to the *Ministry* (Here I suspect the shoe pinches.) Of course I am in a much better position than if I had resigned under the *late* Ministry. John S. Macdonald writes to Wallbridge or Adam Wilson – I forget which – 'I shall not forget the old Sheriff.' Wallbridge says he will keep at them till I get something and will try to get a Registry Office for me if possible. If I can only get some Office which will bring me in say £200 or £250 a year I shall think the exchange a good one coupled with relief from the crushing anxiety I have endured for so many years. Wallbridge made it a condition with George Taylor[2] that he would take Dunbar as his deputy and Bob as Clerk in the Office which he at once agreed to. As for Donald he gets Fifty Pounds a year from Bell[3] which must keep him at present. I should be glad to leave Belleville at once – but all the business in our hands *now* must be finished up. I cannot see how Taylor can take the Office until he gives his Bonds to the Crown-County which must be accepted by the Magistrates at the next Quarter Sessions which will be in March next. I do not know whether he can be gazetted before that time. The people are making a great fuss about the matter in the town particularly Dean and Diamond the Lawyer who supported Wallbridge and are annoyed that the appointment of a New Sheriff should be made without consulting them. It is said Diamond is one of the applicants for the Office. God knows what may happen *in three months. Taylor* may slip up as well as *Levisconte*.[4]

Many thanks My Dearest Katie for your kind offer of an asylum in Toronto of which if necessary we will gladly avail ourselves. Mother thinks of dividing the encumbrances between you and Agnes. Mother herself going to Agnes and I to your house, – but we will have time to talk of that by and by. I have very few debts so I think I can save most of my land. I told Vickers about the mortgage of six acres to the Bulls for £125. It does not run out for a few months yet and the security is excellent if he would take that step so as to give me time to redeem it I would be glad. I would rather depend on him than the Bulls tho' they speak fair.

God bless you my dear child for your affectionate love for your old father and mother. I must write you more fully again as I am afraid of missing the mail. Give my best thanks to dear John Vickers for his kindness in time of need. The affection of you and Agnes at this time has been my greatest comfort and has inspired me with more hope than anything else.

> I remain Ever My Dear Child
> Your Affectionate Father
> *J.W. Dunbar Moodie*

Kiss the dear children for me.

J.W.D.M.

1 John Sandfield MacDonald (1812–72), prime minister from 1862 to 1864 and premier of Ontario from 1867 to 1871. J.S. MacDonald was a Catholic conservative who represented Glengarry, then Cornwall, throughout his political career. He sympathized with the aspirations of Lower Canada and accepted many of the aims of the reformers (*DCB*, 10:462–9).
2 Georqe Taylor succeeded Moodie as sheriff in March 1863.
3 John Bell became a partner in John Ross's legal firm and was solicitor for the Grand Trunk Railroad.
4 Charles G. Levisconte, who was perhaps serving as Taylor's deputy, was a Belleville pharmacist and a leader in the Orange Order there. See Gerald Boyce, *Historic Hastings* (Belleville 1967), 92, 132.

65 John Moodie to John Vickers

Belleville

My Dear Vickers, June 25 1863

I duly recieved yours of the 10th June 1863, but delayed replying to it from time to time awaiting the progress of the Elections.[1] You will now be satisfied that there is no chance for the other party getting in *at present*. I am fully satisfied of Wallbridge's sincere desire to serve me – to which he has, publicly pledged himself at one of his Meetings here. The most artful means have been used to make mischief between us. But knowing what the other party have already done against me it would be worse than folly for me to doubt Wallbridge's sincerity after all his efforts in my behalf – it would be the height of ingratitude. Sometimes Lewis gets cross with me and *I* not having the most passive of tempers get cross with him for a while, – but in all his *actions* disregarding mischief makers who I suppose may have tried to decieve him as well as me – he has steadily stood like a stone wall against all their machinations. I took an opportunity at one of his meetings to show the people my estimation of his friendship as I found some of the raskalls were trying to set me up against him and I wished them to save themselves and me the trouble of putting the saddle on the right horse.

I must take a run up and see you and Katie and all the dear children soon. I am afraid I cannot get my wife to go but I will try. Old Benjamin seems to have fairly burst up and since Cam's election they say he has a bad *Bowell*[2] complaint.

I would rather have had the old beast in than the new one. The people call him one of Benjamin's Pups.

Love to all
I remain Ever Yours very
Sincerely
J.W. Dunbar Moodie

I see old Dr Wolfred Nelson[3] is dead. I do not know whether he resigned his Inspectorship of Prisons. If not there is a chance for some one, but I fear they may reduce the number of the Inspectors for economy.

J.W.D.M.

1 In May 1862 John A. Macdonald's government was defeated in the House of Commons, and John Sandfield MacDonald was asked to form a new government in alliance with Louis Sicotte of Lower Canada. One year later, having lost Sicotte's support, J.S. MacDonald felt obliged to call an election, which returned him to power with Antoine Dorion and his Lower Canada lieutenant.

2 MacKenzie Bowell (1823–1917) became editor of the *Intelligencer* after George Benjamin, as well as grand master of the Orange Order, MP for Hastings North in 1867, cabinet minister, and eventually prime minister (1894–6).

3 Dr Wolfred Nelson (1792–1863) had been a Lower Canada reform politician and was active in the Patriot movement at the time of the rebellion. He had been appointed inspector of provincial penitentiaries and jails as a reward for his services to the La Fontaine–Robert Baldwin administration (*DCB*, 9:593–7).

---

66 John Moodie to the Editor, *Notes and Queries*

Belleville, Canada West
[9 April 1864][1]

BEECH-DROPPINGS (*Epiphegus Virginiana.*) –

Can any medical man give any information respecting the medicinal properties of this curious parasite? It grows as a parasite on the roots of beech trees in Canada.

I find the following description of the plant in the December (1863) number of *The British North American Magazine*, published at Toronto, Canada West: –

'Here, in this wood, is an odd looking plant: a naked and slender thing, with stems which are never covered with leaves, but bear nothing more than small scales in their stead. It is called "beech-drops" (*Epiphegus Virginiana*), and grows as a parasite on the roots of beech trees. In October the plant is full of life and vigour: the stems, which have been hard and brittle the summer through, are now tender and succulent, and shoot out many branches. The flowering season is scarcely over; but the flowers being small, are not readily found. It bears the reputation of *possessing medicinal virtues.*'

So far for this quotation, which creates curiosity without satisfying it in the smallest degree.

Now I happen to know some of the virtues of this valuable plant. It is used by the Indians for curing *hemorrhoids*. An acquaintance of mine in this town, who suffered terribly for months with this most weakening disease, for which he could find no relief from the medical men of the town, was entirely cured by a farmer's son with this plant – the use of which *he* learned from the Indians. As I understood him, he boiled about a handful of the stems in milk, and drank a small quantity two or three times a-day. The cure was effected in two or three days: and years have passed since without any return of the disease. A medicine of such power may, no doubt, be useful in other cases of congestion. I trust, through the medium of 'N. & Q.,' this note will attract the attention of some medical men in England. I shall be only too happy to afford any further information on this subject, either through the post or N. & Q.'

J.W. DUNBAR MOODIE

1 This is the date of the letter's publication in *Notes and Queries*.

---

67 John Moodie to John Vickers

	Belleville
My Dear Vickers	27 Septr 1864

You are still quite in error about the costs of the original suit Queen vs Moodie for which *I* only am liable. You are only liable for the Defence of the Appeal for which we gave Bonds and which amounted to £23.19.0.

As to the costs of the *suit as tried at Belleville* Wallbridge has written (I posted the letter yesterday) to John A. Macdonald asking him to save me from the costs – it will not affect *you at all*, as I am unable to pay them.

On receiving your telegraph last night about 8 O'Clock P.M. I ran down to Wallbridge as fast as my old lame legs would carry me and got the enclosed note in order to satisfy Mrs M. I send it to you and you can keep it or return it to me just as you like. The sum of £48.3.6 taxed off is from the *original costs of the suit* and has nothing to do with those of the *Appeal* which you have already paid.

Nothing further can be done against *me* until next assizes at Toronto, – but I expect the Attorney General will save me from this further aggravation of my troubles – viz. That of asking me to pay the Legal Hangman.

I remain Ever yours truly

P.S. Do or pay nothing without asking Patterson.[1] It seems to me they (Harrison[2] &c.) are trying to make you believe that you are liable for the costs of the original suit.

J.W.D.M.

1 C. Patterson (see next letter) is apparently a Toronto lawyer advising Moodie at this time.
2 Robert Alexander Harrison (1833–78) was at this time in private legal practice in Toronto (*DCB*, 10:336–7).

---

68 John Moodie to Katie Vickers

My Dearest Katie,   Belleville
                                                     Nov 20/64

Mother was expecting to hear from you every day in reply to her letter and I delayed writing you until it should arrive. I also wished to wait until Dunbar should come home, when I might endeavor to make the arrangement about the property we were talking about. He has not yet arrived tho' we are expecting him every day. He is detained by the bad state of the roads at the village of St George on the Kennebec Road.[1] After returning home I was very anxious about Donald who had not written to any of us since writing to Bob while I was at Toronto, stating he would be home the following Saturday. He did not come as he stated and we were in great anxiety about him thinking he might have gone to the States or that some accident had happened to him. At last wrote to Judge Clark to whom he had gone on a visit hoping to some get employment up there. [He] came home the following day and I hope to keep him here until Dunbar comes home. Donald and Bob are quite willing to go into the plan suggested by C. Patterson and I think Dunbar will not stand in the way as it is as much for his interest as for that of the other members of the family. While I am upon this subject I wish to learn from Patterson whether I could not give deeds to you all *simply of one fifth each* of the land contained in the Trust Deed, – without specifying the particular lots. This would save trouble and if they were deeded back to me in the same manner they were to them it would just leave matters as if the Trust Deed had never been executed. This would prevent any tricks supposing D. was set

up to it by Gillett who has just got the length of his foot. I am suspicious of all the Belleville Lawyers – and with some reason.

Now as to the money which has to be paid to R.A. Harrison, – I
am quite willing to give him two lots which will make just about
the sum due him £67.3.3 I believe. I send you one of the plans
printed at the time of the sale (on 26 May 1864) and I make the two
lots for Mr. Harrison just the same price as the opposite lots were
sold at auction. I think he will think this fair. If I had the money I
would much rather pay cash as the property tho' now low from bad
crops and hard times in this part of the Country, – will ultimately
be greatly enhanced in value.

I have marked Lot 20 $140
               Lot 19 $130
                    $270

being precisely the prices at which the opposite lots were sold.

I registered that part of the property about 6/acres held in Vickers
Mortgage from me, at the Registry Office in Belleville on 9th July
1864, so in making the deeds it is only necessary to refer to the plan
made by Messrs Innes and MacLeod Provincial Land *Surveyor[s]* and
Civil Engineers.[2] You do not understand about advertising Lands by
Sheriff's Sale. The Sheriff is required to advertise the land *six* times
6 times in the Canada Gazette and three months in the County
paper (Chronicle in this case). I saw it in the Gazette at the Office,
the sale is some time in the latter end of January next so *that* is all
right so far. I only hope the lands will bring a fair price. After all
Harrison (R A) has been very kind about his claim. If I can only get
the money from O'Hare's Sale I shall be only too glad to keep the
land for better times. John will have to release the claim he holds
on that part of the lands I may sell to Harrison for *his* claim.

I am sorry to learn that Vickers has had trouble this year. I trust
however he will not suffer *ultimately* as I suppose he has got Security from his Agent who 'skedaddled.' I think the war cannot continue much longer and then we shall probably have better times. I
am very sorry that Necessity compelled me to give you all so much
trouble out of which I have been relieved by Vickers generous kindness. Would to God I could make him a suitable return. Mrs Traill
your aunty is now with her daughter and looking very well. I hear
Strickland is gone home to get some plunder I suppose at Reydon.
Mrs Gwillym is to give her share of Reydon proceeds to Strickland.[3]
I think it would have shown more benevolence to have given it to
either of her *Sisters* in Canada who want it *so much more*.

Lizzie is in a great fuss about Donald's constant visits to the gentle Julia and wants us to interfere. I told her she must tell him herself as I well know *she* will back out of any quarrel or trouble and throw it upon us. I told her the surest way to get rid of Donald would be to send Julia away. As soon as Dunbar comes home I suppose there will be a row if Donald does not decamp. Poor boy he is so lazy that I fear there is little chance of his helping himself much. I will have to keep him as long as *I can* and that will not be long. Bob will be leaving soon for Trenton. His partner Rankin is a dear fellow and a good workman and understands all matters pertaining to iron. Nelly has had a miscarriage a few days ago with *two dead boys*. One trouble is enough at a time. I think Bob will get on. Nelly more than does her part. She can get music pupils enough to pay £100 per ann. She is the best of the Belleville daughters in Law.

I must now close my epistle. Mamma will write you herself. She is busy cooking dinner as the old maid is at Church.

I enclose a plan of lots &c. Love to John and Children

> I remain Your Affectionate
> father
> *J.W. Dunbar Moodie*

1 Kennebec Township is north of Frontenac County.
2 Innes and Macleod were Belleville land surveyors with an office in the Dafoe Building.
3 Old Mrs Strickland had died earlier in the year.

---

69 Susanna Moodie to the Royal Literary Fund

> Belleville
> County Hastings
> Canada West
> May 4th 1865

Sir.

I received by the last English mail, a form of Application to the Royal Literary Fund[1] – sent to me, by an old and esteemed friend, Mr. Richard Bentley, of 8 New Burlington Street London, which I have filled up to the best of my ability, and submit for the consideration of your honourable Committee –

I have never asked relief from any Institution of the kind, and feel like a child groping its way in the dark, without any clear perception of stumbling upon the right track – I must therefore trust to your kind forbearance, to excuse my want of experience, in stating the cause which has made such an application necessary, and will proceed to give you the facts of the case, as briefly as I can –

My Husband, John Wedderburn Dunbar Moodie, was appointed Sheriff of the County of Hastings in the year 1839, by Sir George Arthur Governor of the Upper Province – and for 24 years held the office, in which he gave general satisfaction; and was considered by all parties, as a man of strict honour and unflinching integrity. He entered upon its arduous duties, at a time, when party spirit ran very high in the Province, and Tories and Reformers regarded each other with bitter hostility; yet all parties agreed in awarding to him a high character, which indeed, was no more than he deserved. In the year 1860 a fierce persecution was raised against him, by interested persons, who wanted his situation for one of their partizans –

Not possessing private property of his own, sufficient to enable him to cope successfully with such powerful enemies, he was forced to resign his office, on the proceeds of which he entirely depended for his own maintenance, and that of his family.

His resignation was made in the year 1863 – and the mental anxiety which he had suffered during the two preceding years, brought on a severe attack of paralysis, which has partially deprived him of the use of his left hand and side. The enclosed letter, written by our friend the Hon. Lewis Wallbridge Speaker of the Legislative Assembly, who was employed by Mr. Moodie in the suit brought against him, will explain better than I can, the injustice and cruelty, which deprived a good man of the office which he had held for so many years, with credit to himself, and had won for him the good opinion of the public, to wage in his old age a hopeless battle against Poverty and starvation.

I likewise enclose the presentment of the Grand Jury of the County of Hastings, to Judge Haggerty, and that gentleman's reply –

As I have before stated, Mr. Moodie had no income whatever, and what with heavy law expenses, and other losses connected with his removal from office, we have suffered great pecuniary distress for the last two years. A small house and fifteen acres (on which we reside) is heavily mortgaged, and we are unable to redeem this little property, or find the means to pay up the heavy interest on the same.

Unfortunately, the members of our family, are not in circumstances to render us any permanent assistance. Our three sons, though men grown, can barely support themselves. Two of them, are married men with families. My second son, who has successively studied for the law, and the medical profession, has never settled to either, and for many years has been a burthen upon his family.

My eldest daughter, likewise married, and the mother of a large young family, has given us all the assistance in her power, but her heart is larger than her means. My second daughter, has just lost her husband, who held the office under Government, of Clerk of the Court on Probate in Toronto, and is left with six small children, on a scanty income of eighty pounds per annum. It is impossible for her to assist us, though most anxious to do so.

My Husband's mind is still active, but his bodily infirmities incapacitate him, for manual labor. He can still use his head, but has lost power in his left hand.

He has completed his sixty seventh year and I am, myself, a sexigenarian. Under these circumstances, I have been advised to apply to your benevolent Institution, for relief, as an author whose name is not wholly unknown among the writers of my Native Land and the youngest daughter of a well known Literary family, sister to Agnes Strickland the Historian of the Queens of England.

My Husband's claims to Literature are I consider, far greater than my own.

In the year 1835 Mr Bentley published a work in two volumes, from his pen – 'Ten Years In South Africa, including a particular description of the wild sports of that Country. By Lieutenant J.W.D. Moodie 21st Fusileers.' The book was very well received by the public, and highly spoken of by the leading Periodicals of that day, both in England and America, as a work written with considerable ability, and containing much valuable information with regard to the Cape Colony. It has often been referred to by writers on the same subject – Mr. Moodie also contributed two papers to the Athenaeum, on the Cape, one of which, His encounter with a wild Elephant, was reprinted in Knight's Library of Useful and Entertaining Knowledge,[2] and in the Penny Magazine which also extracted largely from 'Ten Years in South Africa.'

In the year 1831 – he sent to the United Service Journal an account of the attack upon Bergen Op Zoom, in which action, he rendered good service by forcing open the waterport gate and lowering the drawbridge, in the midst of a sharp fire from the town, and

received a severe wound in the wrist. This article was republished
by Henry Colburn, and Richard Bentley in a work entitled, 'Memoirs of the Late War Comprising the personal narrative of Captain
Cooke of the 43ᵈ regiment of Light Infantry, The History of the
Campaign in 1809 in Portugal by the Earl of Munster, and a Narrative of the Campaign in Holland, by Lieutenant J.W.D. Moodie, H.P.
21st Fusileers –' Mr. Moodie, also contributed four chapters to my
work, 'Roughing It in the Bush,' The song – 'God Save the Queen' –
written by him, at the end of the last chapter, of the second volume
in the second edition of that work, which also belongs to him a
genuine expression of heartfelt loyalty and Patriotism. We have both
contributed largely to the Literature of Canada –

During the rebellion of 1837, I endeavoured to do some good, by
sending loyal and patriotic poems to the public journals, which
became very popular in the Colony. As a general thing, the people
in these provinces, are too much occupied in obtaining the common
necessaries of life to waste their money in patronizing Literature or
giving any encouragement to Authors. They never have sustained a
lierature of their own, though several excellent Magazines have been
started in the Colony, preferring the cheaper American periodicals
to the productions of native talent. The Canadian Government
never grants pensions to old and faithful servants, when unfitted by
age for the performance of public duties. To render assistance to
such useless people as authors, would be regarded as an absurd
waste of the public money.

I can conscientiously affirm, that in all Mr Moodie's writings and
my own, we have always endeavoured to serve the cause of religion
and morality, and will continue to do so, as long as we have power
to wield the pen.

I am sorry that I am not able to transmit for the inspection of
your honourable Committee copies of the works that have been
published by us, both here and in the old Country. Unfortunately, I
lost in a fire which destroyed our dwelling, most of my books and
papers, together with valuable letters from authors of note, testify-
ing to my literary ability. My kind friend, Mr Bentley, who has published many of my works, will I have no doubt, add his testimony
to the truth of what I have here advanced.

I have no plea to offer as an excuse for my troubling your honorable Committee, but my necessities. While a hope remained of earning a living for my old age with the pen – I worked on, trusting in
the mercy of God, and looking forward to better days, but the mind

is not capable of profitable exertion, while sorely burdened by heavy cares, and I see no way out of the difficulties which surround us. In making this appeal, to your truly benevolent Institution, I feel a conviction that I shall not seek sympathy in vain –

> and I remain,
> Sir –
> Your Ob^t Hum^ble Servant
> Susanna Moodie

1 The Royal Literary Fund to assist impoverished writers operated from 1790 to 1918. See Nigel Cross, *An Introduction to the Fund's History and Archives* (London 1984) and *The Common Reader: Life in Nineteenth-Century Grub Street* (London 1985).
2 John Moodie's elephant sketch had first been published in a volume on elephants in Charles Knight's series 'The Menageries' in London (n.d.). It was republished by Harpers in New York as *Natural History: The Elephant in a Wild State* in 1840.

---

70 John Moodie to Richard Bentley

	Belleville U. Canada
My Dear Sir,	6th May 1865

After perusing your very kind letter to Mrs Moodie of 1st April '65 it occurred to me that from my being engaged for so many years (24 years) in the extremely anxious and responsible duties of a Sheriff in Upper Canada, by no means a merely honorary Office as in England, – I had but little claim to the name of a professional Author, – and that it would therefore, be better for me to state privately to you who have taken such a kind interest in our troubles, the causes which have led to our present almost destitute condition. Poor, as we now are, I have no sense of humiliation for I know that to the very best of my ability I have striven to perform my various duties in the different Offices I have held under the British and Colonial Government with zeal and fidelity. As in writing to you I am not bound down by any particular form, I will give you a brief Narration of my life and Services, leaving my friend The Hon. Lewis Wallbridge, Speaker of the Legislative Assembly of Canada to state the facts of my case from a *Legal* point of view. In plain English it was a conspiracy formed by a hostile party in the Colony, – which

compelled me after a struggle of about three years to resign my
Office of Sheriff after a service of nearly 24 years; *though no indi-*
vidual alleged that I ever injured any one directly or indirectly
through my Office.

Mr Wallbridge, who resides in Belleville, and who was employed
by me in my defence, is better able to state my case, *as a Lawyer,*
than I can myself.

I shall now proceed with the sketch of my life, which has had its
share of adventures and vicissitudes. I was born in 1797 (7 October)
at Melsetter in the Orkney Islands. My father was Major James
Moodie of Melsetter a grandson of Captain James Moodie R.N. a
brave Officer who rendered important services to his country particularly in relieving the town of Denia in Spain while closely
besieged by a French Army. Having landed with all the Sailors and
Marines he could spare from the three line of battle ships he commanded at the time, as Commodore of the Squadron, he headed a
sally of the garrison and townsmen and drove the enemy from the
works. For this Service, the Austrian Claimant to the Spanish
Crown, afterwards Emperor of Germany, presented him with a
splendid sword and Marshal's Baton and an autograph letter of recommendation to Queen Anne, who granted him an honorable Augmentation to his arms. He afterwards had the honor of conveying
George Ist from the Continent to England on his accession to the
Crown, at Queen Annes death. This brave Officer was afterwards
murdered in the streets of Kirkwall by Sir James Stuart and his
brother, two violent Jacobites, when over 80 years of age. This took
place on 26 October, 1725. My Grandfather Capt. Benjamin Moodie,
who was a boy at the time, afterwards became an Officer in the
Guards, and was employed by the Duke of Cumberland against the
rebels in Orkney in 1746 and having surprised Sir James Stewart and
his brother sent them to the Tower, where they bled themselves to
death before their trial, in order to save their property from forfeit-
ure. From that time as before our family were always decidedly
loyal and generally entered into the Service of their Sovereign by sea
or by land. My Grandfather had a number of sons who all died in
the King's Service. I had a brother who was killed at the attack on
Leghorn in 1813 (I believe). He was first Lieutenant to Admiral Sir
Josias Rowley. I had another brother Donald Moodie who at this
time was a Midshipman in the same ship (afterwards Lieutenant).

He emigrated afterwards to South Africa where he held several
important Offices such as District Magistrate or Judge and after-

wards held the office then very necessary & important Protector of Slaves, at Grahamstown.

He was afterwards appointed Secretary to Government under the Governor of Natal. He died there in 1861 broken hearted from the cruel persecution raised against him by the colonists, in consequence of his zealous advocacy of the cause of the Kaffres who had been deprived of the lands granted to them by the British Government.

I had also still another brother a Lieutenant in the E.I. Company's service and Assistant to the Agent of the Governor General in Bundelkund, who recieved his last appointment for his great proficiency in the Native languages, particularly in Persian and Arabic, for which he was highly complimented in a speech of the Governor General. He died of jungle fever at Calpu 27 April 1824. I am come to the only surviving member of my family and now give you a slight sketch of my own history in which I can boast of nothing, – but an anxious desire to serve my country and to do my duty. I entered the army as 2nd Lieutenant of the R.N. British Fusiliers (21st Reg^t of Foot) in 1813 when about 16 years of age. I was at the night attack on Bergen op Zoom in Holland on 8 March 1814 where after entering the works with a small party of soldiers of different regiments who had got mixed in the darkness and confusion I volunteered and succeeded in forcing open the Waaterpoort Gate and in lowering the drawbridge in the midst of a sharp fire from the town. On this occasion I was severely wounded by a musket ball in my left wrist, which partially disabled my left hand. In 1819 while on half pay I emigrated to South Africa to join my eldest brother who had settled in that Country. I returned to England in 1830 – wrote my work 'Ten Years in South Africa' and emigrated to Upper Canada with my wife in 1832. On the Outbreak of the Rebellion in 1837 I, of course, offered my services in the Militia of the Province where I served as Captain on the Niagara Frontier for several months until the reduction of the Regiment in 1838 – when I was appointed Captain and Paymaster to a number of detached Companies of Militia stationed at and near Belleville about 16 Companies scattered along the coasts of Lake Ontario and Bay of Quinte (about 60 miles).

Not being allowed a Paymaster's Sergeant or Clerk I had a most laborious duty to perform for several months, particularly as I was totally unacquainted at that time with money matters and accounts. I payed out, I suppose, over £30,000. (I have not the documents to

refer to as proof that my services met with the approval of the
Gov^t.) I can only say that I was appointed Sheriff of the District of
Victoria (now, the County of Hastings) in November 1839. This
Office I held for nearly 24 years until I resigned it in 1863.

On 28 July 1861 I had a severe attack of paralysis which deprived
me of the use of my left arm and left leg. This attack from which I
have since only partially recovered was occasioned by great mental
anxiety connected with my duties as Returning Officer at a County
Election, coupled with unceasing labour for several days in Copying
the Roll Books for registration within a limited number of days. I
now come to the *cause* of all our misfortunes and present suffering.
From the time of my appointment to the Shrievalty in 1839 I had to
contend with a succession of petty persecutions got up by parties
desirous of holding my Office. A number of *Civil* actions of one
kind or another were one after another instituted against me. I had
never attached myself to either of the violent parties that distracted
the Colony. I only desired to do my duty impartially to both; – and
of course I got the ill will of both, and though I generally managed
to escape the snares laid for me by unscrupulous lawyers I was *poor*
and the tear and wear going on for so many years was undermining
my health and spirits. Desiring some peace and quiet in my old age,
the idea occurred to my mind of employing a Deputy Sheriff, who
instead of recieving one half of the fees in the usual way in Canada,
– should pay me *a certain sum* annually equal to one half of the
fees. I reserved certain duties required of Sheriffs to be performed by
myself personally as heretofore; – such as attending the *two* courts
of Assize and the *four* County Courts; holding Elections for Members of Parliament &c. &c. Having still some doubts as to the strict
legality of the arrangement I consulted a lawyer in whom I had confidence – a confidence sadly misplaced as the sequel will show – and
he assured me over and over again in the presence of my wife, –
that the arrangement was 'perfectly safe and perfectly legal.' The
Deputy I employed was recommended by this lawyer and for whom
he became surety in a Bond to me. In drawing this Bond which was
done *with great care*! the four words which would have made it perfectly safe were omitted, as I found out when too late to save me
from its consequences. These words were '*out of the fees*' which
would have removed the fatal *uncertainty*. The *facts* of the case
were not denied and the verdict of the Jury was against me, the
Judge reserving certain points for the opinion of the full Court at
Toronto. I, of course, appealed and so strong was the feeling of all

the Judges of the great practical injustice done me that the Court of Appeal postponed their decision from Court to Court for nearly two years. I should also observe that the arrangement I made with my Deputy was quite a common one with other Sheriffs in U. Canada many of whom still hold their offices, – until some malicious conspiracy shall be formed against them as in my case. Before Judgement was entered I was advised by the Solicitor General who before he took office in the Ministry was employed by Mr Wallbridge to aid in my defence, – *to resign my office*; so that I would not be debarred from holding another office under Government.

I have applied for various Offices since, but was constantly disappointed, – tho' from the language used by the different Members of the Ministry I had every reason to expect that some Office would be found for one who had served so faithfully and laboriously for so many years. My *mind* is still sound and I am anxious still to work, but like the poor man at the pool of Bethesda 'another steppeth down before me.' I have given you, I think, a more full and intelligible account of my wrongs than my friend Mr Speaker Wallbridge, who to do him justice has done his best to serve me while he was a Member of the Ministry as Solicitor General and since as Speaker of the House. I did not at first wish to speak of this painful subject, but I felt that some explanation was still wanted. The late worthy Chief Justice Sir John Robinson, who under the cold crust of the law was always my warm friend, told my daughter only a few days before he died that 'they (the Judges) had put off their decision from time to time, until they thought the Sheriff was safe' expecting that – the Ministry I supposed the friends to me? – would enter a *noli prosequi* and stop proceedings against me. – I enclose a 'Presentment' of our Grand Jury at Belleville at the last Court I attended before I sent in my resignation. As you may suppose I, as well as the kind Judge Hagarty was much affected when he delivered his most feeling reply to the 'Presentment'.

As to my present circumstances, and property I may state that I hold a few acres of land near Belleville which if I could retain them might in a few years become valuable but from the immediate necessity of procuring the bare necessaries of life, I have been compelled to mortgage heavily. Could I sell the whole of my land at once, which is now impossible I would ask aid from no one. In a very few years this land will be swallowed up by two mortgages of £250 each. I cannot bring my mind down to becoming a burthen on my kind daughter who has already assisted us so much.

I have to thank you from the bottom of my heart for your kind sympathy, – particularly when compared with the hard selfishness of most of the Canadians for many of whom I have so often stood in [place of] to shelter. Praying that as you have suffered like ourselves the Almighty may be pleased to grant you many happy days yet. With kind regards to your son Horace and our respects to the rest of your family, I remain My Dear Sir Ever yours most sincerely

and gratefully
J.W. Dunbar Moodie

P.S. You are perfectly at liberty to use this letter in any manner you may think likely to be beneficial to me or my closest family. I could provide any number of testimonials in my favor if required.

J.W.D.M.

---

71 John Moodie to John Vickers

	Belleville
My Dear Sir,	23 May 1865

You will remember I told you of poor Bob's agreeing with old Cooley at the Trent to carry on an Iron Foundry at that place. After making his bargain with Cooley Bob took a Belleville man who had been foreman at Wallbridge's Foundry in Belleville as a partner with him. This man whose name is Rankins has turned out to be a scoundrell and after making mischief with Cooley is trying to get Bob out of the concern. Neither Bob nor Rankins have any capital, and Cooley has given them both notice that if they do not proceed with the work, he will take the concern into his own hands again. If he gets Bob out I suppose he will either carry on the foundry himself under Rankin's management – or Rankin may find some one with the requisite capital. In the mean time the foundry is likely to turn out a first rate paying concern and they have got it in good working order. I have just been talking to a man of the name of Jordan who for many years carried on the Foundry with a partner of the name of Earl which Wallbridge *now owns*. Now I wish you to try and get some one in Toronto or elsewhere with sufficient means to start the Foundry at the Trent, either taking a third share (or equal) with Bob and Jordan that is to say one third of the profits and any *advances* he should make to start the concern to be paid out of the first proceeds of the concern in such portions or manner as might be agreed on between the parties. Please speak to Mr Armstrong in Young Street about it. There is a first rate chance for any one with a small capital. If you could get any one to find the means and get himself fully secured on the property it could be done in that way if he should prefer it. Mr Jordan whom I have known for many years thoroughly understands his business. Jordan says that they would want $4000 or $5000 to carry on the business to advantage at once and he says he will guarantee 50 per cent profit. However he says for $2000 the Foundry can be started. None of the parties could give security on lands or houses, I therefore thought it would be better for any one that should advance the necessary funds to take a share in the foundry besides getting the terms or sums he might advance paid off gradually. If you have not *time* get Katie to speak to Mr. Armstrong about the business. Bob is honest steady and temperate and I know will do *his* best for the concern. It is really too bad that the poor boy after working like a horse to start the concern – should be chisselled out of it by an ungrateful rascal!

Rankin would sell out his share *now* for a trifle as he finds he cannot find means to carry on the concern after doing his best to get Bob out of it.

I suspect some of the Wallbridges are at the bottom of the trouble between Bob and Rankins, as the establishment of a foundry at the Trent would greatly interfere with their foundry at Belleville – at least *they* think so.

You must know the locale of the Foundry which was formerly a part of Hawley's property at the mouth of the Trent. All they might manufacture can be shipped off at once from the gate of the foundry which is in the wharf.

Do try and do something for poor Bob, – who has been striving hard to make a living.

With love to Katie and the dear children

I remain My Dear Sir

Yours very sincerely
J.W. Dunbar Moodie

Mother will write soon and sends her love.
Write soon as the chance may be lost.

72 Susanna Moodie to the Royal Literary Fund

Belleville
July 10, 1865

To the General Committee of the Royal Literary Fund.
Gentlemen.

Accept my grateful thanks, for the liberal donation of £60 Sterling, which I this day received from the manager of the Bank of Montreal, in this town.

Words would fail to convey to you, the extent of the benefit which you have conferred upon me. May God reward your noble generosity as it deserves.

I remain,
Your deeply obliged
Humble Servant
Susanna Moodie

73 John Moodie to the Editor, Orkney *Herald*

Belleville, Canada West
SIR, –   28ᵗʰ Sept. 1866

Respecting the names of large counties, or large objects on their surface, such as mountains and rivers, &c., the probabilities are that they receive their names from the language of the races who first visited the country. There can be little doubt that the first settlers of Orkney and Zetland, as well as of Iceland, within the historic era, were Irish adventurers, long before the Norsemen had settled in these remote islands. The first Norwegian settlers found *crosses* and *Irish books* in Orkney and Iceland, and two distinct races of men – the 'Peti' and the 'Papae;' the 'Peti,' no doubt the Picts, and the 'Papae,' probably 'Culdees' or Romish priests.

There can be no doubt that the promontory of '*Orcas*' – Dungalaby Head – gave the name 'Orcades' to the islands, being derived from the genitive case of Orcas. But what does 'Orcas' signify? 'Orca' is the Latin name for a great fish – a whale or porpoise. However, I am rather inclined to think that 'Orcas' is a native word which the Romans found already in use. We may readily imagine that the first visitors of Orkney in the summer time found numbers of *eggs* of sea fowls in the heath at that season. Now, *Orc* is the Irish for an *egg*. Placing ourselves in the situation of those who first gave a name to these uninhabited islands, this etymology of the word is, to say the least, *very probable*. From this name of Orkney, or the 'Egg Islands,' the Norsemen, following the genius of *their* language, would naturally form the Ork-in-eya or the Egg Islands – the word 'in' or 'hin' being the article 'the' which generally followed the noun.

I now come to the most remarkable and interesting monument of antiquity in Orkney – 'The Stones of Stenness.' *Stenness* signifies 'the ness or point of the stones.' This implies an antiquity much more remote than the arrival of the Norse settlers. They therefore called them 'The Stones of the Stone-ness.' I pointed out this fact to Professor Daniel Wilson,[1] of Toronto, as confirmatory of his opinion of the great antiquity of this (probably) Druidic temple.

I will now give you some of my antiquarian recollections respecting the southern islands of Orkney. To begin with *Walls*, or more properly 'Waes,' or the 'Island of harbours,' generally called Vaga-land in the Sagas. The most remarkable antiquity in this island is the 'Dwarfie Stone,' respecting which there is no history or *reliable* tradition. It is situated in a deep valley in the northern part of the island, which was called by Norwegians Ha-ey – High Island of Hoy. The southern part of the island was called 'Vaga-land' or 'Voes,' or the 'Island of harbours;' and part of it may, in fact, be considered a separate island, being connected with the rest of the island by an isthmus or '*aith*' or ayre, which is often overflowed at high tides. The little bay outside of this 'aith' is still called Aith-hope. The term 'hop' signifies an inlet, of which there are many in 'Waes,' such as Long-hope, Orc-hope, &c.

'Brim' is the Norse word for the swell of the tide or sea; hence the name Brims, which is a contraction of 'Brim-ness.' 'Osmundwall head' is a corruption of 'Asmundar-vog' or 'Asmundar-voe.' In the account of the summary conversion of the Orkneymen from heathenism by a certain King of Norway, by drawing his sword and threatening to cut off the head of the Earl's son, the scene of this feat was laid by one of the 'Sagas' in Ronald's-voe, and by another,

much more probably, in 'Asmundar-voe' in Waes. The King, finding
the Pentland Firth too rough at the time for crossing over to Scotland, put in to 'Asmundar-voe' with the ships. Near 'Asmundar-voe'
is the castle of Melsetter, now, and for a long time in ruins. This
was the ancient seat of the Mudie or Moodie family, which is certainly one of the most ancient in Orkney. Close to the shore of
'Kirk-hope' there is an old chapel, connected with which is the
tomb of the family. My father, the late James Moodie, of Melsetter,
told me that there were four or five mummies of our ancestors lying
on a stone table in the tomb in a good state of preservation, being
nearly as light and as dry as bladders. An old lady, a relative of the
family, who was left in charge of the house of Melsetter during my
father's absence with his regiment, was greatly scandalized at the
exposure of the remains of our ancestors above the ground, and got
them all buried decently in the earth. I remember seeing the initials
of W.M. and B.S. on the outside of the tomb, and the date 1593.

In my younger days I took a great interest in the etymology of
names of persons, families, and localities. Among the rest I was
curious to discover the origin of the name of Moodie, or Mudie as it
was written originally in Orkney and Scotland. I tried at first to find
the origin of the name in some place, but without success. I then
searched the Norse books relating to Orkney, particularly the
'Orkneyinga Saga,' and there I found the name Harald Modadi, one
of the last of the Norse Earls of Orkney, who died about the year
A.D. 1266. I afterwards found that the letter *o* in Norse is pronounced like *u* or *oo*. This brings the pronunciation of the name
Modadi to *Mudadi*, from which the present name Moodie is a corruption. To go more into detail, Modadi is the Latin genitive of
Modadus, the filius or son being understood. The name Modad is
the Norse name for Mudoch or Mudah, Earl of Athol, who married
Margaret, a daughter of Hacon, Earl of Orkney. Their son Harald
was called Harald Mudadi (filius) after the fashion of the time. Thus
the name Mudie is but a corruption of Mudadi. In the same manner
many other names have originally been formed, such as Petri or
Petrie for Peter-son; Swaney for Swens-son or Swan's-son. Magnus'-
son has been corrupted into Manson; and sometimes the Latin genitive was taken, and sometimes the Norse patronymic son.

I now return to names of places. Beginning with Caithness,
Halkirk, or as it is called in Caithness, *Ha*-krig, is derived from *Ha*-
kirk or High Church, the seat of the bishop being situated there,
where one of them was burnt by the people in a popular rising occa-

sioned by his exactions. The name of Scrabster was originally 'Skar-bolstadr,' or the place of the stair-steps, where a flight of ancient and rude flags are found like a stair from the landing place to the top of the clay bank near the house of Scrabster. The Bishop's Castle there has been in ruins for centuries. The name Melsetter, in the island of Walls, is obviously derived from 'Miab,' the Norse name for a kind of eatable seaweed now called 'mellak,' which is found in great abundance at the head of the bay near the house of Melsetter. 'Setter' or 'Seater' is a place, and the word 'ster' – the termination of most names of places in Orkney – has another meaning, being a corruption of 'stadt' or 'stather,' a place, like the English stead or Dutch 'stadt.' The name of the 'Ord' of Caithness is from the Norse word 'urd,' a strong place.

I shall not tire your readers with more etymologies at present, but will perhaps return to the subject at a future time, as I perceive that some interest is beginning to be felt for such matters. So farewell for the present – I am, &c.,

J.W. DUNBAR MOODIE

1 See *DCB*, 12:1109–14.

---

74 John Moodie to the Editor, Orkney *Herald*

SIR, –

Belville, C.W.,
1st March 1867

In the *Orkney Herald* of Dec. 25, 1866 I observe an account of the murder of my great-grandfather, Captain James Moodie of Melsetter, in the streets of Kirkwall, on the 26th October 1725. As you refer to me for farther information on the subject, I feel great pleasure in complying with your desire, in order to place the character of my gallant ancestor in a truer light.

I can distinctly recollect the oft-repeated statement of my late father, Major James Moodie of Melsetter, who never lost an opportunity of inculcating honest and loyal sentiments into the minds of his children. In a matter of much interest to all of us, it is not therefore likely that any of us would forget his statements. My attention was called more particularly to this subject a few years ago

by an article in *Notes and Queries*, by my friend, W.H. Fotheringhame, Esq., Sheriff-Clerk of Orkney,[1] who had certainly through the
office he holds, the very best means of obtaining correct information. In farther illustration of the subject, I addressed a letter to the
editor of *Notes and Queries*, which, for some reason, seems never to
have reached its destination, though several other communications
from the writer duly appeared in that journal. Having preserved a
copy of my letter, I shall now give all the particulars it contained
nearly in the same words, and thus enable your readers to judge of
the comparative probability of the respective statements.

I shall conclude this note with a few remarks on the late Mr
Vedder's account of 'the murder,' in which account, having great
respect for his genius *as a song writer*, I was sorry to find such a
want of appreciation of the high character of a very brave and honest man and distinguished British officer as Captain Moodie. Besides
this, his statements are exceedingly improbable. Is it likely that
such a man and *at such a time* could have lived on terms of friendship with a known adherent of the despotic Stewarts? But Mr Vedder
says 'the lady of the mansion was a distant relation' of the Stewarts
of Burray. There are no grounds that I can perceive or find for this
assertion. My great-grandfather was first married to a Douglas – of
the Earl of Morton family, I have been informed, with which family
Sir James Stewart appears to have been on anything but friendly
terms, according to the narrative given in your paper, unless the ball
he fired at the Sheriff-clerk of Orkney contained a HUMBLE APOLOGY
to HIS seat of honour for his insult to the Earl of Morton. My ancestor's last wife, Christian Crawford (Lady Melsetter) was certainly
not a person to be influenced by a mean, obsequious feeling towards
Sir James Stewart a bit more than her gallant husband. I extract
from Vedders narrative the following fine model of humility: –
'When the Captain learned to *whom* the arms belonged, *he was
quite confounded*, and well knowing the implacable disposition of
his lady's relations (?), he despatched a boat to the island of Burray
with the fowling-piece, and with a sealed letter containing the most
ample apology, and *inviting them on all occasions, when they so
pleased, to use every liberty on his estate, answering them that
their doing so would be a high compliment!*'

This humility puts me in mind of a story my father used to tell
of some poor serf (I think he must have been from the same parish
as David Vedder). My father was going in a boat to some one of the
North Isles with the grandfather of the present Earl of Caithness,

who was amusing himself by asking the crew, one by one, where each of them was born. They were all humble enough, but on asking the last one where he was born reverently taking off his hat and stroking his hair with his hand in deep humility, he replied: 'O! please your lordship, *it's no for the likes o' me to be born*. I was *foaled* in the poor island of Sanday, and rocked ina caisy!' – I am, &c.,

J.W. DUNBAR MOODIE

In 3d S. III. 31 of *Notes and Queries*, I perceive an account of the murder of Captain James Moodie of Melsetter by Sir James Stewart of Burray. Being a grandson of Captain Moodie, I am enabled to [se]nd a few particulars, which I learned through my father, the late Major James Moodie of Melsetter, who died at Edinburgh in 1819 or 1820, respecting the murder in question; as well as to give a few other particulars respecting a family of upwards of 600 years' standing in Orkney. In the account my late father gave me of the murder, he told me that, after the murder, Sir James Stewart escaped with his brother 'on the Sheriff's horses.' In order to pick a quarrel, Sir James sent one of his servants to shoot grouse on the moors near the house of Melsetter, where he was seized by Captain Moodie's servants, and his gun taken from him. On breaking it over his head, it was discovered that it was loaded with two balls, intended, no doubt, for the especial benefit of the old 'Commodore.'

Shortly afterwards, on going to Stromness, he learned that Sir James Stewart was seeking an opportunity to assassinate him. However, disregarding the entreaties of his wife, who had an ominous dream about him, he proceeded to Kirkwall, at which place Sir James Stewart was awaiting his arrival. The facts are probably given as correctly as might be expected in the communication of my friend Mr Fotheringhame, but he did not know several particulars which seemed to point at treachery on the part of the Sheriff, who was said to have been connected with the family to Sir James Stewart. However this may be, Captain Moodie, who was over eighty years of age at the time of his murder, died of his wounds in eight or nine days. My grandfather, at the time, was a boy of about nine years of age, and he vowed to have his revenge on the cowardly murderer as soon as he should be a man. Sir James Stewart and his brother obtained a pardon at the time; but when the rebellion in favour of the exiled Stewarts again broke out in 1745–6,

they were again engaged in treasonable correspondence with the
rebels.

My grandfather, now a captain in the Guards under the Duke of
Cumberland, after the battle of Culloden, obtained from the Duke
the command of two or three companies of foot and two or three
ships in order to pursue the rebels in Orkney. He surprised Sir
James Stewart in his island of Burray early in the morning as he was
walking in his night-cap near the shore. On perceiving the approach
of the red coats, Sir James fled into the barn of one of his tenants
and endeavoured to conceal himself in a heap of straw. When he
was pulled out, he fell on his knees to my grandfather, acknowledging himself as the murderer of his father, and told him he could
now take his revenge. My grandfather, however, told him that he
must be tried as a rebel and murderer by the laws of his country.

In a few days, both he and his brother, Alexander, were secured
and sent to the Tower to stand their trials for their respective
crimes. In order to save the family property from confiscation, Sir
James and his brother, by the aid of an old servant, while kissing his
old master, managed to convey a lancet into his mouth by which
means they both bled themselves to death in the Tower before the
time appointed for their trial. Besides arresting the murderers of his
father, my grandfather attempted to arrest several of the Orkney
lairds who had assisted the rebels; but as soon as they heard of their
danger, they all concealed themselves in a cave in the island of
Westray, where for six weeks they were fed by a poor tenant of one
of the lairds, who faithfully kept their secret until the danger was
past. Several of them, however, never recovered the effects of their
exposure.

In the year 1819 I visited this miserable place of refuge, before
going to settle at the Cape of Good Hope as a half-pay officer. The
rock at this point hangs over the sea, so that a false step would precipitate any one into the waves beneath. The mouth of the cave is
approached by a narrow path only a few inches wide along the projecting edges of the strata of the rock, which incline at a steep angle
to the Atlantic Ocean. At one point we had to make a jump across a
rift in the rock three or four feet wide, with the wild waves welter-
ing beneath the overhanging precipice. The very thought of that
jump still makes my flesh creep; but I suppose the Orkney lairds
took a short plank with them to enable them to reach their cave
with greater safety. The cave was simply a rent in the rock, with a
quantity of wet clay which had fallen from above, and a long dark

crevice in its interior. Any particulars respecting this 'transition' period between feudal lawlessness and civilisation will not be altogether devoid of interest to your readers.

Captain James Moodie was a good sample of the rough, blunt, and gallant seaman of those times. Stimulated by that craving for the sea and adventurous spirit so natural to Orkneymen, and a descendant of the Norse Vikings, he ran away from school in Edinburgh when he was a little boy, and his family never heard of him again until he had raised himself from before the mast, by his bravery and talents, to be an officer of some rank in the Royal Navy. He served under Sir Charles Rooke and Sir Clondesley Hood, and once saved the Turkish fleet from the enemy by conveying it safely round by the Orkney Islands and through the Pentland Firth, which at that time was considered a daring feat by those unacquainted with the locality.

At the attack on the harbour of Vigo in Spain, his vessel was one of those that broke the boom which protected the entrance to the harbour. On one occasion, while engaged with two men-of-war, he was wounded by a cannon ball, which carried away a part of his thigh. After getting his wound dressed, he ordered an arm chair to be placed for him on his quarter-deck, on which he sat until the engagement terminated with the capture of both of his opponents.

On another occasion, during the war of the Spanish succession, when cruising off the town of Denia in Spain as commodore of a squadron of three ships of the line with a quantity of soldiers' clothing on board, he found that the town was closely beseiged on the land side by the French. Having free access to the town from the sea, he had a number of his sailors dressed in red coats, and after keeping them rowing in his boats between the town and his ships for some hours, he himself landed with all the sailors and marines he could spare, and making a sudden sally from the town at the head of garrisons, the enemy were seized with a panic and he thus relieved a place which was one of great importance at the time to the cause of Charles of Austria. On this occasion Charles presented [the commodore] with his own splendid scimitar, a marshal's baton, a fine Arabian horse, and other articles, together with an autograph letter in French to Queen Anne. All these articles, excepting the Arabian horse, who died greatly regretted in Orkney, are still in the possession of my elder brother's children at the Cape of Good Hope.

The old arms of the Mudie or Moodie family are Cheveron ermine and spheous, with a hunting horn for crest. The motto 'God with us,' an augmentation, was granted by Queen Anne, viz. 1st and 4th quarters, a castle and three ships. The new crest is a Lion *prennent regardient*, holding in his dexter paw a flag with the double headed eagle of Austria, standing on a naval crown, and the motto '*The reward of valour.*'

My father gave me an anecdote of the old Commodore after his retirement from the service. With the prize money he earned, he purchased the estate of Melsetter from his nephew, who was captain in the Guards and member of Parliament for Orkney. On one occasion the old Commodore had a lawsuit with some one before the Court of Session at Edinburgh. He had employed a lawyer, who made some statement in his favour which did not accord with the truth. The old Commodore immediately jumped up in the Court and told him in a loud voice, 'that he had hired him to tell the truth, and not *lies.*' The presiding judge told him that he must not fancy that he was now on his own quarter-deck, and that such language 'could not be tolerated in a court of justice'. The old captain replied that he was quite aware of the distinction, but that he had seen much more substantial justice done on the quarter-deck than he had seen in this Court. The partiality of the Court of session at that period arising out of family alliances was very notorious.

The old Commodore's nephew, known as the young captain, was the laird of Melsetter, and what we would now call '*a fast young man.*' He was a Roman Catholic, and in consequence of being engaged in some conspiracy against the Government, fled to Spain, where he became a Colonel in the service of that Government. He afterwards went into the service of the Venetian Government, and attained the rank of commander-in-chief of their forces. Here all traces of him are lost, and he is supposed to have died unmarried.

In my younger days I took some pains to ascertain the origin of the name and family, but with indifferent success. The name is certainly not derived from any locality in Scotland, and I therefore had recourse to the old Norse, or Icelandic histories of Orkney. In the *Orkneyinga Saga* I find the name of Harald Modadaison, or in the Latin Modadi (*filius*, or son, being understood), the son of Modad. Now, the letter *o* in the old Norse and Swedish languages was pronounced like our *u* or *oo*. It was anciently a common usage of the Northern nations to use the Latin genetive for surnames. Thus, Petri (filius) was used for Peter*son*, and Jacobi (filius) for *Jacobson*. The name Mudadi (as it was pronounced) came thus naturally to be shortened into Mudi. The substitution of the modern *oo* for *u* was only adopted by my great-grandfather. Before his time the name was Mudie, as it is still spelled by some families descended from our family in Forfar. The name of Modad, Mudah, or Mudad, was the Norse version of Mudah, son of Melmare, third son of King Duncan I of Scotland. This Mudah or Mudad was created Earl of Athole, and married Margaret, daughter of Haco, Earl of Orkney.

As an instance of the origin of surnames, I may mention what I learned in Canada, from an Orkneyman of the name of Petrie, settled near Ottawa. He told me that his grandfather's name was *Peter Peterson*, which name became *Petrie*.

It is curious that in the small island of Hunda, near the island of Burray, there is one of those ancient 'Tumuli' so common in Orkney, and there called 'hows' from the old Norse wo[rd] 'Hang,' a burying-place, before the introduction of Christianity about A.D. 1000. On visiting this island, my father was informed by the people that the 'tumulus' was called the cairn or 'How of Muda.' Now *Muda* is the genetive in *Norse* of Mudi.

The grandfather of Duncan I, Malcolm II, was called by Norsemen '*Karl Hundason*,' or Karl the son of *Hundi*. Query – May not the island of Hunda have been called in some way after Hundi?

In order to shew the great insecurity of life in those times, I will just mention that another great-grandfather of the writer, Alexander Sinclair of Olrig in Caithness, fell in a duel by the hand of Captain William Innes of Sandside. It seems Sinclair of Olrig was a quarrelsome character, and possessed of great bodily strength; this, coupled with his great stature – 6 feet 6 inches – made him rather a formidable character, so that few dared encounter him. At last he met with his match in Captain Innes, whom he had insulted at a public meeting, and who was an expert swordsman. This duel was fought at a place called Tongside, where Olrig was run through the body. Calder, in his history of Caithness, says, 'Captain Innes, however, was so much afraid of his life from the relatives of the man whom he had unfortunately slain, that he ever after kept a strong, muscular Highlander as a life guard, who accompanied him wherever he went.'

My grandmother, Henrietta Sinclair, the daughter of the slain man, was a good sample of that gigantic race, as she was fully six feet in height, and with a large share of their high spirits. She bore much of what may be called the common bold character of those rough times, commingled with kindness of heart, and, like many ladies of the present day, loved to have her own way.

On one occasion, having set her mind on a visit to her family in Caithness, go she would if she could get any one to run the risk of crossing the Pentland Firth in an open boat. At last she sent for a noted character in Orkney, called by way of distinction 'Skipper Irving,' probably a relative or ancestor of Washington Irving, whose father was an Orkneyman. The wind was blowing fiercely, and there was a heavy sea running in the Pentland Firth. All this was urged in vain by the 'skipper,' who assured her that no open boat could live in the Firth in such weather. At last, perfectly enraged at my grandmother's obstinacy – drawing himself up with great dignity, he exclaimed: 'Madam, *do you presume to teach ME skippery!*'

My grandmother had a large family of sons, all of whom were in the army or navy. There was one, in particular, my father often spoke of with great pride – Donald, a captain in the 'Ross-shire Buffs' as they were called. He raised fifty men among my father's tenantry, who accompanied him to India. One only of that number ever returned to Orkney, wounded in several places, and full of long yarns about Seringapatam and the bravery of my uncle Donald, who died in India.

When the regiment was ordered for service in India, and were about to embark at Leith, the men of the regiment, who understood that they were enlisted on the condition of not being required to serve in the East or West Indies, mutinied and took up a position on '*Arthur's Seat*,' to which they marched from parade with their bagpipes playing, and refused to obey their officers. This continued for several days, while the townspeople supplied the soldiers with plenty of provisions. At length my uncle, Captain Donald, went up among them, and by means of his great popularity succeeded in persuading them to return to their duty, – which they did, with their pipes playing as when they left their parade ground, and they immediately, cheerfully, embarked for India.

Captain Donald Moodie was a man of a fine, manly figure, and fully six feet six inches in height, so that his mother could not feel ashamed of him in any respect.

To return to my great-grandmother, Christian Crawford, or 'Lady Melsetter' as she was called. She was the daughter and heiress of Crawford of Kerse, in Ayrshire, and lineal representative of Macgill, Viscount Crawford, through her mother, who was his daughter. Of Christian Crawford's first husband, Bellenden of Stenness, there was no issue remaining.

In a late work, *The Scottish Nation*, among numerous other mistakes, I find the following passage in Vol. I., p. 701: – 'This Alexander Crawford appears to have been the last male proprietor of Kerse of the name of Crawford. His only daughter, Christian Crawford of Kerse, married Mr Moodie of Melsetter (Captain James Moodie of Melsetter), and *having no succession*, she disponed the lands of Kerse to William Ross of Shandwick, writer in Edinburgh, who was soon after drowned on his passage to Orkney, when the estate of Kerse devolved on his heirs.'

Now, as already stated, Christian Crawford was twice married – first to Bellenden of Stenness, and second to Captain Moodie, and had issue by both marriages. My grandfather, Captain Benjamin Moodie, was *her* son beyond question. The alienation of the estate of Kerse from *both* families seems to speak of wars and troubles between this very strong-minded lady and her different children. It is only to be regretted by her descendants that 'the writer in Edinburgh' had not been drowned a little earlier.

J.W. DUNBAR MOODIE

1 In *Notes and Queries*, 3d ser., 3:51–4, an article entitled 'Smith of Braco and Stuarts of Burgh and Burray,' signed by 'W.H.F.,' gives an account of the slaughter of Captain Moodie.

---

75 John Moodie to Anna Ricketson

	Belleville, U.C.,
My Dear Miss Ricketson	September 1869

I am so disabled with *paralysis* that I can hardly write. On the other side I give you my words for the sad ballad of 'Lauchlan wi' the raven black hair,'[1] which is somewhat short (not the hair) which with sailors is usually rather long and curiously tied up in a '*queue.*' By the way neither my wife nor I remember to have ever written this word before. We were both puzzled and had to fly to the dictionary, where we found it spelled two ways '*queue*' and '*cue.*' I shall adopt the latter mode in future as the shortest. I shall be glad if you can *fix* the music better. You must excuse my weakness. I wish I could suceed better. Remember me most kindly to your dear father and mother &c. whom may God bless with yourself and remain ever your's most affectionately

J.W. Dunbar Moodie

1 The manuscript poem which John enclosed had appeared in the Orkney *Herald* on
29 March 1864 under the title 'Laughlan wi' the jet-black hair – a ballad.'

76 Susanna Moodie to Daniel Ricketson

Seaforth Station
G.T.R.
Ontario

My Dear Kind Friend,   Nov. 11 1869

I could not write to you while the arrow was in my heart, and the
desolation of bereavement left my mind blank and useless, but I
have had so much to attend to, since he left me, that I can only
indulge the luxury of grief during the solemn night, when my spirit
is alone with his and God. It was so hard to part with him at a
moment's notice and to find myself alone and bereft of his dear
companionship.

But I did bless God, even then and there, that he had granted him
his own earnest desire, a speady and painless exit from this beautiful but *mournful world* –

He had been so well lately, that I did not apprehend by any *physical* token, the near approach of the death angel. How delighted too,
he was with your last kind letter, announcing the safe arrival of the
music, and he felt so proud of your appreciation of his talents as a
poet. How from my *very heart*, I thank the merciful Father, for your
friendship, from which he derived such pleasure, which has so
cheered us in our lonely hours. God bless you dear friend and yours.
I owe you a great debt, which I can only repay with tears. But you
will wish to hear something about the last hours of the dear old
Norseman –

On the 7th of October, he completed his 72nd year. It was a glorious fall day and when I kissed him and wished him joy, hoping that
he might live to see another October. He shook his head, 'Don't
flatter yourself Auld wife. I shall never see another birthday. I shall
not be here long.' And I chid him, as love will chide any one who
checks the joy of hope – Robert, Agnes and Dunbar, always wrote to
him on his birthday, and he sent me down after breakfast for his
letters. But, alas, none were there. He sighed deeply but bore the
disappointment better than I expected. R and A. were very busy and
not well and had forgotten the day. Dunbar did write, but owing to

the floods in Delaware we did not get the letter for some days after. D. did not tell us that he was ill, but his wife put in a postscript. That he was ill with the Delaware fever, and that he was threatened with consumption. Had heavy night sweats and hemmorage of the lungs.

– This I am sure had a deep effect upon his mind. All day he could talk about nothing else. What if that strong man should die before his old father – My poor Dunbar –

He then wrote him a letter with his own hand, the last time he ever put pen to paper. In which he cancelled the obligation under which he lay to keep us in our old age, and sent him his blessing. This was on the Wednesday. He seemed quite happy after writing that letter, especially when I said 'Johnnie, this has made me very happy. You have forgiven poor Dun all his past faults?' – 'Yes all' – I went down and posted the letter early in the morning. When I came back, he was sitting on a chair cutting wood with his right hand, in the verandah, in front of the Kitchen. Passing in that way, I put my hand on his shoulder – 'You naughty creature.' – I said, 'Did you take the opportunity of my being out, to kill yourself –?' He laughed – 'I feel quite well and strong, today. I mean to cut all the wood for the parlor stove, it will give me a good appetite for dinner.' 'You will do no such thing,' I replied, 'while I can earn money to pay for having it cut.' 'Well,' he returned, with one of his brightest smiles, 'I believe old woman you are right, for I can't split it. Have you any letters? –'

'Yes, one from dear Aunt Traill come up and hear it.' My dear good sister had written from a sick bed. Her complaint one of great danger and chronic. He seemed much touched by her letter. 'Susy,' he said, 'Kate will not be long here. We shall all go together – I first, then your sister, then you.'

The day passed pleasantly away as it ever did. He read aloud to me while I knitted new socks for him, that he was never to wear. And he looked so beautiful. The silky snow white hair waving on his shoulders. The noble face illumined by the lamp and the pure fair complexion just tinged with a bright glow, that gave to lip and cheek almost the bloom of youth. I often looked up at him that night, and thought what a picture he would make, and he, generally stern, was as sweet and gentle as a little child.

At nine, I brought him the only stimulant in which he indulged, a pretty large tumbler of new milk, and a bun. 'It is time,' I said 'for respectable old people, like you and I to be in bed.' 'I was thinking so,' and he rose without my help, and walked quite steadily into his bedroom. While undressing him, he remarked 'Dear Susy I give you a deal of trouble.' 'It is no trouble,' I said, 'I always bless God, that I am here to help you.'

When I had fixed his pillows and made all quite comfortable, I kissed the broad, noble brow, and bade God to bless my old darling, and give him a good night's rest. And he put up his dear arms and pulled me down to his breast, and said, 'My dear dear *Auld* wife, may He bless you.'

Those were the last words of love and tenderness, he was ever to say to me. For though I was with him to the last, during the awful death struggle, and held the white hand in mine, long after it was cold, he had no power to give utterance to his thoughts, after the first apparently slight indisposition, had assumed a dangerous character, and he must himself have recognized his approaching change.

I had slept on a low couch near him for the last 16 years, and being a poor sleeper was always within call to attend upon, or help him in and out of bed during the night. He slept very tranquilly, and though I awoke at the usual hours, he did not awake. It was just before 5 o clock when the dark curtain of night was hardly withdrawn from the earth, when I was suddenly roused from sleep by a loud voice calling upon me – '*Mother*!' – A term he often used when he wanted me. I was at his side in a moment trembling from head to foot. 'Dear Johnnie. Are you ill. What is the matter?' He seemed to awake, and said, very calmly, '*What is* the matter? *Mother* I *did not call* you. But I am very thirsty. Have you any drink here?' I got him some cold spring water, that I never failed to bring up at night, for fear that it might be wanted and I always had my lamp and matches at hand.

I lighted the lamp, and brought him the water, but he did not drink it but asked what a clock it was? A question that he had asked of me at intervals during the whole of the past day. I went into the next room to see, for he had forgotten to wind up his watch – 'Just five.' – 'I don't know,' he said, 'what ails me. I find such difficulty in swallowing and my breath comes up as hot as flame.' 'Let me send for Dr Hope.' 'Doctors can do me no good, they kill more than they cure. Get me over the bed and open the window, I want more air.' I put my cloak around him, for the early dawn was cold with a hard frost, and privately went up stairs and told an old woman whom I had taken in on charity to get up and get our neighbour Wilkinson to go for Dr Hope or any medical man he could find. I still did not apprehend any danger, as he looked as well as usual and for the last twelve months had been subject, to what he called fits of weakness. He complained of being very sick at stomach and threw up a quantity of slimy foam, that I had to wipe out of his mouth and began to breathe very heavily. Alas, I knew it all then. He was dying. I laid him down on his pillows and half dressed as I was ran for our neighbor next door, Mr Lane a good pious mechanic, who promised to come directly. I was not gone a minute, but I saw a change he was pale and shivering. I said 'Let me shut the window,' and he answered quite loudly and firmly 'No!' – and motioned for me to get him to the window again.

I raised him with great difficulty, and he stood quite firmly for a moment on his feet leaning upon me. Mr Lane came in, and helped me to place him in his bed.

Death was evidently very near. I asked him to speak to me once more. To send some message of love to his children before he left us for ever. He waved his hand, the other was already cold in mine. Gave two deep inspirations, and closing his eyes passed through the dark river as peacefully as a child going to sleep –

Oh my dear friend, I cannot dwell upon the reaction of that trying hour. It can only be realized by those who have loved and lost.

The mill bell was ringing for six when he passed away. He had not suffered if he did suffer at all, more than one hour. But what voice was it, that called me to his deathbed. That remains an awful mystery –

The midnight train brought dear Agnes and the darling Robert, to my aid, and kind friends and tender hands dressed him for the grave.

Nothing could exceed the majesty of that calm grand face. No crowned King ever wore such a regal look. One old friend repeatedly kissed the marble brow exclaiming, 'You grand beautiful old man – Noble in life but perfectly sublime in death' – The undertaker said, He never had put such a magnificent man into a coffin, that from the crown of his head to the sole of his foot, he was without spot or blemish. In spite of his poverty, he had one of the largest funerals ever known here which reached from our cottage to the English church a full mile in length. Even the men whose persecutions had shortened his days, paid respect to his remains. I could not look at it. The taking him away, was the worst agony of all. While I could look at him for hours, he was still with me. It was a terrible blank to know that he was gone –

Do not think that I murmur at, or resist God's will. I know that he was in mercy taken before perfect helplessness, subdued the fine mind and humbled him to absolute dependence. 'Thank God! – he is gone to a better world, Where the wicked cease from troubling, and the weary are at rest' – It is a satisfaction to know, that he considered the years spent alone with me in the little cottage, the happiest he had known for years. That he was pure and innocent in his pursuits as a little child. Humble with all his wide knowledge, and fine talents, such a man as we seldom meet along the dusty high way of life. Such as I fear I shall never see again.

My poor Robert who is very like the dear old father in moral excellence was terribly cut up by his death and had to be supported, when the honored head was laid in the grave. Besought me so pathetically to come and end my days with him, that I could not resist his tearful entreaties.

I was sorry to leave the dear cottage I loved so well, but perhaps it is all for the best. I am now far west in the Huron District, 230 miles from my old home. Roberts wife is a sweet young woman and they have three lovely young children. The boy named after his grandfather, and when my mind can shake off the gloom of grief I will try to be contented.

Thank the dear daughter for her sweet letter. I cannot write more today. Recalling the past quite upsets me. You will comprehend it all.

Farewell, my dear good friend, I bear you all upon my sorrowful heart and remain your faithfully attached

Susanna Moodie

---

77 Susanna Moodie to Katie Vickers

| | North Douro |
| My Dearest Katie, | June 2 1872 |

I have been thinking of you and the dear children all the week. I hope that the horrid cough is progressing favourably. The weather here has been intensely wet and cold for the time of year. Poor Kate Traill has had several bad fits of the ague, and though we have a fire in the stove mornings and nights one feels very shuddery. The incessant rains have brought out all the forest leaves and the whole world here is intensely green. Oh the dear trees, the bright rushing river with its everlasting song, gleaming under the windows and glancing from among green boughs is a gladsome sight to see love. My eyes are never tired with looking or my ears with hearing. Born and brought up in the Country, how dearly I love it – Nature never yet betrayed the love we feel for her. We are very quiet here, during the past week no one but Mrs Beatty has been to the house, and I was calling at Mr Clementi's when she came.

The parson has a very pretty house and garden, and is at the top of the tree here. He seems a kind man and has lots of beautiful hot-house plants, gold fish, birds, pictures and all sorts of pretty things. He is by no means a poor preacher. Quite equal to the Arch deacon, and far less of a Roman. They have no organ, but a good melodeon and some excellent singers in their quire. The church is very pretty and most comfortably arranged. Mrs Traill was not able to go, and Kate had the ague, but Percy kindly came for me, and walked home with me. Mrs K. Strickland is still at Peterboro', and will not return to the homestead before Henry returns from Montreal. She will keep house for them during their absence. I have not seen any of the Stricklands this week but Percy, who lives quite near to us. Poor James Bird has been desperately ill with lung fever and is still in an uncertain state, and chills and ague are pretty prevalent in the neighborhood.

I have got over my daily shiver, and hope it may not trouble me again, and feel better, but not very strong. I am, however, comfortable and quite at home, nothing could exceed the kindness of my dear sister and her good daughter. We live twice as we[ll] as I did at Mrs. D's, without the miserable and begrudged scarcity and eternal liver and fish dinners. If I feel hungry I can get a bit of bread and butter without having to keep a store of food in private, and Katie washes for me, and I have only to iron my few things which saves me a dollar per month. I am so glad I got away from that stern old woman, and can feel at home once more. Though I see few people here, as they are beyond walking distance for me now, with the eternal shackle that makes me lame and sore. I fancy that my very high hips create a difficulty which other people escape. I cannot bring the pad to bear upon the rupture without great pressure over the abdomen which certainly don't improve my digestion.[1]

I had a letter from dear Robert yesterday dated the 30th of May. He complains of not being well, and has been taking medicine as a preventative from the terrible head epidemic, which has killed so many people both in Seaforth and Clinton. The Doctors give it to hinder people taking it. R. says, it makes you wild but you feel better after it, while the disease is the most terrible state of suffering that can be imagined. Like the dog Maniac,[2] the head is bent back until it touches the heels like a bow, or the face is twisted behind and this state of things lasts until death frees them from agony worse than cholera –

He owns to feeling a little nervous about it. The children are all well, but strange to say – He never mentions poor Nell, so I suppose he has not heard of her lately. I got a newspaper from Donald last week. The Newark Morning Post. So I suppose that he has left New York. I wish he would write and relieve my anxiety, and tell me his whereabouts. No letters this week. No nothing. I got the Weekly Globe yesterday from dear John. Thank the good son for me. He is always thinking of my Comfort God bless him. I have not heard again from Agnes, or even from Maime. I seem beyond the reach of letters here –

Aunt and I and the wee Katie Traill have just been wandering in the sunshine by the banks of the beautiful river. The little copse in front of the house, belongs to Percy, and adds greatly to the beauty of Aunts dear little place. It slopes down to the water covered with soft velvet grass. All splangled with violets and woodland flowers. We have been watching the fish pursuing their prey and flashing their red fins in the sunlight. This is a bright warm day. I hope the Aurora last night brought a good change for us. How I wish you were here with me, and the dear children sporting in the grass. The smell of Aunt's lilac fills the air. Her house is quite large. I had no idea of its size and comfort, besides the large pretty garden full of spring flowers. She has a nice good-sized drawing room not richly, but very nicely furnished, taste supplying the want of luxuries. A good dining room and her own comfortable bedroom on the ground floor. Kate sleeps in one bed with the wee Kate, and old Kate in a single bed. Large door windows open upon the garden. I sleep in a large room over the drawing room. Carpeted and with a stove if required. A nice cherry set of drawers, and all the other conveniences. Far more comfortable than Mrs Dougall's, and then – such a lovely view up and down the lovely river. Lots of birds build in the trees and bushes and waken me at early dawn with their sweet songs. I have slept very well ever since I came here, an exception to my general restless state of a night.

I have painted two small groups of wild flowers that look very pretty, but the power of writing seems to have left me altogether. I fear, I shall never be able to write that memoir of dear Father. If it was for any one else, I might manage it, but, when I know how particular he was, my mental powers seem silenced. I should not [do him] justice I fear.

I am spoken to by everybody in the village for Mrs Traill. I cannot see why for I am dark and much older looking, and she is a pretty old lady with a soft smiling face and nice pink cheeks. Percy took me to see his father's grave. A nice green quiet spot in the old church yard, but now in the very heart of the village. The rail road, comes within half a mile of Mrs Traill's, and the small steamboat starts just on the other side of the river for Julian's landing on Stoney Lake, every other morning. Our post comes in at half past one, is delivered at half past two, and goes out at 8 in the evening.

I want to buy a good, four foot broad, bedstead, to suit my mattress and bedding, but we have no furniture shop here. Tickle of B.V. offered to send me up by freight a good iron bedstead that size, for eight dollars cash. Would that be dear or cheap? – The freight will not cost a dollar, up here. Could I get it cheaper in Toronto? – I expect that I could not, and will send a post card to Tickell when I hear from you. I liked the look of his. It was green and gilt and so nice and low. I could tumble in and out without any trouble. The saving of 3 dollars a month in my board, will soon pay for it. I wonder how the old lady gets on without me? I think she must miss the ready money which they were saving up to buy a new carpet, hence the very meagre board.

We heard to day, that Walter and his family had arrived at the homestead. Perhaps I shall see Walter to day and hear something about you all. Mr Bird was a little better. They got news of his mother's death by the last mail from England. She has outlived her husband nearly 40 years. A beautiful woman to the last.

To day is dear Victor's birthday. Don't forget to kiss him for me, and to wish him many many happy years. I shall be anxious until I get a bulletin from you about their health.

Has Mr. G.V. arrived yet? – and Annie gone off with the little carpenter[?] She ought to have invited Vic to be the best man at the wedding as he made the match. When I come to Toronto again, I shall miss Annie's very kind face. You saw in the Globe the meeting of the Dundee female servants. Was it not rich? [It w]ould make a good comed[y.][3]

Talking of comedies I see Charlotte[4] is now constantly before the public. Does it pay? I should not like to get my living in that way. The theatre always was – and ever will be an immoral school for the young. The success of the comic heroes almost always depends upon rascallity, run away marriages and cheating guardians and parents, its very fascination makes it dangerous –

I would send dear Rob's letter but it is too heavy to enclose.

Monday/ A glorious day at last. River and trees and flowers all alive and glowing in a warm sun. I seem to expand into a second youth at the sight of it.

Walter, George, and Percy were over last night, Walter had no news of you. He goes on Wednesday back to Toronto. I told him to call and tell you all about me. Dear old fellow, he looks ten years younger than he did, and was [so] kind. He is quite a darling. Percy brought over Dolly and Alec the baby. The baby is *superb*, not to be beat for his age, and like my dear father with his brilliant hazel eyes and auburn hair. Dolly is 4 – she is very pretty, with the fine features of her father.

Well, dear Kate is waiting to take this, so I will conclude with love to John and your dear self and the baby up to Jack and Miss V. and remain your ever loving Mother.

S. Moodie

1 In her letters from August 1871 through to early 1872 Susanna frequently reports intestinal difficulties of one kind or another (*LOL*, 294, 296, 299). It may be that she had been advised to wear a truss to support a hernia.
2 This may be a reference to hydrophobia or rabies, since the symptom Susanna describes is opisthotomus, which is also characteristic of tetanus.
3 On 3 June the *Globe* reprinted a report from the London *Times* of an early meeting of a new association of domestic servants in Dundee, Scotland. The women were anxious to ensure fair working conditions, and part of the article lists their grievances against unscrupulous mistresses.
4 Charlotte Nickinson (1832–1902) was a well-known actress, daughter of the theatre manager John Nickinson, who controlled Toronto's Lyceum Theatre during the 1850s. In early 1857 she may have visited the Moodies in Belleville (*LOL*, 174).

---

78 Susanna Moodie to Katie Vickers

Lakefield
North Douro

My Own Beloved Katie   June 8, 1872

I have only just got dear Robert's letter, with the sad news of our dear Johns illness. Too late for any post before tuesday next. Oh, that I had wings to fly to you, for old though I be, I could yet nurse baby, or sit by the dear sufferer's bed and attend to his wants, when you were absent about the house. If I can be of the *least use* or comfort, telegraph for me when you get this. It is very provoking that there is but one post here during the day, which comes in at noon, and goes out at half past two, but generally too late to answer any letters received until the following day.

I have a thousand things to say to you, but I have not the power to write them down. God knows my darling good child, how much I feel for you, and my kind dear son. But keep up your heart. All may yet be well. A few hours may restore your dear one as it did before. I can well imagine that if Fraser has left him, the double trouble and worry has been the cause of his present seizure. He needs rest of both mind and body. Perhaps change and sea air might prove beneficial. That close office is too much for him, and the pressure of his great business. How I wish he could sell his mines and leave it altogether. His life is of more value than millions of dollars. If the anxiety of his office was less, his health would steadily improve. But after all, this is mere conjecture. The future is with God, to Him my darling you must look for help in time of trouble. We may build, and plant and plan, but He only can bless the work of our hands, and if we suffer, it is to bring us nearer to Him. All the riches of earth will appear to us as nothing when we come to bid our last adieu to the world and its fleeting vanities. 'Hold every thing here Susanna, with a loose hand,' dear old Mr Hodson used to say to me, but for all that – I held them tight, and smiled at the admonition – Yet how true it is. –

I have seen everything slip from my hand, and am really more contented than when I had a home, and held a fair position in the world.

I am so glad that dear Robert is with you in your trouble, as I know he loves both you and John with sincere affection, and will do all in his power to help you.

He does not say how the children are getting on with the whooping cough, or how you are off for servants. I was troubled about you after I got your letter, and found that you had lost Annie and that your other servants were going to leave you, but I did not foresee the greater need of help. But cheer up dear heart, I trust the good God ere this has lessened your anxiety, that the dear husband is able to comfort you and raise your spirits. I hope nothing has gone amiss in the office that Fraser left. I thought he was too much

attached to Mr. Vickers ever to leave him. It was a greater loss than
all the house servants.

I have been down this evening to the Village to get a tooth taken
out, but could not find either of the Doctors at home. I have been
suffering with tooth ache for several days and my jaw is terribly
inflamed, healing I fancy by the throbbing.

I received a letter yesterday from Donald. He is still out of
employ and on the eve of starvation. This made me very sad as I
had not the power to help him. I wrote to Allen Ransome enclosing
his letter and asking him to recommend him to any house in
America with which he had dealings. A forlorn Hope, but it was the
only thing I could think of. He has left New Jersey City and is
boarding in cheap lodgings at Newark, New Jersey.

Walter Strickland goes up on Monday morning by the five o'clock
train. How I wish that I were going with him. For though an old
woman is not of much use, I am not too proud to wash dishes and
dress little ones, and if you think I could be of *any use, don't hesitate a moment*, but send for me right away. All here are deeply concerned for your husbands illness, and sympathize with you most
sincerely. This wet weather makes poor Aunt very rhumatic – ...

---

79 Susanna Moodie to John Vickers

My dear Mr Vickers,

Lakefield, North Douro
June 13 [1872]

I feel so glad, at the good news of Katies postal card, that you are
better, that I must write and tell you so. May God grant you my
dear son renewed strength and add many years to your valuable life.
It is good, however, sometimes to stand in the entrance of the dark
valley, and feel how near we are to the unknown future, to deepen
our trust in the unfathomable love of God, and in his mercy shown to
us through his beloved son, and to shew us how little in comparison
is all the wealth of this world. May you dear John, obtain the *true*
riches is my most earnest prayer which comes warm from the heart
of the old mother, that loves you and your dear ones very much.

But I am not going to write a sermon to one better and kinder
than myself who I have no doubt knows and feels more than I can
express upon this momentous subject.

I have felt so anxious about you and Katie and the dear children, that it has made me sick and nervous. Ague chills are very common here, owing I think, to the high back waters flooding a large swamp in our rear, of about a mile in extent, which is full of dead trees and decaying vegetable matter, and the weather between the constant thunder showers is sultry or quite cold. The stinging of the black flies like one of the plagues of Egypt, ditto mosquitoes. In other respects, I am *very comfortable* indeed as my good sister and kind niece do all in their power to make me so. We have a pretty merry little child the size of Ethel, in the house. Poor Harry Traill's little girl, who lives with her grandmother, and makes the house very lively with her original prattle, for it is a clever funny little creature and though only 4 1/2 years old, reads as well as many of the grown up natives, and makes very droll shrewd remarks on what she reads. Her adoration of dolls is most amusing. She has quite a regiment of dolls which she makes out of rags and bits of stick, and to whom she talks and gives most sage advice – and she generally sleeps with them all, but one, she keeps in her arms. Her maternity is most extraordinary. She promises to make a beautiful woman.

And now I must tell you about our trip on tuesday up to Stoney lake in the steamer yclept, The Chippewa. Robert ran in about 10 on tuesday morning and asked us if we could be ready in an hour, and he would send his buggy to take us to the landing. It was not a picnic only a small family party and he would bring all that was necessary. Aunt was quite delighted and little wee Kate was sent to Mrs Percy's who could not go, the house shut up and we were soon ready for the start. Percy called in, and advised me to walk with him, as he thought that the Buggy would scarcely hold two fairies like Aunt and me. I was of his opinion and off we went. The walk was rather long, and the day, the hottest of the season so far. When we reached the landing, we found Mr & Mrs Clementi, their niece Miss Smith, Sherry Macdonald, a pretty young lady and Kate Traill, sitting on a log near the boat, not making love to the black flies, but the black flies paying their *devours* to them. We were soon joined by Robert and his wife, Roland and his Mary, George Strickland, Charles Boker, the two Miss Stricklands Robert's daughters, Mr and Mrs Barlee, and good old Isaac Garbutt who happened to be a passenger on the boat. The only beaus for the three young ladies were George and Mr. Boker.

Well, we had a delicious sail up the lakes to Julians landing on Stoney lake, but though the waters remained the same as of yore, all the scenery I once knew along the shores was quite changed. Our old place I should never have recognized. The woods about it are all gone, and a new growth of small cedars fringes the shore in front. There is a tolerable looking modern cottage on the spot, that the old log house once occupied, and the old barn survives on the same spot on which it was built, more than 30 years ago, but the woods that framed it in, are all down, and it has a bare desolate look, and is used as a place for feeding young cattle. The back waters from the mill dams have drowned all the trees on Moodie's Island[1] which still bears the name, and it has become a very ugly place to what it was in the hand of Nature.

These drowned lands spoil the once pretty shores of the upper Katchewanook lake and the scene is greatly changed all the way up the Young's old place. The falls there have been blasted out to make the canal into Clear lake, and the great beauty of the place, while in the wilderness, is greatly diminished, but a pretty Catholic church and burying ground, and a small picturesque group of cottages, gives an air of civilization to the once romantic place.

At the Lock, Old Garbutt, introduced me to Pat Young, the Lock Master, and the son of the old Miller at the rapids at whose hospitable log house, Katie and Aggie reposed while Pat, Mat and Betty Young, paddled us up in canoes to Stoney lake, and on our return feasted us with all sort of Bush Dainties, and for the first and last time in my life, I drank coffee made in a frying pan. Pat was Young then both by name and nature, he greeted me with intense Irish glee, and asked after the two pretty little girls he carried down in his arms asleep to put in Moodie's canoe at night, and sure, was he not delighted to hear that they both had married Irish husbands and that little Katie was the mother of nine children. 'Sure she was always the clever stirring little thing.' On we went through the grand scenery of Stoney Lake. That is just the same, and its Islands, there are 1200 in it, must remain as they now appear to the end of time. Great bare red granite rocks crowned with scrub oak and pine. Some are many 100 feet high and heave up like the bare bones of some ancient world. It is quite a labyrinth of Islands, how people can find their way through them is the wonder. How I wished that Katie could have seen them. It is a wonderful place, so vast, so wild and lonely, the waters so blue, the dark woods frowning down upon them from their lofty granite ridges that towered far far above us. The time will come when this will be one of the sight seeing places in Canada.

We got our dinner on board, the Parson and Robert S. doing the honors of the place – the prey excellent and every body hungry enough to enjoy it. At Julian's landing, we went ashore, I could not climb the big sugar loaf rock, and I believe that Katie Traill was the only one that did. She said the view from it was magnificent –

Mrs. T. the parson and I, went into the woods to hunt for ferns, but I hunted up a snake, and grew rather shy of the ferns. It is not pleasant to see an emblem of old Scratch wisking his tail among them. But enough of this. I see you are tired. We parted here with Roland and George, who by the bye seemed very sweet upon Miss Smith. On our return I had a long chat with old Isaac Garbutt whom I found a very intelligent man. The wind sprung up to almost a gale and we landed at Lakefield just in time to get home before an awful thunder storm, which returned again in the middle of the night and recommenced bombarding us with renewed vigor. It is raining again today. I shall not be able to post this as it shews no sign of leaving off. It has rained nearly half the time, since I came up to Douro.

Do you know I have been amusing myself with fishing in the river that flows opposite Aunts gate, and succeeded in catching plenty of perch and sunfish. I tried my old receipt of fish soup and found it excellent, far richer and nicer than beef soup. Aunt and Katie thought it very good. The black flies are too bad now for fishing. They will be all away by the end of the month. I have not heard a word of B.V. news since I left. I wonder how all the folks are. You must thank dear Katie and Jack for me for the postal cards which were no small comfort to me. I hope and trust, dear John that this will find you still mending. You should take a trip somewhere when able to walk again, to recover your strength and not work *quite* so hard for the future. You are too precious to us all to throw away your life for the dollars.

My tooth has given over aching at last – and I have not got rid of it. I cannot afford to lose it as long as it will stay in. Goodbye my dear son. May God bless and quickly restore you to health and comfort. With kind love to the darling Katie and all the dear boys and girls and much love to yourself, believe me ever to remain,

Your affectionate Mother
Susanna Moodie

Aunt and Kate beg love and kind regards to all. If Robert is with you

give him my best love. I will write to him soon. I suppose your
visitors were McIntires –

1 Moodie's Island, which retains its name today, is located in Lake Katchewanooka
to the northwest of the Moodie clearing. It was likely drowned with water level
increases in the 1840s. See *Recent Archeological Investigations along the Margins
of Lake Katchewanooka and Select Sections of Smith and Douro Townships and
the City of Peterborough* (York North Archeological Services 1988), map 15.

---

80 Susanna Moodie to Katie Vickers

My dearest Katie,   Feb. 15th 1878

I wanted sadly to come and spend your birthday with you, but feel
so far from well this morning, that to walk from the station would
knock me up entirely, and leave me sick upon your hands. I must
perforce wait until I am better able to undertake the journey – A
great one on foot for me. Now do not think dear child, that I am
seriously ill for I am only weak and deplorable, and my ailments
are confined to fierce cramps in my legs and feet leaving them hot
and swollen, so that to walk is painful. But may every blessing
be yours my beloved and may God grant you many many happy,
peaceful and prosperous years spent with the dear good husband
and the children. I am very anxious to hear of Georgie[1] but fear the
time will not allow of that. I have no news to tell you. Nellie will
most likely be in tomorrow if fine, and I will come if I can manage
it at all.

Our children are all on the lookout for Valentines. Bessie has
had six very pretty ones indeed – Nellie only two. I sent little Aggy
one. As she loves pussies I quite fell in love with the pretty Kitties
myself. I heard from Agnes this week. She was in bed sick. She
wants things for a bazaar, but I don't feel inclined to paint for folk
that don't belong to our section of the Province.

Poor Mr Higgenson is the parson that is in trouble. She does not
mention his crime but says that he has disgraced himself for ever,
and has given up the church and every thing. He was as ugly as
Ben Davy. I should think it could not be a woman scrape. D. was
doing well and was quite steady.

Robert saw one of the Stricklands in town yesterday. One he
never saw before. I think it must be Percy, as he was tall and hand-

some with a beard. Jack is waiting for this. Give my kind love to dear Mr V. and all the dear girls, and with lots of love for your dear self believe me ever your faithfully attached Mother

Susanna Moodie

Mrs Traill is home again and found all right.
Nellie and Rob sent love and kind wishes to you for many happy returns of the day.

1 Georgina Vickers, Katie's daughter, was visiting relatives in Ireland and England and touring the Continent (see *LOL*, 320).

---

81 Susanna Moodie to Dr Edward Chapman

30 Baldwin Street
Toronto
Dear Sir,   Jan. 3rd, 1880 –

With great pleasure I transmit you a copy of the little poem you requested. An almost forgotten trifle, which came warm from the heart in those days when youth and love deify God's glorious hand-made nature and make this world a paradise. I feel greatly flattered, that *you* whose dealings with Nature in her grandest forms should notice my little song – and remain with

Much respect,
Yours truly,
Susanna Moodie

The Canadian Herd Boy

Through the deep woods at peep of day,
The careless Herd-boy wends his way,
By piny ridge and forest stream,
To summon home his roving team –
    Cobos! – Cobos! from distant dell
    Shy echo wafts the cattle bell –

A blythe reply he whistles back,

And follows out the devious track,
O'er fallen tree – and mossy stone,
A path to all save him unknown,
    Cobos! – Cobos! – far down the dell
    Shy echo wafts the cattle bell –

See – the dark swamp before him throws
A tangled maze of cedar boughs
On all around deep silence broods,
In Nature's boundless solitudes –
    Cobos! – Cobos! the breezes swell
    As nearer floats the cattle bell –

He sees them now – beneath yon trees
His motley herd recline at ease
With lazy pace and sullen stare
They slowly leave their shady lair.
    Cobos! – Cobos! – far up the dell,
    Quick jingling floats the cattle bell –

Written in the back woods
1834 –

---

82 Susanna Moodie to Catharine Parr Traill

> [152 Adelaide Street
> Toronto
> 6 December 1880]

... and stamp out the blaze and then get water from the bath house and put it out. A few nights ago – number 10 – the house just above ours [was] on fire. Our house was full of smoke but no one could see where it came from until Robert tore up the boards with the axe and found the middle flooring was burning and the fire not to be put out as easily as ours had been. The fire brigade was given the alarm, and but for prompt measures the whole long row of houses would have gone. The house in which the fire took place, was an *empty* one, and a spark from the fireplace in which the workmen had been burning chips had fallen through the boards and the main beams of the building quite out of sight were burning. This has given us all rather a [scare], and we shall feel less repugnance in having to leave the house, which has been sold over our heads and if we stay until March, when our rent expires we shall have to move again. Think of moving 7 times in less than three years. It involves fearful expense and destruction of property. Poor Rob is not one of the lucky ones – But thank God he is looking well just now. I wish I could say the same of dear Nellie, but she is far from well and I often feel very anxious about her. The girls are hard at their studies and getting into women. Bess is very short, and Nellie very tall, one with jet black hair and a very expressive face the other blue eyed and fair. Bess took a silver medal of Arithmetic which all have quite a genius for, and Nell hopes to get one before the examinations close.

I am glad my dear little Katie likes her school. Give her my kind love, not forgetting Charlie when you see him. I love that fine gentlemanly boy.[1] Boy, he is more like a thoughtful nobleman. I feel certain if he lives he will make a good clever man and better still, a christian. I look in Grip, every week but cannot see Mary's name. If she would write some of her droll sketches I think they would be glad to pay her – for it takes more brains to write a good joke than a romantic tragedy.[2]

I came here yesterday to spend the week. Kind Vickers sent a cab for me for I walk with more trouble than I did. Today, my dear Kate came in with a lovely cap for me and a beautiful chrome and such a pretty breakfast shawl, and John gave me such a nice hymn book with some of our best hymns – Many of Charles Wesleys, who after all is the very *king* of *hymn writers*. I did not know before, that he was the author of 'Hark the Herald Angels Sing' the most triumphant anthem we have in ours, or in any language – Poor young Steel – it is good for him to have passed though the portals of death to heaven I never saw him but once – but was struck by the likeness to my dear friend Mr Pringle. There can be no regret for one so fit to die we feel so sure that all is well with him. I wish I had some patches to help you but I have not a single scrap of print of any kind. There is a strange fascination in patchwork. It is bringing of order and harmony out of disorder and disunion, and you feel certain that the result will fully accomplish the end you desire.

How is dear Susan – Nephew Percy's good wife – for whom I always have a place in my old heart. Give my love and best wishes – not forgetting dear Mary and Tom and little Carrie and the blue-eyed boy with the sweet gracious smile.[3] And so all my playfellows the saucy chicks are dead, and Lorn is left sole master of the field. My little Canary is so fond of me that he chooses to sit and stand on my head or to cuddle under my chin which puts our wee tigress into an extasy of delight.

I have got decent paper but vile ink and pen, the one as thick as mud, the other old and rusty and I feel very old and rusty myself but with many bright gleams of happiness within. I must say good-bye – God bless you and yours my dear old sister and crown your declining years with the peace and love that Jesus alone can give. Katie and all here send love to you and yours ditto my dear Robert and Nell and with fond love, for your own dear self I remain,

Your loving sister
Susanna Moodie

Give my fond love to our darling Robert. I am so glad that his sweet saint, is through her trouble. May the wee lassie prove a treasure to all its parents.[4]

1 Probably Charles Henry Strickland Traill (b. 1865), little Katie's older brother and Catharine's grandson
2 See LOL, 264, 344. Mary (Traill) Muchall published stories and articles in such magazines as the Canadian Monthly and National Review during the 1870s and 1880s. She does not appear in Grip during 1880–1.
3 Mary and Thomas Muchall had moved to Lakefield in 1878. Little Carrie was ten-year-old Caroline Muchall, and the 'blueeyed boy' was probably Hargreave Muchall, age fifteen and a particular favourite of Susanna's (see LOL, 264–5).
4 Susanna's great-niece, Charlotte, Robert Strickland's eldest daughter, had married the Rev. John Charles Taylor in 1879 (LOL, 264).

Sources of Letters and Illustrations

LETTERS

ARCHIVAL SOURCES

British Library, Manuscript Room
Richard Bentley Archives: letters 11, 70
Papers of the Royal Literary Fund: letters 69, 72

Dunedin Public Library, New Zealand: letter 81
See also *Canadian Notes and Queries*, no. 38 (Autumn 1987).

Guelph University Library
Goodwin Haines Collection: letter 82

Houghton Library, Harvard University
Rare Books and Manuscripts: letter 75

Metropolitan Toronto Reference Library, Baldwin Room
Robert Baldwin Papers: letters 40–2, 46–7, 49–53

National Archives, Ottawa
Upper Canada Land Petitions: letters 9, 12, 13, 56
Upper Canada Sundries: letters 15, 37–9, 43–4, 48

National Library, Ottawa
Patrick Hamilton Ewing Collection: letters 1–6, 8, 14, 16–36, 54–6, 62–5, 67–8, 71, 76–80

National Library, Scotland: letter 7

Thomas Fisher Rare Book Library, University of Toronto
Canadian Parliament Legislative Assembly Journals 2 (1842): letter 45

PUBLISHED SOURCES

English Notes and Queries, 3d ser., 5 (9 April 1864): letter 66

Letters and Extracts of Letters from Settlers in Upper Canada (London 1833), 9–12: letter 10

Orkney Herald, 30 October 1866: letter 73
2 April 1867: letter 74

Spiritual Telegraph, 1 May 1858 to 9 July 1859: letters 57–61

ILLUSTRATIONS

ii Susanna and John Moodie, c.1860. Courtesy of the National Library, Ottawa

3 Melsetter House. Reprinted from *Scottish Country Life* (August 1981)

5 Susanna Strickland, c.1828. Courtesy of the National Library, Ottawa

11 Moodies' Douro property showing site of their dug well, c.1909, photographed by George Douglas. Courtesy of Katherine Hooke

62 Colonel William Kingsmill. Courtesy of Nicol G.W. Kingsmill

67 Map of Niagara frontier. Reprinted from E.A. Cruikshank, 'A Memoir of Colonel the Honorable James Kerby: His Life in Letters,' *Welland County Historical Society Papers and Records* 4 (1931), 162

87 Colonel Robert Brown. Courtesy of Lloyd J. Delaney; reprinted from his *Small But Bountiful* (Orillia 1983), 57

93 George, Baron de Rottenburg. Courtesy of the Archives of Ontario

106 Cross-written letter, 1839. Courtesy of the National Library, Ottawa

171 George Benjamin, 1859. Courtesy of the Hastings County Historical Society

173 Robert Baldwin. Courtesy of the National Archives, Ottawa

210 Masthead of the *Spiritual Telegraph*

212 Agnes (Moodie) Chamberlain. Reprinted from H.J. Morgan, *Types of Canadian Women* (Toronto 1903)

285 Vickers family, c.1875. Courtesy of the National Library, Ottawa

287 Moodie family crest. From a reprint of the 1852 edition of *Roughing It in the Bush* (Toronto 1980), 565

Index

Readers will find the major subjects of the Moodies' correspondence tend to occur in chronological groupings related to the chapter divisions as follows: chapter 1 – courtship, family background, emigration and settlement, religion; chapter 2 – the Rebellion of 1837; chapter 3 – rebellion aftermath, colonial administration, settlement life, and migration; chapter 4 – colonial administration, politics, shrievalty; chapter 5 – religion, spiritualism, and related enthusiasms; chapter 6 – family history and literary summaries.

For ease in identifying individuals listed in this Index we have included their location at the time of their mention by the use of the following abbreviations: Bv (Belleville), Cbg (Cobourg), Lkfd (Lakefield and area), Pto (Peterborough), Sfk (Suffolk, England), To (Toronto). Where necessary, other locations have been spelled in full.